"The *Things Unseen* podcast is a very great gift to the church, and now that blessing has been further multiplied in this published format. In these pages, you will not only find the fruit of faithful learning and profound reflection but also, beautifully, the fruit of humble living before the face of God and loving devotion to the Lord Jesus Christ. Winsome and wise, gentle but robust, full of truth and grace, this devotional guide will nourish and edify the youngest believer and the most seasoned saint. You are holding in your hands a treasure to which you will want to return again and again and a wellspring in which you will discover new depths year after year."

—Dr. David Gibson
Minister, Trinity Church
Aberdeen, Scotland

"Imagine spending a few minutes every day for a year with one of today's wisest senior saints. Sinclair Ferguson combines theological depth of insight with pastoral astuteness and a wonderful way with words to produce devotional supplies for a year's growth in Christ. Here is wisdom, light, and encouragement to bring to your daily life."

—Dr. Michael Reeves
President and Professor of Theology
Union School of Theology
Bridgend, Wales

"These wonderful reflections brim with wisdom, encouragement, and challenge. We are repeatedly reminded that our spiritual life is not first about us but about God, about His Son, and about the Holy Spirit. Our first task in life, Dr. Ferguson reminds us, is not to think about ourselves but to see the Lord and to enjoy His presence and to live out the beauty of the Lord's character in our everyday lives. In reading this book, you will meet the Lord, day after day, week after week, month after month. You can't ask for much more than that, and I found these reflections to be a tonic for my own soul."

—Dr. Thomas R. Schreiner
James Buchanan Harrison Professor of New Testament Interpretation
The Southern Baptist Theological Seminary
Louisville, Ky.

"It is difficult to find the correct set of superlatives for these podcasts/devotionals now published as a book. Listening to them as they appeared each day was transformative. Dr. Ferguson has been a friend for more than forty years, but having him in the passenger seat each day as I drove to church was like a throwback to a time when we served together at the same church.

"These are much more than devotionals. They are a digest of bibical and systematic theology in bite-size pieces. Having these podcasts published in a book helps you see that a little clearer. I am tempted to ask, What should every Christian know about the Christian life? Answer: The contents of this book! I have read many devotionals that take you, day by day, through the year. This one exceeds them all. A triumphal achievement."

—Dr. Derek W.H. Thomas
Teaching Fellow, Ligonier Ministries
Chancellor's Professor, Reformed Theological Seminary

"It is a true delight to see Dr. Ferguson's podcast made into a devotional book. As I listened to the daily episodes of *Things Unseen*, I often wished that I could have them in written form, both for looking back over them myself and also for giving them to other people. I'm very grateful to have that become a reality. So much wisdom is packed into this book, and I look forward to passing copies along to others. There is help here: help in knowing, in loving, and in living for the Lord Jesus Christ."

—Rebecca VanDoodewaard
Author and editor
Greer, S.C.

THINGS
UNSEEN

One Year of Reflections on the Christian Life

SINCLAIR B. FERGUSON

 LIGONIER MINISTRIES

Things Unseen: One Year of Reflections on the Christian Life
© 2024 by Sinclair B. Ferguson

Published by Ligonier Ministries
421 Ligonier Court, Sanford, FL 32771
Ligonier.org

Printed in York, Pennsylvania
Maple Press
0001124
First edition

ISBN 978-1-64289-640-4 (Hardcover)
ISBN 978-1-64289-641-1 (ePub)

Cover design: Ligonier Creative
Interior design and typeset: Katherine Lloyd, The DESK

Library of Congress Control Number: 2024936684

TO

The Board and Faithful Staff
of
Ligonier Ministries

whose service is unseen
but whose ministry
reaches
the ends of the earth

CONTENTS

INTRODUCTION

THINGS UNSEEN BEGAN AS A DAILY DEVOTIONAL podcast released each weekday throughout 2023. It contains all 260 episodes edited from the spoken to the written form. I am grateful to the team at Ligonier Ministries, who first suggested the idea of a podcast to me, for allowing me the privilege of entering the lives and sometimes the families of Christian people—and perhaps some non-Christians, too—in many parts of the world. I am also grateful to the staff who in different ways encouraged and helped me in the recording process, to those who worked very much behind the scenes to make the podcast possible, and to those who helped with the editing that has transformed the spoken word into a book. Above all I am grateful for the many listeners who, over the weeks and months, became part of the "podcast community of *Things Unseen.*"

Recording 260 podcasts is a more major undertaking than it might seem, and the sheer number of them helps to explain their format. Rather than attempting to cover 260 random topics during the year, I thought it seemed more helpful to select 52 topics, one for every week of the year, and follow each theme through from Monday to Friday.

In the nature of things, a limited number of the podcasts were "time-sensitive." While the first and last weeks of the year and Christmas week always come at the same point in the calendar, this is not so with Easter week, Ascension week, or Pentecost, which are all "movable feasts" in the Christian year. Some readers may want to take note of these particular weeks and adjust the order in which they read the corresponding podcasts. If so, then Passion and Easter weeks (14 and 15), and also the weeks of Ascension and Pentecost (20 and 22), should be read at the appropriate point in the current year's calendar.

One of the privileges afforded by a podcast is receiving messages from listeners. Some of my favorites reflected the fact that the sound of our voices can divulge not only our nationality but even our age group. Messages to me that reflected this included one from a young student who, listening as she drove to college each day, said that it was like having your grandfather in the back seat. That theme was also echoed by a mother whose children thought it was their grandfather she was listening to—and therefore wanted to know why he never came to visit them!

Now that the podcasts are in readable as well as audible form, I hope that they will continue to be an encouragement and blessing and that readers will find something worth reflecting on each day. But I also pray that, in the kind providence of God, there will be occasions when readers feel that what they have read seems to have been written just for them, and just for today.

So may these daily reflections be a reminder that it is the things that are unseen that are eternal.

—Sinclair B. Ferguson

WEEK 1

Happy New Year

1

Beginning a New Year Well

AS WE BEGIN OUR JOURNEY TOGETHER, I'd like to wish you a blessed and happy new year. In fact, that is going to be our theme this week: a happy new year.

Back when I was a student, I once preached on New Year's Day at a service in a Methodist church in a fishing village in the northeast of Scotland. I didn't know enough about the Methodist tradition to appreciate that it was actually a rather special service.

And although I, and probably they, have completely forgotten what I preached on, the service left an indelible impression on me because it was the church's annual new-year covenant-renewal service. And after the sermon, the whole congregation in unison committed themselves afresh to the Lord with the words of a very personal and moving covenant.

I was quite surprised by that because I associated covenant theology with Presbyterians, the Reformed tradition, and the Puritans—not the Methodists, and certainly not the Wesley brothers. But John Wesley had borrowed the idea of a living covenant from some of the Puritans that he had read at an earlier stage in his life. It deeply impressed me, and I wanted to introduce it to the churches I later served.

Occasionally, I found people objecting to doing this, saying that it wasn't really sincere to commit themselves to the Lord using someone else's words. To be honest, this slightly amused me because I watched them every Lord's Day, morning and evening, heartily singing other people's words of commitment to the Lord Jesus Christ. But the vast majority of us found it very helpful, and I personally found it deeply moving to join with people I loved and to whom I was committed as together we committed ourselves afresh to the Lord for another year.

So I want to begin this new year by sharing that covenant with you, and inviting you to commit yourself to the Lord and to pray for His help through this new year.

> I am no longer my own, but thine.
> Put me to what thou wilt, rank me with whom thou wilt.
> Put me to doing, put me to suffering.
> Let me be employed by thee or laid aside for thee,
> exalted for thee or brought low for thee.
> Let me be full, let me be empty.
> Let me have all things, let me have nothing.
> I freely and heartily yield all things
> to thy pleasure and disposal.
> And now O glorious and blessed God,
> Father, Son, and Holy Spirit,
> thou art mine, and I am thine. So be it.
> And the covenant which I have made on earth,
> let it be ratified in heaven. Amen.

I hope you want to say, "Amen and amen."

2

Growing in Love for the Church

YESTERDAY, I RECOUNTED THE INDELIBLE IMPRESSION made on me at a New Year service in a Methodist church and how moved I was when the whole congregation joined together in the words of a personal covenant. We also sang from the Methodist hymnbook, which I had never used before. But I was so struck by the words we were singing that sometime later I bought a copy.

It came with a bonus that has lasted all through my life.

The Methodist hymnbook not only included the first line of a hymn; it included the first line of every verse of a hymn, which meant that when I could remember how the third verse began but couldn't remember what hymn it came from, I went straight to the Methodist hymnbook to help me.

But the really important thing was the hymn we were singing. It was written by Charles Wesley. His brother used it as the opening item of praise at the annual meeting of the Methodist Societies to help them praise God for the blessings of the previous year. And its first lines express that desire beautifully: "And are we yet alive, and see each other's face? Glory and praise to Jesus give for His redeeming grace."

I wonder if you'll feel that way at the first church service you go to this year. Even better, shouldn't we really feel that way every week when our church family meets together? We tend to live very much outside each other. Paul says in 1 Corinthians 2:11 that no one knows a person's real thoughts except the person himself. We are very much individuals. And yet the wonderful thing that happens to us when we come to faith in Jesus Christ is that not only are we bound together in Him, but because of that, we are bound to one another.

As the Shepherd calls His sheep to come to Him, they come nearer to each other. They are bound together in love, bound together in grace. Isn't it true that you feel nearer to fellow believers who may be a thousand miles away than you often do to the people standing next to you? And that is because we belong to a family—a family that one of my colleagues used to describe as the worldwide, eternity-long family of God.

I hope, therefore, that this new year will be one in which we will grow in love for the church, and that we will express the kind of admiration of God's goodness to us that is found in this hymn. And as we grow in love, we'll be able to sing with one another:

And are we yet alive,
And see each other's face?
Glory and praise to Jesus give
For His redeeming grace.

What troubles have we seen,
What conflicts have we passed,
Fightings without, and fears within,
Since we assembled last.

But out of all the Lord
Hath brought us by His love;
And still He doth His help afford,
And hides our life above.

Then let us make our boast
Of His redeeming power,
Which saves us to the uttermost,
Till we can sin no more.

Let us take up the cross
Till we the crown obtain;
And gladly reckon all things loss,
So we may Jesus gain.

3

A Resolution for the Christian Life

SO FAR THIS WEEK, WE'VE LOOKED at a covenant for a new-year commitment and a hymn for a new-year praise. Today, we'll explore a text for the new year from one of the Apostle Paul's letters. You're probably familiar with it, and perhaps you even know it by heart. But even if you don't know it, I think you'll be able to remember it quite easily. It's Paul's personal resolution in Philippians 3:10–14:

> That I may know him [Christ] and the power of his resurrection, and may share his sufferings, becoming like him in his death, that by any means possible I may attain the resurrection from the dead.
>
> Not that I have already obtained this or am already perfect, but I press on to make it my own, because Christ Jesus has made me his own. Brothers, I do not consider that I have made it my own. But one thing I do: forgetting what lies behind and straining forward to what lies ahead, I press on toward the goal for the prize of the upward call of God in Christ Jesus.

At the beginning of Philippians, Paul indicates that his young colleague Timothy was with him. Paul often dictated his letters, and I've sometimes wondered if he mentions Timothy because he served as his secretary for this letter. It begins with the words "Paul and Timothy," and I wonder if he gave his son in the faith a slight smile when he told him to write his own name down.

But if that were the case, I'm pretty sure that as Paul came to this passage, "But one thing I do," Timothy might well have looked up at Paul with a quizzical stare. And if Paul asked if he'd said something that

Timothy didn't understand, perhaps he would have had the courage to respond: "Paul, do you really want me to say that you do only one thing? As long as I've known you, you've always been doing many things, and at the same time. You're the ultimate multitasking Apostle. You're always traveling; you're always preaching; you're always praying; you're always visiting; you're always counseling. I've never seen you do just one thing."

I think Paul would have smiled back to his young friend Timothy and said: "I know what you mean, Timothy. No one knows better than you what I do and how busy I am. But you need to understand that I'm not busy doing many different things. I'm busy doing one thing in many different ways. And all of them are about getting to know the Lord Jesus Christ better, sharing His life and becoming like Him. That is the heart—in some ways it's the secret—of everything I do, in every waking hour and every different activity. They are all simply different ways of doing this one thing."

When I was a small boy in Scotland, each New Year's Eve (Hogmanay, as it's called), my parents would tell me to go to my room and write out ten New Year's resolutions for the year to come. Looking back, I laugh now when I remember how hard I thought it was to find ten ways that I needed to improve. I could write them out much more easily today, I suspect.

But if you are a Christian, you really need only one New Year's resolution, and Paul's will be a great help to you. Especially if you're a younger Christian or a younger person, few things can be more helpful to you than to understand that this is the way to both simplify and integrate your life. This is what will give you direction. This is what will help you answer the great question, "What am I really here for?"

As one of the older translations puts it, "All I care for is to know Christ and the power of his resurrection, to share the fellowship of his sufferings and be made like him, that one day I may attain to the resurrection."

What a great New Year's resolution. This one thing I do: I want to know Christ.

4

How to Be Happy

I HAVE A LITTLE PROBLEM AT this time of the year. What do I say to people when I meet them for the first time? What words should I use? Maybe you think that is a bit strange, but here's the issue: When I was a young Christian, I was taught that God is more interested in my holiness than He is in my happiness. So I thought it would seem very strange if I started saying to people, "Have a holy new year." Even Christians might have cooled off to me if I'd greeted them in that way. But there is another problem: you could wish someone a happy new year and then later in the year regret that you'd said it because their life had been so filled with unhappiness. So with thoughts like that, you can understand how I sometimes puzzle over what adjective to use when I greet people at the beginning of the new year. I usually end up saying something like, "I hope you have a blessed and happy new year."

But maybe my conscience is too tender, because the Bible does speak about our being happy. Just as it's the desire of every earthly father that his children will be happy, then surely that is all the more true of our heavenly Father. Some of us struggle with the idea of a God who wants us to be happy, perhaps because of our own experience of fatherhood, perhaps because of the doubts and fears of our own hearts.

This is why the Holy Spirit has been sent to us, so that once we have been adopted into God's family, we might be persuaded that He is our loving heavenly Father. Although we cannot fully understand the ways in which He accomplishes this, He does ultimately want us to be happy, to be happy with Him, and to be happy forever.

The thing is, God knows better than we do how we can be truly happy. He knows that we can be truly happy only when we fully belong to Him, only when we are growing in our knowledge of Christ and

9

want to live for Him. There is a real happiness for the Christian to experience, but he or she is brought to experience it in many different ways. And some of them are actually very sore to us because we're still seeking happiness in places where happiness can never be found, rather than seeking it in the Lord.

Augustus Montague Toplady wrote a great hymn titled "A Debtor to Mercy Alone," and there is a verse in it that has always moved me. Toplady writes:

> My name from the palms of his hands
> Eternity will not erase;
> Impressed on his heart it remains,
> In marks of indelible grace.
> Yes, I to the end shall endure,
> As sure as the earnest is giv'n;
> More happy, but not more secure,
> The glorified spirits in heav'n.

Those final lines are ones to remember. They—the saints in heaven—are happier; they see the face of Christ; they are set free from sin. But they are not more secure, because you and I are held in the hollow of His hand. They are happier, but because He is ours and we are His, we can be happy here.

Of course, we'll know perfect happiness only when we are with those saints in glory, when we're perfectly holy, and when we're in the presence of Jesus, the Mediator of the new covenant. That is where our lives are heading: to be conformed to the image of God's Son.

But if we are His, we can already be happy. Happy in Jesus, and learning sometimes through difficult experiences, as many of us will know this year, that our true happiness lies not in the things of this world, but in our fellowship with Jesus Christ. And as we're still in the very first week of this new year, let me wish you a very happy new year.

5

A Life-Changing Experience

MOST OF US FORGET MORE THAN we remember, it seems. But the events that shape our destiny or change our future are events that we remember forever. I suppose most of us can point back to a single moment, a single hour, an experience we had, or someone we met that has radically changed the direction of our lives.

Often at the beginning of the new year, I think about the experience of the prophet Isaiah. If we imagined all the prophets who lived before Jesus climbing a mountain to look over the summit and see His coming, then John the Baptist would be the man standing on the summit, wouldn't he? But I suspect that the man standing right behind him would be the prophet Isaiah, straining his neck to see who the Suffering Servant of his fifty-third chapter really was.

God prepared Isaiah for that ministry very early on in his career.

Isaiah 6 contains the great biblical chapter on the holiness of God, in which Isaiah encounters the manifestation of God's holy majesty—the Holy, Holy, Holy One. Isaiah never forgot that year. It was the year that King Uzziah died, a year of sadness for the people. But it was also a new year that shaped every year of Isaiah's future life—indeed, every single day that he lived from that point onward.

Yesterday, we spoke about being reluctant to wish someone a happy new year when we know that people can't really be happy unless they are holy. And I think it was Isaiah's encounter with God that made him realize he could never be truly happy until he was really holy. For that reason, if you read through the rest of his prophecy, you'll notice that his favorite description for the Lord becomes "the Holy One."

Isaiah 6 teaches us so many things. One of them is how to respond to God. You've probably noticed that Isaiah's response seems to have been three-dimensional. One dimension was an awareness of his own sinfulness. He felt as though he was disintegrating before God.

What interests me as a preacher is that Isaiah was undoubtedly the most eloquent prophet of his day—perhaps, for that matter, of any day in the Old Testament. But what he felt his sin had polluted was the very instrument God had given him to proclaim His word. Isaiah says, "I am a man of unclean lips" (Isa. 6:5). It's very telling that he was conscious that his sinfulness was not just found in what he or others regarded as one of his weaknesses, but actually embedded in his greatest gift and his greatest strength.

If you read through Isaiah from the beginning, you'll notice that in Isaiah 5, he had already pronounced six woes on others. And where there is the number six in the Old Testament, we should always be looking for the seventh. And in chapter 6, he pronounces the climactic seventh woe. But it's not on others; it's on himself. Those whom God uses have always been those who are conscious of their sinfulness.

The second dimension of his experience, of course, was that of God's pardoning grace—that electric moment when the seraph takes the burning coal from the altar with tongs and puts it on Isaiah's lips and cleanses him. That is exactly what he needed, and it's also what we need at the beginning of the year: cleansing. As the hymn "Rock of Ages" teaches us to sing, "Be of sin the double cure, cleanse me from its guilt and pow'r."

But then the third dimension of his experience was this: an unreserved willingness to serve the Lord without question. He didn't even know what God wanted him to do, but he was willing to say: "Here I am! Send me" (Isa. 6:8).

May this new year be one in which God marks our lives in the way He marked the life of the prophet Isaiah.

WEEK 2

Divine Revelation

1

Creation Reveals the Creator

IF YOU'RE NOT A CHRISTIAN, the word *revelation* might prompt you to think of all kinds of things. I remember a friend's receiving a suitcase for her twenty-first birthday, and it had the manufacturer's name embossed on it: Revelation. So I could imagine someone's remembering that brand and thinking "suitcase" when they hear the word *revelation.* Or perhaps someone with a guilty conscience might think "hide." If you're a Christian, you might think of all kinds of things. You might think of Jesus. You might think of the book of Revelation. The word *millennium* might come to mind.

But if you've studied the Bible for any length of time, you know that *revelation* is a word that describes the way in which God has made Himself known to us. And He has done that right from the very beginning.

"In the beginning, God created . . ." (Gen. 1:1). The age-old question that philosophers have always asked and that scientists still seek to penetrate—"Why is there something and not nothing?"—is answered in the very first chapter in the very first verse of the Bible: It is because God has revealed Himself in creation. The uncreated God has made all things.

If you think about it, that inevitably means that everything God has made reveals Him. Created things reveal their creator, just as the work of a great artist reveals the artist himself. As an art expert might say, "I see the characteristic signs of this great artist in this particular painting." If we have eyes to see, then we will recognize that everything in the universe bears the stamp "made by God" and reveals Him.

Paul put it this way in Romans 1:20: "[God's] invisible attributes . . . have been clearly perceived, ever since the creation of the world, in the things that have been made." John Calvin puts it delightfully when he says that the acts of creation were like God's putting on His outside clothes in order that we might see who He is, what He is like, and what He has done.

It's in this way that the invisible God makes His invisible attributes known to us in visible things. That's revelation. However, we are blind to it because of our sin, and our eyes are opened to it only by the grace of Jesus Christ. That is why the hymn writer George W. Robinson once wrote, "Something lives in every hue, Christless eyes have never seen."

As Christians, we certainly don't know everything, but the great thing is that we know something about everything. We know that it's been made by God. We know that we are living in His world. And we know that we are secure with Him.

2

No Real Atheists

THE WORD THAT THE NEW TESTAMENT uses for *revelation* is *apoka-lypsis*. This Greek word gives us the alternative title for the last book of the Bible: the Apocalypse of John. It means "unveiling," disclosing something to us that would otherwise be hidden.

We said yesterday that God reveals Himself in everything that He has made and that His invisible attributes become visible to us in the created order. Isaac Watts wrote a hymn about this titled "I Sing the Almighty Power of God." Its last verse captures this truth:

There's not a plant or flow'r below
But makes Thy glories known,
And clouds arise and tempests blow
By order from Thy throne.

I often think in this connection of the words of the great Dutch theologian Herman Bavinck. He writes in his *Reformed Dogmatics*: "According to Scripture the whole universe is a creation and hence also a revelation of God. In an absolute sense, therefore, nothing is atheistic. . . . There is no atheistic world. There are no atheistic people. Nor are there atheistic persons." That sounds like a staggering claim, but it's actually just a paraphrase of what Paul says in Romans 1:19–21.

If everything has been made by God, then the words of Psalm 139 are true in this particular sense: even if you take the wings of the morning and travel at the speed of light to the farthest part of the earth to flee from God, when you land you will still be confronted by the same revelation of God in creation that you were trying to escape. It's as though God had planted quiet voices in everything in creation to make them say, "There is no last exit from My revelation." And since that is the inescapable environment in which we live, as Bavinck goes on to say: "There are no real atheists. There are only hiding theists."

Now, I'm sure that Bavinck wasn't denying that there are people who *call themselves* atheists. We would probably have to concede that there are people who deceive themselves so fully that they believe themselves to be atheists.

But notice the implications of this: if God's revelation of His eternal power and glory are so real that nothing is atheistic in the absolute sense, and if no one can escape it (so that ultimately there are no real atheists), then those of us who are Christians know something about non-Christians and atheists that they may well be denying about themselves. This is what Paul says in Romans 1:21: They know that God exists. They can deny it to us. They may even deny it to themselves. But ultimately, deep down, they cannot escape this reality.

Why is this important for us as Christians to know? Since this is a God-revealing world, it isn't possible to live in it without that being the basis for everything humans do. And this means that atheists can never really be consistent with their first principles—or at least the first principles they profess to have. They must always be borrowing from the implications of the existence of God and His revelation. Otherwise, nothing makes sense. Nothing is ultimately explicable. Our lives fail to make sense. Our loves fail to make sense. And we have to make up everything as we go along.

It's important to realize that no one can actually live consistently with that presupposition. If you think for ten minutes about living that way—in which nothing makes sense, in which there is no foundation for rationality—I think you will soon be driven to despair. But there is something else that we need to know: Atheists are all inconsistent. They all borrow or steal from the implications of God's existence and from His creation in order to live.

And so inevitably, there are what I call "loose threads" in their lives, inconsistencies. And one of our responsibilities as Christians is to spot these inconsistencies, to gently pull on the loose thread, and to help unravel the falsehood that they have professed to believe so that we can begin to point them to the true and living God, and to pray that as their lives, inconsistent as they are, unravel, they, too, will begin to seek God.

3

Our Identity: The Image of God

THE GREAT DUTCH THEOLOGIAN ABRAHAM KUYPER made a beautiful statement in his *Encyclopedia of Sacred Theology* when he said, "If the cosmos is the theater of revelation, in this theater man is both actor and spectator."

Yesterday, we talked about being spectators of revelation. But we're also actors on the stage. Why is that? Because we are made in the image of God; we're made to reflect God. The creation account in Genesis 1 climaxes with God's making man in a different way than He made other creatures. He created man after holding a divine council, and He made him in His own image, that humanity might reflect and imitate Him.

We read in Genesis 1–2 that as God created all things and filled all things, so man as His image was given a garden to tend, fill, and extend. It's almost as though God wanted Adam and Eve to be able to walk with Him in the cool of the day and discuss the things they had in common. It's a beautiful picture with a significant reality. It means that we can never escape the revelation of God, not only because we are surrounded by it, but because as His image we carry it around with us even though we have defaced and deformed it.

This is exactly the point that Paul makes in his sermon to the Athenians when he quotes pagan writers as saying, "In [God] we live and move and have our being . . . , for we are indeed his offspring" (Acts 17:28). Therefore, not only is there no last exit from divine revelation that surrounds us; it actually invades us.

The book of Ecclesiastes puts it this way: "[God] has put eternity into man's heart" (3:11). As the great theologian Augustine said, "Our hearts are restless until they find their rest in [God]." In our world today, it has become cool and modern to say that one doesn't believe in God. It reminds me of what smoking cigarettes used to be to teenagers. It was cool; it was what everyone else was doing. But ultimately, it became a habit for many that lasted a lifetime until, in many cases, it led to death.

It's rather the same today with atheism. But the Bible teaches that if we deny the existence of God, it's not only that God collapses from our lives and worldviews; it's that our own identities collapse, and we no longer know who we really are. When that happens, we are left to make up our own version of how the world came to be. Not only that, we then have to make up our own identity.

And in the Western world, we are experiencing a pandemic of identity crisis. When we deny God, we lose our identity as His image bearers. We no longer know who we are. We have become lost souls, and the result is that our governments, agencies, programs, and schools spend billions of dollars trying to help young people know what their identity is. But they have cut off the source of that identity in God. Our young people no longer know the answer to the question, "Who am I?"

One of the greatest blessings of being a Christian is that, contrary to the people around you, you know who you are, and you know what you are made for. This truth is especially important for the younger generation to understand. You were made in God's image to know Him, to trust Him, to love Him, to serve Him, and to be with Him.

And that makes all the difference not only in this world, but also in the world to come.

4

Unbelief: A Moral Issue

WE'VE BEEN THINKING THIS WEEK ABOUT God's revelation of Himself in creation, and we've been seeing just how all-embracing that revelation is. It not only surrounds us in the created order, but also invades us because we are part of that created order—and especially because we've been created in the image of God.

The Bible teaches that even though mankind has distorted that image by our sinfulness, it hasn't been completely destroyed. We can try to suppress that fact—the fact that we know that God is and that we are made in His image and likeness—but we can never ultimately destroy it. There is no ultimate escape from revelation. We're both spectators of it and participants in it. All who claim to be atheists will at some time and in some way give themselves away. Somewhere along the line, it becomes clear that the atheism that they claim is simple intellectual honesty actually has deep twisted moral roots. Because deep down, as Paul says in Romans 1:30, they are haters of God.

Do you ever think to yourself: "Why do so many of the people who tell me they don't believe in God get so angry about Him? After all, they've just told me that He doesn't exist."

I remember coming across a very powerful illustration of this in a newspaper article. It reported on a service of tribute held in St. Martin-in-the-Fields Church of England in London. It was a memorial service for the famous English novelist Sir Kingsley Amis. Amis had been knighted by the queen. His son, Martin Amis, who was also a successful novelist, gave an address about his father. In that address, he told the following story.

On one occasion, the Russian poet and playwright Yevgeny Yevtushenko met Martin Amis's father. He said to him, "Sir Kingsley, is it true what I hear about you, that you are an atheist?" And then Martin Amis said something that apparently prompted an outburst of laughter in St. Martin-in-the-Fields. "Well, yes," Kingsley Amis said, "it's true I'm an atheist, but it's more than that. You see, I hate Him." People laughed at the self-contradictory nature of the statement. I'm sure Kingsley Amis's son meant for people to laugh, a great moment in the service. But what he said was not so much funny as tragic. I wonder if any of the A-listers in the congregation that day thought, "How desperately sad."

How stunning an illustration of what Paul says in Romans 1:18–32. Kingsley Amis denied the existence of God, and yet hated the God whose existence he denied. He is simply living (and now dead) proof of what Paul says in Romans 1. He suppressed the truth that he knew, and he did it not because of intellectual honesty but because of unrighteousness. But he could not permanently suppress it.

If Yevgeny Yevtushenko had been a Christian, I think he might have wanted to pull on this loose thread that was so obviously sticking out of the poorly woven garment of Sir Kingsley Amis's bravado and point out the inconsistency between what he professed to believe and what he really believed deep down.

I imagine that would have taken much courage. And sometimes it will take courage for us to do the same with people who are supremely self-confident and hate the hubris of their sinful hearts being unmasked. But we do need to look for and listen for these loose threads. Some of them will be less obvious; some of them will be very obvious.

So let's ask the Lord for eyes to discern them, and courage to begin to pull them, so that we may help people whose foolish hearts, as Paul says, have become darkened—help them to see their need and point them to Jesus Christ.

And let's not forget to thank God daily that we see His handiwork in everything He has made, and that He has made us in His image. And in Jesus Christ, He is transforming us back into that image so that we may be like Him again.

5

Eyes Opened to Christ

WE'VE BEEN THINKING ALL THIS WEEK about the wonder of God's revelation in the cosmos. As Christians, we marvel that we were made in His image so that we might fellowship with Him and be like Him. We've especially been thinking about mankind's rebellion and rejection of this revelation.

But before moving on from this week's theme, let's remember where this story goes in the pages of the Scriptures. For just as the Old Testament begins with the words "In the beginning, God created the heavens and the earth" (Gen. 1:1), there is a very similar beginning to the gospel of John.

John echoes what Moses wrote in Genesis 1 when he tells us that the creation came into being through the instrumentality of God's Word. In his gospel, John shows us that the Word is actually a person. He says that in the beginning, when God created all things, He did it through the person who was face-to-face with Him. In the beginning was the Word, and the Word was face-to-face with God, and the Word was God.

In the prologue to John's gospel, he makes it crystal clear that this Word is none other than our Lord Jesus Christ. He is the One without whom nothing was made that was made. He is the One who sustains all things. And, John adds daringly, He gives light to everyone.

That is something we've been considering, isn't it? Even the people who walk in darkness cannot escape the fact that their thinking, their reasoning, their loving, their living, and their sense that there might be some meaning to life is grounded in the Word who created everything. And now in Jesus Christ the Word, the true Light who enlightens everyone has come into the world.

This is a wonderful thing for us to know: the inescapability of the revelation of God in Jesus Christ. The world owes its existence to our Lord Jesus Christ. The human race owes everything to Him. It's amazing, when you think about it, that the world has rejected Him, and yet He has continued to sustain that world.

It's into that world that the Son, the Word, came to redeem us. John says that there is good news for us in the fallen creation order. And it comes in the prologue to his gospel in two stages. Stage one is wonderful: the Light continues to shine because the darkness can never extinguish it.

But if stage one is wonderful, stage two is absolutely phenomenal. The Light that gives light has come into the world. The Word has become flesh. The eternal God has come to be face-to-face with us.

And the purpose of it all is that those who come to trust in Him might have the right to become children of God.

We learn in the first chapter of John's gospel that we were created to be the children of God. We were meant to live in loving fellowship with Him and to grow in the knowledge of Him. But through Adam's sin, we have now been excluded from that garden of Eden, where Adam and Eve walked together with God in love and faithfulness. And the only way to be restored to that relationship with God is through Jesus Christ.

I don't know how long it took for it to dawn on me that there is something quite spectacular about becoming a Christian. I became a Christian because I was conscious of my sin, and I knew I needed a Savior. And by God's grace, I found the Savior. What I didn't expect to find—and this still opens my mind in awe and wonder—is that in coming to know the Savior, I'd actually come to know the Creator of the whole cosmos. And that coming to know Him as Savior meant that I could now look at creation with fresh eyes. It was created by the One who came into it in order to save me.

That is why one of my most vivid memories as a youngster singing hymns comes in those words I quoted earlier this week from George W. Robinson. When you come to Christ as Savior, you discover that He is also the Creator, and something lives in every hue that Christless eyes have never seen.

I hope that is true for you, too.

WEEK 3

John Newton's Character Types

1

The Faults We Fail to Notice

MOST OF US ARE PROBABLY FAMILIAR with the hymn "Amazing Grace," penned by the great English hymn writer John Newton.

Newton is known for many things. Before his conversion, he captained a slave transporter. After his conversion, he became a minister and preacher in the Church of England. He was a spiritual guide to the great William Wilberforce. He was also a faithful friend to William Cowper, who suffered from very deep depression. Partly in an effort to help Cowper in his depression, Newton cowrote an entire hymnbook with him.

Newton also had another talent that may be less well known, although most of his friends thought it was his greatest talent: he was one of the greatest letter writers of the Christian church. Hundreds of his letters are still available to read, and they are hugely helpful to us as Christians. This week, I want to think with you about one of his letters, which I've found quite interesting. In this letter, he puts into words—and almost into pictures—something you've probably noticed but perhaps haven't been able to put into words yourself.

I wonder if you've ever spilled a tiny blob of soup on your new silk tie, or maybe a small piece of mud gets splashed on your dress, or there is a tiny scratch on your new car. That is very discouraging, but what's even more discouraging is that everyone seems to notice. They don't say, "I like your new car." They say, "There is a scratch on your new car." Or they say: "There is a spot on the tie. Did you notice it?" Or

"What did you do to your dress?" It's this strange phenomenon that very small things can spoil the whole, and everyone notices.

Newton wrote this letter about the spiritual equivalent of this phenomenon in his fellow Christians. Here are Christians who in many respects are admirable, but they have one characteristic that somehow seems to spoil the whole. It's not a gross sin; it's just a blotch, like a scratch on one's car or a stain on one's clothing. But it's the thing that everyone notices about them and remembers, and it distorts everything. It seems far bigger, much more prominent, than any of their graces or their gifts. And yet the sad thing is, we ourselves may not be aware of the fault. We may be ignorant of the atmosphere that we leave behind us and unaware that it isn't the aroma of our Lord Jesus Christ.

We're a bit like people who get into an elevator in an office building, smartly dressed and well groomed, but after a few seconds, everyone's nose tells them that they have been outside smoking. Every breath they take, every breath they breathe out, tells us something they don't notice about themselves. And the odor isn't attractive. In fact, perhaps it repels rather than attracts.

And perhaps you've noticed a spiritual equivalent.

Have you any idea at all if there is a scratch, or a dent, or a mark, or a blotch in your life that you've hardly noticed, but it might be the thing that stands out to others and makes them think that although you profess to be growing in likeness to Jesus Christ, something is hindering you? Maybe even thinking about that will draw something to your attention. And if that is the case, what you really need to do is to tell the Lord Jesus about it because He has promised to forgive you. And He has also promised to begin to cleanse you and make you more like Himself.

This week, we'll talk about some of the people that John Newton describes in his letter, and I think maybe you'll be able to recognize them.

2

The Austere Christian

WHEN OUR CHILDREN WERE YOUNG, we used to read them a series of books by Roger Hargreaves called the Mr. Men books. They were cartoon books in which people's faults seemed to stick out in the pictures—Mr. Nosey, Mr. Fussy, and so on. In John Newton's letter, in a very wonderful and gracious way, he writes a kind of Christian version of the Mr. Men books, and he gives Christians some rather interesting names. Since he was writing in the eighteenth century and had a good sense of humor, all these names are in Latin. But don't worry about that; you'll recognize these people immediately.

One of the people he talks about is Mr. Austerus. You probably know someone like him. In many respects, Mr. Austerus, or maybe Mrs. Austerus, is an admirable Christian who knows the Bible well, is committed to living according to God's Word, studies the Scriptures, prays, and is disciplined in giving. And the one thing you can be sure about Mr. Austerus is that he won't bend to the prevailing winds in society. He knows that we've moved a lot closer to George Orwell's *1984* than we were when Orwell wrote it in 1949. And he is not impressed by fads in the church either. He doesn't like worship that resembles a pop concert or preachers who remind him of T-shirt-wearing stand-up comedians. Not Mr. Austerus.

And you know, there is probably a good deal to admire in Mr. Austerus's principles and courage. He'd die rather than compromise.

But Newton says something very insightful about Mr. Austerus. He says he prizes the precepts of God's Word, but there is one thing he seems to have forgotten: he has forgotten to be courteous and loving. And instead of his having the gentleness of the Lord Jesus, there is something about him that seems to demand attention but never stimulates love for him. For all his admirable qualities, there is a kind of armor-platedness about him that repels rather than attracts.

Newton puts it like this:

His intimate friends are satisfied that he is no stranger to true humility of heart, but these friends are few. By others, he is thought proud, dogmatic, and self-important. Nor can this prejudice against him be easily removed until he can lay aside that cynical air which he has unhappily contracted.

The problem with Mr. Austerus is that he doesn't realize that his virtue has been twisted out of shape. It's become disconnected from the other graces that are so vital to a Christlike life. That is the problem, and that is actually why he doesn't have many intimate friends—unlike Jesus, the friend of sinners. But Mr. Austerus doesn't see this about himself yet.

If you were Mr. Austerus, here's one way you might begin to recognize yourself: if what I've just said irritates you a little and you want to defend him. I can imagine that Mr. Austerus's self-defense might be, "But Jesus was austere, too." Yes, Jesus could set His face like flint to go to Jerusalem. But the same Jesus could say, "I am meek and gentle in heart, and you will find My presence restful." That is what Mr. Austerus is missing, and that is why people don't unburden themselves to him. He has forgotten what the Savior is really like, and that he needs to be made like that, too.

3

Can You Keep a Secret?

WE'VE BEEN TALKING THIS WEEK ABOUT a letter written by John Newton around two hundred years ago. It's a letter about people whose problem is that they sing about amazing grace, but they haven't themselves become amazingly gracious. Newton had some clever Latin names for these people. Yesterday, we talked about Mr. Austerus. Another person that Newton mentions in his letter is almost at the opposite end of the spectrum: Mr. Humanus.

Mr. Humanus is a people person. He is the kind of person, as is Mrs. Humanus, who is all over new visitors to the church, giving them a warm welcome. He is gregarious and friendly, but here's the problem: there is a seam of inconsistency in his Christian life. Newton captures it like this: If you trusted Mr. Humanus with your gold, there would be no risk at all. It would be perfectly safe. With money, he is a model of integrity. But entrust him with a secret, and you put your secret into the public domain. He just can't keep it to himself.

Some time ago, I was having dinner with some Christian friends. At one point in the conversation, they expressed interest in something that had happened in my life when I was a teenager. And I said to them: "I'll tell you what it is as long as you promise never to tell anyone. Promise me?" None of them promised. They were all mature Christians. Most of them were pastors. And I think most of them had read some of John Newton's letters. I wonder if they were thinking: "I don't think I can trust myself to keep Sinclair's secret. I think I'd be tempted to share it."

This was the problem with Mr. Humanus. He trusted himself too much, and he had lost control of his tongue. And that means he had actually lost control of his heart, because spiritually, the tongue is directly connected to the heart. As a result, eventually his fellow Christians realized they couldn't share their secrets with him. For all his friendliness, they could never unburden themselves to him. And so they never told him about their struggles, their problems, their failures, or their deepest needs, and he was left wondering, "Why do they share these things with other people and never with me?"

Keeping secrets is a small thing. Failing to keep them is a big thing. Because faithfulness isn't really faithfulness unless it's faithfulness in everything. Being faithful in the big things doesn't minimize the importance of being faithful in the small things.

Do you ever wonder why there are some people in your church family to whom other people tend to go? One reason is that people trust them to keep their secrets, and the reason is that faithful people guard their hearts and their lips as though they were Fort Knox.

You and I need to learn to do the same. So remember Jesus' words, "One who is faithful in a very little is also faithful in much" (Luke 16:10).

4

Loud Opinions and Little Prayer

WE'VE ALREADY MET MR. AUSTERUS, the austere Christian, and Mr. Humanus, the gregarious Christian. John Newton also wants us to meet Mr. Querulus, and perhaps Mrs. Querulus, too. What is Mr. Querulus's problem? Newton says, "He wastes much of his precious time in declaiming against the management of public affairs." Or to put it in contemporary terms, he is always expressing opinions about what governments, authorities, educational systems, or churches are doing wrong. And he always seems to know what they should be doing right.

Newton has the courage to say that Mr. Querulus is just wasting his time, and our time, too. And the reason he gives is this: Mr. Querulus has no expert knowledge or any personally researched information on which he bases his judgment. He simply parrots things he picks up from talk shows on television, or on the radio, or in the particular kind of literature he reads. And Newton says he is just wasting his time.

I imagine if Mr. Querulus heard Newton say that, it would be something of a body blow to him. And Newton didn't say this because he was uninterested in the affairs of life. He is the one who discouraged

William Wilberforce from leaving Parliament—and perhaps going into the ministry—and told him to stay in politics. Newton really cared about the affairs of the world, and he really was concerned about the good of the city.

Here's what he says about Mr. Querulus: "Our national concerns are no more affected by the remonstrances of Querulus than the heavenly bodies are by the disputes of astronomers." In other words, Mr. Querulus is much talk without any transformation. Of course, Newton is not saying that these things are unimportant. As I said, he encouraged William Wilberforce to stay in politics and continue his opposition to the slave trade.

But I think if Newton were alive today, he would be worried about the equivalent of Mr. Querulus, and perhaps especially in the ministry—ministers whose tweets and blogs and videos and programs rather suggest that they think the world is waiting to hear their opinions, although their opinions will do little to transform the world in which they live. And Newton says something in many ways much more cutting. He says that what Mr. Querulus is doing is a sinful conformity to the men of this world.

Newton says: "There are people enough to make a noise about political matters, who know not how to employ their time to a better purpose. Our Lord's kingdom is not of this world; and most of these people may do their country much more essential service by pleading for it in prayer, than by finding fault with things which they have no power to alter."

I wonder how many websites you visit, or tweets you see, or programs you watch on YouTube or other channels, where the mastermind is always pulling other people down and expressing his opinions. And there is the rub: the Mr. Queruluses of this world—and within the Christian church—spend a lot more time telling people what's wrong than they tend to spend speaking about the beauties and glories and graces of the Lord Jesus Christ.

And maybe Newton points us to the litmus test: How loud am I in my opinions? How long am I in expressing them? And how little am I upon my knees?

That is a word in season, don't you think?

5

Give Sin a Name

IN NEWTON'S COLLECTED WORKS, THE TITLE of the letter we've been discussing this week is, "On Some Blemishes in Christian Character." And perhaps you've recognized yourself, or at least parts of yourself, in one or another of these characters. As we come to the end of the week, I want to ask a question: "If we recognize a blemish in our Christian character, something that seems to obscure the grace and graciousness of Jesus Christ, is there a remedy? Is there a pathway we can follow to spiritual transformation?"

We know that being a Christian isn't a matter of following a checklist, but the Scriptures are full of helpful and wise directives for us to follow, and I want to suggest a few principles to you.

The first is this: whatever you come to realize is distorting the image of the Lord Jesus in you, be sure to give it a name. I think it's part of the wisdom of John Newton that when he described these people, he specified their names. And in fact, that is what Scripture does. Scripture encourages us to confess our faults, and it actually encourages us not to be vague about them. Rather than confessing our faults in general, we should specify them and give them names.

It's always intrigued me that in Ephesians 5, the Apostle Paul says there are things that shouldn't be named among believers (v. 3), and yet in Colossians 3:5, he actually names those very things! What explains the paradox? It's this: if we don't have a clear sight of the target that we want to destroy in our lives, then we will miss it. Unless we confess to the Lord, "Lord, the blemish on my Christian character and walk is called . . . (whatever it is)," it's unlikely that we will really be delivered from it. So we need to learn to name the distortion.

Here's a second principle that I think is helpful: write down on a piece of paper the nature of your blemish, and then write down the name of the opposite grace to your blemish. What grace of the Lord Jesus Christ is the opposite of your blemish? And when you have done that, commit yourself before God to seeking it. This is a principle that we need to keep coming back to. We are not transformed merely by avoiding the works of the flesh; we need to simultaneously seek the fruit of the Spirit. Just trying to get rid of the blemish may actually make it worse and no more likely to transform us than scratching an itch will make it go away. As you read through Paul's letters, you'll notice that he does this constantly. We are to put off, but we are also to put on.

And here's a third principle: we need to realize that the resources for lasting transformation are found in the Lord Jesus Christ. Having named our sinful blemish and named the opposite grace, we should then turn perhaps particularly to the Gospels and read about the Lord Jesus Christ. As we see how that opposite grace is manifested in His life, we can pray the simple prayer, "Lord God, make me more like my Lord Jesus Christ."

And if we make that prayer without any strings attached, and if we don't try to second-guess how the Lord is going to do it, He surely will do it.

WEEK 4

Things We Have Forgotten

1

A Day to Remember

THIS WEEK, WE'RE GOING TO EXPLORE some things that Scripture urges us to remember—things that we shouldn't forget. If you looked in a Bible concordance, I think you'd find that the words related to remembering and forgetting appear about two hundred times. Remembering is a fundamental Christian spiritual duty. Some of these verses may come to mind. For example, "Remember also your Creator in the days of your youth" (Eccl. 12:1).

But how do we remember? It's all very well to be told to do it, but how do we do it? Can we really make ourselves remember?

When I was a child, I was taught that if I needed to remember something, I should tie a knot in my handkerchief and put it in my pocket. And when I needed to remember whatever it was, I should take out the handkerchief, and I would remember it. It worked for a while. Later on, when it stopped working, I developed the technique of going to the spot where I thought I had last remembered what I had forgotten. And sometimes I stood there for quite a long time forgetting.

What was I trying to do when I did that? I was trying to, as it were, click on the file of the information to get it to open up so that I could remember what I should be doing or thinking, or where I should be going. In other words, I was trying to stimulate my memory banks. Now, is there some kind of spiritual equivalent of that?

The Scriptures do teach us how to develop a healthy spiritual memory. It's important to note that we don't do this in the same way the Eastern mystics would—that is, by emptying our minds. In fact, it's the very reverse.

Scripture teaches us that the key to remembering is to fill our minds with the truth of God and then to employ the stimulants that God has given us to remember the things we must never forget.

What must we never forget? We'll talk about one or two of them later this week, but we'll briefly discuss one of them today. This may come as something of a surprise, but it's actually one of the most helpful things that the Bible tells us, and it's one of the most important verses about remembering that we find in the Old Testament.

In Exodus 20:8–11, we read the commandment to remember the Sabbath day, to keep it holy. Why is that so important? I think it's a key to remembering for this reason: from the very dawn of creation, God has given us one entire day every week to set aside our work and have time to think about Him, read His Word, fellowship with other believers, and sit under the ministry of His Word.

Through these different avenues, God stores up in our minds the truth that He wants us to know and remember.

I think that people often make the mistake of thinking that the Sabbath commandment is about one day in the week. But if you read it carefully, you'll notice that it's actually about seven days in the week: six days we work; one day we rest. And if you think about it, Adam's first full day was his day of rest.

Adam was called to live on the basis of a day on which he could reflect on God's creation and goodness, store his mind with reflections on who God is, and then work through the rest of the week with that mindset. And that rhythm is really very important. We need that space to have our minds decluttered and then filled with the truth of God's Word. It's the day when our whole beings are intended to be recalibrated into this weekly rhythm of rest and work.

I wonder if you've discovered what to do when the cursor on your computer screen freezes up. I remember how amazed I was, after trying all kinds of things, when I found the instructions saying, "Close the program, turn off the computer, take out the plug for thirty seconds, then reverse the process and reboot." And lo and behold, things worked very smoothly again. The Sabbath day is that kind of command. It's saying, "Close the program of the other six days, turn that off, wait for thirty seconds, reboot, and you'll be recalibrated in such a way that you'll be able to live with greater pleasure for the glory of God."

I think that one of the saddest things about evangelical Christianity is that we see this commandment as probably the darkest of commandments. It's almost the commandment that you dare not mention among evangelical Christians. And I say it's sad not because I think we should get back to legalism or some dark form of Sabbatarianism, but because we fail to recalibrate our lives as God intended, and the evidence of it shows in many different ways. There are so many things that we forget because of this one thing that we haven't remembered.

So if you're reading this on a Monday, put something in the pocket of what you'll wear this coming Sunday, just in case you forget to remember!

2

Lest You Forget the Lord

YESTERDAY, WE TALKED ABOUT THE CONCEPT of remembering and how important memory is in the Bible. I mentioned one of the great master keys that God has given to help us improve our spiritual memory: we need the space of one day in seven that we may remember well the other six days.

Here's another key to remembering, and for some reason, the Bible puts it negatively. Perhaps this is to emphasize it to people who tend to assume that it's something we'd never forget. It's the words of

Deuteronomy 6:12: "Take care lest you forget the LORD." The same words appear again a couple of chapters later in Deuteronomy 8:11: "Take care lest you forget the LORD."

Why should God have issued such a wake-up call to His people and, through them, to us? I think perhaps because it's so easy for us to think, "The one thing I'll never forget is the Lord." Perhaps He has intervened in your life in some way, and you've said, "From now on, it is impossible for me ever to forget the Lord." And yet before too long, you've begun to forget Him again. I don't mean that we become atheists. We don't forget God in that sense. What I mean is that we forget what He is like, and that sometimes means we end up thinking He has forgotten us. It's one of the great paradoxes of spiritual life: we have forgotten Him, but we misinterpret reality and we think He has forgotten us.

There is a very moving illustration of this in Psalm 102. It's not only a great psalm, but also a great example of how to remember what we have forgotten and the difference that remembering the Lord makes.

The first eleven verses are perhaps the most melancholy poetry we could imagine reading. The psalmist is distressed and depressed. He says that his days pass like smoke. He is not eating. He is lonely. He is not sleeping well. And he basically feels that no one understands him. He is withering away like grass. And worst of all, he feels that God has forgotten him. And yet the man is obviously a believer. So what's wrong?

Part of the answer is this: in the space of these eleven verses, he uses the word "I" seven times, the word "me" seven times, and the word "my" fourteen times. And that is the problem. As Martin Luther used to say, in some ways, it's our biggest problem. We are, as he put it, *incurvatus in se*, "turned in upon ourselves." We're remembering ourselves, but we are not remembering the Lord.

After eleven verses of sinking down, the psalmist comes to the answer. Yes, it is going to take time for him to recover fully, but here is how the transformation begins. It's actually just two words in Hebrew: "But You, O LORD." It's as if He has pressed the ignition switch. The engine of grace has been fired up. The spiritual memory file has unfrozen. He looks outward and upward. He looks Bibleward, and he begins to remember. God is enthroned; God is the Lord; God has been remembered throughout the generations; God is merciful and will have pity on him; God is from everlasting to everlasting.

Earlier in the psalm, he felt isolated and turned in on himself. He had forgotten God, and life was no longer worth living. But when he remembers God, by the end of the psalm, he is talking about his grandchildren knowing the Lord's blessing. He is talking about the people of God having a future.

No wonder we're told not to forget the Lord. Because we're so prone to.

But if we have forgotten Him, the first step of recovery is this: to say out loud: "But You, O Lord! Lord, I remember You, and I know You have never forgotten me, and that You are there. And I'm coming to You now. Lift me up and restore me." And just as He did for the man who wrote Psalm 102, He will surely do for you.

3

Storing Up Scripture in Our Hearts

WE'VE BEEN THINKING THIS WEEK ABOUT the way the Bible places a premium on our ability to remember. And yet the question that we've been trying to answer in different ways is, "How do we do that?" It's all very well to be told to remember, but how can we begin to remember when our problem is actually that we keep on forgetting?

We saw that part of the answer is having our minds and hearts well stocked with the knowledge of who God is and what God is like.

I wonder if you know the great old Scottish hymn that is called "'Twixt Gleams of Joy and Clouds of Doubt." Here's the first verse:

'Twixt gleams of joy and clouds of doubt,
Our feelings come and go;
Our best estate is toss'd about
In ceaseless ebb and flow.
No mood of feeling, form of thought,
Is constant for a day;
But Thou, O Lord, Thou changest not:
The same Thou art alway.

These are the words of a man who found himself in difficulties and was struggling. He eventually realized that he had forgotten something: his Lord was the same yesterday, today, and forever. And that knowledge recalibrated his thinking and his emotions. It stabilized him. And all because in the past he had stored up Scripture in his mind and heart.

I don't think it's possible to overemphasize how important this is for days when we may be forgetful. It reminds me of something that Charles Spurgeon, the nineteenth-century Baptist minister, once said about John Bunyan, the author of *The Pilgrim's Progress*. He said, "Prick Bunyan anywhere, and he bleeds bibline." He was really saying that John Bunyan was so saturated with Scripture that it simply flowed out of him because it had flowed into him.

The Christian life isn't lived in a robotic fashion where we're constantly thinking, "Is there a verse of the Bible that will help me in this situation?" That would make for very artificial Christian living. What we really need is to so absorb Scripture that it becomes part of us. Then in a sense, we become a walking Bible in human form, and it begins to flow out of us instinctively the way that a concert pianist's knowledge of the great work he is playing seems to become part of him, and he plays almost by instinct. He doesn't even need the score in front of him.

The Scriptures urge us to develop that kind of knowledge of them. And that is why, for example, Psalm 119 was originally written in the form that we have it. It was meant to be memorized by young people. That is why there are verses like this: "How can a young man keep his way pure? By guarding it according to your word" (v. 9). Its emphasis is on storing up the words of Scripture in our minds and in our hearts. Job had done that. He said, "I have treasured the words of [God's] mouth more than my portion of food" (Job 23:12).

When you get to know older saints, you realize how fruitful this is. I've known people whose minds seem to have gone and who can't even remember the names of their nearest and dearest relatives. But if you begin to quote a verse of Scripture, they will join in. It's as though the Word of God has gone deeply into their souls. And when they are almost beyond fellowship of any coherent kind with others, they are clearly still engaged in profound fellowship with the Lord.

We tend not to think about that when we're younger, but we are sowing the seeds of the harvest that we will reap in the future, and we desperately need to sow the seeds of the Word of God in our hearts. And that, as we soon begin to discover, is a lifelong process. So we'll think a little more about that tomorrow.

4

Remembering the Covenant

WE'VE BEEN THINKING ALL WEEK ABOUT the importance of remembering in the Christian life.

Years ago, we carpooled with another family for school, and I was driving our son and their daughter home on the very last day of class. The little girl was expressing considerable anxiety about how difficult their next year at school was going to be. And to my complete astonishment, my young son turned to her and said, "There is nothing to worry about next year because it's all a matter of revision."

I don't think he knew at the age of eight or nine that he was embracing a rather well-known and particular point of view of a philosophical school. Because some philosophers have held the view that the human mind at birth is a *tabula rasa*. It's a totally blank slate, like an empty computer disk that needs to be programmed and populated with information. But other philosophers, and some neuroscientists as well, have held the view that the human brain, at least to some extent, comes preprogrammed and already hardwired. Otherwise, how can you explain that human beings everywhere with very different languages seem by and large to think in the same ways?

No matter whether the empiricists or the innatists, as they are called, are right, one thing is for sure: none of us is born with the Bible already in our memory banks. We need to put it there. We need to program our memories with the truth of Scripture, and as we know from God's Word, this is how our lives are transformed. Transformation takes place by the renewal of the mind, and the renewal of the mind takes place through the truth of Scripture. Therefore, we must hide God's Word in our hearts.

I don't know if you've ever thought about this, but it's not only true of us that we don't come preprogrammed with the Bible in our minds. It was true of the Lord Jesus. In His humanity, He had to program His mind with the truth of Scripture. And He must have known from early days that this, in fact, was prophesied of Him in those lovely Servant Songs that we find in the second half of the prophecy of Isaiah.

Here are some words that Isaiah puts into the mouth of our Lord Jesus: "The Lord GOD has given me the tongue of those who are taught, that I may know how to sustain with a word him who is weary" (Isa. 50:4). Isn't that a beautiful description of Jesus, the meek and the lowly, sustaining those who are weary?

How did that come about? Here is how the verse continues: "Morning by morning he awakens; he awakens my ear to hear as those who are taught." And if that was true of the Lord Jesus in His perfect humanity, how much more true it needs to be of us as we battle against our inward temptations and native sin and seek to live for God's glory. We need to hide the Word of God in our hearts.

We find another passage about remembering and forgetting in Deuteronomy 4: "Take care, lest you forget the covenant of the LORD your God" (v. 23). The word "LORD" in this verse is "Yahweh"—the covenant name of God. That was a very important command that the Lord was giving to His people.

There is a remarkable passage later on in 2 Kings 17, in which the author interjects his own voice into the story to remind his readers just how important these words were for God's people. But then he adds—you can almost imagine with a slight shake of his head—"However, they would not listen" (v. 40). They didn't take care. They forgot the covenant of the Lord their God, and spiritual disaster followed.

I wonder when you last remembered the covenant of the Lord, or even last thought about it. I think your answer will probably tell you a good deal about how much or how little the Lord's covenant means to you. But here's something wonderful: the Lord not only urges us in Scripture to remember His covenant; He helps us to remember it.

Every time we come to the Lord's Table, through the bread and the wine, the Lord Jesus is whispering to us, "Remember the covenant in My blood." What we see in the bread and wine stimulates our memories, and we remember Christ's death until He comes. The bread is placed in our hands, the cup on our lips, and we are given these remembrances by Jesus of His covenant love for us.

We are so much more privileged than those old covenant saints who were told to remember the Lord's covenant. He knows how forgetful we are, and He helps us. And it is, I think, one of the most wonderful things in the world for us to remember that He is a covenant-making and covenant-keeping God. And the covenant He has kept has been the most difficult covenant in human history to keep because it cost Him His Son.

He has remembered His covenant, and we should remember it, too.

5

I Will Remember Their Sins No More

AS WE APPROACH THE END OF THE WEEK, we're going to think about something that we actually need to forget. Yesterday, we talked about remembering God's covenant with us because He remembers that covenant with us, and He promises that He will never forget it. But I find it intriguing that in that covenant, He actually promises that there is something He *will* forget.

In the promise of the new covenant made in Jeremiah 31:34, quoted in the New Testament in Hebrews 8:12 because it is fulfilled in Jesus Christ, God says, "I will remember their sins no more." He makes a similar promise in Isaiah 43:25: "I am he who blots out your transgressions for my own sake, and I will not remember your sins." We can think about it this way: the only thing that God says He forgets is our sins. He has blotted them out with the blood of His Son, Jesus Christ.

That is a very important promise to remember because some of us—I suspect more than might be prepared to admit in public—are haunted by the memory of our past sins. Remember how that was true of King David. In Psalm 51:3, he wrote that his sins were ever before him. He could be paralyzed by the memory of them. Perhaps there were days when he was not thinking much about his past, and then all of a sudden out of nowhere, the memory of his sins was like a fiery dart in his mind, paralyzing his sense of fellowship with God. And so David needed to know day by day that his sins were blotted out and that the Lord remembered them no more.

In the United Kingdom, people sometimes invest in what are usually called *gilts*. Gilt-edged securities are very high-grade government-issued stock. I think they are called that because originally the paper on which they were printed was gilt-edged, like some of the old Bibles. And

I sometimes think that the devil, who is described as the accuser of the brethren, is an investor in guilt-edged stock—not *gilt*, but *guilt*.

When Satan tempts us to sin, he tells us, "This isn't such a big deal." But then when we fail and fall, he capitalizes on our sin and emphasizes our guilt. He comes to us and almost seems to screw into us our deep incapacity and, as John Calvin once said, seeks to drive us to despair. We can be paralyzed with shame, and it can be a frightening thing to experience. We're like Joshua the high priest in Zechariah 3. There we are before God, clothed with filthy garments, and Satan is standing at our side accusing us.

We need to remember what happens next in that passage. The Lord said to Satan, "The LORD rebuke you, O Satan!" (v. 2), and the angel of the Lord took off Joshua's filthy garments. He then spoke these beautiful, heart-melting words: "Behold, I have taken your iniquity away from you, and I will clothe you with pure vestments" (v. 4). What a picture that is of the believer clothed in the filthy garments of sin, but now, through Jesus Christ, clothed in pure vestments from head to toe.

I wonder if you can see yourself standing before the throne of God and hearing God say: "But I don't see any sin. I see only purity. I've covered your sin with the blood of Christ and clothed you in His righteousness." Does God really forget your sin as you trust Him? Yes, indeed. He tells us that He removes our sin as far as the east is from the west (Ps. 103:12). I wonder if you have forgotten what God says He will forget. God remembers our sins no more.

So perhaps the thing we need to remember most of all is the one thing the Lord tells us He remembers no more. There is nothing more glorious than to be living a paralysis-free Christian life in the presence of the heavenly Father, knowing that He loves us more than we will ever know; and that He has given His Son to cover our sins; and that He says to us, "Your sins I remember no more."

I do hope you know the peace that brings.

WEEK 5

Scripture

1

The Mouth of God

SOMETIMES THE WORD *DOCTRINE* IS HEARD as though it were a slightly nasty word. But it's far too important in the Bible for that to be true. Knowing biblical doctrine is like having the architect's drawings for a building. If we don't have the architect's drawings, we don't know what we're building, and we're not going to be very successful. And if we have bad drawings, the building is going to be faulty.

The same is true in the Christian life. There is a close relationship between our understanding of Christian doctrine and the way we live the Christian life. I know that people often say, "Doctrine divides; experience unites." But that is not only far from the truth; it's almost the reverse of the truth. The reality is that true doctrine unites, and the New Testament itself teaches us that.

Years ago, I read the Scots Confession, which was written in 1560. There were six authors, and they all had the name John: John Winram, John Spottiswood, John Willock, John Douglas, John Row, and John Knox. This confession was a guiding light to Scottish Christians, pointing them to Christ and the faith once delivered to the saints. What struck me the first time I read it was the introduction, in which Knox and his friends wrote that if anyone found anything misleading in the confession, he should tell the authors, and they would respond to him "from the mouth of God."

They were talking about the Bible, of course. I remember that my instant thought was, "What a tremendous way to describe the Bible—the mouth of God." But my next thought was: "It wasn't John Knox who came up with that expression! It's how Jesus described the Bible." When Jesus was tempted by Satan in the wilderness, He said, "Man shall not live by bread alone, but by every word that comes from the mouth of God" (Matt. 4:4). Jesus Himself was actually quoting from Deuteronomy 8:3. Of course, Paul puts it the same way but in different words. He tells us that the Scriptures are "breathed out by God" (2 Tim. 3:16).

As we think today about the doctrine of Scripture, perhaps the simplest and most helpful way for us to read the Bible is to think of it as "the mouth of God." When we read it, we should think of ourselves as listening to God Himself speak, because indeed He does speak through the Bible. And because that is true, it tells us a lot about the authority and reliability of the Bible. If God is speaking through it, we can trust it. And if God is telling us something by it, we should do it.

This little phrase "the mouth of God" has the power not only to instruct the way we think about the nature of the Bible, but also to help us read the Bible. I quoted the other day some words written by Isaiah about the coming Savior: that morning by morning, the Lord opened His ear and He heard as one who was taught (Isa. 50:4). He listened through the Word to the voice of God.

Think about the Bible this way, and you'll likely find yourself paying more attention to it. More than that, you'll begin to realize that there are few greater privileges in all the world than sitting with your Bible and listening to your heavenly Father speaking to you through it. Remember in Hebrews 12 where the author of Hebrews quotes from the book of Proverbs? He doesn't say, "This is what God said." He says, "And have you forgotten the exhortation that *addresses* you as sons?" (v. 5, emphasis added). The verb is in the present tense. He is now, through the Scriptures, addressing us as sons. I think we need to recover that sense of the amazing privilege we have in possessing the Bible.

There are more editions of the Bible, more shapes and sizes of the Bible, than ever before. Christians own more copies of the Bible than ever before. But all the statistics tell us that we are a generation that knows so little about the Bible. And perhaps it's because we've forgotten what the Bible really is. It's the mouth of God. We need to learn to say with the Lord Jesus, in the words of Isaiah 50:4, "Morning by morning . . . he awakens my ear to hear as those who are taught."

And if we do that, we'll begin to grow and become more like our Lord Jesus.

2

God's Word at Work in Us

YESTERDAY, WE TALKED ABOUT ONE OF the best ways to think about the Bible: it is "the mouth of God." The Apostle Paul thought about it that way, too. He said that it was the God-breathed Word (2 Tim. 3:16). When Paul speaks that way, he is not saying that the Bible is inspiring—although in many parts it is inspiring—but rather that God has spoken to us, that His words are carried to us, by the Holy Spirit. And as God said to Jeremiah, He has put His words into the mouths of those who wrote the Scriptures in order that we may hear God's voice (Jer. 1:9).

So although the Bible was written by different men at different times, they were carried along by the Holy Spirit (2 Peter 1:21). That is why John Calvin says in his *Institutes of the Christian Religion* that we should give the Scriptures the same reverence we give to God. Not because the Scriptures are God, but because the Scriptures are the mouth of God, the Word of God. And as God's Word, it is full of God's promises, and it directs us in God's will. Most of all, it shows us God's Son. It's given to us chiefly in order to make us like Jesus.

We've already looked at the passage in Isaiah, referring to Jesus, that says that morning by morning He listened to the voice of His heavenly Father and treasured up His Father's words (Isa. 50:4). And if you read the Gospels, it's striking that although Jesus never had a Bible of His own, He clearly treasured up Scripture. My own conviction is that He probably knew all the Old Testament by heart. He wanted the Scriptures to shape His life in obedience to His Father, and He wanted to mine the Scriptures to be able to instruct and teach others. He wanted to live by every word that came out of the mouth of God, and He believed in the absolute authority of Scripture. That is why it was said of Him that He spoke with authority and not as the scribes did.

I owe a great debt to the man who was my minister when I was in my teens. When he saw that I had come to believe that the Bible was fully inspired and finally authoritative, he took me aside one day and said, "How you view these issues doesn't really affect the way you preach." I had heard very few people preach at that point in my Christian life, so I wasn't able to debate him on the basis of personal evidence. But I'd become convinced that he couldn't possibly be right and that it must affect the way people preach. But I couldn't point to other preachers and say, "Listen to their preaching, and you'll be able to tell the difference."

But in my later teen years, I did hear other preachers. And even as a teenager, I could tell the difference. Only when and where the Scriptures are believed as absolutely reliable will we hear the kind of preaching that God intends us to hear. That is why it's so important to be in a church where the Word of God is believed to have come from the mouth of God. That explains the authority of the preaching, the fullness of the preaching, and the benefit of the preaching.

Only then do we begin to understand what Paul was talking about when he wrote to the Thessalonians and said, "And we also thank God constantly for this, that when you received the word of God, which you heard from us, you accepted it not as the word of men but as what it really is, the word of God" (1 Thess. 2:13). And then he added something very significant. He said "which is at work in you believers." And that is the big difference.

Many Christians believe that reading the Bible and hearing the preaching of the Bible is simply a matter of the Bible's telling us what to do and our going and doing it. But where the Bible is believed to be the living Word of God, we begin to experience what Paul is talking about here. It's not just that we do the work that the Scriptures tell us to perform. It's that the exposition of the Word does the work on us. It works in us. It transforms us. It shapes us to be more like Jesus.

That is why we need to believe in the authority of Scripture, and that is why we need to place our lives under a ministry of the Word that shares that conviction, in order that the Word will do its own work in us.

I wonder if that is your experience, too. I hope so.

3

Teaching and Reproof

AS WE DISCUSSED YESTERDAY, THE WORD of God isn't inert and powerless. Rather, Paul said that it's at work in believers (1 Thess. 2:13). If you've been a Christian for some time, you're probably familiar with the Old Testament version of that statement: "So shall my word be that goes out from my mouth; it shall not return to me empty, but it shall accomplish that which I purpose, and shall succeed in the thing for which I sent it" (Isa. 55:11). That is a verse worth memorizing.

But when the Word of God works, what does it accomplish? That question brings Paul's important words to Timothy to mind, where he talks about the Scripture being breathed out by God and profitable (2 Tim. 3:16–17).

The Greek word he uses there means "useful." Paul rarely uses this word in his letters. Interestingly, when he does, it's always in the pastoral letters, the letters he wrote to the pastors Timothy and Titus. And here he is telling Timothy, and by extension telling us, something very important. If something has a specific use, then we need to understand what that use is. So what is the Word of God for? What is it useful for? What does it accomplish?

Paul gives several answers: doctrine, or teaching; reproof, or convicting us of our faults; correction; and training in righteousness. He goes on to say, "That the man of God may be complete, equipped for every good work."

God's Word teaches us doctrine. But then Paul adds a second word: "reproof." In other words, if we're going to be healthy Christians, we're going to need God to perform spiritual surgery to deal with the malignancies in our lives. God's Word is like a surgeon's scalpel, whether He holds it in His hand directly or operates by some providential means. And that is the kind of healing that causes pain before it brings cure. God's Word can hurt in order to heal. In fact, it needs to hurt because we need to discover what's wrong with us in order to experience conviction, which means being made aware of our sin, that we may learn our need of Jesus Christ.

Martin Luther says in the very first of his famous Ninety-Five Theses that when our Lord Jesus Christ said "Repent," He meant that the whole of the Christian life should be repentance. I wish every Christian understood that. Yes, repentance begins at conversion, but it's not just a thing of the past. It goes through the rest of our lives, and that is why we need the Word of God to continue to reprove us. The Christian life is an ongoing cycle of discovering our sinfulness in order that we may seek Christ, experience God's grace, and turn away from sin. And as we grow and God's Word does its work in us, we realize that our sin goes down even deeper than we ever imagined.

We live the Christian life convicted of our sin, confessing our sin, repenting of our sin, and enjoying forgiveness. That is why when we read the Bible, we should always hold it up as a mirror to our own soul and ask ourselves: "Is there something amiss, Lord? Are You pointing out my sin here?" And even saying: "Lord, it hurts to see how much I have failed You. Help me to turn to You again for Your forgiveness and to turn away from my sin."

I wonder if even as I say that, God is touching your conscience. If that is the case, then the Word of God is reproving you to bring you to repentance so that you may enjoy His forgiveness and new life.

4

Correction: A Healing Word

WE NOTED YESTERDAY HOW THE APOSTLE PAUL said that the Scriptures are profitable, or useful, for us. They teach us doctrine. They reveal our sinfulness. They reprove us. They show us our failures and lead us to turn back to the Lord and turn away from our sin. In a word, they help us to keep on living a life of repentance.

But Paul also tells us that Scripture is useful for other things, and one of them is what most of our translations call "correction." To be honest, that word always makes me wince a little. I suppose that is because when I was in elementary school, we spoke of our teachers "correcting" our exams, and I felt more or less that the word *correct* was the same as the word *reprove*. Correcting my exams meant that there were red crosses down the side of the page and that something had gone wrong. But I could hardly be further from understanding what Paul means when he speaks about correction.

I'm glad, therefore, that I know some Greek, because the Greek word Paul uses here has a completely different atmosphere about it. It's a wonderfully positive word—*epanorthōsis*. Did you hear the word *orthos* right in the middle? Even if you don't know any Greek, you can guess what that means from the English words you know. When we break our arm or leg, we go to an *ortho*pedic surgeon and he sets it. Or if there is something wrong with our bite, the dentist sends us to the *ortho*dontist. And although it might be expensive, we end up not only with a healthy bite, but also with a beautiful smile. We no longer need to be embarrassed.

That is the atmosphere of Paul's word here. It's used outside the New Testament in a medical context. It's a healing word: setting a broken bone or straightening something that has become deformed. And that is what the Word of God does. It straightens what has become deformed. It heals what has become sick. I think we could also say it improves our bite as Christians because people see the difference it makes. And it also produces a kind of beauty in us, a kind of smile.

Incidentally, there is another word that has *orthos* at its root. It's the word *orthodoxy*. To some people, that is a very cold word. But I hope you see now that it really means something very beautiful. It means that our thinking, speaking, and feeling about the triune God, the gospel, the Christian life, and the future have all been healed, straightened, and mended. So although I used to find the word "correction" very difficult as a youngster when I read 2 Timothy 3:16–17, it's a word I've come to love. God's Word works in our lives to bring healing and transformation. It brings correction where things have gone wrong.

Most of my life, I've been a teacher, preacher, and pastor. So perhaps you would allow me to briefly apply this to those who are teachers, preachers, and pastors. I become increasingly concerned when I hear preaching that is full of rebuke. The preaching of God's Word does bring rebuke, but if it doesn't also bring healing and mend what is broken, then there is something lacking in it. There is something lacking in our use of Scripture.

And so this is a challenge for those of us who preach and teach: we should use the Word of God the way that God intends it to be used: for teaching, for reproving, but also for correcting, so that people may be trained in righteousness and live fully for the glory of God. So let's never forget that the Scriptures and the preaching of the Scriptures are profitable for correction.

5

Training in Righteousness

THE PAST FEW DAYS, WE'VE BEEN REMINDING ourselves of Paul's famous words to Timothy about the Scriptures being useful in our lives. And today, we'll look at the last word he mentions in 2 Timothy 3:16. He says that the Scriptures ultimately have this in view: training us in righteousness. The word he uses here really means "child-training." God's instruction is that of a Father to His children, bringing us up in the family likeness, that we may be more like our Elder Brother, the Lord Jesus Christ.

The Bible is God's Word and His words. It's His mouth. And the words are carried to us by the breath of the Holy Spirit. As Christians, we sense that as we respond to it, we are always saying: "Abba, Father, teach me more. Make me more like Jesus." The wonderful thing is that the Scriptures instruct us whether we are rocket scientists or very simple people.

When I was a teenager, one of the books that we used to help us understand Christian doctrine was called *In Understanding Be Men*. It was written by an Irish minister named T.C. Hammond. He eventually went to Australia and became the principal of Moore College in Sydney. He was a remarkable Irishman, and at one time he ran a club in Dublin for boys—for boys from the worst part of town.

Hammond taught them what became known as the "one hundred texts": they memorized one hundred texts of Scripture. One day, the bishop visited, and he was pretty unsympathetic to Hammond's gospel preaching. But when Hammond told him that these boys knew one hundred texts of Scripture, the bishop simply didn't believe him. The bishop rather snootily said that he'd test these boys.

He turned to the boys and said, "Boys, can any of you tell me what Timothy says about the Bible?" Total silence reigned. He asked them again. More silence. Then he turned and rather demeaningly spoke to T.C. Hammond as though Hammond's deceit had been exposed. These boys didn't know one hundred texts at all. It was all a lie. And seeing this, one of the little street boys piped up and said to the bishop: "Sir, *Timothy* didn't say anything about Scripture. But in 2 Timothy 3:16–17, *the Apostle Paul* said, 'All scripture is given by inspiration of God and is profitable for doctrine, reproof, correction, and training in righteousness that the man of God may be thoroughly furnished for every good work.'"

Here was a learned bishop looking down his nose at these boys, and this little boy actually had a more accurate knowledge of Scripture than he did. The Word of God had made him wiser than his teachers. Isn't that what Psalm 119:99 says? "I have more understanding than all my teachers, for your testimonies are my meditation."

Let's remember that as we think about the Bible and as we turn to the Bible more often: It's God's Word, and it's doing God's work. And it will give us wisdom that enables us to navigate the world in which we live and see through the falsehoods of the world.

WEEK 6

Worship

1

Let Us Worship God

WHAT WAS THE REFORMATION ALL ABOUT? We might say that it was about the authority of the Bible over the authority of the Roman Catholic Church. We could say that it was all about justification by faith alone in Christ alone. And certainly, these are both good and true answers.

But years ago, I was struck by something I read in a book by the Reformer John Calvin. He said that what really lies at the heart of things is worship. I must confess that for a moment that took me aback. But then I realized what Calvin was saying. The Bible, after all, is a means to an end, and the end is worship. That is the goal.

Justification—our being counted as righteous, and our sins being forgiven—is also a means to an end, isn't it? And that end is fellowship with God and worship. So in a sense, both Scripture and justification are given to us so that through the Spirit we will love the Lord our God with all our heart, soul, mind, and strength. In other words, to lead us to worship Him.

Worship has been a prominent topic in the church over the last fifty years. We probably talk more about how we do it than any generation since the Reformation. We now talk about worship "styles." For example, someone might ask you, "Is your church's worship a traditional style or a contemporary style?"

And it's important for us to think about this topic, because a great deal of that kind of talk about worship isn't really about God at all. It's about us. It's often about what *we* like and what is according to *our* taste rather than about what *He* actually likes. To be honest, I suspect that in many churches, the fundamental questions were never even asked: "What does God actually like? What does He want? What kind of directives has He given to us?"

Yet those are the questions we should ask, aren't they? Because we're not worshiping worship. We're not worshiping one another. We're not worshiping ourselves. We're worshiping God the Father, Son, and Holy Spirit. Therefore, our worship should be shaped according to who He is and what He wants.

For about the first half of my life, almost every church service I attended began with exactly the same four words—words that I rarely hear nowadays. Of course, it's true that the Scriptures don't tell us what words to use to begin our worship services, but in many ways, how we begin explains what we intend to do. And I think the fact that I heard these words every week of my life, but now hardly ever hear them, is significant.

You may be wondering, "What were these words?" I think you can probably guess what they were, and you would also likely agree that they've largely disappeared. And you will probably understand why I think it's significant that we don't so often hear them. The words were these: "Let us worship God."

2

The Quality of Our Worship

HAVE YOU EVER FLOWN ON A PRIVATE JET? It's the way to beat the crowds lining up at check-in. It's a breeze through security, and it's unbelievable to walk out onto the tarmac and be greeted by the pilot. It's fantastic to be on a small jet with a few friends. I know because it once happened to me in another country far away. What an experience!

The only thing is, flying economy never seems to be the same again. You might think I'm telling you this to make you envious, but my motive is actually more spiritual than that! It's to make this point: Sometimes in life, we have experiences so wonderful that our normal experience seems pretty poor by comparison. But we really see the normal experience in its true light only when we've had the wonderful experience.

In many ways, the same is true of our worship of God. I think we'd be surprised to discover how content we can be as worshipers with what actually may be profoundly impoverished worship. But then we experience something different: the presence of God. We find ourselves bowed down before Him in worship and in silence at the end of the service. And then we realize that we've really been in a service of worship.

Sadly, at least in my experience, what people are often talking about when they assess worship are matters of personal satisfaction or preference. Was the singing enthusiastic? Was there a choir? Did we like the choice of songs? Did the organist or band play well? Was the person who nowadays seems to be known as the "worship leader" outstanding? Was the liturgy well crafted?

I've had more than one minister say to me that they've had expert church analysts tell them that the worship in their morning service was excellent. And almost before they finish their sentence, I'm wishing that the heavens would open and a voice would come from above, saying, "Let Me be the assessor of the quality of your worship." Because at the end of the day, what they are assessing is largely a performance factor. Not a sense of the majesty of God and His glory, or a sense of the exaltation of the Father, Son, and Holy Spirit. That is why what mattered to the Apostle Paul was that when people attended the worship service, they found themselves bowed down and saying, "God is really among you" (1 Cor. 14:25).

When that happens, we are inwardly humbled in heart, filled with a sense of awe before God, realizing we have had the extraordinary privilege of joining with the angels and archangels, led by our exalted Savior Jesus Christ, to adore our glorious God. We are, as the hymn says, "lost in wonder, love, and praise," and wanting it all to go on and not wanting to leave.

I suspect that if you've ever tasted that in worship, you feel that much of our worship—our own worship, not just other people's worship—seems flimsy and horizontal. So as we reflect on these things, this is an exhortation to us to recalibrate our thinking about worship. Worship is about Him and how badly we need to hear—at least in our own hearts if we no longer hear them in our churches—these great words: "Let us worship God."

3

Bowed Down in the Presence of God

WHAT HAVE BEEN YOUR MOST MEMORABLE experiences of worship? If we were discussing this together in a group, I imagine we could spend hours listening to each other tell very different stories about memories of worship that has brought us into the presence of God.

For some of us, it might be the first time we were in a large gathering and listening to people praising God together. For others, it might have been worship in a rural place in a faraway country with Christians who had very little but hearts full of praise. For some of us, it might have been an occasion when we felt the density of worship in the singing, or the power of the Word of God in the preaching, or the presence of the Lord Jesus Christ in the celebration of the Lord's Supper.

No doubt each one of us has his or her own special memory. But the thing that binds them together, as we've been reflecting, is that on those occasions, we have become conscious of the presence of the Lord with us. He has promised always to be with us, but He has also promised to manifest Himself to us as we respond to Him in love and worship. Remember how Jesus says in His Farewell Discourse that when we come to Him in obedience, trust, and love through the Holy Spirit, the Father and Son come to us and make Their home with us? When we engage in that kind of worship, I think we feel at last that we have come home.

There is a very interesting statement in the Westminster Confession of Faith about the sacraments, which I think also applies to our worship in general. It says that the efficacy—the power, the influence, the impact—of the sacraments is not tied to the moment of administration. Rather, the significance of our baptism lasts the whole of our

Christian life. The pleasure of being at the Lord's Table endures even when we get up and leave. And the same is true of preaching, isn't it? A sermon that lasts only as long as the church service has had very little power and efficacy in our lives. The same is true of worship.

It's like the taste of really good coffee at the end of a meal. It lingers, and we continue to taste it. In worship, that sense of awe, reverence, solemn joy, and pleasure at the presence of God lingers with us, transforms our lives, shapes our character, and puts dignity and reverence into our lives. Why? Because it has begun to dawn on us that little you and little me have been in the presence of the Creator of the cosmos, and that He has come to us as our loving heavenly Father to receive our worship.

As a teenager and into my early twenties, I had the privilege of being in a church where, at the end of the services, I think we always felt bowed down with this sense of awe. Sometimes the hymns were more uplifting. Sometimes, yes, the sermons were more or less applicable to my situation. Sometimes we had the Lord's Supper. But this one thing was constant: God seemed to break through the veil between heaven and earth, between eternity and time, and bow us down in His presence. And when you have tasted that, you can never be fully content until you taste it again.

Years later, I came across a statement by Dr. Martyn Lloyd-Jones, the famous Welsh preacher of the twentieth century. He said, "I can forgive almost anything in a service so long as there is a sense of the presence of God." I don't suppose he was indifferent to how services were conducted or whether the sermon was a good exposition of Scripture. He meant that these are really means to this glorious end: that we meet with God. How sad it would be if, spiritually, Absalom-like, we lived in the city of God but never actually saw the king's face (see 2 Samuel 14:28).

And that is what worship is about: seeing the King's face.

4

Principles for Worship

I'VE ALWAYS LOVED WORSHIPING WITH GOD'S people at Saint Andrew's
Chapel in Sanford, Fla., the church where Dr. R.C. Sproul served as
minister. This is true for many reasons, but one reason is that it's the
only church I have ever attended where the congregation sings the
"Sanctus":

> Holy, holy, holy, holy is the Lord.
> Holy, holy, holy, holy is the Lord.
> Holy is the Father, holy is the Son,
> holy is the Spirit; blessed Three in One.

Sometimes we speak about what's called "the regulative principle"
in our worship. Some people think that it's only Presbyterians who
have a regulative principle! But in reality, all of us have a regulative
principle. Sometimes it's more obvious, and sometimes, alas, it's a regulative principle that seems chaotic.

We need a regulative principle; otherwise, every single one of us
would end up starting his or her own denomination. We need principles that guide and govern what we do in worship. As we've been
discussing this week, sometimes this principle is focused on the wrong
things, such as our own personal preferences or what we think will
appeal to unbelievers. These rather suggest that our worship is going
to be about *us* rather than about *God*.

But the true basic regulative principle for worship is based on
these questions: " What does God tell us He likes? What does God
tell us He wants? What does God tell us will be most helpful to us to
be able to come into His presence and to praise Him?" There is only
one way to discover the answer to those questions. It's by searching

the Scriptures and reflecting on their teaching and applying it to our churches so that ultimately our regulative principle is the one that God gives to us.

If we search the Scriptures, we will find two things. First, we will see certain constants in a worship service, sometimes called *elements*. And these are (or should be) in every service no matter who we are, where we are, or how many or few of us are in attendance. There will be singing praise. There will be praying. There will be the exposition of Scripture. On some occasions there will be baptism and the Lord's Supper. These are constants.

And then there will be variables—and there are many variables. For example, the time of day that we gather for worship is variable. For the first half of my life without fail, the morning worship service began at 11 a.m. I think it traditionally began then because the farmers needed time to milk their cows. But now, even though no one in the congregation owns a cow, we have kept up the tradition and treated it as a constant, although it's really a variable.

There are other variables. The Scriptures don't tell us what tunes we need to use to sing God's praise. The Scriptures don't tell us when we should stand and when we should sit. And so as the Westminster Confession of Faith says, it's legitimate and appropriate for these things to be "ordered by the light of nature." These characteristics may differ from place to place, and from culture to culture.

But there are other aspects of our worship that should be fixed. That is where sometimes Christians tend to go adrift, thinking that if God hasn't given us clear instructions, then we can do whatever we want. In fact, the Corinthian church said that to the Apostle Paul. He responded by saying that even in areas of life and worship where God has not given specific instructions, we are still called to apply general biblical principles to every one of these specific occasions.

In his first letter to the Corinthians, he told them (and by extension, tells us) how to do that. He raises two questions. The first is, "Is this really going to be edifying for the church?" And the second is, "Is this really going to be for the glory of God?" That second question should always be the dominant question we ask, even when Scripture doesn't give us specific directives about our worship. What is most going to tend to the glory of God? What is most going to enable us to sing, "Holy is the Father, holy is the Son, holy is the Spirit; blessed Three in One"?

When we ask what will tend to the glory of God, we are likely to be able to worship Him in spirit and in truth.

5

Cleansed and Renewed

I MENTIONED YESTERDAY HOW MUCH I'VE loved singing the "Sanctus" at Saint Andrew's Chapel. Of course, the words are based on Isaiah 6. In this passage, we read that Isaiah, in the year that King Uzziah died, saw the true King, the Lord seated on a throne in His temple, and heard the voices of the seraphim chanting these words: "Holy, holy, holy" (v. 3).

In chapter 1, Isaiah spoke of the impoverished worship taking place in the Jerusalem temple in his own day. But by chapter 6, he has seen his own impoverishment because he saw and heard the worship of the holy seraphim as they praised God as the Great Holy One.

It must have struck him that these seraphim covered their faces with two of their wings.

I wonder what that really means. After all, they were permanently holy. They were perfectly holy. I think it's probably an indication that perfectly holy creatures, these seraphim, needed to veil their faces before the *uncreated* holiness of this thrice-holy God. So it's not surprising that when Isaiah saw and heard this, he cried out that he was a man of unclean lips and felt he was disintegrating. I'm pretty sure that when he left the temple, he must have felt that he had been in the presence of God in a completely new way and that he could never be the same man again.

That is what worship is for. That is why God calls us to worship regularly and not to forsake the assembling of ourselves together (Heb. 10:25). Because in the rhythm of our worship week by week, Lord's Day by Lord's Day, we find ourselves cleansed and renewed.

If you belong to a church that has not only a morning service but also an evening service, let me encourage you to attend both. After the morning service, you are really just a little cleaner than you were when the day started. You are just ready to worship. And if we love the Lord, we will want to worship Him more. That is why our forefathers recognized the wisdom not only in gathering together once, but in gathering together twice on the Lord's Day, so that we might experience this wonderful paradox that Isaiah experienced.

What is this paradox? On the one hand, in God's presence we become conscious of our sinfulness. And yet the glory of the gospel is that Christ—not merely a seraph, but Christ Himself—comes to us by the Spirit, puts His gospel into our hearts, and says: "Lo, this has touched your life. Your sins are forgiven."

Going out into the week knowing that your sins are forgiven, that you have been strengthened by the presence of the Lord, is surely the most wonderful way to live the rhythms of the Christian life. To go as Isaiah did, not saying, "This is my special gift, and I'm going to use this exclusively," but rather saying: "Lord, whatever You want me to do, wherever there is need that I can meet, whatever You hold for me in this week, here am I. Send me."

That is a great way to leave our church services—with the words ringing in our ears, "Now go forth to love and to serve the Lord."

WEEK 7

Fruit of the Spirit, Part 1

1

Introducing the Fruit of the Spirit

THIS WEEK, WE'LL BE LOOKING AT what the Apostle Paul calls the fruit of the Spirit: "But the fruit of the Spirit is love, joy, peace, patience, kindness, goodness, faithfulness, gentleness, self-control; against such things there is no law" (Gal. 5:22–23). These words are worth memorizing, and we'll repeat them every day this week.

It's interesting that Paul calls these nine qualities "fruit." That is, he refers to them in the singular rather than the plural "fruits." Earlier in chapter 5, he spoke of "works" (plural) of the flesh, not just the "work" (singular) of the flesh. I think what he is suggesting by using "fruit" in the singular is that all these qualities belong together. They are meant to grow on the same tree, as it were. We can't really develop one of them fully without having all of them.

At the same time, I wonder if the reason he calls them "fruit" is that they take time to grow and need to be nourished. It's interesting that he uses a horticultural metaphor here rather than a mechanical one. These qualities can't be artificially produced; they need to be developed in us by God's grace.

When I think of these words in Galatians 5, I'm often reminded of two comments made by two rather remarkable Christian ministers. The first was made by the great eighteenth-century Anglican minister Charles Simeon of Cambridge. He was speaking about a young man named Henry Martyn who became a great missionary and translator of the Scriptures. Martyn was a brilliant young man who was the outstanding mathematics graduate of his time at Cambridge. He chose to become a missionary, and he died as a young man.

Charles Simeon commented that what struck him about Henry Martyn was not just how tall he had grown spiritually, but how the fruit of the Spirit in his life seemed to be perfectly proportionate. I think that is a beautiful description of a Christian, don't you? Someone in whom all the graces of God, the fruit of the Spirit, are growing in a wonderfully balanced way, showing that they grow on the same tree.

The other comment was made by my own minister when I was a student in Scotland. He said that the growing Christian is someone who has learned to do the natural thing spiritually, and the spiritual thing naturally. That is a good way of thinking about the fruit of the Spirit, isn't it? It's not a matter of just trying to do the right thing—trying to be this, or trying to be that. It's much more organic.

It's this ninefold fruit of the Spirit that the Holy Spirit produces in us as we grow in our love for the Lord Jesus, as our hearts and minds and wills submit to Scripture, as our affections are suffused with the teaching of Scripture and the knowledge of the Lord Jesus. There is a kind of "spiritual-natural" way in which we grow to be more like Him. Ultimately, that is what this fruit of the Spirit adds up to: likeness to the Lord Jesus.

So as we think about the fruit this week, let's pray that the Lord will make us more like Him.

2

Do You Have Love?

YESTERDAY, WE BEGAN SOME REFLECTIONS ON the fruit of the Spirit, and I mentioned that we would repeat these words each day: "The fruit of the Spirit is love, joy, peace, patience, kindness, goodness, faithfulness, gentleness, self-control" (Gal. 5:22–23). Fruit grows on trees. But we might say that in this instance, fruit grows in threes, because this ninefold fruit of the Spirit seems to divide into three sections. The first three are love, joy, and peace—a trilogy. And this isn't the only place that Paul mentions them together.

You might immediately think of Romans 5:

> Therefore, since we have been justified by faith, we have *peace* with God through our Lord Jesus Christ. Through him we have also obtained access by faith into this grace in which we stand, and we *rejoice* in hope of the glory of God. Not only that, but we rejoice in our sufferings, knowing that suffering produces endurance, and endurance produces character, and character produces hope, and hope does not put us to shame, because God's *love* has been poured into our hearts through the Holy Spirit who has been given to us. (vv. 1–5, emphasis added)

What's interesting is that the order in Romans 5—peace, joy, love—is different from the order in Galatians 5, where the order is love, joy, peace. Why is that?

I suspect it's because in Romans 5, Paul is talking about the *roots* of our Christian experience. We have peace with God, and that leads us to rejoice. And as we rejoice, our hearts are filled with the love of God for us poured into us by the Holy Spirit. But in Galatians 5, Paul is speaking about the *fruit* that flows from these roots. So when the Spirit unites us to the Lord Jesus Christ, our hearts are filled with love, we begin to rejoice, and our lives are marked by peace.

The New Testament places massive emphasis on the importance of love. We learn that from the Lord Jesus in John 15: "As the Father has loved me, so have I loved you. . . . This is my commandment, that you love one another as I have loved you" (vv. 9, 12). Paul devotes a whole chapter to love in 1 Corinthians 13, explaining why love is the greatest. And the Apostle John tells us, "Beloved, let us love one another, for love is from God, and whoever loves has been born of God and knows God" (1 John 4:7).

But what is love? Ultimately, it's not an emotion so much as forgetting about ourselves and living for others, being like Jesus in our devotion and care. And yes, love is also all the things Paul says it is in 1 Corinthians 13. It's being patient and kind, not envying or boasting, not being arrogant or rude. It's being taken up with devotion to others, and that is why it doesn't insist on its own way. It's not irritable or resentful. It doesn't rejoice at wrongdoing, but rejoices with the truth. It bears all things, believes all things, hopes all things, and endures all things.

None of these things is actually complicated, is it? But the problem is, we are desperately complicated by our sin. But when the Holy Spirit begins to work in us, He uncomplicates us. He begins to fill us with love for others and forgetfulness of self.

I can't help but think about a comment made by Peter the Venerable, the abbot of the great monastery of Cluny in the medieval days, about his much more famous friend, Bernard of Clairvaux: "Bernard, you do all the difficult and complicated things well. But you're failing in the simple thing. You don't love." When I first read these words, they were like an arrow in my heart—doing the difficult things, but not doing the simple thing well.

I wonder if that is true of you. Perhaps you almost pride yourself in doing the difficult things well. But have you been uncomplicated by the Lord Jesus? Are you doing the simple thing? Do you have love?

3

A Supernatural Joy

"THE FRUIT OF THE SPIRIT IS love, joy, peace, patience, kindness, goodness, faithfulness, gentleness, self-control" (Gal. 5:22–23). Yesterday, we looked at love, and today, we'll explore joy. Perhaps we think of joy as the kind of characteristic some people have by nature, and others don't. And maybe you feel that you fit into the second category. If so, I can sympathize with you. I doubt if joy is one of the leading characteristics of people who have Celtic blood in them.

But the joy that Paul speaks about here is not the natural characteristic of a sunny disposition. How do we know that? Because in Romans 5, Paul describes a triple joy that has very little to do with a sunny disposition. He says: "We rejoice in hope of the glory of God. Not only that, but we rejoice in our sufferings" (vv. 2–3). And he adds that we also rejoice in God Himself (v. 11).

The joy that is a fruit of the Spirit is the result not of our genetic structure but of our being justified by faith in Christ (Rom. 5:1). And because of this, we have a new relationship to God and are at peace with Him. And that is not just a sunny disposition, is it? You and I know people who have sunny dispositions, but they don't rejoice in any of these things.

As people might say at home in Scotland, "Christian joy's no natural." It's not natural. It's something that is produced in us by the Holy Spirit. And joy is produced in us only when we've been brought to faith in the Lord Jesus Christ. We rejoice because our sins have been forgiven; because we've been counted righteous; and because we've begun to understand that through difficulties, trials, friction, sufferings, and affliction, the Spirit is working to make us more and more like Jesus. He is producing endurance, character, and hope in us.

Chiefly, we have joy because we know that God loves us, and we have the ultimate proof of His love in that He gave His Son for us. So the joy of which Paul speaks is "no natural." It's spiritual. It's the fruit of the Spirit.

And so as a waiter in a restaurant might say when he puts the meal down before you, "Enjoy."

4

Peace Be with You

"**THE FRUIT OF THE SPIRIT IS** love, joy, peace, patience, kindness, goodness, faithfulness, gentleness, self-control" (Gal. 5:22–23). We've been thinking this week about the fact that there seems to be a shape to this fruit. There are nine of them, but they belong to three triplets. We're looking at the first triplet this week: love, joy, and peace.

In Romans 5:1, Paul spoke about peace in an objective way: Being justified by faith, we have peace with God. The alienation and enmity are ended. Paul is speaking here not about something that we feel, but about a new state of affairs: peace has been declared; the battle is over; the war is finished. But in Galatians 5, he takes that further. He is saying that not only *are* we at peace with God, but we actually *experience* peace with God.

I'm sure that at the back of his mind is the Old Testament word *shalom*, which means far more than simply a feeling of being at peace. It is the experience of being made whole and well. It is coming home, knowing that you belong. It is no longer being a stranger, but being a member of the family. It is the sense that there is a well-being in your life that wasn't there before.

After the Old Testament sacrifices had been accepted, the high priest would come forth, lift up his hands, bless the people, and say to them: "The LORD bless you and keep you; the LORD make his face to shine upon you and be gracious to you; the LORD lift up his countenance upon you and give you peace [*shalom*]" (Num. 6:24–26).

This might be the best way to think about the peace that the Christian enjoys: not that Aaron has come forth to pronounce the benediction, but One who is greater than Aaron—our High Priest, the Lord Jesus Christ—has come forth from His death and resurrection. And

His first word to us is: "*Shalom*. Enjoy the peace. I am doing all things well in your life, and I will make you whole."

When Jesus appeared to the disciples on the evening of His resurrection, this was the first word He said: *peace*. And this is what the Apostle Paul is speaking about here. It's the same thing that the great early Christian theologian Augustine experienced. He says in his *Confessions*, "You have made us for Yourself, O Lord, and our hearts are restless until they find their rest in You."

I was brought up as a teenager on the words of the Rolling Stones' song "Satisfaction," which became an anthem of the sixties. No matter where or how they tried, they couldn't get any satisfaction. And where there is no satisfaction, there can be no peace. But every believer has the privilege and blessing of the gospel, and the Lord Jesus says to us, "My peace is now yours."

5

The Patience of God and of His Children

I HOPE YOU'VE BEEN ABLE TO memorize these words as we've repeated them this week: "The fruit of the Spirit is love, joy, peace, patience, kindness, goodness, faithfulness, gentleness, self-control" (Gal. 5:22–23). We've come now to the second triplet of these Spirit-nurtured graces: patience, kindness, and goodness. They do seem somehow or another to belong together.

The New Testament has two different Greek words that can be translated by our English word *patience*. The word that Paul uses here is *makrothymia*. It's a compound word from *makros*, which means "long, long in time," or "long in space, far away," and *thymos*, which means "anger" or "passion." The Bible teaches us that God is patient:

"The LORD is merciful and gracious, slow to anger and abounding in steadfast love" (Ps. 103:8).

We sometimes speak about people who have a short fuse. This word *patience* suggests that a Christian is someone whose fuse gets longer and longer and longer, even in the face of provocation. You can see where the motivation for this grace comes from, can't you? It's because God has been so patient with us. So as His children, we breathe in the family atmosphere, and we learn by the Holy Spirit to mimic Him.

This brings a couple of thoughts to mind. One is that I've met proficient Christians who have said quite openly and without embarrassment (and almost with a touch of pride), "I'm the kind of person who doesn't suffer fools gladly." I always want to say three words: "Well, Jesus did." The darker side of me wants to add, "And you're one of those fools." Not being patient with others is not a virtue. It's a blemish because it means we're not being like the Lord Jesus.

You may be thinking: "But what about this or that situation? Isn't there righteous anger?" Of course, that is true. But what Paul is speaking about here is our basic, day-to-day instinct and reaction to people and to situations that are challenging or frustrating. I wonder if you've ever been with a Christian who, because of something that happened, just lost the plot, and a fuse has been lit, and they've reacted badly in the moment. Then realizing you are there, they become flustered, and they say something like this: "I don't know what came over me. I'm really a very patient person."

You know what we all want to say, don't you? It's this: "Actually, you're not really a very patient person at all. You're an impatient person whose patience level has never really been tested. It's been tested now, and you've just failed the test."

This leads to what I think is a very important thought—that patience can develop only through being in situations likely to create impatience in us. So long as our patience is never tested, it never grows.

When Paul says that the fruit of the Spirit is patience, it's not as though the Holy Spirit gives us a permanent commodity. It is that the

Spirit works in us, transforming us gradually—perhaps even gently and slowly, but surely—bringing us into situations that might tempt us to be impatient. But as He works in our lives and we reflect on how wonderfully patient the Lord has been with us, we find that we are able to take the strain, and patience begins to develop.

Perhaps your patience will be tested between now and the next time you pick up this devotional. Perhaps mine will be tested too. But let's pray together that by God's grace, our patience will also grow.

WEEK 8

Fruit of the Spirit, Part 2

1

Kindness: Simple Yet Significant

THIS WEEK, WE'RE CONTINUING OUR STUDY of the fruit of the Spirit in Galatians 5:22–23. Kindness is our theme today. These three graces—patience, kindness, and goodness—form the second of three trilogies in the Apostle Paul's list. You can't be kind unless you're patient, can you? In some circumstances, simply being patient with a difficult person is being kind to them.

Kindness is a beautiful thing. I think there is some evidence that it is related to the old word *cynn*, or *kin*, which refers to one's relatives. It means treating people as family. Kindness often translates one of the greatest words in the Hebrew Bible, *hesed*, which can be translated as "loyal love."

It's both important and encouraging to recognize that kindness isn't something spectacular. It isn't about appearing on the big stage, being fawned over by adoring fans as though you were some kind of celebrity. But kindness is what really matters. This is what the Holy Spirit most delights to produce in us—not kudos, but kindness.

The book of Ruth is all about kindness—how Ruth showed kindness to her bereaved mother-in-law, Naomi; how Boaz showed kindness to Ruth; how Boaz felt that Ruth had shown kindness to him; and all because of the God who is kind to His people. The Holy Spirit wants to inject that into our spiritual DNA so that it's embedded in all that we are, in everything we do, and in all the words we say. Kindness is a simple thing, but it's a beautiful grace.

I've noticed over the years that in all the different personalities and temperaments of outstanding Christians I've known, there is always this common feature: they are kind and they show kindness.

I wonder if it's ever dawned on you how much, humanly speaking, the Christian church owes to one man's kindness long ago.

When Augustine's wanderings and searchings eventually led him to Milan, he encountered the bishop Ambrose, one of the great preachers of his day. Augustine was tremendously impressed by his eloquence. Augustine hung on his diction with rapt attention, but he was pretty bored by what Ambrose said. What Augustine loved was only the charm in Ambrose's language, but he was relatively indifferent to what Ambrose said.

But then as Augustine got to know Ambrose, things changed. He says toward the end of book 5 of his *Confessions*: "I began to like him, at first indeed not as a teacher of the truth, for I had absolutely no confidence in your church, but as a human being who was kind to me." Isn't that something? The milk of human kindness in Ambrose—rather than his great preaching—was what God first used to bring to faith a man whose Christian life, witness, and writings have shaped the history of the Western world for seventeen hundred years.

Who knows what your kindness today to someone might mean?

2

Reflecting God's Goodness

TODAY, WE REACH THE END OF the second triad in the fruit of the Spirit: patience, kindness, and goodness. Many of the questions that philosophers have asked over the centuries pertain to the true, the good, and the beautiful: what we call *epistemology* (How do we know things?), *aesthetics* (How do we assess things?), and *ethics* (What is the good life? And what, after all, do we mean when we say "good"?).

If you studied moral philosophy in college, you may think of some of the different answers that philosophers have given to questions such as these: "What is good? What is the good life? What principles should guide our decisions and our actions? Is goodness objective, or (like what some say of beauty) is it only in the eye of the beholder?" That certainly seems to be a common enough view today: good is what I like, what I think is good for me, what I think will make me happy. But that is not an option for a Christian, is it?

Where do we begin untangling this twisted ball of philosophical wool? The answer is found where we should always begin: with God. Psalm 34 is instructive here. It urges us, "Oh, taste and see that the LORD is good!" (v. 8). But what does that mean? It isn't easy to answer in just a few words. In fact, the Bible uses the word *good* in a variety of ways. It means that something is attractive, that it's free from defects, that it's morally upright, that it's as it should be. Ultimately, of course, it means that something expresses and reflects God's character and will because He is good. Everything He created was good. When He spoke the universe into being, the whole creation was very good.

John Calvin used to speak about the world's being the theater of God's glory. But when He created it, the world was also the theater of God's goodness. So when we say that someone is good or exhibits the quality of goodness, what we're ultimately saying is that a person is living as the image of God should, reflecting His character in his or her words and actions. God is perfect goodness in Himself, and we were created as reflected goodness.

Apart from the rich young ruler who addressed Jesus as "Good Teacher," it's not often that anyone is called good in the New Testament. But one man who did receive this designation was Joseph of Arimathea. He is the one who went to Pontius Pilate and asked if he could take Jesus' body and bury it in his own tomb. Mark's gospel gives us a beautiful description of Joseph: he was a respected member of the council, looking for the kingdom of God (Mark 15:43). But although he was a member of the Sanhedrin, he had not consented to their decision to crucify the Lord Jesus. Instead, he took courage and asked Pilate for the body of the Lord. Luke says it best: he was "a good and righteous man" (Luke 23:50).

A lot must have been going on in the heart of Joseph of Arimathea. He was a person who—like Elizabeth and Zechariah earlier in the gospel of Luke—was looking for the fulfillment of God's promises and the coming of the messianic kingdom. I wonder if his friend Nicodemus, who helped him late that afternoon, told him what Jesus had said about entering the kingdom. I think that is highly likely. Joseph could see that an injustice had been done, a great non-good.

But there is something else we should notice because it tells us something important about Joseph's real goodness. Real goodness cares, and real goodness acts, even if it's going to cost. Who knows what it cost Joseph to step out of line with the Sanhedrin and do what he did for the Lord Jesus? But that is what good men and women do.

I wonder: "Is goodness part of the fruit of the Spirit in your life?"

3

Faithful, Trusted, and True

WE'VE COME TODAY TO THE THIRD and last triad of graces in Paul's description of the fruit of the Spirit: faithfulness, gentleness, and self-control. Today, we'll look at faithfulness.

It's always been interesting to me that the words for *faithfulness* and *faith* in the Old Testament have the same root as the word *amen*. Faithfulness is just saying an ongoing "amen" to the commitments that we've made. God has given us a model of what this means, and we see it perfectly expressed in the life and ministry of the Lord Jesus.

The author of Hebrews tells us that, as the Apostle and High Priest of our confession, Jesus was faithful to Him who appointed Him (Heb. 3:2). He was determined to say "amen" in His own life to every aspect of His Father's covenant promises and covenant commands. Indeed, Paul says that all the promises of God find an answering "Yes" and "Amen" in Jesus Christ (2 Cor. 1:20). This was especially true when it came to the hardest-to-keep promise of all: going to the cross to die for our sins.

When Paul says that Jesus became obedient to the point of death, even death on the cross, He is actually describing Jesus' faithfulness. And because Jesus has been faithful to that promise, we can be sure He will be faithful to every one of His promises. And it's in light of His faithfulness that you and I are called to be faithful.

As I was searching my mind for another word to convey what faithfulness looks like in daily life, my wife, Dorothy, happened to use the word *inconsistent* during a casual conversation. That switched on a light for me.

Faithfulness means being consistent, reliable, trustworthy, and dependable. Consistent in our work because someone is paying us for it. Consistent in our churches to the vows we've taken to the Lord and to each other. Consistent in our friendships. Consistent with our wife or husband. Consistent with our children and grandchildren. And consistent and faithful to the Savior who has been so perfectly consistent and faithful to us.

We need the help of the Holy Spirit to be consistent and faithful in all our relationships. Paul isn't telling us here that we're to depend on our own resources. Rather, he is telling us about a quality that the Spirit of Christ produces in us precisely because He is the Spirit of the Lord Jesus Christ.

So today, let's trust the Holy Spirit to produce faithfulness in us as He works in our hearts and lives to make us more and more like our Lord Jesus.

4

Soft-Handed Gentleness

TODAY'S FRUIT IS SURELY ONE OF the most attractive. It's not the biggest or brightest-looking, but I wouldn't be surprised if it's one that the Spirit especially delights to produce in us. What is this fruit? It's gentleness.

The Apostle Paul uses this word several times, but it's not always translated in the same way. Sometimes it's translated as "kindness." I suppose the tradition of the translation "gentleness" instead of "kindness" is just to distinguish two qualities that really belong together. Kind people are gentle, and gentle people are kind. And like all the other fruit of the Spirit, they belong together.

If you watch golf on TV, you'll hear the commentators say that a particular player has "soft hands." This means that even though the player grips the club securely, he or she also grips it gently. It's kind of counterintuitive when one begins playing golf (and alas, it remains counterintuitive for many golfers). They think that the most important thing is how tightly they hold the club, and they don't understand that the truly important thing is how the other end of the club, the club face, makes contact with the ball. A tight grip rather than a gentle one often means that the ball veers off to the right or to the left and ends up in the rough, in a sand trap, or even out of bounds.

I think that this may be a parable of the Christian life. If you don't live with a gentle spirit, if you grip things tightly in order to control them, and if that is how you relate to other people, then things will veer out of control. A person can wrongly believe that the way to live is by having a tight grip. But then they discover, perhaps when it's too late, that what they really needed was gentleness.

Psalm 18 begins with these words: "I love you, O LORD, my strength. The LORD is my rock and my fortress and my deliverer" (vv. 1–2). It's a wonderful psalm, but there is no statement in it more moving than the last words of verse 35: "Your gentleness made me great."

When you think about it, it was God's gentleness with David that must have enabled him to be gentle with Saul. You remember that Saul was within his grasp at the cave of Engedi in 1 Samuel 24. David could have tightened his grip and killed Saul, but he used soft hands. God had used soft hands to protect David, and David used soft hands to protect Saul. In fact, his hands became so soft that he felt ashamed that he'd even cut off the corner of Saul's robe and probably made Saul look like a fool in the eyes of his men.

There is a kind of Christian whose only concern is being right and, too frequently, trying to show that others are wrong. Too many of them have become self-appointed gurus on social media. But when we're trying to discern the spirits, as the Apostle John tells us to, we must not only ask the question, "What is being said?" We should ask two other questions as well. The first is, "What isn't being said?" And the second is, "How is what he or she says being said?"

You see, we need to discern whether or not something is true, but we also need to discern whether the person who says it is gentle like

Christ. That is a sobering thought about others. I find it a sobering thought about myself, too. Don't you?

5

The Heavenly Music of Self-Control

TODAY, WE COME TO THE END OF these two weeks in which we've studied the fruit of the Spirit. Let's read Paul's words one last time: "The fruit of the Spirit is love, joy, peace, patience, kindness, goodness, faithfulness, gentleness, self-control; against such things there is no law" (Gal. 5:22–23).

Fruits are all different, aren't they? Not only that, each piece of fruit has its own distinctive shape, size, and sometimes even taste. The different fruits are just like that. Each one has its own special quality. You might even say that each one leaves a kind of taste in your mouth when you meet someone who shows it. God produces a far greater variety of fruit than fruit farmers do, and that is an encouraging thing to think about and to look for in people.

The last variety of fruit in Paul's list is self-control. However, we could get the wrong impression of what this term means. Self-control was a virtue admired by some of the philosophers and moralists of antiquity, especially the Stoics. For them, the model person had self-control. It was a sign of real strength. But precisely for that reason, self-control can seem metallic. The self-controlled person can be a strong-willed person and maybe even an intimidating kind of person—someone who leaves you feeling small.

But think about this: if that is true of someone in the church, it's a sign they are bearing all the fruit of the Spirit. Because while there are all kinds of fruit, there is really only one fruit of the Spirit, and it's this: being more like the Lord Jesus.

The life of the Lord Jesus was one of perfect self-control. But what that meant was that He possessed and expressed all aspects of the fruit of the Spirit fully and in perfect balance with each other. The result was that even though His presence made people conscious of their sin and need, Jesus never demeaned them. He didn't repel the weak and the needy. No, there was something magnetically attractive about Him, not metallic. His self-control meant that He was able to express all the fruit of the Spirit in a way that must have felt like listening to beautiful voices singing in harmony, weaving in and out of each other to enhance every single voice.

That is how the fruit of the Spirit functions. When love, joy, and peace sing together, the harmony enhances the quality of each of their voices. And then we can triple that: love, joy, peace, patience, kindness, goodness, faithfulness, gentleness, self-control—three groups singing three-part harmony, uniting together to sing nine-part harmony. And that is how self-control functions.

No wonder Paul adds here, perhaps unexpectedly, the comment "against such things there is no law" (Gal. 5:23). Does that strike you as strange? A kind of loose end hanging out here inexplicably?

To understand Paul's words here, we must remember what his letter to the Galatians is all about. It's about a misuse of the law. And what he is saying here so wonderfully is that the Spirit of God works within the believer to produce a conformity to God's law that God's law itself could never reproduce.

It's the same as what he says in Romans 8:3–4: "For God has done what the law, weakened by the flesh, could not do. By sending his own Son in the likeness of sinful flesh and for sin, he condemned sin in the flesh, in order that the righteous requirement of the law might be fulfilled in us, who walk not according to the flesh but according to the Spirit."

Only the Spirit of the Lord Jesus can make us like Jesus and produce in us the fruit of the Spirit. And when He does that, our lives become like trees that are bearing fruit and blossoming wonderfully.

WEEK 9

Who Is God?

1

The Most Important Question

WHAT WOULD YOU SAY IS THE most important question a Christian can ask? Maybe there is no single right answer to that question. Some philosophers have thought that the most important question is this: "Why is there something and not nothing?"

That is a great question to ask people, because it gives us the opportunity to point out that an answer such as the big bang or evolution can't possibly be right. Even if there were a big bang at the beginning of the cosmos or if things did evolve, neither big bangs nor things evolving come from nothing. And nothing is no thing—nothing. The wise old Latin adage is correct: *ex nihilo nihil fit*—nothing comes from nothing.

But for the Christian, perhaps the most important question we could ask is, "What is God really like?" We'll think about that question this week, and we'll begin with a negative. By that, I don't mean describing God by saying what He isn't, which is what theologians call "apophatic theology" or the *via negativa*. The negative I'm thinking about is that the answer to the questions, "What is God like?" and "Who is God?" should never begin with the words, "Well, the way I like to think about God is . . ."

How we like to think about God isn't really a relevant factor when it comes to the question of what God is actually like. After all, God isn't the result of what I like or don't like to think. He isn't in the business of saying, "If that is the way you'd like Me to be, well, of course I'll become like that." That is utterly ridiculous, isn't it?

Throughout church history, whenever catechisms were written, this issue of who God is was often one of the first questions they asked. In the Westminster Shorter Catechism, it appears as the fourth question: "What is God?" Its answer is majestic: "God is a Spirit, infinite, eternal, and unchangeable, in his being, wisdom, power, holiness, justice, goodness, and truth."

I wonder if you noticed, however, the subtle difference between the question I asked at the beginning of today's reflections and the one the Shorter Catechism asks. I didn't ask, "What is God?" but "Who is God?"

One of the great moments in the Bible occurs when God appears to Moses at the burning bush. God tells Moses that He is going to deliver His persecuted people, and He commands Moses to go to the Israelites, telling them that God has appeared to him and has given him a message.

Do you remember Moses' reply? "If I come to the people of Israel and say to them, 'The God of your fathers has sent me to you,' and they ask me, 'What is his name?' what shall I say to them?" (Ex. 3:13).

That is a tremendously important question for us, too, because in many ways, our Christian lives are determined by what we think about who God is and what He is really like. As the psalm puts it, we tend to become like whatever we worship (Ps. 135:18). Our beliefs about who God is and what He is like are bound to shape who we are and what we are like.

We'll return to this topic tomorrow. In the meantime, perhaps ask yourself the questions, "Who is God?" and "What is God like?"

2

I Am Who I Am

YESTERDAY, WE STARTED CONSIDERING THE QUESTIONS of who God is and what He is like. We saw that Moses asked God this exact question at the burning bush. What was God's answer? He said to Moses: "I AM WHO I AM. . . . Say this to the people of Israel: 'I AM has sent me to you. . . . The LORD, the God of your fathers, the God of Abraham, the God of Isaac, and the God of Jacob, has sent me to you.' This is my name forever" (Ex. 3:14–15).

God is the great I Am. The Jews came to treat this name with such reverence that they wouldn't even pronounce it. When reading aloud from the Hebrew Bible, they say *hashem* "the name" instead. While their respect for God's name is admirable, we need to remember that He specifically said, "This is my name forever, and thus I am to be remembered throughout all generations" (v. 15). He meant for His people to know Him as "I Am" and to call Him "I Am"—not to hide His name. We are to say it and proclaim it throughout all generations and to the ends of the earth.

And yet there are some quite mysterious things about this revelation of who God really is. If you were to ask me who I was and I replied, "I am who I am," it would be true. After all, I am who I am! But it's probably not the kind of answer you want. It might even seem to amount to saying: "I'm not telling you. I'm going to hide my identity from you." Some Bible readers have thought that is what God was saying to Moses. But that cannot be the case because here God is revealing Himself to Moses, not hiding Himself from him.

What does this name mean? I think it means several things, but let's choose one to reflect on today: "I Am" means exactly that. You and I *became*. Our existence had a beginning, and we are changing every day. We are becoming. And one day, we'll die, and people will talk about us in the past tense. We became, we are becoming, and we were.

But God is simply I Am. He is the great I Am. He didn't become, He is not becoming, and He has no ending. God simply is. He is all He is, and He always is all He is.

However simple the words "I Am" seem to be, they are really beyond our grasp. His greatness none can fathom. It's just too much for our little minds to comprehend, and that is why we speak about the incomprehensibility of God. We can truly know Him, but we can't fully wrap our minds around the I Am.

If I try to think simply of that name, my mind begins to reel and stagger. Doesn't yours? I'm able to grasp only things that have come into being, change, and die. The harder I try to understand One who is without beginning or ending, who is not a being caused by something else, the more I'm likely to get a headache. How can there be anything that doesn't have a beginning or a prior cause? Someone who simply is? When I think of that, I realize it's beyond me.

But here's something that saves us from getting a headache that might make our brains explode: I Am wanted Moses and the people to know who He really is. He wanted them to know Him. What He also makes clear is that He wanted them to know that He saw their need, He cared about them, and He was going to save them.

Some Old Testament scholars have suggested that when God said to Moses, "I AM WHO I AM," one of the things Moses was meant to understand was, "I Am exactly who I will be in what I'm about to do." To know God better, Moses needed to know both what He said and what He would do.

The same is true for us, except that by God's grace, you and I know so much more than even Moses did.

3

Knowing More of God

MOST OF US FIND OURSELVES BEING asked from time to time, "What do you mean?" We might respond a bit like Augustine when he was asked to explain the nature of time. He replied, "I thought I knew what it was until you asked me." I sometimes wonder if the same is true when someone asks, "What is God like?"

From one point of view, the answer is that He is actually not like anything. After all, He is God. But it also works the other way around: what He creates and what He does are like what He is. Only when we begin with God, and then move to what He creates and does, are we really ready to move back again from those things and understand how the Bible uses them to teach us what God is like. That is a very basic principle. If we're going to think biblically, and if our theology is going to be honoring to God, then we should begin with God Himself.

Yesterday, we discussed the great name of God in the Old Testament, the name "I Am," or "Yahweh." I noted that some biblical scholars have thought that when God says, "I AM WHO I AM," He is telling Moses and the people to keep their eyes and their ears open, to listen to what God says about Himself, and to watch what He does in history. From these two realities—God's acts and God's words interpreting His acts—they would get to know who He really is.

This helps us understand what is meant later in Exodus 6. Here, God tells Moses that although He appeared to Abraham, Isaac, and Jacob "by my name the LORD" (that is, I Am, or Yahweh), "I did not make myself known to them" (v. 3). Yet the name Yahweh has been used dozens of times already in Genesis. It's possible, of course, that the people at that time didn't know this name of God and had never heard it. Perhaps Moses wrote Genesis as he did after the exodus and chose to use "Yahweh" all the way through.

Or perhaps Moses simply wanted to indicate that the God of Exodus was also the God of creation, covenant, and providence in the lives of Abraham, Isaac, and Jacob. Another possibility is that although the patriarchs knew the covenant name Yahweh, they couldn't understand its meaning the way Moses and his generation would when they experienced the promises of God coming to pass with mighty power in the events of the exodus.

In any case, it's clear in Genesis that I Am was already at work. The exodus wasn't the first time that God had revealed Himself to His people. This wasn't the first covenant He ever made with them. They weren't the first people He had helped. The patriarchs knew I Am, but they didn't yet know just how great He is as the One whom the hymn calls "Jehovah! Great I AM." And that is actually how God's revelation of Himself works in the Bible. It's progressive and cumulative until He fully reveals Himself as the I Am in our Lord Jesus Christ.

In the former days, God revealed Himself to His people at various times and in fragmentary ways (see Heb. 1:1–2). Abraham didn't know the greatness of I Am to the degree that Moses did. And truth be told, neither Abraham nor Moses knew His greatness the way Isaiah did. In the same way, not even Isaiah knew the meaning of I Am the way you and I do.

There is a lesson for us here. Because God is the great I Am, there is no end to our growing in knowing who He is. He is even greater than we can comprehend, and that is one of the marvelous things about being a Christian. Day by day, month by month, and year by year, we can get to know God better, appreciate Him more fully, and love Him more deeply.

Richard of Chichester wrote the following prayer: "Lord, for these three things I pray: to see Thee more clearly, to love Thee more dearly, and to follow Thee more nearly." Let's make that our prayer today.

4

Burning, Yet Not Consumed

KNOWING THAT GOD IS I AM is just the beginning. It certainly was for Moses. If we could take a mental helicopter ride over the Pentateuch (the first five books of the Bible), we'd be amazed at just how much Moses learned in the next forty years about the character of God.

Moses must have reflected often on the meaning of the dramatic experience he had at Mount Horeb. What initiated it was the sight of a bush that was on fire but was not consumed. It must have taken at least a few minutes before it dawned on him that here was a bush burning, but apparently the fire was self-propagating. It was in the bush, and yet the bush wasn't the fuel that kept the flame alight.

In fact, the bush was burning, but it wasn't burning up. A fire was present in the middle of the bush, yet the fire was completely independent of the bush for its existence. This was a fire like no fire Moses had ever seen. I suspect that the more Moses thought about this—the more he played the scene over and over in his mind in later months and years—the more he understood what was happening.

It was as though I Am, Yahweh, the Lord, were saying: "Moses, there is none like Me in heaven or on earth. I Am who I Am. But I want you to know who I am. I want you to understand as far as you are able what kind of God I Am is."

And so He created something like Himself as a kind of picture, an active parable of a God who is absolutely independent, uncaused, in need of nothing, sufficient for Himself: a fire who simply burns. Uncreated fire. And yet at the same time, He is the I Am who makes Himself present in history and among His people, like the fire in the bush, without them being consumed. In fact, He comes not to consume them, but to preserve and save them.

He is infinite and independent, but He is not a prisoner of His infinity. In the mystery of His being, He can make Himself known in history. And more than that, He can come to be with His needy people and save them.

This reminds me of the piece of paper that was found sewn into the coat lining of Blaise Pascal when he died. Here's part of what was written on it:

The year of grace, 1654,

Monday, November the 23rd. From about ten-thirty in the evening to about half an hour after midnight.

Fire.

God of Abraham, God of Isaac, God of Jacob, not of the philosophers and savants.

Certitude. Certitude. Feeling. Joy. Peace.

God of Jesus Christ. *Deum meum et Deum vestrum.*

Your God will be my God. My God will be your God.

Forgetting the world and everything, except God.

He is only found by the paths taught in the gospel.

Grandeur of the human soul.

Righteous Father, the world has not known you, but I have
known you.

Joy, joy, joy, tears of joy.

This is eternal life, that they know you, the only true God, and
whom you have sent, Jesus Christ.

Jesus Christ.

Jesus Christ.

I separated myself from Him. I fled Him, renounced Him,
crucified Him.

May I never be separated from Him.

He is only kept by the paths taught in the gospel.

Total and sweet renunciation.

Total submission to Jesus Christ.

Eternally in joy for a day of trial on earth.

Moses met with God as the Fire that burned but was burning, in
a bush that was not consumed. The Fire that came to save the people.
The Fire that transforms our lives.

I think we want to say a simple "amen" to that.

5

The Lord Will Provide

WHEN I THINK ABOUT THE BIG THEMES in the Bible, there seems to be no end to them. This week, we've been like theological gemologists holding up a precious stone to the light and admiring some of its facets. In this case, we've been mining in Exodus 3, examining the precious jewel buried deep in that chapter: the great name Yahweh, the Lord, I Am, what used to be translated as "Jehovah."

If your first Bible was a King James Version, you remember that in Genesis there is one place where this name is expanded. It's expanded into "Jehovah-jireh" in Genesis 22:14: "And Abraham called the name of that place Jehovah-jireh [the LORD will provide]." This took place on Mount Moriah, where Abraham went to offer his son Isaac, the son of the promise, as a sacrifice to God. The angel of the Lord intervened, and as Abraham turned around, there was a ram caught in the bushes, a divinely provided substitute for his son. And so he called the place "The LORD will provide." He must have hardly been able to believe that his own words had been fulfilled.

As they had climbed the mountain, Isaac had said to Abraham, "Father, we have everything we need here for the sacrifice except the sacrifice." Abraham had responded, "God Himself will provide a lamb for the sacrifice." Haunting words. But if Abraham reflected on this dramatic experience of the angel of the Lord, I wonder if he ever thought, "I told Isaac that the Lord would Himself provide a lamb for the sacrifice, but it was a ram, not a lamb, that He provided." Is there something significant in this detail?

Later on, hidden away in 2 Chronicles 3:1, we discover that Mount Moriah was the area where Solomon began to build the house of the Lord in Jerusalem. It was therefore the area where Jesus spent the last week of His ministry. It's where He went through His agony in Gethsemane. It's where He was arrested, condemned, crucified, buried, and then wonderfully raised from the dead. Truly, on the mountain of the Lord it came to pass: God did provide for Himself the Lamb.

There on Mount Moriah, on the edge of King David's city, took place the event that all history had awaited since Abraham had spoken to his son as they climbed the barren wastes of that elevated ground. There, the words of the greatest of the prophets of the old covenant era, John the Baptist, were fulfilled: "Behold, the Lamb of God, who takes away the sin of the world!" (John 1:29). Jehovah-jireh, the Lord, will provide the Lamb for the sacrifice.

We began this week by asking what God is like, and we should end it by saying that this is what He is like: He is the God we can trust to provide us with everything we need, because, as Paul says: "If God is for us, who can be against us? He who did not spare his own Son but gave him up for us all, how will he not also with him graciously give us all things?" (Rom. 8:31–32).

May these two words be fixed into our hearts: *Jehovah-jireh*, the Lord will provide. And if we want to be sure that He will, we must look nowhere else than to the cross of Jesus Christ, for there He has proved beyond any doubt that He will provide.

WEEK 10

Ten Commandments, Part 1

1

The Commandments of God

IF YOUR PASTOR ANNOUNCED THIS SUNDAY that he was going to preach for the next three months on the Ten Commandments, what would your reaction be? Would you be thinking, "Oh, that is great!" or would you say, "Oh, not again"?

The commandments get a mixed review these days, even among some Christians. There is a kind of atmosphere that surrounds the expression "the Ten Commandments," and rightly so, because when we read the account of God's giving them at Mount Sinai, Moses' experience is even more spectacular than it was at the burning bush.

The giving of the Ten Commandments was surrounded by thunder, lightning, and a thick cloud. At the foot of Sinai, the people trembled. God revealed Himself as a God of power, might, holiness, and righteousness. But we should notice something important about the Ten Commandments: they were given by the God of infinite holiness and righteousness, but they were also given in a context of grace. This is perhaps the single most important thing for us to remember: God's law is given in the context of God's grace. How so? Before the giving of the Ten Commandments, God first says, "I am the LORD your God, who brought you out of the land of Egypt, out of the house of slavery" (Ex. 20:2).

This is the same great I Am who earlier told Moses that He had heard the groaning of the people of Israel and remembered His covenant. God instructed Moses to say to the people of Israel: "I am the LORD, and I will bring you out from under the burdens of the Egyptians, and I will deliver you from slavery to them, and I will redeem you with an outstretched arm and with great acts of judgment. I will take you to be my people, and I will be your God, and you shall know that I am the LORD your God, who has brought you out from under the burdens of the Egyptians" (Ex. 6:6–7).

If that isn't grace, I'm not sure what is. It's amazing grace. It's grace that the children of Israel needed to drink in and to keep drinking in. Therefore, when God says, "You shall have no other gods before me" (Ex. 20:3), nothing could be more rational. The logic is this: "Because of who I am to you, My people, you should reflect that character as a son reflects the character of his father."

And here's something else: nothing could be safer than obeying this command. For other gods, no matter what they are, ancient or modern, can only harm and damage us.

The first commandment teaches us that putting the Lord first is not only the right way to live; it's the best way to live. It's also the safest way to live, and we'll learn more about that in the rest of this week.

2

The Danger of Idolatry

YESTERDAY, WE SAID THAT LIVING BY the Ten Commandments is both the best way to live and also the safest way to live. Think about it this way: as Christians, we know that we can live for God's glory only with the help of the indwelling Spirit of Jesus Christ. He gives us the power to do that. To run properly, trains need tracks as well as power, don't they? In the same way, the commandments of God keep us on the right lines.

In the second commandment, God instructs His people not to make images or bow down to them. We might think that as Christian believers, we are not in danger of doing that. But when Moses later came down the mountain, this is exactly what the people who had experienced dramatic salvation from Egypt were doing. John Calvin was surely right when he wrote in book 1 of his *Institutes of the Christian Religion* that our hearts are a perpetual factory of idols.

In the Western world, our idols don't take the shape of golden calves, but they take other forms. If we look back to the era of Elvis or the Beatles, or even consider some of the massive music performances by the great pop stars of today, we notice that the crowd often looks as though they are at a charismatic worship service, adoring their idols.

If we're more straitlaced, then our idols can be as diverse as our job, our bank balance, our home, or our car. An idol is just about anything or anyone that we think about more often than we think about God—anything that stimulates our affections more than God does.

Why does God warn us about this? One reason is simply that it's wrong. But there is something else. It's that it's neither safe nor healthy for us. Idols can never satisfy, whether they are idols of wood and stone, or what the prophet Ezekiel calls "idols of the heart." Why not?

Let's look at two similar answers from men who thought long and hard about this question. Augustine writes in his *Confessions*, "You have made us for Yourself, O Lord, and our hearts are restless until they find their rest in You." The author of Ecclesiastes puts it this way: "[God] has put eternity into man's heart" (Eccl. 3:11).

That is our burden: if we were made for eternity—for faith in, love for, and fellowship with the living and loving God—then nothing less can ever be adequate for us or ever satisfy us. We are lost without Him precisely because we were made for Him and made to know Him and to love Him.

It's actually dangerous for us to have an idol. Our safety lies only in God. In fact, He tells us that He is jealous for us because He wants us to be safe with Him.

So I wonder, "Are you safe with Him or in danger with an idol?"

3

Taking God's Name in Vain

THE THIRD COMMANDMENT INSTRUCTS US NOT to take the name of the Lord in vain. I suppose for most people, that means only one thing: don't use swear words, and especially don't use God's name as a swear word. Of course, that is right. But it's more than that.

What God is forbidding here is using His name lightly or thoughtlessly, as though neither God nor His name were of any importance to us. What marks out the true believer is that he or she loves the Lord's name and exults in Him (see Ps. 5:11).

We can think about this in terms of the two Testaments of the Bible, Old and New. In the days of the Old Testament, the high priest was to bless the people. The specific blessing, sometimes called the Aaronic benediction, is recorded in Numbers 6:24–26:

> The LORD bless you and keep you;
> the LORD make his face to shine upon you and be gracious
>   to you;
> the LORD lift up his countenance upon you and give you peace.

These are beautiful words, and they describe the wonderful privilege of God shining on His people. Think about it: the face of God turning toward His people in love and smiling at them. But do you remember the words that follow?

God says this about the priests: "So shall they put my name upon the people of Israel, and I will bless them" (Num. 6:27). When the people of God received this blessing, God was putting His name on them. Therefore, to take the name of the Lord in vain was to accept the Lord's benediction, and then go off and live as if one had never received it. It seems almost impossible that someone would feel the smile of God in His benediction and then live as though it really didn't mean anything to him or to her.

But before we look down our noses at Old Testament believers, let's remember the other occasion when God's name is said to be put on people—and this time, it's referring to people like you and me, New Testament believers. It happened when you were baptized into the name of the Father, the Son, and the Holy Spirit. I hope we all understand that this is a bigger blessing than the Aaronic blessing.

But here's the challenge: Am I living as though that never happened? Am I living as though my baptism was just an empty sign, or merely a sign of something I did in the past that doesn't really matter today? If so, I couldn't be further from the truth or more deluded. I'm no longer on safe ground. In fact, Exodus 20 tells me that I'm on dangerous ground. I've emptied the name of God that was put upon me of all its significance. He has pronounced a benediction, but I've forfeited the blessing by the way I live.

Paul wrote about this in Romans 6 to counteract the idea that because God has been gracious to us, it doesn't really matter how we live, or even if we dishonor God's name. He says, "Do you not know that all of us who have been baptized into Christ Jesus were baptized into his death?" (Rom. 6:3). In other words, don't you know the meaning of your baptism? Don't you know that the name of Christ was placed upon you? If the name of the Lord has been put on you in baptism, then the rest of your life should be one in which you give yourself entirely to the Lord, whose name has been placed upon you.

Perhaps today you are tempted to take the Lord's name in vain, to empty your baptism of all its significance. Don't do that. Remember the family name that has been placed on you, and live as a member of the family of God.

4

A Pattern for Our Days

PERHAPS OF ALL THE COMMANDMENTS, the commandment about the Sabbath gets some Christians hot under the collar. No stealing, no adultery, no bearing false witness, no coveting—we understand these. We never dream of openly ignoring them. But the commandment about keeping the Sabbath requires some additional explanation to clarify what it says (and also what it doesn't say). While we can't get into all the issues, let me say a few things that I hope might be helpful.

The first is this: it's a mistake to think that the Sabbath commandment is either *only about* or *all about* one day in the week. Rather, it's actually about every day of the week: six days of labor, and one day of rest from that labor (see Ex. 20:9–10). In this law, God is giving us a kind of tool for balancing our lives. If you were to ask me, "Is it OK to do such-and-such a thing on Sunday?," I would respond, "Well, why are you thinking of doing that on Sunday?" Often the answer to this question is, "I don't have time during the rest of the week."

And that is the problem. If this is our answer to that question, then it's not just that we may be misusing the Sabbath. It's that we are misusing the whole week. Therefore, the Sabbath commandment isn't just about keeping or guarding the Sabbath; it's about living a healthy, balanced life all week long.

Here's a second thing to remember: the command implies that we've been given the six-plus-one pattern because we've been created as the image of God. It reminds us of this because it's grounded in the pattern by which God created the world—six days of divine activity, and one day to rest, admire, and enjoy it. When we follow that pattern, we are being what we were made to be: the children of God, made as His image and likeness, patterning our lives after His activity. This is a commandment that reminds us of our dignity and destiny as men and women. We've been created as the miniature image and likeness of the Creator, and as a result, we live after His pattern.

Here's something else that I find quite interesting. The first Sabbath day was not Adam's seventh day. It was God's seventh day, but it was Adam's first full day. It was as though God were saying to him, "I want your existence to begin with a time to admire everything I have made, and then you can go on from there and imitate Me."

What a gift the Sabbath is, and what a marvelous safeguard for our lives. I hope you feel it really is a gift to you, and I hope you find it really does safeguard the way you live the whole week.

5

Honor Your Father and Mother

SOMETIMES CHRISTIANS THINK ABOUT GOD'S LAW in the same way many of us think about police officers. They tend to make us feel on edge and fearful that we have done, or might do, something wrong. And of course, the Ten Commandments do function that way. They show us our sin for what it is, and that can be a very unpleasant experience—but it's a necessary one.

The police officer doesn't exist simply to make people feel guilty. He or she is there for the protection of the public. And in the same way, the Ten Commandments function like a well-trained divine police force, protecting us from moral harm and from making a shipwreck of our lives.

"Honor your father and your mother" is the fifth commandment (Ex. 20:12). The first four commandments are about our relationship with God, and the next six are about our relationships with one another. And the first of these human-relationship commandments has to do with our relationship with our parents. We are to honor them. Let's note a few observations about this command.

First, we should notice that God doesn't say, "Obey your parents." He says, "Honor your father and your mother." There is a reason for that. We are always to honor our parents because they gave us life and nurtured us. When we're young and at home, that honor takes the form of obedience. When we're older and perhaps married with our own children, we've begun a new family group. We're no longer under the authority of our parents the way we once were. We have left that family structure and started a new one. That is why the Bible never says to adults, "Obey your parents." But we are still to honor them.

Sometimes both parents and children can give themselves problems by not understanding that. The Christian parent who doesn't understand this may turn out to be a real problem to his or her children. And the husband or wife who doesn't understand this may become a real problem to their spouse. So this is an important distinction. Always honor your parents, no matter what age you are. And when you are young, that means obeying them as a way of pleasing the Lord and blessing them.

There is one more thing that I've always thought rather wonderful. After the four commandments dealing with our relationship to God—our Creator, Redeemer, and Lord—there are six commandments about dealing with each other. And if you're a young child, that is quite a lot to take in: no murder, no adultery, no stealing, no lying, no coveting.

But the way the fifth commandment works for a child is this: If my mom and dad love the Lord, and if I honor them, then these other commandments will naturally fit into place almost without my thinking about them. It's as though the fifth commandment were like a very tall, kind police officer whose special job is to guard our children from sin and spiritual danger.

But then there is this: If you are a mom or a dad, will you live in such a way that you're worthy of being honored by your children?

WEEK 11

Ten Commandments, Part 2

1

Murdering in Our Hearts

THE TEN COMMANDMENTS ARE THE CHRISTIAN'S FRIENDS, not his enemies. They function like guards posted around our lives to keep us safe and faithful. And so it's worth lingering over them and reflecting on them one by one. Today, we've come to the sixth commandment: "You shall not murder" (Ex. 20:13).

I remember my parents taking me to the famous Cecil B. DeMille movie *The Ten Commandments* with Charlton Heston, the magnificent, eighty-year-old Moses. I think I was only eight at the time, but the voice of God booming down on Mount Sinai held no surprises for me because I'd memorized the Ten Commandments long before then.

If you were anything like me and had to learn the Ten Commandments as a child, you probably shared my relief when you got to number six. You might not have loved God with all your heart and soul and strength, and you had not fully obeyed your parents, but at least with number six, you could relax and say with the rich young ruler, "This commandment I have kept from my childhood upwards" (see Mark 10:20). But now we know better, don't we?

When we look at the Sermon on the Mount, we learn that we can murder with our mouths as well as with a machine gun. We can lacerate with a look as well as with a knife. And we can kill with a computer keyboard as well as with a blunt instrument. That is what Jesus said this commandment really meant. When we realize this, we begin to see that the Ten Commandments all have an inside as well as an outside, and we find a clue that helps us understand and apply them to our lives. They all come alive with instruction for us.

The Westminster Larger Catechism is helpful at just this point. Question 99 asks, "What rules are to be observed for the right understanding of the Ten Commandments?" The answer begins, "For the right understanding of the Ten Commandments, these rules are to be observed . . ."

The second rule reads, "That it is spiritual, and so reacheth the understanding, will, affections, and all other powers of the soul; as well as words, works, and gestures."

The fourth rule states, "That as, where a duty is commanded, the contrary sin is forbidden; and, where a sin is forbidden, the contrary duty is commanded: so, where a promise is annexed, the contrary threatening is included; and, where a threatening is annexed, the contrary promise is included."

The sixth rule says, "That under one sin or duty, all of the same kind are forbidden or commanded; together with all the causes, means, occasions, and appearances thereof, and provocations thereunto."

And the seventh rule tells us, "That what is forbidden or commanded to ourselves, we are bound, according to our places, to endeavor that it may be avoided or performed by others, according to the duty of their places."

I think you can tell that the Westminster divines had been listening to the Lord Jesus, for they knew that every commandment has both an outside and an inside. The real significance, as well as the real challenge, of the commandments is not just about our outward behavior. It's also about our inner spiritual condition.

I hope that you see the inside as well as the outside. It's not enough for the outside to be washed. The inside needs to be washed too. And that is why we constantly need to remind ourselves that it's only by the Spirit of the Lord Jesus Christ that the righteous requirements of the law will ever be fulfilled in us (Rom. 8:3–4). So let's look to the Spirit of Christ today to enable us to live like Christ.

2

The Beginning of Lust

THE SEVENTH COMMANDMENT SAYS, "You shall not commit adultery" (Ex. 20:14). If you remember how Jesus taught us to understand these commandments, you know that this goes much deeper than the physical act: "I say to you that everyone who looks at a woman with lustful intent has already committed adultery with her in his heart" (Matt. 5:28).

I know what some people say when they hear the Christian sexual ethic: "There are other sins. Why do you Christians obsess over sexual ones?" There is a famous Latin expression *corruptio optimi pessima est*: the worst is the corruption of the best. That is not only morally true; it's theologically true as well. When God had finished His creating work by making man and woman as His image, everything was said to be "very good."

Since Satan knew that he could not overcome the Creator, he simply moved on to the next stage: he sought to destroy what God had made very good and for our blessing. It's illuminating to see the pattern. First, he spoiled the marriage. In Genesis 3, Adam and Eve have started a blame game. Then Satan moved on to the family and incited Cain to slay his brother Abel. And before we've reached the end of Genesis 4, we're hearing Lamech serenading his wives (plural) with tales of his murdering vengeance.

The point to notice is that now we have a further attack on marriage and family life with adultery. If we're inclined to say, "But don't we have to wait until Moses before the law condemns it?," the answer is surely to think the way the Lord Jesus thought and ask the question, "What did God intend at the beginning?"

The answer to that is found in Genesis 2. A man leaves his family home, marries one woman, holds fast to his wife, and they become one flesh. The truth is that adultery is destructive of God's best purposes.

It's as simple as that. In the nature of the case, it isn't a private matter. Whatever people may say, it destroys at least one marriage, and perhaps two. It inevitably has an effect on any children, on parents, on friends. It has financial repercussions as well as familial ones. It strikes at the very fabric of society, which can be strong and happy only when the marriage bond is held in honor.

Yes, there can be forgiveness even for adultery. But in God's economy, forgiveness isn't like a computer program that can switch everything back to an earlier date so that you can begin again. There will be lasting repercussions for the rest of our lives, and perhaps for the rest of others' lives, too.

Jesus says that it all begins, and always begins, with a look. It does, doesn't it? Yes, there may be many other dimensions, but it begins with a look. That is why the next verse in the Sermon on the Mount records Jesus as saying, "If your right eye causes you to sin, tear it out and throw it away" (Matt. 5:29). Of course, He doesn't mean that literally. What He is saying is that so long as my eye lingers, my heart will yearn and not be satisfied until I have what my eye sees. We need to begin there, and then work backward to our hearts.

I'm often reminded of a little verse in a poem that John Bunyan wrote:

Sin, rather than 'twill out of action be,
Will pray to stay, though but a while with thee;
One night, one hour, one moment, will it cry,
Embrace me in thy bosom, else I die:
Time to repent (saith it) I will allow,
And help, if to repent thou know'st not how.
But if you give it entrance at the door,
It will come in, and may go out no more.

Wise words in this context, don't you think? And in many other contexts, too. May God keep us all safe today.

3

Theft and Generosity

HAVE YOU EVER WONDERED WHY the Ten Commandments include so many negatives? There are ten "you shall nots" plus one "no," and that is a lot of what people nowadays call "negativity." It's very countercultural today to say it, but I'm going to say it nonetheless: negativity can be very positive for your spiritual health.

Of course, there are negative thoughts and feelings that are harmful. But in the Ten Commandments, God is teaching us not to throw the baby out with the bathwater. He is saying that there are some things we need to be negative about because they will destroy us or someone else—and perhaps both. Here are two reflections that may help us.

The first is this: Why all this negative language? Well, it's the clearest and simplest way to put things, isn't it? I'm sure that Einstein's dad wouldn't have sat him down when he was three and explain how electricity works to stop him from pushing a screwdriver into the electric socket. Presumably he would have said, "Albert, don't do that." There'll be time enough for Albert to learn how electricity works. But if Albert sticks his little screwdriver into the socket, Mrs. Einstein will be calling for the emergency services, and little Albert will wish that he'd listened to his father's negativity.

The same is true of the Ten Commandments. Their negatives say: "Danger! Don't cross the barrier." We are still spiritual children, growing only slowly to understand how much damage sin does. But here God gives us ten simple, straightforward statements to protect us.

The second reflection is this: in Ephesians 6:2, Paul calls the fifth commandment (to honor our father and mother) the first commandment with a promise. But it's also the first commandment without a negative. In fact, it's the only commandment without a negative. But if we remember the principles the Westminster divines gave us in the

Larger Catechism, we realize that the commandments all have this character—that every negative involves a positive, just as every positive involves a negative.

The eighth commandment tells us, "You shall not steal" (Ex. 20:15). What I find wonderful about this commandment applies to us from the time we are young children. It's not negative; it's wonderfully positive. It's saying something about life, and it's saying something about God: that God Himself positively loves us and wants to keep us safe, and He wants us to keep other people safe too.

He keeps things simple for us. He gives us only ten commandments, and this one tells us that from the beginning of life to its end, life is precious—and that is a wonderful expression of His kindness to us. This command is expressed in the negative, but it also implies something positive, just as the Apostle Paul in the New Testament tells us to put off sinful ways, yet he also tells us to put on Christlike ways.

And so this eighth commandment implicitly calls us to generosity. Saying no to stealing from others means saying yes to giving to others; otherwise, we're likely to become very metallic Christians. Here's the challenge: if my saying no is becoming rigorous in my life, is my saying yes becoming generous in my life? That is the litmus test.

4

Is It Ever Right to Lie?

IF YOU'RE FROM THE UNITED STATES, you're probably more familiar with the name Mason Locke Weems than I am. He wrote the book *The Life of George Washington*, which has the delicious subtitle *With Curious Anecdotes, Equally Honorable to Himself and Exemplary to His Young Countrymen*. With a title like that, how could it possibly fail to be a bestseller? It actually was when it first appeared in 1800.

But it wasn't until a few years later, in the fifth edition, that Weems included the story about six-year-old George Washington, his new hatchet, and his father's cherry tree that has become so famous: "I cannot tell a lie. I cut down the cherry tree." What makes these famous words somewhat humorous is that, apparently, they are a fabrication. I hesitate to call them a straight-out lie.

I don't mean that Washington was telling a lie; I mean that Mason Locke Weems apparently made up the story. His motives were good. He wanted to set Washington before young people as a fine moral example to follow. But what is slightly curious and ironic about this story is that Mason Locke Weems was an itinerant preacher, and McGuffey, who reworked the story in his famous reader, was a Presbyterian minister. Yet they didn't seem to be telling the full truth about George Washington. I think that is sometimes true when we come to the ninth commandment: "You shall not bear false witness against your neighbor" (Ex. 20:16).

One of the questions that often arises in connection with this commandment is, "Well, is it ever right to lie?" The question becomes pressing because people often answer it by appealing to examples in Scripture of people's telling lies, and good seems to result.

Here are a couple of considerations to bear in mind. The fact that good follows a person's telling a lie is no more a justification of the lie than that the blessing of God, seen when Joseph becomes prime minister, resulted from Joseph's brothers selling him as a slave. We can't argue backward from what God does in His providence to justify everything that we or other people do. To use a more specific example, the fact that Rahab seems to have told a lie and the aftermath was that spies escaped, Israel conquered Jericho, and she was saved doesn't in itself justify her lying. Rahab's bearing false witness was never the *sine qua non* of God's overcoming Jericho, and we need to bear that in mind.

But the second thing to say is that while we should never bear false witness, this does not mean that we are not permitted to ever withhold information or that we are obliged to tell people anything we know that they want to know. Remember Jesus' own words about not casting pearls before pigs who will devour them and then trample you? Christians are to be resolutely committed to not bearing malicious false witness. We are to be committed to telling the truth. But we're under no obligation to tell the truth to anyone who wants to know it.

If the local Christian busybody in your church asks you about someone you know well—and about whom you know more than perhaps anyone else does—and then says, "Tell me the truth about them; don't bear false witness," you and I are not under any obligation to tell them anything. There is a time to speak and a time to keep silent, and we need to know the difference. We also need to be able to discern people's spirits.

We've been learning that every commandment implies its opposite, so it's not enough to refrain from lying speech as we seek to obey this command. As the book of Proverbs tells us, we need to learn how to use truthful words in a way that both blesses and heals others, and that is part of our growing Christian maturity. So let's remember that every time we open our mouths to speak today.

5

From Covetous to Christlike

AS LIFE BECOMES MORE COMPLEX, the principles and laws we use to regulate it are bound to increase in number. If no one had ever put anything in space or traveled there, then we wouldn't need any space law. If there were no computers, World Wide Web, or social media, we wouldn't need laws to regulate them. But they do exist, and we all understand that we need to agree on how best to handle them.

As we've been studying for the past two weeks, God gave us ten basic laws to govern our lives. But when these ten big laws are ignored, demeaned, or rejected—as often happens in our society today—something else inevitably happens: our governments have to introduce more and more laws to try to cope with the moral and social chaos that results. They simply don't know what they are doing because they have no moral rudder calibrated to God's Word and wisdom. Ignore, demean, or destroy the big ten, and you inevitably have to produce more and more laws.

The truth of the matter is, as Chief Justice John Roberts famously wrote in one of his opinions, that we are doing things simply because we want to. And the more the things that we want to do are against what God wants us to do, the more we will create laws yet find ourselves in moral chaos.

This reminds me of the Hans Christian Andersen story about the emperor's new clothes. Two swindlers had made "clothes" for the emperor that didn't really exist, and they told him that only those who were stupid couldn't see them. That left everyone sycophantically telling the king how marvelous he looked. It took a clear-sighted little boy to pull the wool from their eyes by pointing out that the king had nothing on.

That is our world today, and we need to look out for the inevitable entail of rejecting the big ten. It's always going to be more laws, unworkable laws, and further laws to deal with unworkable laws, a process that gradually undermines the stability and safety of society. Yes, only the gospel can save us. But the gospel that saves us teaches us to please God by obedience to His commandments.

The last of the Ten Commandments says, "You shall not covet" (Ex. 20:17). We covet when we are not content with what we have and want to have what belongs to someone else. This commandment is the one that seemed to break through the hardness of the heart of Saul of Tarsus. He says as much in Romans 7:7–12: when the law came, sin revived and he died. And the particular law that came was, "You shall not covet" (v. 7). He suggests that it was this that laid the foundation for his Damascus Road experience.

But what was Saul coveting? I believe the answer is that without fully realizing it, he was coveting what he had seen in Stephen, something that Saul didn't himself possess. No one had ever made that kind of impression on him. Stephen was a young contemporary who was full of grace, full of the Holy Spirit, and full of God's Word—everything that Saul actually wasn't.

In Stephen, Saul saw illustrated firsthand what he would later write about in Romans 8. It was a lifestyle that expressed beautiful obedience to the law, but that lifestyle was effected only through faith in Jesus Christ. That was what Saul lacked, and that was what he saw. And probably before he even knew it, that was what he coveted. And that word from God, "You shall not covet," brought him to realize his need.

There is an important lesson here for us as Christians. It's that what best shows people both the beauty of the law, and that they've broken it, is seeing that law fulfilled by the Spirit of Christ in our lives as we become more like Jesus. Because ultimately, that is what the law is about: Jesus Christ is the end of the law.

WEEK 12

Christians Love to Sing

1

Singing Christians

CHRISTIANS LOVE TO SING. But why is that? Before I came to faith, I enjoyed listening to music, but I didn't like singing. If I were to break out into song, you would understand why. I wouldn't say that regeneration on its own improved my voice, but it did make me *want* to sing. And in particular, it made me want to sing Christ's praises.

I imagine the very fact that I wanted to sing probably did help a little. It wasn't that I felt under obligation to sing or that I'd worked it out theologically. I was only a young teenager. It was simply an inner urge, a new desire to express praise, admiration, and gratitude for what the Lord Jesus had done for me, for all that the Father had come to mean to me, and for all that the Spirit was beginning to work into my life.

I remember a friend of mine who is a minister telling me about a young man with no church background who started coming to their church. Eventually, the man said he wanted to become a member. When the elders met with him and asked about his spiritual journey, he told them how dramatically their church had changed since he started attending. The services were much livelier than when he had first come. The hymns were much better as well, and he enjoyed singing them much more than the ones they had sung when he first came. He even said to my friend that his sermons had become much more interesting in recent weeks.

You know what had happened to him, don't you? The elders were too kind to embarrass him by telling him that they were still singing the same old hymns, and my friend was far too wise to get upset about the fact that his sermons had apparently dramatically improved. The real truth, of course, was that the young man had been born again. The old had passed away, and the new had arrived. The tunes were just the same. What had changed was that he now understood the words and realized that they matched his own experience. There was music in his soul now, and that music matched the music of the hymns.

When you become a Christian, you want to sing. This leads me to a couple of questions I want to ask. I think these questions are more important than they might at first appear.

The first question is this: Do you sing hymns? By that, I mean psalms, hymns, and spiritual songs. I don't just mean in church, but as you go through life. Is there music in your soul only when others are present and when there are instruments? If that is the case, then something has gone out of your soul, and you need to get it back. You need to sing.

What is the remedy for someone who has stopped singing? It's simple: start singing again. Don't wait for inspiration. Sing. The singing will give you inspiration. Praising God is a command; it's not an optional luxury in our Christian lives.

Here's the second question, and I think it's just as important: Do you own a hymnbook? I suspect that next to a Bible, a good concordance, and a decent whole-Bible commentary, the most important book you should own is a good hymnbook. That is a strong statement, I know. Why do I say that? We'll talk about that more tomorrow.

2

Do You Have a Hymnbook?

I'VE COME TO SUSPECT THAT MANY Christians today don't possess a hymnbook. That is a huge contrast with the church culture of previous generations. When I became a Christian, many Bibles were published with a built-in hymnbook at the back. You took not only your own Bible to church, but your own hymnbook, too.

I realize there is something convenient about the church's supplying everything you need for the worship service, but I think there has been a cost as well. For example, it's no longer clear to your neighbors that you're going to church because they don't see a book in your hand. But there is something else. Part of the loss in some churches is that you end up at the mercy of seeing the words you're singing only on a screen, and you can become a victim of the law of unintended consequences.

If your church uses a screen, let me urge you today to buy a hymn-book. You owe it to your Christian growth to own one. Why do I make that radical and rather countercultural, old-fashioned suggestion? Because I'm an old man? It's simple, really. In all likelihood, if you don't have a hymnbook, then you don't know the vast majority of the great hymns of the Christian church, and you don't know the hymns that never go up on the screen. In fact, you don't know if you're being fully nurtured by what you're singing or starved by whoever chooses what goes on the screen.

But there is another reason for having a good hymnbook. If your church uses a screen, you probably see only one verse of a hymn at a time, never the whole hymn. All you see are single verses, and that means you're being deprived of what Christians have valued for centuries: seeing and understanding the flow and logic of a great hymn as it moves from verse to verse. It's all in front of you. You see the whole.

The great hymn writers were students of Scripture. Some of them were not only gifted poets but fine theologians capable of developing an idea and illuminating biblical truth. We're always at the mercy of whoever is responsible to choose the praise in our congregation, whether we use a hymnbook or not. And everyone—and for that matter, every congregation—tends to have favorites. But knowledge of your hymnbook means you can still get to know all the hymns, reflect on them, and grow through their teaching because often they are sermons in song. You can follow the theological reasoning of the hymn.

With a hymnbook, you get almost twenty centuries of hymns, not just the last twenty years. When you sing your way through a hymn-book, you begin to appreciate that in your praise, you belong to the vast company of believers through the centuries. And that is so important for us today, because it reminds us that the church is far bigger than we ever imagined. There has perhaps never been a day when that is more important, because the contemporary church's thirst is to be exactly that—contemporary in everything. That often means that Christians are deprived of the wisdom of the ages.

Please don't misunderstand me. This is not an attempt to demean all modern songwriters and modern songs. But if that is all that we sing and know, we are rejecting a wisdom practice of the church throughout the ages. We're the first generation in three hundred years to do that, and frankly, we're not a smart enough or a spiritual enough generation to do that. In addition, as a number of commentators point out, our praise is more likely to reflect the deep subjectivism and individualism of much contemporary Christianity.

So here's today's message: if you don't have a hymnbook, please get one.

3

Singing with the Son of God

HAVE YOU EVER HAD THIS EXPERIENCE? You're in church singing "How Great Thou Art," "A Mighty Fortress Is Our God," or perhaps something more modern, and the question pops into your mind: "Does God actually *like* this? Does this please God?" We may not be very good singers. And God is eternal, the One without beginning or end or cause. So why should we think that our singing praise to Him would give Him any pleasure?

Scripture gives us some interesting reasons for believing that God loves it when His people praise Him. One reason is that Scripture itself urges us to praise Him. When words breathed out by God and written down by men tell us to praise Him, then we can safely assume that He wants us to do it and that it gives Him pleasure—the kind of pleasure that a father has when his three-year-old daughter starts singing to him and tells him, "I love you, Daddy."

Another reason is that the Bible contains an entire book, the Psalms, that is composed of songs of praises, requests, and laments. That would hardly be the case unless God desired to listen to us. In fact, He has such a desire that He has provided us with the very words we need for every season and stage of life from beginning to end, from gladness to sadness. Yes, God wants us to sing.

There is a third reason. We know that the Lord Jesus, who always did the will of His Father and lived to please Him, sang praises to Him. There is one place in the Gospels that tells us very specifically that He did so. At the end of the Passover meal, as He was about to go to the garden of Gethsemane, He and His disciples sang a hymn. We know what they probably sang because the same praise was sung year after year at Passover. It was called the *Hallel* (like the word *hallel-u-jah*), and it begins:

> Praise the LORD!
> Praise, O servants of the LORD,
> > praise the name of the LORD!
>
> Blessed be the name of the LORD
> > from this time forth and forevermore!
> From the rising of the sun to its setting,
> > the name of the LORD is to be praised! (Ps. 113:1–3)

If the Son of God sang praises to God, then we can be sure that God loves to hear and enjoys the praises of His people, just as a father loves the love of his children.

The upper room was not the last time our Lord Jesus led the praises of His children. Psalm 22 begins with an anticipation of Jesus' cry of dereliction on the cross: "My God, my God, why have you forsaken me?" (v. 1). But the psalm concludes by looking forward to the resurrection and to another cry—this time a cry of delight. Our Lord Jesus says, "I will tell of your name to my brothers; in the midst of the congregation I will praise you" (v. 22). This is a lovely description of what happens when we meet together in worship. Jesus preaches His

Word, and He stands in the midst of the congregation and leads our praises.

The author of Hebrews quotes this psalm in Hebrews 2:12. These words are not only a picture of what Jesus was doing with the Apostles in the upper room, but also a statement about what He is doing now as He is present with us in worship. He is with us, and He leads our praises.

Think of it this way: when we lift our voices together in praise, assisted by the Holy Spirit to praise our Lord Jesus Christ, we're brought into the presence of God. We're actually sharing in the worship of heaven, and Jesus is with us. Or better said, we are with Jesus. We surround Him, and He is leading our praises.

If anything should make you want to sing in worship, it's knowing that He is the real praise leader.

4

Christians Sing Differently

I FIND IT REMARKABLE THAT THE AVERAGE Christian probably sings many more times in the week than the person who isn't a Christian. There are certainly exceptions. I realize that some non-Christians sing a great deal and that some Christians don't sing nearly enough. But generally speaking, I believe this principle holds true.

But even more significant is the fact that Christians sing differently. The teenager enjoying the latest rap song, the would-be operatic tenor singing "Nessun Dorma" in the shower, or the seventy-something-year-old retiree humming Beatles or Beach Boys tunes from the sixties and seventies—none of them sings the way Christians sing.

What do I mean by that? Non-Christians always sing on a horizontal plane. The songs they sing are about me, or you, or them, or it. Christians also at times sing horizontally. Think about some of the Psalms. We are singing horizontally when we sing, "O come, my soul, bless thou the Lord . . . , and all within me bless his holy name" (or if you prefer contemporary wording, when you sing, "Bless the Lord, O my soul"). We're talking first to ourselves when we sing these words. We are also singing horizontally when we sing, "Come, we that love the Lord, and let our joys be known," or "Come, people of the risen King." We're talking to others, to our fellow believers, and we're saying to them, "Come on, now, let's sing together." But that, too, is on the horizontal plane.

Is that wrong? Not at all. In fact, the way that Christians sing on a horizontal plane is actually not the same as how non-Christians sing on a horizontal plane. Because when Christians sing on a horizontal plane, we don't stay on that horizontal plane. We sing to ourselves, and we sing to others, but we do so to encourage both ourselves and others to sing vertically, to sing in the presence of the Lord and upward to the Lord.

Many of the spiritual songs we sing begin in a horizontal direction, singing to ourselves or to others, perhaps even about our own lives. Secular songs do that, too. But while secular songs end that way, Christians are always singing upward to God, for in the songs that begin with singing about ourselves and others, we actually end up singing about and to God, praising Him for His goodness and grace or seeking His help. In addition, no matter what we are singing about, we know we are singing in His presence.

Even if we find ourselves singing exactly the same songs as non-Christians, we never sing them in exactly the same way. Here's a simple personal example. When I think back to my first conversation with the fellow student who became my wife, I often think of a song made famous by Roberta Flack, "The First Time Ever I Saw Your Face."

My point is not that I'm secretly the great romantic. It's this: those words have a vertical, God-centered meaning to me, not simply a horizontal one. I was a Christian, and yes, I certainly liked her face, but I couldn't think "I want to spend my life with you" without knowing that the real reason I felt this was because of her trust in and her love for the Lord. So even what began on a horizontal plane was taking place on a vertical plane.

When you become a Christian, you live *coram Deo*—before the face of God, in His presence. And when you do, that changes everything. Including the way you sing.

5

Let the Word of Christ Dwell in You Richly

YESTERDAY, I SAID THAT SECULAR SONGS have a horizontal direction. We sing about ourselves or what's around us, or we sing to each other. There is nothing wrong with that, but there is a whole missing dimension. By contrast, when a Christian sings in a horizontal direction, even singing the very same songs as unbelievers, there is always a vertical direction. And the reason is that we live before the face of God and in His presence. We know that when we are singing, He is listening. When we are singing, we're singing to Him and about Him, for Him, or in His presence. Therefore, all of the Christian's singing is different.

When we sing Christian praise—psalms and hymns and spiritual songs—it's very different. In Colossians 3:16, Paul writes some of the most important words in the New Testament about singing: "Let the word of Christ dwell in you richly, teaching and admonishing one another in all wisdom, singing psalms and hymns and spiritual songs, with thankfulness in your hearts to God."

There is a whole theology of singing in this one verse. What is Paul teaching us? First, that our singing needs to be informed and directed by the Word of Christ, by the teaching He gives us in Scripture. Scripture is profitable for doctrine, reproof, correction, and training in righteousness to equip us for every good work. That is true when we sing the truths that Scripture teaches us as well as when we hear the preaching of these truths. That is the first thing we should ask when we read a hymn. Yes, we know that hymns are poetic, and that can involve a special use of language. But we also need to be just as discerning about what we sing as we are about what we hear. We should always be asking: "Is this song biblical? Is it profitable for doctrine, for reproof, for correction, and for training in righteousness?" That is a fundamental issue.

The second thing to notice is that Paul shows us here that our singing is actually part of the whole congregation's ministry of the Word. It's a ministry that we exercise toward each other. We may not be using our own words, but we need to understand that when we all sing the same words, we're meant to be thinking and praying: "Lord, help us learn what this hymn is saying. Help us, through the singing of this song, to teach one another. Help me minister to my brothers and sisters about You, Your Son, Your Spirit, our church, our needs, and the ways that You will meet them."

There is a third lesson here, and it's an important one, too. We are to sing with thankfulness in our hearts to God. Paul makes the same point in the parallel passage in Ephesians 5:19, where he talks about making melody to the Lord with all our hearts when we sing psalms, hymns, and spiritual songs. We're to lift up our hearts to God when we lift up our voices in praise. What He is listening for is the melody in our souls. That is why Paul writes in 1 Corinthians 14:15: "What am I to do? . . . I will sing praise with my spirit, but I will sing with my mind also."

I hope you'll set your mind on what we've been thinking about this week, and when you sing on Sunday, you'll want to sing more thankfully and enthusiastically, and with a better understanding of what you're doing. And don't forget who the real worship leader will be: the Lord Jesus will be with you. When you listen to the sermon, remember the Lord's words, "I will tell of your name to my brothers" (Ps. 22:22).

When you sing, remember He is the real praise leader. He is saying in the midst of the congregation, "I will praise you." That should energize your singing.

WEEK 13

The Attributes of God

1

Knowing God

AT TIMES, WE SPEAK ABOUT GOD too casually, don't we? Sometimes even Christians are guilty of this and empty God's name of content. We forget that it's God we're talking about, not our next-door neighbor. The problem with our assumed familiarity and easy talk is that it actually diminishes and almost destroys our sense of the privilege of knowing Him. That privilege is created not by our sense of familiarity but by His identity—who He is that we have come to know.

I sometimes think of it this way: When my shadow falls on a line of ants scurrying across the ground, I'm sure it doesn't cross their minds to ask: "Why does Sinclair keep blocking out the sun? We need to tell him that we are fed up with the way he towers over our lives." That an ant would talk about me is ridiculous. There is no comparison between an ant and me, no comparison between his brain and mine.

But the gulf between God the Creator and us as creatures is immeasurably greater. We're talking about the God who spoke the cosmos into being in all its vastness and diversity, the One whose imagination is of such genius that He created the seemingly endless variety that exists in the world. We take it for granted that we know what we mean when we say "God." As long as we do that, we never really feel the sheer wonder of what it actually means to be able to say, "I have come to know God."

Remember how God takes Job outside in Job 38–39, invites him to look at some of the wonders of creation, and asks him: "Where were you when I did this? What did you contribute? What do you understand, really? I invented and created all this, and did it just with a few words." And the answer to those questions is that Job didn't actually understand very much of it. Neither do we.

I have a wonderful Christian friend who has devoted his academic life to the study of the human brain. He very kindly gave me a copy of the textbook that he'd written, but I hardly understood any of it. In his introduction, he says a very striking thing: he says that he hopes his book will help students and practitioners understand something more of the little we really know about the human brain.

Staggering, isn't it? The brainiest people we know don't know all that much about the brain that makes them so brainy. The human brain is only one element in the sheer vastness and variety of the cosmos that God imagined and then brought into being with a few words.

In light of these realities, what should be lesson number one when we think about God? Augustine taught it, and John Calvin echoed it. Just as when the famous Greek orator Demosthenes was asked the secret of oratory and responded, "Action, action, action," if these masters of the Christian faith were asked the secret of the Christian life, they would say, "Humility, humility, humility."

The call for the those who engage in theology is humility. And if you're familiar with the title of what I think is one of Dr. R.C. Sproul's best books, you'll realize that this applies to you, too, because "everyone's a theologian."

2

The Simplicity of God

YESTERDAY, WE BEGAN REFLECTING ON THE difference between the Creator and the creature. We are, as the hymn "O Worship the King" says, "frail children of dust, and feeble as frail." We grasp the privilege of knowing God, then, not by making Him small, but by realizing the sheer greatness of the One we've come to know.

But what is involved in knowing who God is and what He is like? We can come to know Him only because He has condescended to reveal Himself to us, and because He has made us as His image and likeness, giving us the capacity to know Him. He is the original person, and He has made us as image persons, miniature likenesses of Himself. Though we are of a different genre from God, we have been created by Him to know and love Him.

One way that we come to know and love each other as persons is through what we might call our "attributes." The same is true with God. When we speak about the attributes of God, we're not talking about characteristics we attribute to him, characteristics we think He has but He might not have; we're talking about characteristics He displays. We're talking about what Scripture teaches us about Him.

In the same way, we as humans also have attributes—kindness, trustworthiness, patience, and so on. But there is a difference between us and God. In other words, I might be kind and patient today, but tomorrow I might become someone who's cruel and irritable. Yet I'd still be the same person if I had different attributes. But God isn't like that.

One reason why God isn't like that is that in God, all His attributes are Himself. They are simply who and what He is. His goodness, faithfulness, omnipotence, holiness, and unchanging character—they are all who He is. Theologians call this the "simplicity" of God. In saying that, they don't mean He is simpleminded; rather, the very opposite.

Imagine two balls: one is large; the other is tiny—like a round speck of dust so small you can hardly see it. I ask you to lift them one at a time. You manage, with some effort, to lift the big one. "Well done," I say. "Now relax for a minute and lift the small one." "This will be easy," you think. But when you try, you can't lift it. You try and try but fail each time. Why?

This tiny ball is simply too dense for you to lift. It's as though all the weight in the world had been concentrated into one tiny point. It's all one tiny, indivisible reality, and its mass is enormous. All illustrations have their limitations, and this one certainly does. But what I'm trying to say is that when we speak of the simplicity of God, we mean the immense density of all His attributes concentrated into one unimaginably great Being.

When the Westminster Shorter Catechism says, "God is . . . infinite, eternal, and unchangeable, in his being, wisdom, power, holiness, justice, goodness, and truth," these are not elements that when added together make up God's being so that He gets bigger and bigger. They are really ways of expressing the sheer density, the simplicity, of the perfection of His being.

It shouldn't surprise us when we are told in Isaiah 6 that the seraphim, who are perfectly holy, veil their faces in God's presence. It's not that He is holy and they are not. They are perfectly holy, too. But their holiness is light when compared to the density in Him. There is an eternal density in the way all of God's attributes are simply who He is.

Therefore, it's no wonder that the seraphim repeat the word "holy" and then repeat it again. When we turn to the end of our Bibles, they are still repeating it in Revelation 4:8. It's as though they can never get to the bottom of the density of the being of God. And it's that greatness that makes John 1:18 such wonderful news: "No one has ever seen God; the only God, who is at the Father's side"—that is, the Lord Jesus—"he has made him known."

3

The Thrice-Holy God

I REMEMBER OUR PRINCIPAL CLASSICS MASTER in high school telling us what happened when a Roman general won a great victory and rode into Rome with his troops and the spoils of battle. The prisoners followed behind, but they always put a slave in the chariot beside the general. The slave would repeat two words, *homo es*, which means "You're only a man."

The Apostle Paul says the same to anyone who would argue with God because he or she can't understand what He is doing: "Who are you, O man . . . ?" (Rom. 9:20). When we speak about the infinite greatness of God—that He is far beyond us, far beyond our being, far beyond our understanding—we have a tendency to try to bring Him down to our size so that we can think of Him as essentially someone just like us, perhaps a little bit bigger. We want to be that big. But God isn't like that. He is the infinite One.

This is why Christian theology, and perhaps especially the doctrine of God, is so very important. Its beauty lies in the fact that by instructing us about Him, it humbles us. In humbling us before God, it can then exalt us into His presence so that we develop an increased sense of wonder that we can speak of Him, and even speak to Him, because we know Him. Our sense of privilege depends on our sense of His greatness.

What do we know about God? God is holy. Indeed, in both the Old and New Testaments, we hear heavenly creatures praise Him as thrice holy, intensely holy—holy, holy, holy to the ultimate power, as it were.

But what do we mean when we speak about the holiness of God? We often and rightly say that the word *holy* in the Bible means something like "separate" or "cut off from." It's certainly true that at least one major implication of the word is the idea of separation from sin. He is "of purer eyes than to see evil" (Hab. 1:13). We're so used to sin that we find holiness difficult to imagine.

I used to live in a part of the United States that was really hot in the summer months. Perhaps I felt it more because I'd spent the first thirty years of my life in a country where it was considered a heat wave if the temperature got above fifty or sixty degrees Fahrenheit. Usually, I didn't really notice the color of grass in the United States until I was landing at a Scottish airport and looked out of the window. The deep, deep greenness of the grass was so dense, it was almost pulling out my eyeballs. The grass I'd left behind was a kind of brownish shade of green, but this was greenest green. It was green to the third power. It was green, green, green. It was green without brown, green separated from all brown.

In a way, God's holiness is like that. It's like light that never varies, light without any darkness. It's unimaginably bright, deep, and intense light. That is why Malachi says that when God appears, no sinner can stand the day of His coming (see Mal. 3:2). God's holiness is intense holiness, meaning that His presence is unbearable to anything that is even tinged, never mind deeply tainted, with sin.

I think that is also why Isaiah, who was surely a holy prophet, felt as if he was disintegrating when he encountered the holy God. There is something telling about the fact that the man who expressed the most exalted views of God of all the prophets is the man who felt himself coming apart in the presence of God.

The point is this: God's holiness is overwhelming. In His presence, we feel we are disintegrating. Yet often that is the first step to coming to know who He really is and that He really is God.

4

Dwelling in Eternal Light

EVER SINCE I WAS A TEENAGE CHRISTIAN, one particular hymn about God's holiness has meant a great deal to me. It was written by the nineteenth-century English Congregationalist minister Thomas Binney and titled "Eternal Light! Eternal Light!" Here are two of its verses:

> Eternal Light! Eternal Light!
> How pure the soul must be,
> When, placed within Thy searching sight,
> It shrinks not, but with calm delight
> Can live and look on Thee.

> The spirits that surround Thy throne
> May bear the burning bliss;
> But that is surely theirs alone,
> Since they have never, never known
> A fallen world like this.

I love these words, but they don't tell the whole story. It might be too strong a statement to say that these words are wrong, but if you read Isaiah 6, you'll see that the heavenly seraphim—who indeed have never known a fallen world like this and who are perfectly holy creatures—don't seem to feel that they can bear the burning bliss. While they use two of their wings to keep flying or perhaps to hover in midair and two other wings to cover their feet, with the last two wings they cover their faces.

Try to picture these seraphim. What does their posture say? To give you a hint, consider what your children or grandchildren think they are doing when they cover their faces: they are hiding, aren't they? What do we do when there is a sudden flash of light? We cover our eyes. We know that we can't bear the burning bliss. In fact, we don't "shrink not, but with calm delight . . . bear the burning bliss." Not at all. Rather, our instinct is, "I can't bear this."

My point is simply this: These seraphim have never sinned. They are perfectly holy creatures. There is no shadow of sin in them. But apparently, created holiness feels itself somehow almost threatened by, unworthy of, not able to bear the intense brightness of uncreated, original holiness.

God is other than we are. His holiness is infinite and dense holiness, and in His presence, even the holiness of seraphim seems fragile.

Here's how Thomas Binney's lovely hymn ends:

Oh, how shall I, whose native sphere
Is dark, whose mind is dim,
Before th' Ineffable appear
And on my naked spirit bear
The uncreated beam?

There is a way for man to rise
To that sublime Abode;
An Offering and a Sacrifice,
A Holy Spirit's energies,
An Advocate with God:

These, these prepare us for the sight
Of holiness above;
The sons of ignorance and night
May dwell in the eternal Light
Through the eternal Love.

5

Consecrated to God

AS WE DISCUSSED YESTERDAY, Isaiah's vision suggests that even the unfallen, perfectly holy spirits surrounding the throne feel that they cannot bear the burning bliss of God's holiness. Isaiah felt it was unbearable because he was a sinner, but there must be a different reason that the seraphim respond the way they do. It's not their sin that makes them shield their faces. They've never sinned, never known a fallen world like this. This vision helps us understand that there is another dimension to God's holiness.

It's not only separation *from* something; it's also consecration *to* something that gives God's holiness its deep intensity.

We get a helpful hint of this in Jesus' prayer for His disciples in John 17. He prays, "Sanctify them," and then He goes on to say, "For their sakes I sanctify Myself, that they also may be sanctified" (John 17:19, NKJV). The same verb is used three times here. The translators of the ESV render the words of Jesus, "For their sake I consecrate myself," perhaps because they wanted to avoid using the word "sanctify" so that readers wouldn't mistakenly think that Jesus was sinful and needed to be sanctified. It's perfectly understandable that they would want to avoid that confusion. But when we realize it's the same word used three times, that brings out a nuance in the idea of holiness that we might otherwise miss.

Jesus is not only separating Himself *from* something—in this case, sin. He never sinned. Rather, He is separating Himself *for* something. Or to put it more accurately, He is separating Himself for Someone. Jesus is speaking not only about His holiness, but also about the intense zeal of His loving commitment to His heavenly Father. He is also thinking about His loving commitment to us.

In other words, the holiness of the Lord Jesus is seen in the totality of His love for and devotion to His Father, and also to us. He calls His Father "holy Father" in John 17:11 because He knows that His Father loves Him and is devoted to Him. And let's not forget the title given to the Spirit of God: He is the *Holy* Spirit. Like the Father and the Son, He is devoted to the other two persons in the eternal Trinity.

I wonder if that is another reason that the seraphim felt that they had to veil their faces from the holiness of God. They felt they couldn't gaze upon or pry into that holy devotion.

There is a point in most wedding services when the minister says to the groom, "You may now kiss your bride." Who gets the best view of that kiss? Actually, it's the minister. He is three feet away from it.

I confess that I've always looked down at that point. I've always felt that it's not a moment for me to be watching. That moment is about the devoted self-giving of this man to this woman. I, at least metaphorically, cover my eyes. Now magnify that moment of deep human love, mutual commitment, and self-giving devotion to infinity, and that magnification will give you only a glimpse of the wonder of the holiness of God: the consecration of the Father to His Son and the Son to His Father, and the consecration of both to the Holy Spirit and His consecration to them.

I suspect it was something of that order that both the seraphim and Isaiah felt.

We sometimes mistakenly think that it's the severity of God's holiness that we're not able to behold, but it's more than that. It's the sheer intensity of the mutual love of the Father and the Son and the Spirit for one another that makes us feel that we lack love, that we lack integrity, that we are disintegrating, and that we are undone. It's that pure love that makes us feel the ugliness of our own self-love, the self-love that pollutes even our very best gifts. In Isaiah's case, since he was a preacher, these gifts were expressed through his lips. He needed a burning coal from the altar of sacrifice to touch his lips and to bring him cleansing and pardon.

How much more can we thank God that we have come to a greater altar—Calvary—and to a greater sacrifice—our Lord Jesus Christ—and experience the work of a greater seraph—the Holy Spirit—as He has applied pardon and salvation to us? Let's thank God that Thomas Binney was right. There is a way for man to rise "to that sublime Abode; an Offering and a Sacrifice, a Holy Spirit's energies, an Advocate with God." These prepare us for the sight of holiness above:

> The sons of ignorance and night
> May dwell in the eternal Light
> Through the eternal Love.

May that be true for us, too.

WEEK 14

Passion Week

1

Judas, Who Betrayed Him

EACH SPRING, THE CHURCH CELEBRATES PASSION WEEK, or Easter Week. On Palm Sunday, Jesus entered Jerusalem and was hailed as King. Five days later, there would be an official notice posted on His cross by command of the Roman governor: "Jesus of Nazareth, the King of the Jews" (John 19:19). The sign drew loud protests from religious leaders, but it was still there when He breathed His last.

One of the most distinctive things about the four Gospels is that they devote so much space to this one week. Matthew devotes about a quarter of his gospel; Mark, three-eighths; Luke, about a quarter; and John, almost half. No other week in Jesus' life is given such detailed coverage, and there are many different strands in the story. This week, we'll pick up just one of these strands, which has five threads woven into it.

Specifically, we will reflect on some of the people who encountered the Lord Jesus during Passion Week.

We begin today on the dark side with Judas Iscariot. His name probably means "the man from Kerioth," although some have thought it might mean "the knife man." Whatever the origin of the name, there was certainly something of the night about him. He constantly drags behind him the ball and chain of the words "who betrayed Jesus" (see John 18:2).

Years ago in a sermon, I referred to Judas as an Apostle. Afterward, I was roundly corrected at the church door by a woman who insisted that Judas was not an Apostle. But she was wrong. He was an Apostle, and therein lies both the mystery and the tragedy. As Jesus put it as early as John 6:70: "Did I not choose you, the twelve? And yet one of you is a devil."

There is something mysterious, as well as tragic, about Judas's sin. Paul speaks about the mystery of iniquity (see 2 Thess. 2:7), and it was surely at work in Judas's betrayal—an action he later regretted and yet apparently never repented of. Mystery though it may be, we can trace the progress of his sin. Judas was the treasurer of the disciple band. John tells us he had the moneybag, and it looks as though that was a permanent arrangement.

Judas's complaints, then, might have seemed justified when Mary of Bethany lavished her expensive ointment on the feet of Jesus. The ointment could have been sold for a year's wages and the proceeds given to the poor. But it was all a cover-up, because by that time he had been regularly putting his hand into the bag. What was Judas doing with the money? Perhaps it had proved too much for him, to use Peter's words, to have left everything to follow Jesus. Perhaps he wanted something tangible in return.

The song "I Have Decided to Follow Jesus," which speaks about not turning back, was popular during my teenage years. But the reality is that some who say that they follow Jesus do turn back, and Judas was one of them. Like Demas later in the New Testament, he loved this world rather than Christ's appearing. He covered it up, of course. Like the other Apostles, when Jesus said, "One of you will betray me" (Matt. 26:21), Judas asked the question out loud when his turn came: "Is it I?" (v. 25). But Judas already knew that Jesus was speaking about him.

He had already arranged to sell Jesus for thirty pieces of silver, which he later threw down in the temple before taking his own life. It seems he did that in despair. It is apparently possible to reach a point of no return. There was regret, but there was no turning back, no real repentance. Judas failed to deal with the first rising of sin, and he didn't realize that he wasn't just backsliding—he was committing apostasy. At the beginning, the two things are indistinguishable.

This reminds me of John Bunyan's poem titled "A Caution to Stir Up to Watch against Sin." I have quoted it before; but it's worth repeating:

> Sin, rather than 'twill out of action be,
> Will pray to stay, though but a while with thee;
> One night, one hour, one moment, will it cry,
> Embrace me in thy bosom, else I die:
> Time to repent (saith it) I will allow,
> And help, if to repent thou know'st not how.
> But if you give it entrance at the door,
> It will come in, and may go out no more.

It's sobering to see that in Judas's life, isn't it? He stands as a real warning sign as we begin to consider Passion Week.

2

Peter, Who Denied Him

WE'RE REFLECTING THIS WEEK ON SOME of the people who interacted with Jesus during the last week of His life. Some of them, like Judas, had known Him for a few years. Today, we will look at someone else who had probably known Him even longer: Simon Peter.

It's interesting that in Matthew's gospel, the verb *betrayed* is used in connection with Judas's act about fourteen times, but the verb *deny* is used in connection with Simon Peter only twice: once when Peter says that he would die before denying Jesus, and again when Jesus tells him that he will deny Him three times by cock crow.

If you'd been walking the streets of Jerusalem after Jesus' arrest and trial, you might well have encountered two very distraught Apostles full of self-recrimination. We're told that Judas regretted what he had done, and we're told that after Simon Peter denied Jesus he went out and wept bitterly. If you'd encountered both of these men, would you have been able to tell that one would take his life in despair, while the other would be saved?

To ask it another way, is the difference between denying Jesus and betraying Jesus a difference in magnitude, or a difference in kind? Perhaps the simplest way to put the question is this: Why is it that Peter denied Jesus yet was saved, while Judas betrayed Jesus and was damned?

I mentioned yesterday that there is a mystery to Judas's sin. We're told that Satan was instrumental in what happened, but Satan was also involved in Peter's sin. Jesus told Peter that Satan had demanded to have him to sift him like wheat. And in some ways, Peter's failure was much more straightforward, wasn't it? He crumbled before a servant girl. The stakes were high, and he must have feared that if he confessed he was a disciple of Jesus, he might suffer the same fate as Jesus. He didn't have a deep-seated, complex motivation to deny he knew Jesus; he was simply afraid.

But Scripture doesn't tell us that Peter was saved because his failure was more straightforward or normal than Judas's failure. Nor does Scripture say that Peter was saved because he was regenerate, although Jesus made it clear in the upper room that Peter was saved, whereas Judas was not.

Jesus explained to Peter why and how he would be saved, and this explanation must have been an anchor to his soul that dark Jerusalem night. Peter was saved because Jesus prayed for him. In other words, Peter's salvation was guaranteed not by what was done *in* him but by what Jesus did *for* him.

There is a message there for all of us: Our security doesn't lie in ourselves. It doesn't even lie in what God has done in us, wonderful though that is. It lies in Jesus and His intercession for us. Remember what Hebrews says: "He is able to save to the uttermost those who draw near to God through him, *since he always lives to make intercession for them*" (Heb. 7:25, emphasis added).

Peter was learning a great lesson that we need to learn too. It's not by our regeneration that we are preserved. It's not even by our faith that we are preserved, though the power of God that keeps us does work through faith. It's Christ who saves us—the Christ who died for us, who rose again for us, who is at God's right hand for us, who makes intercession for us. That is why nothing can separate us from the love of God, and that is why we can sing the hymn by Charitie Bancroft:

> When Satan tempts me to despair
> And tells me of the guilt within,
> Upward I look and see him there,
> Who made an end to all my sin.
> Because the sinless Savior died,
> My sinful soul is counted free;
> For God, the just, is satisfied
> To look on him and pardon me.

That is Jesus' intercession for us. His very presence before God, the Lion-King who became the Lamb who was slain—that is the intercession we need.

Remember that if you've stumbled and fallen. Look to Him, and you will live.

3

Pilate, Who Condemned Him

NEXT TO THE LORD JESUS AND the Virgin Mary, whose name is most frequently on the lips of Christians? It's not Augustine, or Thomas

Aquinas, or even Martin Luther. Every Sunday in churches around the world, countless Christians say these words: "I believe ... in Jesus Christ, His only begotten Son ... ; who was conceived by the Holy Ghost, born of the virgin Mary; *suffered under Pontius Pilate.*" Every Sunday in the Apostles' Creed, Pontius Pilate is remembered.

Media reporters love few things better than a trapped politician. Sometimes they try to trap them by the questions they ask. Sometimes they run stories about an entrapped politician until something or someone else is worth headline attention. The world seems to love trapped politicians but loves to despise them, too.

Pontius Pilate was the most famous trapped politician in human history.

Pilate was governor of the Roman province of Judea for about ten years. That was by no means an easy posting. Jewish monotheism, like modern-day genuine Christianity, can be a thorn in the flesh to a pluralistic society. People who believe that God has revealed Himself in space and time in very definite and particular ways, and that He sovereignly instructs us in how to live for His glory and for our blessing—well, those people can be a real irritant. Indeed, as in many parts of the world today, and increasingly in the Western world, they are regarded as enemies of the state. They don't fit in.

Pilate was governing a territory occupied by Rome but inhabited by Abraham's descendants in the days of the Lord Jesus Christ, and he tried to find some way to keep the peace. Might was right. Sometimes he tried to use it sparingly, although he could be naively insensitive. But at other times, he used it to the full. Remember Luke 13:1, where some people told Jesus about the Galileans whose blood Pilate had mingled with their sacrifices?

The one thing that Pilate feared most, however, was not the Jews but what they could do to his career. While there are legends about the rest of his life, including the possibility that he ended it badly at his own hand, there is one thing we can be sure of: outwitted by the cunning maneuvering of the religious leaders, Pontius Pilate tried to find a way out by asking, "Then what shall I do with Jesus who is called Christ?" (Matt. 27:22).

Perhaps the very moment the words came out of his mouth, he realized that whatever answer the crowd gave, the only answer that mattered was his own. And so a name that otherwise would probably have sunk into oblivion, even in the Roman Empire, is on many of our lips Sunday by Sunday: Jesus Christ, God's Son, "suffered under Pontius Pilate, was crucified."

The Gospel writers tell Pilate's story in a way that makes us realize why the Bible is compared to a mirror. We read about Pilate, and we feel as though we're watching scenes that reflect moments in our own life, moments that nothing can really prepare us for. We're confronted by a question that will determine what happens to us in the future. There is no escape from it. It's clear who Jesus really is, and the question is, "What will I do with Jesus who is called Christ?"

Hebrews 6 is a passage that Christians have sometimes found very difficult to understand, but I think it may be relevant here. In some ways, Pilate's experience sheds light on the text. It says, "For it is impossible, in the case of those who have once been enlightened, who have tasted the heavenly gift, and have shared in the Holy Spirit, and have tasted the goodness of the Word of God and the powers of the age to come, and then have fallen away, to restore them again to repentance, since they are crucifying once again the Son of God to their own harm and holding him up to contempt" (vv. 4–6).

I'm sure that the author of Hebrews wasn't thinking specifically about Pilate, although he might have been thinking about Judas Iscariot. But some of these things apply to Pilate as well. He'd conversed with the living Word of God, and in a sense, he was enlightened about His identity. He recognized that Jesus was the King of the Jews—at least, that is what he wrote about Him and refused to change. In Jesus' presence, he must have been able to taste the goodness and sense the powers of the age to come. But when push came to shove, he turned away. He fell away, and there was no way back.

Pilate is surely another warning to us to make sure that we respond in faith to his own question: "What shall I do with Jesus who is called Christ?" I hope what the author of Hebrews says in Hebrews 6 is true for you: "Though we speak in this way, yet in your case, beloved, we feel sure of better things—things that belong to salvation" (v. 9).

4

Simon, Who Carried His Cross

AS WE THINK ABOUT SOME OF THE PEOPLE who form part of the drama of Jesus' journey to the cross, we have a great deal to learn from them. But we have even more to learn from Jesus Himself and the great issues involved in either trusting Him or rejecting Him.

Today, I want to think with you about a "what-if." You probably know what I mean by that. I have a book that imagines some of the "what-if" moments in history: What if Julius Caesar had never crossed the Rubicon? What if the emperor Constantine had never been converted? What if Muhammad had been ignored? What if Martin Luther had decided to keep his Ninety-Five Theses to himself?

We all have personal "what-ifs," too, don't we? What if we'd arrived late? What if that person had changed his plans? Maybe you wouldn't have the job you have, live where you do, or even be married to the person who is your husband or wife.

I wonder if you can guess from that introduction the person we will be looking at today. The answer comes from these words in Mark 15:21: "Simon of Cyrene, who was coming in from the country."

Most of us have to consult a reference book to even know where Cyrene was. It's in what we now call Libya. In our Lord's day, there was a large Jewish population there. It looks as though Simon was visiting for the Passover. There he was, making his way to the temple to celebrate the Passover, and the rest is history.

But what if he'd come half an hour or even just five minutes later or earlier? We would never have heard of Simon of Cyrene, and obliterated from Mark's gospel would be the words, "And they [the Roman execution squad] compelled a passerby, Simon of Cyrene, who was coming in from the country, . . . to carry [Jesus'] cross" (Mark 15:21). If you know Mark's gospel, you might notice that I've omitted some words from Mark's account that are really amazing. Mark says that Simon was "the father of Alexander and Rufus."

What's so amazing about that? Our instinctive reaction today might be, "Who were Alexander and Rufus?" Of course, that is the point. Mark's first readers and hearers probably didn't need to ask that question. They probably thought, "You mean he was the father of Alexander and Rufus?" I suspect Mark's words can mean only one thing: Alexander and Rufus must have become Christians. That reminds me of something hidden away in the closing greetings of Paul's great letter to the Romans. Remember that long list of names in Romans 16? Here's Romans 16:13: "Greet Rufus, chosen in the Lord; also his mother, who has been a mother to me as well."

It is surely too much of a coincidence to be a coincidence. It looks as though the first cross-bearer, Simon of Cyrene, became a believer, as did his wife and sons. God's grace reached and transformed this family. Simon's wife became a real mother in Israel, and now apparently she was in Rome. Paul had never been to Rome, so he must have met her elsewhere.

A moment that turned Simon's plans for the day upside down and forced him to head in another direction than the one he intended actually turned his whole life, and that of his family, in the right direction. His plans for his own life that day, and every day afterward, evaporated. That day, he began to take his first steps to fulfilling Jesus' words: "If anyone would come after me, let him deny himself and take up his cross and follow me. For whoever would save his life will lose it, but whoever loses his life for my sake and the gospel's will save it" (Mark 8:34–35).

I wonder if there are "what-if" moments in your life, perhaps one in particular, that has changed everything. It's even conceivable that someone reading this book right now didn't intend to. Perhaps it's you. It's a "what-if" moment. You're hearing about a man who followed Jesus. You're hearing about Jesus and His crucifixion, His death for our sins, and His promise of new life. Perhaps you're hearing a voice that really isn't mine saying to you, as He has said to so many: "Follow Me. Take up the cross and follow Me. It's the only way to eternal life."

If that is true, don't let this "what-if" moment become one you look back on later and think, "I wonder what would have happened." Don't let this "what-if" moment become one that you look back on later and think, "I wonder what would have happened if I had responded to the voice of Jesus and come to trust Him." Take up the cross and follow Jesus now. It's the way to eternal life.

5

The Man Who Was Crucified beside Him

THE FRIDAY OF PASSION WEEK IS KNOWN as Good Friday. The origin of the term is uncertain. Most of us have heard at least one sermon about what makes Good Friday good, the answer being that on that day the greatest good since the creation of the world was accomplished. But there is another tradition that suggests the origin lies in the Old English: God's Friday. This day commemorates the work of God for our salvation.

But did anyone who participated in the events that day think of it as a good Friday? It certainly didn't seem good for any of the people we've been looking at this week—Judas Iscariot, Simon Peter, Pontius Pilate, Simon of Cyrene, and others. Mary was losing her Son. John was watching his best friend die. The Roman centurion might have looked back on it as a turning point in his life, but we can't be sure. Even the religious leaders who engineered our Lord's crucifixion had all kinds of anxieties about the day. After all, they'd been trying to avoid Jesus being executed at the time of the Feast of the Passover.

But there was one man for whom the day started as the *worst* day of his life but ended as the *best* (as well as the *last*) day of his life. In the morning, he had been dragged with two others from his prison cell and forced to carry the instrument of his own crucifixion. From around midday, he began to experience the agony of crucifixion, a torturous form of execution that led the great Roman orator Cicero to say that the very word should be absent from the lips of a Roman citizen.

Sometimes it could take days for a man to die, ultimately by asphyxiation. Perhaps all this man could hope for was that since Passover was about to begin, the execution squad would show mercy and do something to hasten his end. At first, he had the strength to curse anything and everything. He noticed that the crowd that had gathered seemed focused on the man hanging on the cross beside him. They were mocking Him.

What must have struck him was that the chief priests were there, too. That was strange. Wasn't one of the most sacred days in the year about to begin? What were they doing there, and why were they mocking Him? He could surely hear what they were shouting: "So You saved others, did You? Let's see You save Yourself" and: "If He is the King of Israel, let Him come down now from the cross. Then we'll believe in Him. He trusts in God. Let's see if God really cares about Him. He said He was the Son of God. Look at the Son of God now" (see Matt. 27:40–43).

At first, he joined in the shouts. He was in agony, and he was angry. But then he heard an echo of his own words from the other criminal being executed along with him: "Are you not the Christ? Save yourself and us!" (Luke 23:39). The words were bitter. They were words of anger and hatred. But the man hanging on the center cross beside him was without anger or bitterness. He had prayed, "Father, forgive them, for they know not what they do" (v. 34). And something happened in the man's heart. He shouted over to the criminal on the other side: "We deserve this, but He doesn't. He has done nothing wrong" (see vv. 40–41).

It felt as though he'd been struggling in his pain to solve a puzzle, and now the pieces were beginning to come together. This man who had somehow saved others must be Jesus of Nazareth. Most people in Jerusalem seemed to know what He had done. Could that notice on His cross be true: "This is the King of the Jews" (v. 38)? And that prayer for the forgiveness of those who were crucifying Him—that was amazing.

I don't suppose he could put it all completely together, but this much was clear: this was the King, the Messiah who had been promised, who could open the gate to the kingdom of God. What should he do? What could he say? He turned his head to Jesus and said these never-to-be-forgotten words: "Jesus, remember me when you come into your kingdom" (v. 42).

That Friday began as the worst day of his life. It was the last day of his life. But it was the best day of his life because the Lord Jesus said to him, "Today, you will be with me in paradise" (v. 43).

It wasn't an easy road that brought him to Jesus. It was strewn with his own sin and failure. But at last, he was brought near to Jesus to recognize Him as Savior and King, to turn to Him, to cast himself on His mercy, and to find forgiveness and eternal life. And now he is with Jesus in paradise. That is what made this Friday "Good Friday" for him, and it's the only thing that can make it good for us, too.

WEEK 15

Coming Down from Calvary

1

Mary Knew Her Master's Voice

LAST WEEK, WE LOOKED AT SOME of the people who encountered Jesus on His road to Calvary. This week, we will continue that journey by thinking about some of the people who encountered Jesus after His resurrection.

If John wrote his gospel when he was an older man, he probably assumed that most of his readers were familiar with at least one of the other Gospels. Many of his earliest readers would not yet have been born at the time of the crucifixion. They belonged to the second generation of Christians. Perhaps not many people who had personally met the risen Christ were still alive, and John wanted them to feel the wonder of what happened. And so he lingers on some parts of the Easter story in particular.

His account in John 20 has all the marks of authenticity. Think of the way he describes Mary Magdalene as coming back to the garden tomb. In the darkness, she saw that the stone covering the entrance had been moved. She rushed to Peter and John to tell them that the body of the Lord had been taken away. They ran to the tomb. John arrived first, stooped to look in the tomb, and saw the grave clothes lying there.

Peter then arrived, but he didn't merely stoop to look in the tomb; he ran straight past John and went inside the tomb. He apparently saw something more. Then John went inside as well and believed. The truth was beginning to dawn. But by the time Mary Magdalene returned to the garden, the two disciples had gone home.

Here is Mary Magdalene. She is the first person to meet the risen Christ, the very first witness to the resurrection. But from a human point of view, she has several strikes against her. First, she is a woman, which meant that according to the judicial system at that time, her testimony would have no standing in a Jewish law court. Second, she was there alone and was obviously in a state of great distress. Who would believe her? Yet John makes a point of saying that she was the first witness to the resurrection.

The important and impressive point to grasp is this: in John's time and culture, no one who seriously wanted people to come to faith in the risen Christ would fabricate a story like this one. No one would record that a woman with no position, and in a state of shock, was the first witness to the resurrection—unless, of course, it was the unvarnished truth. We should trust what John says and trust that Mary's testimony is reliable for that very simple reason.

In his gospel, John describes events in a way that makes us, his readers, reflect and meditate on what Jesus did and said. That is true of the resurrection account as well. Perhaps because Mary had just met these amazing, apparently supernatural, creatures and talked with them, it is not so surprising that she didn't recognize Jesus at first when He asked her what she was looking for. She mistook Him for the gardener. But when He said, "Mary," she recognized His voice immediately and responded, "Rabboni; which is to say, Master" (John 20:16, KJV).

If we were in one of the early churches where John's gospel was being read to the congregation all the way through from the beginning, we might immediately remember some words we'd heard an hour or so beforehand in chapter 10:

He who enters by the door is the shepherd of the sheep. . . . The sheep hear his voice, and he calls his own sheep by name and leads them out. . . .

> I am the good shepherd. The good shepherd lays down his
> life for the sheep. . . . I know my own and my own know me,
> . . . and I lay down my life for the sheep. . . . I lay down my life
> that I may take it up again. No one takes it from me, but I lay it
> down of my own accord. I have authority to lay it down, and I
> have authority to take it up again. (John 10:2–3, 11, 14–15, 17–18)

That is exactly what was happening to Mary. We still hear that voice today. When the Word of God is preached in the power of the Spirit, the human accent of the speaker begins to fade into the background. We begin to hear the voice of our Lord Jesus Christ, the Good Shepherd, speaking to us.

I wonder if that is your experience. I wonder if you've recognized Him speaking to you and calling you by name. And I wonder how you are responding. Have you, too, called Jesus "Master"?

2

John Saw and Believed

WHEN MARY MAGDALENE TOLD PETER AND JOHN that the body of Jesus had been moved, they both ran to the garden. There is a delightful little human touch in John's gospel at this point. John tells us that he beat Peter there, and he looked in and saw the linen grave cloths. Peter, who is always mentioned first in the Gospel stories, came in second in the race, but he was the first to go into the tomb, perhaps breathlessly running past his friend.

It seems that Peter saw something that John hadn't noticed at first. John 20:6 tells us that "he saw the linen cloths lying there." Those same words are used to describe what John had seen as well. But then Peter saw something else, something that John had not seen: "and the face cloth, which had been on Jesus' head, not lying with the linen cloths but folded up in a place by itself" (v. 7).

Did Peter say something to John? Did he stay in the tomb, staring? Did he come out to let John in? We don't know what Peter did, but we do know what John did when he went inside the tomb. It's at this point that John's gospel makes the comment "and he saw and believed" (v. 8). John had seen mighty works performed by Jesus before. Why did he believe only now? John says that they didn't yet understand the Scriptures, which said that Jesus would rise from the dead (see v. 9). Up to this point, they hadn't fully understood the prophecies about Jesus, but now things were beginning to fall into place.

It looks as though the trigger was that John saw not only that the linen cloths were there but also that the face cloth was not lying with the linen cloths. It was folded up in a place by itself. At the very least, this was a sure sign that the body had not been stolen. We're not told how the linen cloths were left, but the face cloth was neatly folded up, and it doesn't make any sense to unwrap a corpse if you're stealing it. Maybe that thought didn't immediately cross John's mind, but the neatly folded face cloth—that could mean only one thing.

I've sometimes wondered about this detail in John's account because most of us have little habits that mark us out. Was there something familiar about the way Jesus broke bread that made the two disciples on the road to Emmaus think, "Oh, it's Jesus, it's Jesus"? And could it have been the same with this folded cloth?

Had they seen Jesus lie down to sleep some nights and carefully fold His neck cloth? Or had they been in His carpenter shop at the end of the day and noticed how He took off the sweat cloth He wore around His neck or forehead, carefully folded it, and put it in the same place every day? And hadn't the Carpenter said that when His enemies destroyed the temple—meaning His body—in three days, He would rebuild it? That is actually what He had done. It was as if He had folded the sweat cloth that had been soaked in the blood of His labor.

Maybe that is the case and maybe it isn't, but the important point is this: Jesus left behind evidence that He was risen from the dead and was alive.

Sometimes He leaves other evidence of His risen presence, doesn't He? The circumstances and events into which He sovereignly brings us, the people we meet, the joys and sorrows that seem to say to us: "Jesus has been here before you. He has left these evidences that He is at work in your life to bring you to Himself and to bring you to live for His glory."

You and I haven't seen what John saw. But aren't the footprints and fingerprints of Jesus still leaving evidences of His risen presence in our lives as well? Perhaps for us, too, there is much in life and in Scripture that we don't yet fully understand. But like John, we'll discover more and more that Christ has risen and that He plans to make Himself known to us and lead us into the future.

That is the very good news of the gospel.

3

The Disciples' Hearts Burned within Them

DON'T YOU WISH THAT YOU COULD have been a little bird flying behind the two disciples who walked to Emmaus on Easter Sunday? They were dispirited because they had hoped that Jesus was the Messiah, and they were confused because they had heard a rumor among the disciples that Jesus was not dead, but alive. And as they journeyed, Jesus joined them (though they didn't recognize Him yet) and explained that the Messiah had to die and rise again. The prophets had said as much. And for an hour, or perhaps more, He interpreted their Hebrew Bible to show them how that was true. But they still did not recognize Him.

It was probably dark when they reached Emmaus, so they invited Jesus to stay with them for a meal. At this meal, Jesus seemed to become the host—or at least, they invited Him to act as host—and as He broke the bread, they recognized Him. Then just as mysteriously as He had appeared on the road, He disappeared again.

The two disciples were so excited that they got up and made the return journey to Jerusalem. They burst into a room where the other disciples were gathered, and they were about to say: "We met Jesus on the way home, and He sat at our table! He is alive!" Then they must have realized that the atmosphere in the room was entirely different from what they had expected. The disciples in Jerusalem already knew that Jesus was alive and that He had appeared to Simon Peter.

In many seminaries and training courses for preachers and teachers, this passage has become a proof text for preaching from the Old Testament. It's become a major emphasis for pastors to preach Jesus from the Old Testament. People who speak on preaching to preachers often choose to speak about this, and that is all well and good. There are even books that will tell you how to preach Christ from virtually anywhere in the Old Testament.

But there is a problem, and I think a misunderstanding, that is sometimes evident.

What is often forgotten is that in this passage, it's the Jesus of the Gospels who's explaining how the Old Testament bore witness to Him. I say that because too often, this kind of preaching sounds as though the Old Testament is like a puzzle whose solution is Jesus, and then the sermon stops. Little or nothing is said about the Jesus who appears in the Gospels. The result is that in the end, Christ, who is Himself the Incarnate One, is not really preached to us, but the Christ we hear about is simply the solution to the plotline problem.

But it's the incarnate Christ that we need, not the explanation of the plotline or the solution to a literary riddle. We need the Christ proclaimed in the Gospels, the flesh-and-blood Christ. The Christ who was tempted in all points as we are and who can be touched with the feeling of our infirmities because He felt them Himself. We need the Christ who touched lepers, who delivered men and women captured by Satan and in bondage in sin, who loved with a love that drew people to Him.

I sometimes wish that those who teach preaching and teaching in whatever context emphasized the absolute necessity of knowing how to preach Christ from the New Testament. Because too often, the same preacher who is determined to show how to get to Christ from the Old Testament doesn't actually seem so determined to get to Christ from the New Testament, particularly from the Gospels.

We should never forget that it was the Christ of the Gospels who helped these two disciples see how the various parts of the Old Testament bore witness to Him.

In fact, in Luke 24, the litmus test that Christ has been preached is not in verse 27, which says, "And beginning with Moses and all the Prophets, he interpreted to them in all the Scriptures the things concerning himself." Rather, the litmus test is found in verse 32, which says, "They said to each other, 'Did not our hearts burn within us while he talked to us on the road, while he opened to us the Scriptures?'"

That is the preaching that we need and the preaching for which we should pray—heart-burning preaching. So whether we're preachers or hearers, let's pray that we'll hear that kind of preaching.

4

Peter's Failure Was Not Final

THE EVENTS OF EASTER DAY ARE recorded in four different Gospels. And since they don't all give us every single detail, it's sometimes difficult to piece the picture together. That is actually quite natural and a confirmation that these are authentic accounts.

There are some details in one gospel that aren't in the others. And perhaps, like me, you've been struck by one such detail in Mark's account. It has to do with the women who came to the tomb: "And entering the tomb, they saw a young man sitting on the right side, dressed in a white robe, and they were alarmed. And he said to them, 'Do not be alarmed. You seek Jesus of Nazareth, who was crucified. He has risen; he is not here. See the place where they laid him. But go, tell his disciples and Peter that he is going before you to Galilee. There you will see him, just as he told you'" (Mark 16:5–7).

What strikes me is the words "go, tell his disciples *and Peter*." Every time the disciples' names are listed, Peter is always first in the list. But here, Peter comes last, a kind of added extra. Yet even though he is listed last, he is the first one to be called by name. I think the message is fairly clear. It's this: "Make sure that Simon Peter, especially, hears this."

Later, after the great fish-sandwich breakfast beside the fire on the shore of Galilee (see John 21), Jesus took Peter aside and painfully yet lovingly worked through his failure on the evening of our Lord's crucifixion. On that night, Peter, beside another fire, had three times denied his Lord. But that breakfast by the sea had not yet occurred at this point in the story.

At this point, it has been less than forty-eight hours since Peter had denied that he even knew Jesus, and he also realized that Jesus had seen and heard him do so. And I sometimes wonder, "Did anyone apart from Jesus know that Peter had denied Him?" If not, then these words take on a special significance, don't they? No mention of the details of Peter's failure, just: "Tell Peter I'm risen. Make sure Peter knows. Make sure he knows that there is still hope for him."

Simon Peter was given a special role in the disciple band. He was the first to open the doors of the kingdom to those who believed on the day of Pentecost. He was the first Apostle to preach the gospel to gentiles in the house of Cornelius. But on that Sunday, all this lay in an unknown and—he must have felt, at least—hopeless future.

Peter must have been a broken man at this point. So sure of himself, yet so disastrously wrong about himself. Surely he could still feel the rush of shame that came over him when he realized that Jesus had been watching him across the courtyard and heard him denying that he knew Him. It's hardly surprising that Peter fled from the high priest's courtyard into the darkness of the Jerusalem night to weep his heart out. Was he another Judas?

That is why the angel's words must have meant a great deal to him. Not only was Jesus alive, but He had a special message for him: "Peter, the Lord you denied is not dead. He has been raised from the dead and will meet His band of disciples again. And He wants you, you in particular, Peter, to know it. Your denying Him may have added to His sorrows, but it has not destroyed His love for you."

I think I was twenty-three years old and just a very young minister when my senior minister preached a sermon on the book of Jonah. The title he gave it has lodged itself permanently in my memory banks: "Failure Need Not Be Final." That was the message for Peter. Peter's failure need not be final—nor yours either. That is the good news that comes to you today from the risen Savior.

So whatever your failure has been, come and tell Him all about it. Your failure need not be final, because Jesus is risen.

5

James Reunited with His Brother and Lord

YESTERDAY, WE LOOKED AT THE LOVING way in which Peter was singled out after Jesus' resurrection. But there is more than one singling out in the resurrection narratives, and the person we'll look at today is someone we might tend to overlook.

When Paul lists Jesus' resurrection appearances in 1 Corinthians 15:3–8, he tells us that Jesus appeared on one occasion to over five hundred disciples, and that most of them were still alive—the implication to the original audience being, "You can go and ask them." But then he adds, "Then he appeared to James." No explanation. Not even a clear indication of which James he was talking about. Simply, "Then he appeared to James."

Who was this James that Paul knew? It's clear that Paul assumed that his audience knew who he was talking about. Because of the way he words it—"To James, then to all the apostles"—I think he is probably indicating that this James was not one of the original Apostles. In other words, he was not referring to James, the brother of John. That James had been killed by Herod, and the Corinthians would have heard of him as a martyr rather than as a contemporary.

The James of which Paul spoke was still alive, and he was well known enough for Paul to assume that the Corinthians knew who he was. I think he was almost certainly James, the half-brother of the Lord Jesus, probably the eldest of Jesus' half-brothers.

But why a special appearance to him? The New Testament doesn't directly tell us, but there seems to be a common thread running through our Lord's appearances to individuals—Mary Magdalene, Simon Peter, James, Saul of Tarsus. We could put it this way: each of them had a past. I suppose each of them may have felt themselves, to use Paul's words, the foremost of sinners (see 1 Tim. 1:15).

Perhaps the explanation for this special appearance to James is found in John 7:5: "Not even his brothers believed in him." And perhaps, since James was the eldest of the brothers, they all took their lead from him. I have the impression from the rest of the New Testament that, humanly speaking, James was a very impressive and indeed powerful and persuasive individual. So it may well be that if James was to find his place in Christ's purposes, the Lord needed to speak to him personally and privately, as He did with Mary, Peter, and Saul of Tarsus.

Apart from that, there is something else here that is very moving—it's the loving concern that Jesus had for His own family. Part of me wishes that we knew a lot more about Jesus' parents and siblings. But more important than knowing about them is learning about Jesus—His patience with them all when they misunderstood Him and didn't yet fully trust Him; His special loving care in His dying moments for His mother, Mary, whose soul was being pierced by a sword, as Simeon had prophesied; and now His appearance to James. What a tender love He has.

When we think about this, let us remember that He has put all who believe in the category of belonging to His own dearly loved family. Remember how He said: " 'Who are my mother and my brothers?' And looking about at those who sat around him, he said, 'Here are my mother and my brothers! For whoever does the will of God, he is my brother and sister and mother' " (Mark 3:33–35).

Remember that today. Think of the love that you have for your own family, imperfect though it is. Then think of the love that Jesus had for His own family—absolutely perfect, completely constant, and always faithful, even though it was sometimes sorely tried. If you trust Him, then you belong to His family, and He loves you as a family member.

He is the same today in His resurrection power as He was when He walked this earth, and He will be the same forever. That is surely one of the greatest of all the implications of the Easter message if you're a member of the family.

WEEK 16

What Is Man?

1

Who Am I?

I ATTENDED A STATE SCHOOL IN SCOTLAND where relatively few students were what people used to call "out-and-out" Christians. But as I was leaving school, one of my teachers gave me a book that I still own and prize. It was Dietrich Bonhoeffer's book *The Cost of Discipleship*.

The book also included some lesser-known works by Bonhoeffer, including a poem he wrote titled "Who Am I?" It's a very striking poem, written in the 1940s when he was in prison camp prior to his execution. In it, he reflects on whether he is actually the person people think he is. The poem engages in genuine spiritual self-examination.

About fifty years or so after Bonhoeffer wrote that poem, I heard that the words "Who Am I?" had become the most frequently used title for poems written by teenagers. These poems, however, were not a form of self-examination as Bonhoeffer's was. Rather, they were a quest for identity and often an expression of identity confusion. Bonhoeffer was asking about the consistency of his own life, but these young people were asking "Who am I?" because they no longer knew the answer.

I don't know whether that statistic is still true about teenagers' poetry today, but I do know that this question now haunts the younger generation. In fact, the world today actually tells them to be haunted by this question. We are no longer people who are given an identity; rather, it's said to be our personal project to find it. We must decide who we are. Are we male, female, transgender, lesbian, homosexual, or one of the other supposed varieties of subgenders? And this is just the tip of the iceberg.

My question is: "Why has this transformation—indeed, revolution—taken place? Why is it that we have a society of so many troubled young people? Why is it that, despite governments and organizations spending endless millions of dollars, the situation is getting worse rather than better?" Our society has become like the woman with the issue of blood in the Gospels. The more she spent on trying to get better, the worse she got.

How this has happened is actually relatively simple to explain. The people who are now called "influencers" told us, "If we just get rid of the Christian faith and the God of the Bible, we'll return to the basically good, happy, well-adjusted people we were before the gospel ever came." Sadly, they were not thinking either clearly or historically. We weren't that before the gospel came; we were pagans. So it's hardly surprising that there has been a massive loss of certainty today about who we are.

When a society gets rid of God's identity, when a society gets rid of God Himself, what logically and inevitably follows is that we get rid of our own identity, too. Why? Because as Genesis 1:26–28 teaches us, mankind—male and female—was made as the image and likeness of God. If we get rid of God, then however gradually it happens, man's basic identity also begins to fragment and crumble. If we reject who we really are, then we're bound to stumble in the dark trying to discover who we are.

It's significant that when Scripture says "man" in this context in Genesis 1, it means mankind created as male and female. Two things have been built into our deep-down, created consciousness. First, we are the image and likeness of God. Second, He has made us male and female—not one kind or three kinds, but two kinds.

As His image, reflecting His character, we are either male or female. But what is now happening in the Western world, in all its assumed modernity, is that when we lose hold of God, we lose hold of our identity as His image. Then we lose hold of the clear-cut distinctions between male and female that are embedded in every molecule of our being. Until there is a recovery of the knowledge of God, there is really no remedy for this sickness.

That is why the biblical teaching on man as the *imago Dei*, the image of God, is so very important. This is a vital and wonderful doctrine for young Christians to get a hold of because knowing who I am—that I'm made as the image and likeness of God, that I'm created male or female in a way that is embedded into the depth of my physical being, and possessing this wonderfully dignifying knowledge of who I am—gives me the stability and the dignity that I need. That is exactly what our world needs today.

2

Male and Female He Created Them

THE FIRST QUESTION OF THE Westminster Shorter Catechism asks, "What is the chief end of man?" This is a rich question, and the answer is even richer: "Man's chief end is to glorify God, and to enjoy him forever."

In the opening chapters of the Bible, we are told that God made man from the dust of the earth (see Gen. 2:7). That is why it shouldn't surprise us that we humans have much in common with the other living creatures that God brought forth from the earth. But that statement about our origin is set in a larger and more fundamental context.

God created man in His image and likeness in a miniature form. We saw yesterday how vital this truth is, not only for ourselves, but perhaps especially for young Christians today.

But not only does Genesis 2 explain that God made man from the

dust, it tells us that God also created the woman, and the story is exqui-
sitely told.

The only "not good" that God noticed in the original creation was
that Adam, the man, was on his own (2:18). Why was that a "not good"?
Perhaps the reason has already been hinted at in Genesis 1:26, where
God said, "Let *us* make man in *our* image, after *our* likeness" (emphasis
added). God does not dwell in solitude but rather dwells in the personal relationships of the Father, the Son, and the Holy Spirit. The one
God is alone God, but not lonely as God. And so God made companions
for Adam.

First, He made wonderful animals. I wonder if you've ever played
the game "Name That Tune." God seems to have had a little fun with
Adam in the garden. They played a game of "Name That Animal." Genesis 2:19 tells us how God brought the animals to Adam and asked him
to name them. What fun that must have been! But as Genesis 2:20 says,
none of them was really a perfect fit for Adam.

And so God made a woman. The text actually says that He *built* a
woman for him. It wasn't haphazard. She was carefully created, Genesis tells us, out of Adam's rib. Bone of his bone, flesh of his flesh; she
was perfectly fitted for him. And when Adam saw her, he knew immediately that she was different and that she was just what he needed.
Unlike the animals, she was like him, made, we might say, in his likeness. Not identical to him, but like him.

I think that is one of the things Paul meant when he said in 1 Corinthians 11:7 that man is the image and glory of God, but woman is
the glory of man. He is not demeaning women here, as though only
men were made in God's image. Genesis teaches us that both male and
female are made in God's image.

Rather, Paul is saying that just as God made Adam to reflect Him
as His image and likeness, and therefore to be an expression of His
glory (although that is also true of woman), in the special relationship between Adam and Eve, she reflected him, just as in Adam, God

reflected His glory. God showed how marvelous He was by making this man in His image, so as far as Adam was concerned, Eve was his glory. She was the one who showed his dignity to him.

This is the foundation for the biblical teaching on the relationship between a man and a woman. In a way, it's a description of the first romance and all romance since then. The man saw the woman, and he knew that in this woman's friendship, he would find glory. I've mentioned before the song "The First Time Ever I Saw Your Face." That is what Adam must have felt when he saw the woman who was to be his glory. No wonder he wanted to be with her and be one with her.

There is more to say on this topic, but today, let's just linger on the wonder of our creation in the image of God, male and female. That difference in unity is basic to our humanity. And whether you're married or not, it's a difference we were all created to enjoy. That is why the church, where male and female are one in Christ, is such a glorious place to be.

3

The Inconsistent Atheist

THIS WEEK, WE'RE THINKING ABOUT THE QUESTION, "What is man?" Yesterday, we reflected on the sheer wonder of being created as male and female, two kinds of the same being made to belong together, to glorify God together, and to enjoy Him together. That last part is what unbelievers can never understand: when we come to know God, we enjoy Him. And no wonder, because we come to realize how loving, kind, and generous He has been to us.

I've often thought that agnostics and atheists can't really live consistently on the basis of their own agnostic or atheistic presuppositions. They've got to beg, borrow, or steal from a biblical worldview—of course, without admitting it and often without realizing it. Their pre-supposition is that we are just a mass of stuff and that all we are and do is determined by the stuff that is built into us from our conception. But one can't really live consistently with that worldview.

I'm reminded of a lecture given by my professor of psychology at university. She was a well-known British humanist who had written on the subject of humanism and its virtues. One day, she gave a lecture on biological determinism, arguing that everything we think, feel, and do is essentially biologically determined. The idea that we have free will, she said, is a figment of our biologically determined imagination.

The effect on my class was electrifying. There was an uproar after-ward. No free will? It was as though someone had given a lecture in an Arminian college on predestination and election. I've never forgotten the outrage. But the interesting thing was that this occurred in a class-room of students who mostly prided themselves in adopting a secular, atheistic, scientific view of the universe. But they couldn't stand the implications of their own presuppositions.

I recognize that as one gets older, too many sentences begin with the fatal words "I remember." But there is a reason I'm dragging up this memory from the past. Some weeks after the lecture, I was in the university bookshop, and over the other side of a bookcase, I heard an immediately recognizable voice. It was my biologically determined, humanist psychology professor.

I couldn't see her, but I could hear her say very distinctly to one of the staff, "Do you sell Christmas cards here?" Inwardly, I wanted to jump over the bookcase with an angelic leap and say: "Caught you! Why are you stealing Christmas joy from the worldview you've rejected?" I'm not an angel, and I suppose it wouldn't have done my grades any good if I'd leapt over the bookcase, but you see the point.

That is only an illustration of inconsistency, so let's think of this more broadly. We're created as God's image and likeness. We can't escape the fact that life was created to have meaning, no matter how much we try to deny it. Try to think consistently from a presupposition of atheism and its partner, biological determinism, and the result will be an intolerable darkness and despair. I do not recommend the thought experiment of consistently working out what it means that you're simply an accident.

As Paul says in Romans 1, the only way to sustain atheism is to hold back, hold down, suppress, and eventually repress the truth in unrighteousness. If you've professed to be that kind of unbeliever, you need to remember that you are actually a kind of believer—this is what you profess to believe. But you can't live that way consistently, can you? You're always going to need to borrow from a Christian worldview, the Christian view of mankind as male and female.

If that is who you are, I hope you're willing to be honest enough with yourself to rethink things. And I hope you'll come to see how wonderful it is to discover the biblical answer to this ancient question, "What is man?"

4

Jesus' Teaching on Marriage and Gender

AS WE DISCUSS THE REMARKABLE FACT that God created mankind as male and female, it's important to recognize that this isn't just the view of Genesis 2. It was also the view of Jesus on the basis of Genesis 2. He said to the Pharisees: "Have you not read that he who created them from the beginning made them male and female, and said, 'Therefore a man shall leave his father and his mother and hold fast to his wife, and the two shall become one flesh'? So they are no longer two but one flesh. What therefore God has joined together, let not man separate" (Matt. 19:4–6).

Jesus could not have made it clearer that the teaching God gave in the beginning—far from being contradicted, changed, or adapted by

Jesus, as people sometimes say—is the very teaching of Jesus. Why is this so important? Because it establishes the Christian view that marriage is between a man and a woman.

There is another implication of this passage as well: there were ever meant to be only two created genders. Human beings come in only two created sexes. Anything other than this is a distortion and disordering of the creation and God's purposes for it. This, too, is the view endorsed by Jesus.

We can draw several conclusions from this. First, our governments are mistaken when they endorse any other view. More than that, they are rejecting the Word and wisdom of God and of our Lord Jesus Christ. Second, it's simply not true that love takes a different view today. Neither God's loving Word nor human anatomy has changed.

The One who is love incarnate affirms this view. Jesus' affirmation of Genesis 2 outlaws what is today called "gay marriage." It also outlaws no-fault divorce. Jesus didn't believe that the individual's demand for, or even the individual's understanding of, his or her own happiness is the most important consideration, for incarnate love does not tolerate the disordering of God's creation order.

We live in an era when that is an unpopular thing to say, for powerful forces have been released in our society. We need to take a leaf out of Jesus' book. Or to put it another way, we need to take a leaf out of Jesus' logic to unmask the deception that quotes "Love conquers all things"—in this case, referring to conquering all obstacles and barriers to what a person wants to do. Seven words are all that the biblically instructed Christian needs: "From the beginning it was not so" (Matt. 19:8). That is it.

Today, we see women exchange relations with men and vice versa for same-sex relationships, and instead of the threatened thunder and lightning of God's judgment, there is happiness. But if Romans 1:18–32 makes one thing clear, it's this: God's present-day judgments are usually manifested not in cataclysmic destruction but in giving people over to their own desires to do what they want to do.

Three times in Romans 1—verses 24, 26, and 28—Paul tells us this: God simply gave them over to their own desires and to the consequences of those desires. As C.S. Lewis once put it, there is a sense in which the most terrible words in the universe are when God Himself says to us, "Thy will be done."

It's very telling how Paul ends his exposition of Romans 1:18–32. He says that those who break God's law in this way not only do it themselves, but give approval to those who do the same. In a sense, they've got to. Rebellion against God must have company. It must make its own way normal and, if possible, normative.

But as has often been said, we can never really break God's law because it is indestructible. We can only break ourselves against it. And we need to pray with great compassion that our world will soon realize this before more people destroy themselves.

5

Created for Glory

TODAY, I WANT TO DRAW YOUR ATTENTION to a pattern embedded in the biblical account of creation: it's that Adam was created to be the prophet, priest, and king of creation. What marvelous dignity!

People often think of prophets as men who foretell the future. But much biblical prophecy is not so much foretelling but forthtelling— applying God's truth to every situation. In other words, a prophet is someone who speaks God's word. It's about the present as much as it is about the future. In the Genesis narrative, we find Adam being called to the prophetic task of naming the animals, and to pass on, first to Eve and then to his family, what God had revealed to him.

Adam was also a priest. We tend to think of a priest only as someone who made a sacrifice for sin. That is certainly true. But a priest was also a person who representatively led the people in worship. In that sense, Adam was the priest of the original creation. He supremely and representatively led and expressed the worship of God that the whole animal creation expressed in their own beautiful, but limited, way. The later tabernacle and temple were built in a way that reflected the beauty of the garden of Eden, and the Levitical family was responsible to "look after" the tabernacle and temple—the very same expression that describes Adam's priestly ministry in the garden in Genesis 2:15.

And then most obvious of all, Adam was called to be the king of creation. He was given dominion and authority. He was, in his own sphere, a miniature reflection of what God is to the whole created cosmos. Like a father who is a gardener, God gave His child, Adam, a miniature garden of his own to take care of and to expand: the garden of Eden. Adam and Eve, and presumably their family line through the generations, were to expand that garden until it filled the whole earth with beauty and order.

Adam was to express his authority on earth lovingly and creatively, and to do so to the ends of the earth. But then what would he have done after that? Adam was a human son of God, a child of God. Surely he would have come to his heavenly Father, leading the whole created order as its prophet, priest, and king, and said to his Father, "Father, we finished the work." Then like a child, he would have handed it all back to God as the love gift of an obedient creation.

That reminds me of the first question and answer to the Westminster Shorter Catechism, which we mentioned earlier this week: Adam was made for God's glory and to enjoy Him. The picture we see in Genesis 3 is of the Lord God walking in the garden in the cool of the day, calling out: "Adam, Adam, where are you today? I'm here." That invites us to think of a daily conversation between the Father, who has been upholding the whole cosmos, and the human son, who has been working away at his own little garden. The conversation may have looked something like this: "What have you been doing in the garden today, Adam? How much more have you and the family expanded it?"

Alas, we don't know how it all would have developed. The fall intervened. But I think the way that Paul puts things in Romans 3:23 is especially telling. He says there that all have sinned. Adam and Eve sinned. Their descendants sinned. You and I have sinned. But then he goes on to say something that I might not have said, because I think I would have written, "All have sinned and broken the commands of God." But no; what Paul says is that "all have sinned and fall short of the glory of God."

There is wickedness and perversity in our sin, but in some ways, there is an even greater tragedy in it. Created for enjoyment, even for glory, we have forfeited it all by our sin. But thankfully, that is not where the story ends. Because another Prophet, Priest, and King has come, a better One—"the proper Man whom God Himself hath bidden," as Martin Luther put it—and He has dealt with Adam's sin and ours. He has finished the work His Father gave Him to do, and He is able to restore us to the pattern God originally intended for us. One day, He will cover the entire cosmos in His glory. Thanks be to God.

WEEK 17

The Spine That Holds Your Old Testament Together

1

The Central Promise of Scripture

EVERY BOOK HAS PAGES THAT ARE held together at the spine. Sometimes the publisher will say that the book has been "Smyth-sewn," which refers to a process in which the pages are bound together by groups of pages being sewn together. A Smyth-sewn book will hold together for many years, perhaps even for centuries. This process was performed by hand until an American named David McConnell Smyth invented a machine that could do the work. Ever since, people have spoken about books being Smyth-sewn. If you have a high-quality Bible, it may well be Smyth-sewn.

But regardless of whether the Bible you use is physically Smyth-sewn, you can be sure that it is theologically Smyth-sewn. By that, I mean that the content of those pages is held together by strong threads, and one of the strongest of these threads is found in Genesis 3:15. After the fall, God addressed the serpent and said: "I will put enmity between you and the woman, and between your offspring and her offspring; he shall bruise your head, and you shall bruise his heel."

The rest of the Bible makes clear that the serpent is an instrument and representative of Satan. The book of Revelation notes that the dragon who appears in John's vision is the ancient serpent, the devil. After the serpent deceived Eve and lured Adam into eating the fruit of the Tree of Knowledge of Good and Evil, God pronounced the curse of Genesis 3:15 on the serpent.

But these words are more than a curse; they are also a prophecy. They contain a promise of ongoing conflict between the serpent's seed and Eve's offspring, which will eventually climax in a one-on-one conflict between the serpent and a single, particular offspring. Of that offspring, God says, "He shall bruise your head, and you shall bruise his heel."

There are many reasons that this verse is so important, the most obvious being that it indicates that the plotline of the whole drama of Scripture will involve ongoing conflict. That is a great clue to reading the Old Testament: its many conflict events are not isolated incidents but are part of this history-long struggle between the two seeds.

To give one example of this principle, the fight between Goliath and David was not just an isolated event. Rather, it was part of this long story of the efforts of the serpent and his seed to destroy the seed of God's promise, represented by His chosen people. When we look for this theme, we begin to notice a whole array of examples in our Bibles, and we start to see them in a new light. We begin to realize that the whole Bible story can't be understood merely on the human level; rather, what happens in history is the spillover of Satan's hostility to God.

Satan acts behind the scenes. He doesn't have God's power, but, blinded by hatred and pride, he seeks to destroy God's purposes. If he can't destroy God, he'll seek to destroy us because we're part of the creation in which God most delights.

That is why Genesis 3:15 has often been called the *proto-euangelion*—the first announcement of the gospel. Perhaps some rainy Sunday afternoon, you can take out a piece of paper and trace through the Bible as many conflict situations as you can spot or remember. Keep that page in your Bible, and as you do your regular Bible reading, note more of them as you read. Once you start looking, you'll be surprised how many there are. They are all an important part of this single plotline.

But what you mustn't lose sight of is this: there are wins and there are losses; there are winners and there are losers in these events; but from the beginning, there has never been any doubt that in the end, the seed of the woman will triumph. And if you turn to the end of your Bible in the book of Revelation, you'll see exactly that.

2

God's Unfailing Promise

YESTERDAY, I NOTED THAT GENESIS 3:15 IS basic to our understanding of the entire plotline of the Bible's drama. Every conflict in the Bible, big or small, is an unfolding of this prophecy. While it was a curse, it also contained a wonderful promise to Adam and Eve. Here they were, "fast bound in sin and nature's night," in a condition that was hopeless and helpless. But God promised to intervene. Yes, there would be conflict, but one of Eve's offspring would prevail.

That must have been glorious good news for our first parents. But while it was good news, the promise came in a very condensed form. Think of the questions that reporters are trained to ask: Who? What? Where? When? How? and Why? There is not much in the way of detail in Genesis 3:15. Of course, we now know the answers. But no one in the Old Testament had all those answers, least of all Adam and Eve.

Did Adam and Eve actually believe this promise from God? I think they did. That is the only answer that makes sense of Genesis 4:1: "Now Adam knew Eve his wife, and she conceived and bore Cain, saying, 'I have gotten a man with the help of the LORD.'" A footnote in the English Standard Version says that the name "Cain" sounds like the Hebrew word for "gotten."

It would have seemed very strange if my wife and I had called our firstborn son *Gotcha Ferguson*. But it would certainly make you ask, "Why on earth did you name him *Gotcha*?" You would assume there must be a story behind the name, and I think that is the point of Genesis 4:1. There is a story behind the name *Cain*.

Childbirth must have been a very frightening experience for Eve, but she is doing more here than simply thanking God for getting her through it. If that was all she meant, her son would probably have been given a name like Azariah or even Ezra, both of which reflect the idea of God's help.

Rather, the choice of name had to do with God's promise that she would bear a seed who would crush the serpent's head: "I've got him." Her hopes had been raised. Perhaps soon the conflict would be over and the tragedy of their sin would be behind them. There would be victory, and with victory would come restoration to begin again.

What Eve didn't realize until later was that her firstborn son was not the seed of the promised victory but rather was the seed of the serpent. The sad conflict promised would continue right before Eve's very eyes in her own family. Cain displeased the Lord, developed a hatred of Him, and expressed it by murdering the brother who trusted in the Lord, as Hebrews 11:4 indicates.

Did Adam and Eve perhaps feel that God's promise had failed? No, they continued to believe it. Eve gave birth to Seth, and that name sounds like the Hebrew word for "he appointed." Again, imagine if I called a son *Appointed Ferguson*. People would surely assume that there was a reason. And indeed, there was a reason why he was called *Seth*. They believed that God's appointed promise would not fail.

But this promise had a much longer history in view than they anticipated, so they and their descendants had to keep trusting that God would send the seed to crush the serpent's head, even if they had unanswered questions: "Who is he? What will he do? When will he come? Where will he be? How will he do it?"

They knew only the answer to the question, "Why?" How privileged we are to know that the Lord Jesus answers all these questions.

3

He Will Give Us Rest

GENESIS 3:15 IS A BIT LIKE A TIGHTLY WOUND BALL of thread that is slowly unwound by God throughout the Old Testament. At times, it looks as though the thread has snapped. Other times, it seems to become invisible but then reappears.

Yesterday, we saw that Eve hoped that her firstborn son, Cain, might be the deliverer. But he turned out to be a murderer who belonged to the seed of the serpent, not the seed of the woman. As the story of the promised seed continued, generation after generation seemed to end not in final victory and life, but in death.

Remember the drumbeat running through Genesis 5: "Adam died. Seth died. Enosh died. Jared died. Methuselah died. Lamech died." There is only one missed beat; it occurs in the description of Enoch, who "walked with God, and he was not, for God took him" (v. 24). But even if that meant he didn't die in the same way the others did, not even Enoch was the promised conqueror.

While the godly seed continued, so did the seed of the serpent. And in Genesis 6:5, we read some of the darkest words in the whole Bible: "The Lord saw that the wickedness of man was great in the earth, and that every intention of the thoughts of his heart was only evil continually." Then came what Genesis 6:7 calls the "blotting out" of man: the flood.

It appears as though God's patience has been exhausted and that He has decided to call "time" on His promise and just end it all. Could it be that the words to the serpent didn't mean salvation but pointed to the mutual destruction of both seeds? Even if the serpent's head was crushed, would the seed of the woman just slowly bleed to death from the heel?

But despite the drumbeats of "he died," we come across another boy who was given an unusual name: "When Lamech had lived 182 years, he fathered a son and called his name Noah, saying, 'Out of the ground that the Lord has cursed, this one shall bring us relief from our work and from the painful toil of our hands'" (Gen. 5:28–29).

If you read the footnote in the English Standard Version, you'll find that *Noah* sounds like the Hebrew word for "rest." Can you imagine me calling my son *Relief Ferguson*? It would sound as though I was hoping he would be a baseball "relief pitcher" who would win the World Series in a dramatic final strikeout when the bases were loaded at the bottom of the ninth inning.

These words actually reflect Lamech's hope that Noah would be the one to reverse the curse of Genesis 3:15 and bring rest. The promise was still there. Faith had not died out. Noah's father hoped that Noah might be the promised seed, but Noah was simply an interim climax to the conflict. God's enemies were overwhelmed in the flood. The true seed of the woman—Noah, his little family, and the animal kingdom they possessed—were certainly being mightily bruised, but they emerged. And indeed, the land had rest.

After the flood in Genesis 9:1–7, God gave similar commands to Noah as the ones He gave to Adam and Eve. He spoke of a new covenant and a new kind of new creation that signified that the promise was still intact. But as wonderful as this was, it was still preliminary— just another stage in the outworking of Genesis 3:15.

As we have been considering this theme, we've reached only Genesis 9 so far, and there are more than nine hundred chapters to go in the Bible before we read the name *Jesus*. But finally, the day came when the true Noah appeared on the stage of history, saying: "Come to me, all who labor and are heavy laden, and *I will give you rest*. Take my yoke upon you and learn from me, for I am gentle and lowly in heart, and *you will find rest* for your souls" (Matt. 11:28–29, emphasis added).

What Noah only pictured, the Lord Jesus provided—rest. At last, the promise was fulfilled. I think that is thrilling, and I hope it thrills you too.

4

The Blessing of Abraham

THE NEW TESTAMENT SEES THE PROMISE of Genesis 3:15 as being fulfilled in Jesus Christ. But when it speaks explicitly about the story of a seed, it tends to focus on the way this seed came through Abraham.

There are several reasons for this, one of which is polemical. The opponents of both Jesus' and Paul's ministries claimed that physical connection to Abraham was what really mattered. John 8:31–59 tells us about this conflict. But Cain's connection to Adam and Eve should have been enough to teach anyone that physical connection is no substitute for living faith.

But there is another reason that Abraham gets so much attention. It's that when the story gets to him, God gives significant fuller revelation of how the promise is going to be fulfilled. Today, we are going to look at two elements of that fuller revelation.

The first is given on Mount Moriah, the scene of the binding of Isaac. It's an event full of electric moments. Abraham has been told to sacrifice his son Isaac, the son who carries the seed of promise. As Abraham is about to plunge the knife into Isaac, the angel of the Lord stops him. Abraham turns around and sees a ram caught in the thicket, and he offers the ram instead of Isaac.

This is a moment that brings into full relief Isaac's earlier question and his father's answer. "My father," Isaac said, "we have the fire and the wood, but where is the lamb for a burnt offering?" And Abraham said, "God will provide for himself the lamb" (see Gen. 22:7–8).

Abraham said that God would provide the lamb. But it was a ram that God provided, so where is the lamb? That question was partly answered by Isaiah, who spoke about the Suffering Servant, saying, "Yet he opened not his mouth; like a lamb that is led to the slaughter, and like a sheep that before its shearers is silent, so he opened not his mouth" (Isa. 53:7). John the Baptist would answer Isaac's question even more clearly when "he saw Jesus coming toward him, and said, 'Behold, the Lamb of God, who takes away the sin of the world!'" (John 1:29).

A second element of the new revelation to Abraham lies in that word *world*. Jesus is the Lamb of God who takes away not only the sins of Jewish believers but also the sins of all believers, wherever they are and whoever they are in the whole wide world. Abraham was given a hint of this when God told him that "in your offspring shall all the nations of the earth be blessed" (Gen. 22:18). Psalm 2 later made clear that this was a reflection of the promise that the Father had given to

His Son: "The LORD said to me, 'You are my Son. . . . Ask of me, and I will make the nations your heritage'" (vv. 7–8).

God always had in view the day when the message of the conquering seed of the woman, the Lord Jesus Christ, would go into the whole world. Jesus reflected that in the Great Commission. The gospel was to be taken to all the families of the earth because it was the whole world that had been alienated from God in the garden of Eden. The promise of the coming seed, the conqueror, the Redeemer, was a promise for all who believed in Him: "For God so loved the world, that he gave his only Son, that whoever believes in him should not perish but have eternal life" (John 3:16).

I hope and pray—whoever you are, wherever in the world you are, whatever family of the earth you belong to—that you believe in Jesus as your Savior and Lord. Because if you do, you will have the eternal life that He promised.

That is what the promise of Genesis 3:15 is all about, and that is why it's so very important.

5

Worthy Is the Lamb

GENESIS 3:15 ANNOUNCED A CONFLICT THAT RUNS throughout Scripture all the way to its climax in Jesus' ministry. We need to remember that from beginning to end, Jesus' life was marked by conflict. It emerged in Herod's early attempts to kill Him. It reappeared in His wilderness temptations. He was in conflict with demons and with the religious leaders. Ultimately, His conflict was with Satan himself. Satan stood behind the other conflicts that Jesus experienced.

This helps to explain the vision statement that Jesus announced at Caesarea Philippi: "I will build my church, and the gates of hell shall not prevail against it" (Matt. 16:18). The goal of Jesus' ministry was to build the church, an assembly of God's people. Notice that Jesus says He will do that in enemy-occupied territory, but the serpent will not be able to withstand the seed of the woman. Nothing will prevent Christ's ultimate victory and His building of His church.

The Apostle John expresses all this very pointedly in 1 John 3:8: "The reason the Son of God appeared was to destroy the works of the devil." John saw this in dramatic form in the amazing vision he had on the island of Patmos. He saw a great red dragon, that ancient serpent who is called the devil and Satan, the deceiver of the whole world, being thrown down to the earth. John sees Satan, having failed to destroy the child who came to rule the nations, pursuing the woman from whose womb He came, but she, too, is wonderfully preserved (see Rev. 12:7–17).

That is where the church is now. She is the woman in need of protection against the dragon, the serpent, the devil, until the day dawns when he will be thrown into the lake of fire and sulfur, where the beast and the false prophet are, tormented day and night forever and ever. That will be the signal for the coming of the new heavens and the new earth, for the city of God to appear, for the bride of Christ to begin her honeymoon in the new garden of Eden (see Rev. 21–22). What becomes clear in this picture is that at the center of all history stands the One who holds the end of this ball of thread that unravels from Genesis 3:15 to the end of Revelation: our Lord Jesus Christ.

Eve's son Cain murdered her son Abel, and she must have wondered where the promise was heading. Lamech hoped that perhaps his son Noah would be the one who would bring rest. As Abraham returned from Mount Moriah, he must have wondered when and where God would provide the lamb for all peoples. Did he catch any glimpse that the ultimate reason that he was allowed to spare his son was that God the Father was willing not to spare His own Son but to deliver Him up for us all (see Rom. 8:32)?

In Revelation 5, one of the heavenly elders says to John, "The Lion of the tribe of Judah, the Root of David, has conquered, so that he can open the scroll and its seven seals" (v. 5). John continues: "I saw a Lamb standing, as though it had been slain. . . . And he went and took the scroll" (vv. 6–7). This is why the story ends with the living creatures, the elders, and myriads of saints singing, "Worthy is the Lamb who was slain, to receive power and wealth and wisdom and might and honor and glory and blessing!" (v. 12).

That is where Genesis 3:15 was heading all along. May that truth encourage you to join in heaven's song of praise to the Lamb who was slain.

WEEK 18

The Lord's Prayer

1

Our Father in Heaven

THIS WEEK, WE'RE GOING TO SPEND some time reflecting on the Lord's Prayer. You might be tempted to think, "Oh, no, not the Lord's Prayer again." I understand that. Many of us say it every week in church, and perhaps some of us say it privately every day. From that point of view, we might think that we are very familiar with the Lord's Prayer. But I think it's important to discuss this prayer because it is fundamental to our Christian life. Not only is it a prayer, but it's a prayer that reflects a basic guide to living the Christian life.

Before we look at the Lord's Prayer, I want to try to clear up a misunderstanding. People sometimes say that we shouldn't use these words because it's insincere to use someone else's words when we pray. But that is kind of odd, isn't it? Don't we sing someone else's words in church? And don't the songs that we sing reflect the words of the Lord's Prayer in different ways?

Someone once complained to me about the introduction of a confession of sin into the liturgy of worship. They were upset because they said it isn't sincere to confess our sins using someone else's words. And yet that same person heartily and cheerfully sang Augustus Toplady's hymn "Rock of Ages." And each time they sang, "Foul, I to the Fountain fly," they confessed their sins in someone else's words. So I think we can see that it's appropriate to use someone else's words, especially when they are the words the Lord Jesus taught us.

The prayer begins with an address to God: "Our Father in heaven, hallowed be your name" (Matt. 6:9). This is a wonderful reminder that when we pray to the God who made the cosmos, we're invited to call Him our Father. Believers are His children. We belong to His family. We're His. We're not on our own. Yet it's also a marvelous reminder that He is far above us. He is in heaven. Therefore, our first petition is a prayer that His name be kept holy: "Hallowed be your name."

Jesus is teaching His disciples here to pray the way that He did. In John 17:11, Jesus addresses God as "holy Father." When Jesus teaches us the Lord's Prayer, the first thing that it does is bring us into the presence of the great, majestic Creator and encourage us to speak to Him.

When we realize who God is, we instinctively think: "How can I speak to Him? I don't even know how to address Him, what to call Him, or what to pray." Jesus is saying to us, "My child, say what I say, and call Him what I call Him." So in the lovely words of the old liturgy attributed to John Chrysostom, "We dare to call upon the heavenly God as Father and say, 'Our Father who art in heaven.'"

That single word "Father" is one of the most cherished words in the gospel. But what do you do if the word "Father" is a problem for you—a word that causes you pain or embarrassment, or just leaves you cold because of the kind of father you had (or maybe the father you didn't have)?

First of all, you need to remember that you're not praying to your natural father. And remember, too, that we're not to think that God is just like the earthly father we had, only more so. The way to think about God as Father is by remembering that He was and is the Father of the Lord Jesus. You're being invited to know *that* Father.

Remember what Jesus replied when Philip said to Him, "Show us the Father, and it is enough for us" (John 14:8)? Jesus said, "Whoever has seen me has seen the Father" (v. 9). Like Father, like Son. There is nothing un-Jesus-like in the Father. How good and kind, then, must this Father be?

As Jesus is teaching us how to pray, He is also teaching us how to live. He is telling us, first of all, to speak to our Father the way that He Himself did: to call on Him as our holy Father. The great seventeenth-century pastor-theologian John Owen puts it beautifully. He says, "If the love of a father will not make a child delight in him, what will?"

So let's take to heart the words of Matthew 6:9: "Pray then like this: 'Our Father in heaven, hallowed be your name.'"

2

On Earth As It Is in Heaven

WHEN LUKE RECORDS THE LORD'S PRAYER, he tells us that Jesus taught it in response to a request: "Lord, teach us to pray" (Luke 11:1). In other words, it's a kind of model prayer. "Pray like this," says our Lord Jesus (see Matt. 6:9). I mentioned yesterday that the prayer has an additional function as well. Because it teaches us the shape of our praying, it also teaches us the shape of our living as disciples of the Lord. What is that shape? You might be able to guess the answer by now. Our chief end is to glorify God and to enjoy Him forever. And we enjoy Him only when we live for Him and glorify Him.

The masters of the spiritual life have all recognized that our lives by nature are disordered. Our minds, our wills, and our affections are disordered, and they need to be regenerated and refashioned. That is what Romans 12:1–2 is all about. The transformation of our life—its reconstruction, reshaping, and reordering—takes place by the renewal of our minds.

That is one of the blessings of praying the Lord's Prayer. It begins to renew our minds. It shapes how we think about life. It reorders our priorities. It recenters us on the Father. It sets our affections on the right things and in the right order. And that is why we pray for God's name to be holy, to be reverenced, to be treated with awe—to use Martin Luther's words, to "let God be God."

It then follows that the heart centered on God's glory in this way will want to see that glory manifested in the world. And so Jesus continues, "Your kingdom come, your will be done, on earth as it is in heaven" (Matt. 6:10).

The kingdom of God is His reign. It's what Adam and Eve were commissioned to bring about in the world when God created them and gave them dominion. They were to extend the garden to the ends of the earth. Then the earth would be full of the glory of God as the waters cover the sea. As we know, Adam and Eve failed in this regard. But through Jesus Christ, the second man, God is going to accomplish what they failed to do.

Paul envisions this in 1 Corinthians 15:20–28. He looks forward to the end of history, when everything is subjected to the Lord Jesus as the last Adam. On that day, He will present a renewed and reordered world as God's vice-regent. He will present all this to His Father. And then, Paul says, "God [will] be all in all" (v. 28). That is what we're praying for when we say, "Your kingdom come."

But we also know something that the disciples discovered only slowly. We know from the New Testament that the kingdom comes in stages. It was inaugurated by Jesus, it is now being extended in and through His people in the church, and it will be consummated when He returns in glory. Therefore, praying "Your kingdom come" presents a thrilling vision, but this is not merely a vision of "pie in the sky when you die."

Don't get me wrong; there is pie in the sky when we die—a glorious future, indeed. But we also need to see that there is pie now, for this petition is part of a parallelism like those we find in the Psalms. The first line says one thing, and then the second line often explains or develops the first line. Take Psalm 23, for example. Line 1 says, "The LORD is my shepherd," and line 2 develops this thought by adding, "I shall not want."

A similar thing is happening here in the Lord's Prayer. "Your kingdom come" is developed by the next statement, "Your will be done, on earth as it is in heaven" (Matt. 6:10). In other words, what we're praying for here is help to know and to do God's will.

And that brings us right back to Romans 12:1–2. Our lives are transformed by the renewing of our minds. It's in this way that we discover the will of God, what is good and acceptable and perfect. And all this is rooted in our yielding ourselves to the Lord and not being conformed to the will and ways of the world.

So, when we pray, "Your will be done," we are submitting to the Lord's *decretive will*—that is, His sovereign purposes. But we're also asking for the help we need to understand and pursue His *revealed will*, which we find in the pattern of life He has set before us in Scripture, together with its rich and varied and many individual applications to our own lives.

That is why we need to pray today and every day: "Our Father in heaven, hallowed be your name. Your kingdom come, your will be done" (Matt. 6:9–10).

3

Our Daily Bread

SOMETIMES KNOWING IS NOT REALLY OUR PROBLEM. Our problem is applying what we know. I remember a TV commercial for Kellogg's Corn Flakes in which a young man sits down for breakfast with a bowl of Corn Flakes. He then looks up and says to the camera, "I'd forgotten how good they tasted."

I remember having breakfast once in a hotel and thinking, "I'm going to try the Corn Flakes." I hadn't eaten them in years, and the words of the TV commercial came back to me. And yes, actually, I had forgotten how good they tasted! But how does this commercial relate to our study of the Lord's Prayer? Well, perhaps you've forgotten how good the Lord's Prayer tastes. And perhaps you've forgotten to pray.

Speaking of taste, the next part of the Lord's Prayer says, "Give us this day our daily bread" (Matt. 6:11). There has been a lot of discussion over the years about this phrase "daily bread." Some of those discussions pertain to whether that refers to the Lord's Supper. Other discussions have revolved around the various possible meanings of the word "daily." Does that mean today's bread, or does it mean bread for tomorrow?

To be honest, I don't think all that need bother us very much. What we are asking for here is for the provision we need for each day so that we can have the daily strength to honor God's name, to serve His kingdom, and to do His will.

There are many kinds of applications to these words. We could focus on the word "us." It's not just me. In fact, I could be the hands that answer that prayer for someone else. Or we might remind ourselves that our bread doesn't actually come from the supermarket where we bought it; it comes from the fields that God has providentially superintended. We are dependent on Him.

Or if this is a general prayer for what sustains life, we might remind ourselves that we can eat and drink and yet not be nourished or strengthened by what we eat or drink. Our bodies are ultimately dependent on the Lord to function well in that way.

Perhaps your daily bread—the nourishment your body needs in order for you to live—includes the medicines you take. Do you ever ask the Lord to sanctify them? Are you ever thankful for them? Do you ever pray that they'll be instruments of health for you?

And then, of course, there is the application that you've probably heard a dozen times but perhaps have not really taken to heart: Jesus teaches us to pray for basic things, and praying that way should simplify life. It should help us focus on what we need and only on what we need.

Here's another important application. This prayer reminds me of Proverbs 17:1: "Better is a dry morsel with quiet than a house full of feasting with strife." Do we really need all that we want? That is part of the challenge of this prayer, "Give us this day our daily bread." It helps us to focus. It helps us to simplify. It helps us live one day at a time. It helps us in so many different ways to live an uncomplicated life.

I suspect that there is a connection between simplification and sanctification. Sin complicates our lives and our desires, and it confuses our vision. But the petition "Give us this day our daily bread" helps reorder our lives daily so that we live in a sweet simplicity before the face of God. It uncomplicates us, and that is one of the things that make our lives reflect the Lord Jesus to others.

I need these words again and again because they teach me how to pray and how to live. And I hope you feel the same way as I do.

4

Forgive Us Our Debts

TODAY, WE ARE GOING TO LOOK AT HOW the Lord's Prayer teaches us about a life of forgiveness. It's often said by Christians, as well as by others, that we're living today in a culture where the concept of shame is more relevant than the concept of guilt. But I'm not so sure about that, for a couple of reasons.

One reason is that shame and guilt are intimately related to each other. Another reason is that guilt is actually still a major factor in the world today; the only difference is that we've just changed the basis on which we count people guilty. In other words, our culture today says that if you are not on board with the social agenda of certain pressure groups, then you should be ashamed of yourself, and you may even be shamed by others.

But more than that, you'll be treated as guilty of transgressing the law of the new norms that have been set for you, and that is why you should feel ashamed. You should feel ashamed because you're guilty, and because you are guilty, you may find yourself both shamed and condemned. Therefore, guilt is very much alive and well in the twenty-first century.

It's our *real* guilt, however, that Jesus' prayer now comes to focus on in the words "Forgive us our debts, as we also have forgiven our debtors" (Matt. 6:12).

Do you remember Jesus' parable of the two debtors? The master of one of them forgave him a vast debt. But then that debtor insisted that another man who owed him a relative pittance should pay every last cent.

The parable ends with the lesson that a man who is offered forgiveness but who does not forgive others is a man who will at the end discover that he is unforgiven. It isn't that our forgiving others causes God to forgive us; it's that not forgiving others is a sign that we've never really received forgiveness ourselves.

My parents' generation, by and large, hated being in debt. We are a different generation. I suppose credit cards have changed everything. I remember that one of the earliest credit cards advertised itself as taking the waiting out of wanting. These cards made it possible to have all your debts consolidated under one simple agreement, sometimes with extraordinarily extortionate interest payments. But most people got used to being in debt.

I suppose the majority of us, certainly if we are under fifty, are debtors, whether it's a mortgage on our house or the balance on our credit card. It's just part of life, and it has created a different attitude toward debt. Debt has become normal, and we're comfortable with it. In fact, we budget for it. We know we can manage our debt.

Perhaps that is why we need this prayer more than ever. It's a daily reminder to us that we have a debt that we can't manage, one that we can't pay off. Because we are sinners, we can't pay back what we owe for our past sins. None of our efforts and accomplishments can ever balance our failure, nor can this debt be canceled by any compensatory efforts we make to be holy.

That is a mistake that many people who are spiritually awakened make. They think, "I'll do better and cancel the debt." But like the national debt, each day our liability simply increases. We cannot pay the debt, and there is nothing we can do to earn enough to pay it back.

Our situation is helpless and hopeless. What we need is not strength to do better but mercy, pardon, and forgiveness. When we understand this, the relief of God's forgiveness is enormous. The joy is wonderful. The new life is freedom. And then, instinctively, we want to forgive others who have become debtors to us.

Today, as we reflect on these words, "Forgive us our debts, as we also have forgiven our debtors," I wonder if you feel a stab of pain in your conscience because there is someone you haven't forgiven. If so, you know what to do. Ask for the Father's forgiveness, bathe in it, and then forgive.

5

Lead Us Not into Temptation

WE'VE REACHED THE CONCLUSION OF A WEEK of reflections on the Lord's Prayer, and we've come to the final petition. The doxology at the end, "For Thine is the kingdom and the power and the glory forever. Amen," was probably added by the early church. The last original petition is, "And lead us not into temptation, but deliver us from evil" (Matt. 6:13) or "from the evil one."

These may be two petitions, but if so, they are a parallelism. The second request fills out the first one: "Don't lead us into temptation, but if we are led into temptation, deliver us from its evil" or "from the evil one."

This petition raises a few questions, one of them being this: "What is meant by 'temptation'?" The Greek word that is used here, *peirasmos*, can mean simply "a test" or "a trial," or it can mean "solicitation to sin." So which is it here?

We're all weak, and no matter how strong we may think we are, there are situations in life that can very easily break us. And so at one level, we want to ask God to protect us. At the same time, we know that difficult experiences will come. So we ask Him to protect us from any evil in them. In a sense, we're simply praying, "Father, make Psalm 23 come true in my life so that even if I walk through the valley of deep darkness, I'll fear no evil because You are with me, and Your rod and Your staff comfort me."

If that is true of trials, it's also true of temptations to sin. One of the older writers says that we are brought into temptation when desire meets opportunity. Sometimes there seems to be a desire in us, but we lack the opportunity to sin. And sometimes there is the opportunity, and in God's mercy, we lack the desire. But when both are present, then we've been brought into temptation and are in special danger. It's this that we are praying about. We're praying to be delivered from the strategies of the evil one.

But there is another question I think these words raise in our minds: "Why does Jesus teach us to pray, 'Lead us not into temptation'? Does God ever lead us into situations of temptation?" Well, He certainly leads us into situations that will test us. But James 1:13 makes it clear that God doesn't Himself tempt us or solicit us to sin.

But if that is so, what does it mean when Matthew 4:1 tells us that Jesus was led up by the Spirit into the wilderness to be tempted by the devil? This is amazing. Jesus was led into temptation by the third person of the Godhead. And Mark's account uses even stronger language: "The Spirit immediately drove [Jesus] out into the wilderness. And he was in the wilderness forty days, being tempted by Satan. And he was with the wild animals" (Mark 1:12–13).

That little footnote, "He was with the wild animals," gives us a clue to what was happening here. Jesus was reversing the tragic and sinful act of Adam and Eve. They were tested by Satan in a garden of plenty. They were surrounded by a docile animal kingdom that was under their authority.

But the second man, the last Adam, in order to recover us, was led into a wilderness, the wilderness that Adam and Eve had created. He was without nourishment for forty days. He was surrounded by wild animals, an animal kingdom now participating in the effects of the fall. What Jesus experienced under the guidance of the Holy Spirit, He experienced in order to bring us back to God.

But what about us? There do seem to be occasions when God providentially places us in temptation's way. He may have various reasons for doing so. Perhaps it's to encourage us that we can be more than conquerors through Christ. Perhaps it's to make us more conscious of our vulnerability than we have been. Perhaps it's to bring us to look to Him more consistently. Perhaps, as in the case of Job, it's to put His own power and glory on display.

But the point we need to remember is this: even if God leads us into situations where there is temptation, He never, ever leads us in the sense of soliciting us to sin.

Jesus Himself knew how fierce the battle could be. I think that is probably why He taught us to pray that the Father would deliver us both from evil in the sense of falling into sin, and from the evil one who seeks to devour us.

Martin Luther said of the devil, "One little word shall fell him." But what word can we use to fell Satan? This word: "Deliver us from the evil one." And God will, because His is the kingdom and the power and the glory forever. Amen.

WEEK 19

The Fall: Reflections on Genesis 3

1

The Tragedy of the Fall

A FEW WEEKS AGO, WE LOOKED at Genesis 1:26–28 and discussed what it means to be created in the image of God. While Genesis 1 emphasizes that God created us with two different genders, it's both interesting and important that the first thing it mentions is what we have in common.

We are persons made in God's image and likeness, and that is the most significant and fundamental truth about us.

As we've noted before, when we lose hold of God Himself, our identity as His image bearers also gets lost, resulting in societies where gender issues become far more important than anything we have in common. It's strange that this-worldly people tend to complain that Christians are always concerned about sex, when in reality the shoe is on the other foot.

We live in a time when the loss of the sense of God, and therefore the loss of the sense that we are made in the image of God, has led to all kinds of alienations and antagonisms, not just among people in general but between male and female as well. Therefore, it's a great thing for Christians to know that we are all made in the image of God and that we're called to reflect Him and to live for His glory according to His Word.

When we refuse to do that, then we no longer enjoy Him. And when we don't enjoy Him, things begin to disintegrate all around us— vertically in relationship to God, and horizontally in our relationships with one another. That is our world today.

What brings us stability as Christians in a world like this is that the Bible gives us an explanation for why things are not the way they were meant to be. Although Genesis doesn't use this specific term, we know that behind our human situation is what we traditionally refer to as the tragedy of the fall, and that is what we'll reflect on this week.

What's the fall all about? It's the story of how we were made for glory but have fallen into a deep tragedy.

But before we get into that, I first want to clear up an issue that sometimes bothers or angers people. It's the fact that when (in 1 Timothy 2:14) the Apostle Paul comments on the significance of the fall, he says this: "Adam was not deceived, but the woman was deceived and became a transgressor."

I don't need to tell you why that creates a fair amount of heat for the Apostle Paul. He gets called a misogynist, a woman hater, and a bigot. And what I want to do today is to help us see why these accusations are so false. In fact, they display a sad illiteracy. Why? Because Paul is simply quoting Eve. This isn't Paul's interpretation of the fall; it's Eve's. It's not misogynistic; it's simply factual reporting. It's almost a quotation. It's there in Genesis 3:13: "The woman said, 'The serpent deceived me, and I ate.'"

There are two points worth making here. The first is that we must know our Bibles as well as we possibly can. The more we know them, the better equipped we'll be to deal not only with opposition to the Christian worldview but with a twisting of the teaching of Scripture. When we are equipped in that way, we are able to expose the opposition for what it really is—factual ignorance of the truth claims of Christianity. We're seeing more and more of that Scripture twisting in the secular media today, and the better we know the Scriptures, the better prepared we'll be to handle that twisting.

The second point is, in some ways, a deeper issue: Why did the serpent, the instrument of Satan, approach the woman first? Indeed, why would he do that when the Bible tells us that the first human being and the representative head of the whole human family was not Eve, but Adam? After all, Paul says that it's in *Adam* all die, not that in *Eve* all die.

The Bible doesn't directly give us the answer to this question, so we need to work it out from what it does say. I think the answer is this: What would give the devil the strongest leverage to help him pry Adam away from love for and obedience to his Creator and Sustainer? It would be using the very best gift the Creator had given to Adam and making him choose between the Lord who had given him life and the woman who was bone of his bone, flesh of his flesh, and the source of so much of his happiness. Satan used God's very best gift to Adam to steal Adam away from the Giver of that best gift.

There are many lessons for us to learn here, but let me leave you with this one today: sometimes Satan uses the best gifts God has given us to draw us away from God Himself. He is, as Genesis 3 tells us, very skilled at his craft.

We need to be alert, and we need to make sure that it's the Lord who comes first in our affections.

2

The Strategies of Satan

AS A YOUNG CHRISTIAN, I GREW UP not knowing one Bible commentary from another. I confess that the first one-volume commentary I bought when I was in my mid-teens was chosen because it was cheap. I didn't know that it was full of old-fashioned liberalism until I took it home and discovered that it viewed the events of Genesis 3 as what they called "etiological myths"—that is, for example, a story made up to explain why snakes slither rather than walk.

But the truth is that if Genesis doesn't record actual historical events, the rest of the Bible begins to fall to pieces, including the teaching of Jesus and the Apostles. So for example, while Genesis 3:21 doesn't give us details of the divine tailoring by which God made garments of skins for Adam and Eve after they had sinned, it does tell us that these events really took place in our world.

What we read in the early chapters of Genesis is a record of once-and-for-all events, just as once and for all as the incarnation, crucifixion, and resurrection of Jesus Christ. But at the same time, it's clear that there are important patterns in what happened in the garden of Eden. Scripture teaches us that there is a pattern of disobedience and its consequences that Christ had to reverse in order to save and restore us and the world, and the New Testament records and explains how He did that.

So while Genesis 3 records specific events in the temptation of

Adam and Eve, I think we're right to see a pattern here of the way in which Satan continues to tempt us as God's people. We saw one element of that yesterday: he uses God's best gifts to tempt us to make bad choices. No wonder Genesis 3 calls the serpent the craftiest beast of the field.

Today, I want to draw our attention to a statement Paul makes in 2 Corinthians 2:11. He says to the Corinthians that he doesn't want them to be "outwitted by Satan," for, he says, "we are not ignorant of his designs." I think that Paul is suggesting here that Satan has regular ways of pulling the saints down into sin. He uses the same strategies again and again. But Paul adds that our strength lies in this fact: "we are not ignorant of his [strategies or] designs."

Sometimes I wonder if that is true of us as Christians today. It might make for an interesting fifteen minutes of your life to take a blank piece of paper, title it "A Checklist of Satan's Strategies," and make a list of them. It would certainly help us to be on the lookout for him and to detect his clammy hand at work.

I wonder if James had Genesis 3–4 in mind when he spoke about the strategies of Satan in how temptation takes place. In James 1:14–15, he doesn't specifically mention the devil, but he does seem to outline his strategy: "Each person is tempted when he is lured and enticed by his own desire. Then desire when it has conceived gives birth to sin, and sin when it is fully grown brings forth death." There is a kind of echo there of Genesis 3–4. And don't you think it's significant that James's next words are, "Do not be *deceived*, my beloved brothers"?

Those words echo Eve's words in Genesis 3:13, where she says that the serpent deceived her. She was lured, wasn't she? In Genesis 3, you can almost see the serpent leading her right through the garden to the Tree of Knowledge of Good and Evil so that she would see how delicious the fruit was instead of remembering what God had said about it. Then her desire was stimulated, the desire for something the serpent said was better than what she already had: being as God rather than being made in the image of God. And then the conception took place: the seed of opportunity was joined to the egg of desire. And finally, death followed—the death of her happy fellowship with God, the death of her sweet relationship with Adam, and then, alas, the violent death of her second son recorded in Genesis 4.

"We are not ignorant of his designs," Paul says. But is that really true? There are some basic factors in military strategy that are certainly true of the Christian warfare. One of them is, "Know your enemy." So let's not be ignorant of Satan's devices.

3

The Enemy of Our Souls

THIS WEEK, WE'VE BEEN THINKING ABOUT the description of the fall in Genesis 3. It's surely one of the most important chapters in the Bible, and it's foundational to everything that follows. But here's a question: "Why did Satan do this? Why did he entrap Adam and Eve?"

Earlier in the week, I suggested that the reason that he enticed Eve first was that she was the very best gift the Lord had given to Adam. It was a really hateful way of dragging Adam from his love and loyalty to God. But what the serpent was doing as an instrument of Satan didn't stop at Adam or, for that matter, at Adam and Eve's family. Why this destructive hatred for them and for the entire human race?

It wasn't just about them or about us. Ultimately, Satan's hatred is directed against God.

The Apostle Paul speaks about a mystery in connection with Satan's work, the mystery of iniquity. It's true that we have questions about Satan that Scripture doesn't directly answer, but there are some important things that we do know.

First, we know that he was created by God because God is the

Creator of all things in the heavens and on the earth. God created a heavenly family of creatures—angels, archangels, cherubim, and seraphim—as well as an earthly family of human beings. The angels are sometimes referred to as God's sons, His family. And clearly, they are wonderful, glorious, varied creatures with a nature and powers that seem different from ours.

Second, we know that Satan rebelled against God. He was not always Satan, the adversary, or Apollyon, the destroyer. The Apostle John tells us that he did not remain in the truth and that his lies in the garden of Eden were an expression of a perversion that had taken place in his character.

Third, we know that as a rebel against God, Satan never wants to be alone—no rebel against God ever does. And so it seems that he incited other angelic creatures to join him. The Lord Jesus speaks about those who will share the final judgment of "the devil and his angels" (Matt. 25:41), and the Apostle John caught a glimpse of the rebellion in his vision in Revelation 12.

Fourth, we know that Satan is the *devil*. That word conveys the idea of throwing something against someone else. That is why he is called the "accuser of our brothers" in Revelation 12. In the dramatic description in Zechariah 3, we see him throw accusations at Joshua the high priest.

How does all this shed light on why Satan would, through the serpent, attack Adam and Eve? I've already noted that he attacked Adam through God's best gift to him, his wife. That actually reflects his nature. We might say that in this, Satan was ultimately attacking God the Father, Son, and Holy Spirit through the very best gift They had given to Themselves: human beings. For after God had made all other things visible and invisible, the divine Trinity held counsel and said: "Now let Us make the best of all for Ourselves. Let Us make man as Our image and likeness to know Us, love Us, trust Us, and have fellowship with Us, and let Us make man as male and female."

To use an illustration—a poor one, but a real one—imagine that a man and a woman in love with each other get married. But then what? They instinctively want to have a child in their image and likeness, and what joy that gives them. We all understand that whether we're married and have children or not. A child of love brings joy—unless (as sometimes happens) it reveals our own unhappy, sinful, and perhaps jealous hearts.

But why is that? It's because, despite our fallen condition, we've been made as the image of God. And that is what Satan hated: God's joy in His children, Adam and Eve, and the joy He would have in their children, too. He hated that, and he hates it still.

We need to see that and learn to recognize and to hate his strategies.

4

The Deceiver's Great Lie

WE NOTED YESTERDAY THAT SATAN'S CHIEF MOTIVE in dragging Adam and Eve into sin was not just his hatred of them but, behind that, his hatred of God. He desperately wanted to destroy what gave God so much pleasure: the man and woman He had made in His image and likeness, made for fellowship with Him, made to love Him.

It's actually very difficult for us to understand how much Satan hated, and hates, God. Surely one of the devices that he uses to deceive us is that we often reserve all our blame for things for other people, and sadly, sometimes for our fellow believers. We forget that we have a supernatural enemy who wants to stir us up in hostility so that we no longer reflect the image of God. So we need to remember Paul's words that we wrestle not against flesh and blood, but against principalities and powers in the heavenly places.

One of the reasons that we need to learn about Satan's hatred is that he is a deceiver. Therefore, I want to think with you today about one important aspect of this: the great deceit of the great deceiver.

This is what Paul refers to in Romans 1:25. He says that men "exchanged the truth about God for a lie," which resulted in their being deceived. They "worshiped and served the creature rather than the Creator, who is blessed forever!" That is an amazing deceit, when you think about it. How could this be? Satan's object was to get Adam and Eve to make what is the ultimately irrational exchange: to exchange the truth about God for the lie. The Greek text uses the definite article here, saying that they exchanged the truth about God for *the* lie about God. Not just *a* lie, but *the* lie, the big lie, the fundamental lie.

So the question is, "What is the lie?" We surely need to be able to recognize it when we see it.

It's important for us to remember that the Apostle Paul had given very careful attention to reading and studying the early chapters of Genesis. So we're not left to our own devices to say, "Well, the way I like to think about it is . . ." What we need to do is to get back to Genesis 3 and ask, "What is the lie that Satan was purveying?"

We find it in these words: "Did God actually say, 'You shall not eat of any tree in the garden'?" (Gen. 3:1). Eve puts up a defense, but the seed thought is already planted. It's significant that when she responds, she adds something to what God had said—not only that they should not eat but that they should not even touch the tree, lest they die. It was almost as though she were adding a law to the commandment that God had given.

I wonder if that little addition is an indication that the seed was beginning to take root. I know it seems trivial, but it is a little step toward the lie that the serpent has been purveying to her, which is this: "God says He is loving and generous, but He is actually mean and restrictive. Is He really the kind of God who would put you in this magnificent garden and then say, 'Ah, none of it is to be yours,'" as though He were some kind of twisted, malicious father taking his little boy into a toy store at Christmas, showing him the toys, and then laughing in his face and saying, "And none of this will be yours"?

What's the point? It is that Satan so hates God that he wants you to hate God, too. To do that, he wants to twist your view of God from that of a loving, generous heavenly Father into someone you can't fully trust because you're not fully sure He really wants the best for you. So you suspect that He basically wants to restrict your joy and pleasure, and you cease to love Him and begin to hate Him.

It's very interesting to me that the great masters of pastoral ministry have often noticed that this suspicion of God the Father is not always immediately removed by regeneration. It can remain deeply embedded in many Christian souls. So I suspect that maybe we should draw our reflections today to a close by simply asking ourselves, "Have I, too, continued to exchange the truth about God for the lie?"

That is worth reflecting on, isn't it? And we'll return to that again tomorrow.

5

Looking to Our Loving Father

YESTERDAY, WE BEGAN TO TOUCH ON SOMETHING of great spiritual importance to us. We looked at how Paul speaks about exchanging the truth about God for the lie—that is, the lie that He isn't in fact a wonderfully kind and generous Father. I suggested that many of the great pastoral masters of the spiritual life have noted that this can become a kind of spiritual pandemic among Christians. And perhaps similar to a chronic disease, the effects sometimes go down pretty deep and linger long.

The great English theologian John Owen noted:

Christians are but little exercised . . . in holding immediate communion with the Father in love. Unacquaintedness with our mercies, our privileges, is our sin as well as our trouble. We hearken not to the voice of the Spirit which is given unto us, "that we may know the things that are freely bestowed on us by God." This makes us go heavily, when we might rejoice; and to be weak, where we might be strong in the Lord.

Then he says this:

How few of the saints are experimentally acquainted with this privilege of holding immediate communion with the Father in love! With what anxious, doubtful thoughts do they look upon him! What fears, what questionings are there, of his good-will and kindness!

He adds:

At the best, many think there is no sweetness at all in Him towards us, but what is purchased at the high price of the blood of Jesus. It is true, that alone is the way of communication; but the free foundation and spring of all is in the bosom of the Father.

Then Owen goes on to offer us the solution to this affliction. He says, "Eye the Father as love." That is to say, keep your gaze fixed on your loving Father. And that, of course, is exactly what Satan was attacking in Eden: the love of the Father for Adam and Eve. He sought to deceive Eve into doubting this love and then to entrap Adam to choose a lesser love.

They both lost their grip on the assurance of God's love for them, and when God came looking for them in the evening, they had pathetically covered themselves in fig leaves and were hiding from Him. They were no longer eyeing the Father in love.

The same can be true for us. We experience the influences of the Spirit. We believe in the grace of the Son. But somehow, sometimes we're not so sure of the love of the Father. After all, we think, "Didn't Jesus have to die to persuade the Father to love us?" No, no, no! Never! It's the other way around. God the Father so loved the world that He gave His only begotten Son for us. God the Father proves His love for us in that while we were still sinners, Christ died for us.

Poor Adam and Eve in their fig leaves. They'd lost the sense that the Father is love. At least for the time being, they'd exchanged the truth about God for the lie. And even when they were restored, that lie was now in the bloodstream of the human race.

People say they believe in a God of love, but their lives often give the lie to what their lips say. And often, their attitude to the Father proves it.

So if you meditate on just one thing we've discussed this week, make it John Owen's quaint but vital statement, his wonderful counsel, "Eye the Father as love."

WEEK 20

The Ascension

1

He Ascended into Heaven

IN SOME CHURCH TRADITIONS, the ascension of Christ is celebrated, just as Easter and Christmas Day are widely celebrated. Whatever your thoughts about observing the event, the ascension of our Lord Jesus Christ does really matter. It's an important moment in the gospel and therefore a significant event for our Christian living.

Have you given much thought to the ascension of Jesus? If not, I hope that our reflections this week will be helpful to you.

How important was Jesus' ascension to the authors of the New Testament? Luke certainly thought that it was. The last paragraph in his gospel describes it, and right at the beginning of Acts, he describes it in even greater length. Peter refers to it in his sermon on the day of Pentecost; he also assumes the ascension when he explains the miracle at the Beautiful Gate of the temple (see Acts 3). The ascension of Christ also lies behind Stephen's experience as he was being martyred, as well as Saul of Tarsus' experience on the Damascus Road. John tells us how Jesus spoke about His ascension during His ministry and after His resurrection (see John 6:62; 20:17).

The ascended Christ is now seated at the Father's right hand (Eph. 1:20–23; Col. 3:1). The ascended Christ is highly exalted (Phil. 2:9). The ascension is also implied in various places in Hebrews. We read in Hebrews 4:14 that Jesus has passed through the heavens and is at God's right hand. Also, Jesus is portrayed in Revelation 12 as being caught up to heaven, where He has ascended to the throne of God.

So yes, the ascension really is important. It was the next stage in the work of the Lord Jesus after His birth, ministry, death, and resurrection. In fact, it marked the completion of His present work here on earth. Just as the hymn says:

All his work is ended, joyfully we sing:
Jesus has ascended: Glory to our King!

As John says in his gospel, Jesus came from God, and He was going back to God (John 13:3). His resurrection tells us that His atoning sacrifice has been accepted. His ascension tells us that He has completed all the work His Father gave Him to do on earth.

Jesus was taken up into heaven in a cloud, and there is a reason for that. It wasn't just to hide Him from sight. Throughout Scripture, we see that a cloud regularly appears during God's mighty acts. It's sometimes called the shekinah cloud, the bright shining cloud that manifests the presence of the invisible glory of God. Our Lord went into heaven, riding on a kind of triumphal chariot of glory.

The church fathers in the early centuries loved to think of the words of Psalm 24 in this regard. As Jesus approaches the summit of the hill of the Lord, the angels accompanying Him cry out, "Lift up your heads, O gates . . . , that the King of glory may come in" (v. 9). Like an antiphonal choir, the angels in heaven call back, "Who is this King of glory who seeks entry?" The answer is given: "The LORD, strong and mighty, the LORD, mighty in battle! . . . The LORD of hosts, he is the King of glory!" (vv. 8–10). The doors of heaven swing open, and Jesus, who has conquered sin and death and Satan, comes to His coronation. What a scene! Magnificent, isn't it?

The ascension means that Jesus, who was crucified for us, now occupies the throne of heaven and reigns over all things for us. That is something worth remembering, whatever you're doing today. And it's a wonderful thought to have at the end of the day when you lay your head on your pillow. It really is true:

All his work is ended, joyfully we sing:
Jesus has ascended: Glory to our King!

2

Dominion Regained

I SUSPECT THAT MOST OF US don't pay much attention to Ascension Day, which commemorates the ascension of the Lord Jesus, despite the fact that it's mentioned quite frequently in Scripture.

The opening verses of Acts tell us that for forty days after His resurrection, Jesus met with His disciples and taught them more about the kingdom of God. I think that is the explanation for the amazing biblical theology of Simon Peter's sermon on the day of Pentecost. It wasn't just that he was now filled with the Spirit; it was that Jesus had filled him with Scripture. The rich biblical theology of his sermon didn't come to him on the spur of the moment. It was surely what he had been taught by the Lord Jesus during those weeks after His resurrection and before His ascension.

But why didn't Jesus conclude His last day of instruction by simply saying to them: "That is the end of the seminars, and you won't see Me again. I'm going back to the Father permanently now"? I think there are two reasons.

First, He wanted to make clear to them, not just by word but also by action, that He really was leaving them permanently until His second coming. Jesus could have just said His farewells to the Apostles and the other believers in a relatively undramatic fashion and then left them, as He had apparently been doing for those six weeks. But if that is what He had done, some of them would undoubtedly have entertained hopes that perhaps He was just testing them to see whether they wanted Him to keep coming back, and when He saw that they did, He'd have come back again. And so our Lord left the Apostles and the young church in a very decisive way—in an event that, in its own way, was like His incarnation, crucifixion, and resurrection—a once-for-all event.

But second, I think there is another reason that the ascension took the shape it did, because the ascension event marked a new era in our Lord Jesus' ministry. Just as His incarnation, ministry, death, and resurrection fulfilled specific Scriptures, so, too, did His ascension. It is the event that some of the so-called royal psalms point to: the King coming to His coronation.

The most frequently quoted or alluded-to words in the Psalms are the first words of Psalm 110, where David says, "The LORD says to my

Lord: 'Sit at my right hand, until I make your enemies your footstool.'"
That is what is happening in the ascension. Jesus is not just leaving the world; He is going to heaven. Indeed, it's even more than that: Jesus is going to His coronation.

Remember how He made that point? Just before the ascension, Jesus said, "All authority in heaven and on earth has been given to me" (Matt. 28:18). The majesty of the way He leaves the disciples is an outward expression of that very thing. He is no ordinary king exalted on a throne; He is being raised to the throne of heaven and earth.

I want to call your attention to two things in Matthew 28:18. First, we can easily miss the deep significance of that word "authority." Second, we can easily miss the significance of the verb "given." After all, Jesus is the Son of God. Doesn't He already have all dominion as God? He doesn't need to be given it, does He?

That's true, but there seems to be more to what Jesus is saying here than meets the eye.

What if we substituted the word *dominion* for "authority"? "All *dominion* in heaven and on earth has been given to me." Does that remind you of Genesis 1:26–28, where God made Adam and Eve in His image and gave them dominion over the earth? But of course, they forfeited that dominion, and Satan instead gained it. Satan actually offered this dominion back to Jesus in the wilderness temptations if Jesus would just bow down and worship him.

That was a real temptation because that is exactly what the Son of God came into the world to regain. He came to regain the dominion that Adam had lost. Yet He came to regain it by His death and resurrection, not by aligning Himself with Satan. But now sin has been atoned for, death has been overcome, and Satan has been conquered. Jesus, the second man, the last Adam, has now regained the dominion that was lost. That is why in His ascension the coronation takes place. That is why He ascends to the throne in this dramatic way.

No wonder Luke tells us that the disciples had a threefold response:

they worshiped Him, they experienced great joy, and they went back to the temple to praise God (Luke 24:52–53). I think that when we are really gripped by the reality of Jesus' ascension, we begin to echo that response.

Yes, Jesus has ascended—glory to our King. And yes, joy to us as well, and worship to God.

3

The Heavenly Ministry of Christ

THE ASCENSION RAISES A PRACTICAL QUESTION FOR US: "What has Jesus been doing since His ascension, and what is He doing now?"

Sometimes we talk about the work of Christ in terms of His three-fold office. Adam was created to be the prophet, priest, and king of creation, but he failed in that ministry. When Jesus undertook our salvation and restoration, He fulfilled these three roles in a new and redeeming and restoring way. He did it through His incarnation, life, death, resurrection, and ascension, and now through His heavenly session and reign. He has done everything needed to accomplish our redemption.

This means that there is even more to the good news than the fact that Christ has accomplished our redemption. He has now ascended and gone to heaven to apply that redemption to us. And one of the ways that He does this is by continuing His ministry as Prophet, Priest, and King.

How does Jesus continue to be a Prophet? He did it first of all by giving us His Word in the pages of the New Testament. He told the Apostles in the upper room that when the Holy Spirit came to them—and He was speaking particularly and uniquely to them—they would be able to give the New Testament to the church. The Spirit would remind them of everything Jesus said (John 14:26), and we find that in the Gospels. He would lead them into an understanding of the truth about Himself (16:13), which we find in the Gospels and in the Epistles. And He would show them things to come (16:13), which we find in the book of Revelation, as well as elsewhere. These words are as good a summary of what's in the New Testament as you'll find anywhere. That is the work of Jesus as the ongoing Prophet of the church.

But He also continues to exercise this prophetic ministry in the exposition of the Scriptures He has given to us.

I wonder if you've ever thought about Paul's words to the Ephesians when he says, "[Christ] came and preached peace to you who were far off and peace to those who were near" (Eph. 2:17). When did Christ do that? Did He visit Ephesus during His ministry or between His resurrection and ascension? No. Paul is speaking here about what had happened when he and his companions came to Ephesus. Paul preached, and through Paul's preaching of the gospel, Christ's voice was heard as he proclaimed peace and salvation.

I think that the Ephesians could have sung Horatius Bonar's hymn:

I heard the voice of Jesus say,
"Come unto me and rest;
Lay down, thou weary one, lay down
Thy head upon my breast."
I came to Jesus as I was,
Weary and worn and sad;
I found in him a resting place,
And he has made me glad.

Isn't this exactly the experience we all have under a living ministry of the Word of God? It makes us say to one another, "The Lord was speaking to us today." It isn't that we hear sounds other than the words that are spoken but rather that by the Holy Spirit, within and beyond the preacher's accent, we recognize the accent of the Lord Jesus. There are many times, I suspect, when we scarcely notice that our own preachers have an accent at all. When that happens, we realize that through His Word, it's the Lord Jesus detecting, analyzing, reaching, and healing the sicknesses of our souls, getting into places that no human being could possibly know even exist.

There are two important implications of this present ministry of Jesus as Prophet. The first is that we have a primary need and responsibility, wherever and whenever possible, to place our own lives under a living ministry of God's Word. When we do that, we'll begin to be delivered from the all-too-common idea that sermons explain what God has done, and then preachers tell us what we are supposed to do. We'll discover that because Christ speaks in God's Word when it's preached in the power of God's Spirit, God's Word begins to do its own work in us, shaping and reshaping our thinking, transforming our affections, melting our wills, and renewing our minds.

The second implication is that we need to pray for such ministries to be raised up and sustained in our own time.

Incidentally, I wonder if you pray for the preaching of the Word in your own congregation. And I wonder, "Have you ever encouraged your pastor?"

4

Interceding from Heaven

YESTERDAY, WE LOOKED AT THE TWO ASPECTS to the work of our Lord Jesus as Prophet, Priest, and King: His finished work and His unfinished, or ongoing, work. We saw yesterday that as Prophet, the Lord Jesus continues to speak to His church through the ministry of His Word to us. Today, we'll look at how He continues His priestly ministry.

When we think about priestly ministry, we tend to focus on sacrifice. And certainly, our Lord Jesus, at the heart of His priestly ministry, has sacrificed Himself for our sins. That was fundamental to the work of the old covenant priests, and it's certainly fundamental to the ministry of our Lord Jesus. The old covenant priests kept standing because theirs was not the real sacrifice. They continued to make it daily. The book of Hebrews tells us that our Lord Jesus Christ has made a sacrifice of Himself, once and for all. And now after His ascension, He has sat down at the right hand of the Majesty on high.

Christ has made a sacrifice and finished His work, but that isn't the end of our Lord Jesus' priestly ministry. Making sacrifices for sins was only one part of the priest's regular ministry. The other part was making intercession for the people. It was his responsibility to care for the people, and he did this in a variety of ways. But central to those duties was that the priests interceded for the people, which means that they expressed to God their care and love for the people and carried their needs into His presence.

This was highlighted in a very visible way in the person of the high priest. He wore a breastplate on which twelve different kinds of stones were each engraved with the name of one of the tribes of Israel. There were shoulder pieces on his garment that had two onyx stones. On the first was engraved the names of six of the tribes, and on the second, the names of the other six tribes.

That must have been a wonderful sight—to see the high priest of Israel with all the people on his heart and carrying all the people on his shoulders. What a wonderful picture of our Lord Jesus, not only in His earthly priestly ministry, but in His ongoing heavenly ministry. As Hebrews 7:25 says, "He is able to save to the uttermost those who draw near to God through him, since he always lives to make intercession for them."

The author of Hebrews doesn't explain exactly how Jesus intercedes, so we shouldn't overspeculate. But to me, what makes this one of the most encouraging and reassuring verses in the whole Bible is that it tells me that the Lord Jesus is in heaven, before His Father, and He is there for me in all my need. He'll never let me go. He'll never stop caring.

Perhaps we can think about it like this: When someone you love is in difficulty—perhaps sick, or facing a personal crisis, or going through a testing experience—you feel as if they are constantly on your mind and on your heart. Sometimes you speak words in prayer for them and about them. But there is also a sense in which you're caring constantly for them, isn't there? You're in the Lord's presence, and they are on your heart, and you know He sees that. That is the kind of ministry that Jesus exercises for you, for me, today. We're always on His heart.

There is something else we need to know. Paul tells us that when we feel condemned—maybe because others condemn us, maybe because we feel that Satan condemns us, maybe because we condemn ourselves—we need to know that there is no condemnation for us. Jesus Christ, who alone can ultimately condemn us since the Father has placed all judgment into His hands, not only has died for us, but is now at the right hand of God, interceding for us (Rom. 8:34).

I feel fairly sure that more than one of us will need to remember that today.

5

He Must Reign

THE WESTMINSTER ASSEMBLY'S TWO CATECHISMS contain some fine explanations of Jesus' continuing ministry as Prophet, Priest, and King. I recommend to you questions 43–45 in the Westminster Larger Catechism and questions 23–26 in the Westminster Shorter Catechism. But I especially love the answer that the Shorter Catechism gives to the question, "How doth Christ execute the office of a king?" It focuses on what Jesus is doing now: "Christ executeth the office of a king, in subduing us to himself, in ruling and defending us, and in restraining and conquering all his and our enemies."

Earlier this week, when I said that Christ's ascension was His journey through the heavens to His coronation at the right hand of God, I hinted at the big picture of Christ's kingly ministry. He has now begun to exercise the dominion, or authority, that He won as the second man and the last Adam, recovering and then completing the dominion that Adam was given but failed to accomplish. And Jesus is doing that now, according to Matthew 28:18–20, through the spread of the gospel. But what does this mean for us as individuals when we become Christians?

The first implication is that when we become Christians, we come under the dominion or lordship of Christ. He subdues us to Himself. Despite what some people might claim, we don't come to trust Christ as our Savior without simultaneously coming to Him as our Lord. You can't have half a Christ any more than you can have half a wife. If we have come to trust Him, He immediately subdues us to Himself.

At the same time, we must remember that our trust in and fellowship with the Lord Jesus is a progressive reality. As His Spirit works in our hearts, we find that He is uncovering elements of hidden sin and resistance so that Christ may rule over every aspect of our lives more and more. We're called to grow in our trust and to express that more and more fully in His lordship over us. It's a relationship that deepens over time, just as our human relationships do. For example, you might be a son, but perhaps you don't always behave like a son. Perhaps you don't always appreciate your parents. But you grow in these things. New challenges and changes don't alter the relationship itself: you were a son, and you're still a son.

So it is with the lordship of Jesus Christ. He is always your Lord from the beginning of your Christian life. But there is always going to be more in us to subdue, more challenges to attempt, more ways in which to serve Him. And that is why His kingly ministry is challenging to us.

Yet His kingly ministry is also very comforting because He is defending us. He is restraining our enemies. He is conquering them. Who are these enemies? There is a well-known phrase that sums up who they are: the world that seeks to conform us to itself, the flesh that seeks to drag us down into sin, and the devil who seeks to draw us away from our trust in and love for the Lord. And as we yield day by day in love to the Lord Jesus Christ, we discover more and more how He exercises His kingly power over His and our enemies.

Sometimes we feel that we fail so badly that we almost feel dominated by the world, paralyzed by our sin, and even taken captive by the devil. That is why we need to set our minds on what's above, remembering that Christ is there, seated at the right hand of God, and He is subduing us to Himself (see Col. 3:2). We're already living in His kingdom. We have a King, and He reigns. He has promised to subdue all His and our enemies. He is ascended. He is at God's right hand. And He is reigning until all His enemies become a stool for His feet.

So this week, let's thank God for the ascension of Christ. And indeed, let's thank God every day, every week, every year, that He has highly exalted His Son, Jesus, and given Him the name that is above every name. Blessed be that name.

WEEK 21

The Trinity

1

Knowing the Trinity

I SUSPECT THAT MANY CHRISTIANS CONSIDER the doctrine of the Trinity the most obscure and speculative—and therefore the least practical—of all the major Christian doctrines. Three in one, and one in three. That doesn't compute in the mathematics that most of us use. And unfortunately, we tend to operate on the theological principle that if we don't understand something, it can't be all that important.

We fail to realize that if that were our guiding principle for all of life, we wouldn't be using our computers or cell phones. We wouldn't be flying in airplanes. Most of us wouldn't be using electricity. There are hundreds of things that we wouldn't be using or doing daily if we had to understand exactly how they operated. Therefore, the fact that we may not fully understand the Trinity doesn't mean that the Trinity isn't essential to us.

Perhaps it's worth pausing to ask this question: "Has the fact that God is Trinity crossed your mind in the past week? If so, has it made any difference to the way that you think and live?" Many of us would almost die to defend the doctrine of the Trinity. But the question here is, "Does the doctrine of the Trinity really make any practical difference to us?"

When we speak about the Trinity, we're not claiming that we fully understand the Trinity. The Bible makes it clear that we would need to *be* the Trinity to fully understand the Trinity. But we do know that there is only one God, and that this one God exists eternally in a unity of three persons—the Father, the Son, and the Holy Spirit—and that each of these persons has a distinct relationship to the other two. We also believe that this truth is only gradually revealed to us in the pages of Scripture until it is then fully revealed to us in the person of the Lord Jesus Christ.

B.B. Warfield, the great twentieth-century American theologian, used a helpful illustration here. He wrote: "The Old Testament may be likened to a chamber richly furnished but dimly lighted; the introduction of light brings into it nothing which was not in it before; but it brings out into clearer view much of what is in it but was only dimly or not at all perceived before."

The mystery of the Trinity is not revealed in the Old Testament, but the mystery of the Trinity underlies the Old Testament revelation and comes into view here and there. Thus, the Old Testament revelation is not corrected by the fuller revelation that follows. Rather, it is perfected, extended, and enlarged. That fits the opening words of the letter to the Hebrews. God revealed Himself in gradual, partial ways in the Old Testament. But now He reveals Himself by Himself in the incarnation of the Son, our Lord Jesus Christ.

This is a wonderful thing for us to understand. We can describe the Trinity, yet we recognize that the Trinity remains a mystery to us. We can know that God is Trinity and know God the Trinity, but we also know that we can't fully comprehend Him. After all, even the seraphim veil their faces in the presence of the One who is holy, holy, holy.

I remember, when our children were young, saying goodnight one evening to one of our sons. He was sitting up in bed, looking a bit puzzled. "Dad," he said, "is this right that God is three persons in one?" "That is right," I replied. To which he said, with the trusting innocence of a five-year-old, "Dad, that is a very difficult thing for a wee boy like me to understand." Of course, I told him, "It doesn't get any easier when you get older."

But that is the point, isn't it? God's Trinitarian nature reminds us that while we can know Him truly, we do not, cannot, and never will fully comprehend Him because He is God and we are not. We are finite created beings. He is the infinite uncreated One. In seeking to know Him, we must not fall into the error of reducing Him to our own size. How foolish we would be to think that we are wise when we insist that we would believe in God only if we understood Him. Who do we think we are?

There is something humbling about the doctrine of the Trinity, but there is also something wonderful. If you think about it, only a three-person God can fully experience what it really means to love. Otherwise, He is dependent on creating us in order to love.

Think about that today, because we'll return to it again tomorrow.

2

The Triune God of Love

YESTERDAY, I RAISED THIS QUESTION: "Does this doctrine of the Trinity make any difference to us?" One barometer of our theology and our Christianity can be measured by the content of the hymns and songs that we sing together in church. I wonder, "How many modern Christian songs are obviously Trinitarian?" Compare that with the way that the Apostle Paul just loves to weave references to the Father, Son, and Holy Spirit into his teaching. Shouldn't we do the same in our singing?

In seeking to answer this question of why the doctrine of the Trinity is so important, I want to mention one theological reason that I've hinted at already, and I want to explain this reason by talking about a theologian with whom you may not be familiar: Richard the Scot of Saint-Victor. Richard was Scottish, though for most of his life he didn't live in Scotland. He eventually became prior of the Abbey of Saint-Victor on the outskirts of Paris around the second half of the twelfth century. He died in 1173.

Richard the Scot belonged to the Augustinian Order of monks, and one of the big emphases in the Augustinian Order—going all the way back to Augustine himself—was the love of God. Therefore, it's not surprising that Richard loved to think about the love of God and what it meant.

We often tend to think about the implications of God's love *for us*: "God so loved the world" (John 3:16). But Richard thought about the implication of God's love *for Himself*; by that, I mean the implications *for God* regarding the fact that God is love. Richard thought this way: If God is love, as the Apostle John tells us, what does that imply about God Himself?

Here is Richard's answer: If God is love, then while He is one God numerically, He must also be three persons. Of course, Richard knew that the Bible taught that God was Father, Son, and Holy Spirit. He wasn't saying that apart from the Bible we can work out that God is Trinity; he was saying that the fact that Scripture tells us God is love helps us to see why it is that God is three persons, God the Trinity.

His reasoning was really quite simple: If God is love, then He must love. But by its very nature, love isn't self-absorbed. I sometimes say that this is why I could never be a Unitarian. Unitarians always insist that God is love, but the Unitarian god is like someone who is all dressed up with nowhere to go. He has an attribute—love—but there is absolutely nothing he can do with it. He becomes dependent on creating us in order to have someone or something to love. Otherwise, he is totally self-absorbed. And that is the point: the Unitarian god needs me to be happy and therefore by definition isn't really God.

By contrast, you can see why Richard saw great beauty in the doctrine of the Trinity. The Father loves His Son and the Holy Spirit. The Son loves the Father and the Spirit. The Spirit loves the Father and the Son. Not only is there mutual love, but there is a dynamic love.

One can't help but wonder, "Since God made us as His image as male and female, is this something that He echoed into our existence?"

That is, when a man and a woman are bound together in love, their natural instinct is to extend the love they share toward each other, resulting in the birth of a child. And so there is in the created order of our own lives a kind of miniature reflection of what is eternally true in God Himself.

This is something that helps us to adore God the Trinity. He doesn't need to *become* love. He has always *been* love. He doesn't need to be satisfied by the created order because He is always satisfied in Himself—God the Father, Son, and Spirit dwelling in love. The marvelous truth of the gospel is that God the Father loves us, Jesus Christ has acted to save us, and His Spirit is sent to bring us to Himself.

It's no wonder that we love God the Trinity, and it's no wonder that we love the fact that God is Trinity.

3

Baptized into the Triune Name

I LOVE WHAT AUGUSTINE SAID ABOUT THE TRINITY: no doctrine is more difficult or more dangerous than the doctrine of the Trinity, yet at the same time, no doctrine is more rewarding.

I hope we caught a glimpse of that yesterday when we saw that God is love, and being love is Trinity, and that these two truths mesh together beautifully.

There is an obvious reason that we should be more Trinitarian in our thinking than I suspect we actually are. The reason is so obvious that we rarely notice it, and sometimes we tend to obscure it or divert people away from it. I wonder if you can guess what it is.

What I'm talking about is baptism, which is something that all Christians have in common. I'm not thinking here about the elements of baptism that Christians disagree on—who should be baptized and how we should baptize. Rather, I'm talking about the words that we all use at a baptism—"I baptize you in the name [singular] of the Father, and of the Son, and of the Holy Spirit." These words are from Jesus' Great Commission in Matthew 28.

It's wonderful to remember that this was the first time (if I can put it this way) that the full name of God was ever pronounced. We're baptized into this one name of God, but it's pronounced Father, Son, and Holy Spirit. Right from the beginning of the Christian life, you and I are called to live in fellowship with the Trinity. The Trinity is the bedrock of the believer's life.

It would be a great pity if I as a minister spent most of my time defending my view of baptism when I preached at baptisms or about baptism but never spoke about the wonder and importance of the fact that we are baptized into the one name of the three persons. This is the foundation of our entire Christian lives and our communion with God. I wonder if, when we talk about baptism, we spend so much time on things about which we differ that we don't spend enough time on the things that would cause us to rejoice: living in and acting out the blessedness of our fellowship with the Trinity.

Baptism is a naming ceremony. The water doesn't change us inside, yet something does happen in our baptism. We're being given a name; we're being named for the Trinity. For example, at some point in the first few days of my life, I went through a naming ceremony. The city registrar asked my father and mother, "What is the name of your child?" They replied, "Sinclair Buchanan Ferguson."

It's a grand-sounding name, but it didn't change anything inside me. I'm sure that my mom must have sometimes wished it had! But ever since that moment, whenever I hear the words *Sinclair Ferguson*, I inwardly respond: "That is me. That is who I am. That is my identity." If my mom said to me, as she sometimes did, "Sinclair Ferguson," in the way that mothers sometimes do, I knew she was really saying this: "You've been named for this family, but you're not living as though you were named for this family." Therefore, baptism is a naming ceremony, but it doesn't change us inside.

Yet in another sense, it changes everything. It tells us that our lives have been claimed by God the Trinity to live in His family, to live out His lifestyle, to live for His praise and glory, and to enjoy Him forever. And it tells us that as we live the Christian life, we know that the Father loves us and cares for us, the Son loves us and has died for us, and the Spirit loves us and is willing to lead us.

That is probably what Martin Luther was thinking about in the times when he was despondent. He went outside and said two Latin words, *baptizatus sum*, "I've been baptized." I think he was really saying this: "Martin, remember God the Trinity. Remember that you belong to His family. Remember that you have the privilege of fellowship with the Father, Son, and Holy Spirit. Now, Martin, enjoy it and live it out."

That is a lesson for us today. May our baptisms remind us of this absolutely fundamental truth about us: we've been named for God the Trinity, for the Father, for the Son, and for the Holy Spirit.

Surely there is nothing more practical than that.

4

What Jesus Taught about the Trinity

I'VE MENTIONED A FEW TIMES THIS WEEK that I think many Christians view the Trinity as a somewhat speculative and impractical doctrine, and I've been trying to prove that it's really the very opposite. Today, I want to try to show in another way why it's so practical. My response to someone who didn't see the Trinity as relevant or significant might be this: "You think the Trinity is the least practical doctrine? Tell that to Jesus."

When another Christian expresses a negative opinion about any Christian doctrine, it's always a good pastoral move to ask, "Did Jesus say anything about this?" After all, as Christians we understand that we love and trust Jesus. If He believed something, then we are called to believe it. If He thought that something was important, then surely we should, too.

So where does that take us in regard to the Trinity?

One place it takes us to is the upper room and to the last few hours before Jesus was arrested. Read through John 13–17 and ask yourself these questions: "Did Jesus think that the Trinity is important? Did Jesus think that knowing the Trinity would make any difference to the Christian life?" I think what you'll find in these chapters is a magnificent tapestry of gospel grace woven from three threads: the work of the Father, the work of the Son, and the work of the Holy Spirit.

Those hours in the upper room were the most sacred hours the disciples had spent with Jesus thus far, and this was certainly the most profound instruction He'd ever given them. He was teaching them what they needed to know to live at a time of great crisis. He was teaching them what was really important, and what He spoke about was the Trinity.

Jesus told them about His own relationship with the Father and the Spirit. He told them how the Father loved Him and had committed to Him the work of redemption. He told them how He Himself had honored and glorified the Father. And He told them how the Holy Spirit was *His* Holy Spirit, and that He would send that Holy Spirit to them. In other words, in the upper room, Jesus spoke about the Trinity.

In Jesus, the disciples had seen the Father. In John 14:8, Philip asked, "Lord, show us the Father, and it is enough for us." Jesus replied, in effect, "But Philip, you've seen who the Father is by watching Me, by My relationship to Him." In a sense, Jesus is answering this same question about the Holy Spirit in John 13–16 when He says, "You know him, for he dwells with you and will be in you" (John 14:17). The Spirit of the Father and the Spirit of the Son, one Spirit, had dwelt on Jesus' life for these thirty-three years. "And now," Jesus says, "He is going to come to indwell you. And when He comes to indwell you, your life will become a place, a home, where the Father and the Son will come to dwell."

This is absolutely extraordinary and wonderful teaching. Do you see what it means? Yesterday, when we talked about baptism, I said that we're called to live the Christian life as those who belong to the family of God. We've been named for the Father, the Son, and the Holy Spirit—for the Trinity. That is our new family name. But this is not just a formal thing. It's a glorious reality in which, by the indwelling of the Spirit, not only does He indwell us, but through the Spirit, both the Father and the Son come to make our lives their home.

I don't think there is anything more practical than knowing that that is true of you.

Many years ago, J.B. Phillips, famous for his paraphrase of the New Testament, wrote a little book with the title *Your God Is Too Small*. It's not really about the Trinity, but those words apply to our appreciation of the Trinity.

If we've thought about the Trinity as a speculative and impractical doctrine, then our God is too small.

5

Praise Father, Son, and Holy Ghost

HAVE YOU EVER SEEN THOSE PUZZLES where there are a number of hidden items in the picture that you have to find? When I did those puzzles, it would take me a minute or two to spot one, or maybe two, of the items. Then I would see another and another and another quite quickly. And finally, things would slow down before I might (or might not) spot the last one or two items.

Spotting the Trinity in the pages of the New Testament is a bit like that. I suspect that there are some Christians who faithfully read the New Testament but hardly ever think about the Trinity. But then someone might say to them: "Do you see that? Look at this passage. It's about the Trinity. Do you see the Father and the Son and the Holy Spirit here?" That person then spots a reference or two, and then somehow they get it. They start finding references to the Father, Son, and Spirit all over the place. They begin to see that the Father, Son, and Spirit—one God—are present everywhere they look, even when they are not specifically mentioned.

We see this, for example, in Galatians 4:4–5, a great text about the coming of Christ: "But when the fullness of time had come, God sent forth his Son, born of woman, born under the law, . . . so that we might receive adoption as sons." That is often used as a Christmas text about the incarnation of Jesus, but it's actually also about the Father. It's the Father who sent the Son. Paul says elsewhere that when we receive adoption as sons, the Spirit comes into our hearts, crying, "Abba! Father!" (Rom. 8:15; Gal. 4:6).

In other words, Paul is saying that for us to be conscious of what it means to have God as our Father in Jesus Christ—God as the Father who sent His Son into the world for our salvation—the Spirit also has to minister in our hearts to give us a consciousness of His fatherly love so that we call out, "Abba! Father!" So there is a text about Christmas that actually has to do with the Trinity.

The Apostle Paul works this out in some detail in Romans 8. That may be one of your favorite chapters in the Bible, but I wonder if you've ever noticed that it's full of references to the Trinity. The Father, Son, and Holy Spirit weave their way into almost everything Paul says.

And it isn't just Paul the great theologian who teaches us this. It's also the man who had a fishing business in Galilee and perhaps only a synagogue-school-level education: Simon Peter.

Have you ever noticed how his first letter begins? It's rooted in the Trinity: "Peter, an apostle of Jesus Christ, to those who are elect exiles of the Dispersion in Pontus, Galatia, Cappadocia, Asia, and Bithynia, according to the foreknowledge of *God the Father*, in the sanctification of *the Spirit*, for obedience to *Jesus Christ* and for sprinkling with his blood" (1 Peter 1:1–2, emphasis added). No wonder he adds, "May grace and peace be multiplied to you" (v. 2), because when the Trinity—the Father, the Son, and the Holy Spirit—engage together for your salvation, then indeed grace and peace are multiplied to you.

I value a work written more than 350 years ago by the great Puritan theologian John Owen. It has a rather quaint title, probably because it didn't have a table-of-contents page. It's this: *Of Communion with God the Father, Son, and Holy Ghost, Each Person Distinctly, in Love, Grace, and Consolation; Or, the Saints' Fellowship with the Father, Son, and Holy Ghost Unfolded.*

John Owen's thesis is actually quite simple, but it's wonderfully profound. He argues that since each person in the Trinity has a particular role in the work of God, we can worship the one God with respect to what each person does. We praise God the Trinity for saving us, but we especially praise the Father for planning redemption and sending the Lord Jesus to us. We especially praise the Son for coming to us and dying and rising. We especially praise the Spirit for revealing truth and indwelling us.

What Owen is saying, therefore, is that it's the Son we thank for dying on the cross. We don't thank the Father for doing that, but we do thank Him for sending His Son to die on the cross. When you think about the various operations of the Trinity in that way, what happens is that your sense of wonder and appreciation of who God is as Trinity and what He has done in this marvelous Trinitarian conspiracy to bring us salvation fills your heart with joy, love, adoration, and praise. Your fellowship with God is therefore wonderfully enhanced.

Let's end this week about the Trinity with the words of the doxology:

Praise God from whom all blessings flow;
Praise him, all creatures here below;
Praise him above, ye heav'nly host:
Praise Father, Son, and Holy Ghost.
Amen.

WEEK 22

Pentecost

1

What Was Pentecost All About?

ALL TRUE CHURCHES ARE, in a manner of speaking, Pentecostal churches because Pentecost belongs to all true churches. Without it, there wouldn't be a worldwide church. If we lack the Holy Spirit whom our Lord sent at Pentecost, then we also lack the gospel.

Pentecost was an event that happened only once. We shouldn't think of it as happening again and again any more than we believe the death of Christ happens again and again.

Before His ascension, Jesus told the disciples to stay in Jerusalem until He baptized them with the Holy Spirit. When that happened, they would receive power to be His witnesses to the ends of the earth. On the day of Pentecost, there was the sound of a mighty rushing wind. Something like tongues of fire fell on the disciples, and they began speaking in languages other than their own local Aramaic. Peter explained what this meant to the astonished crowds in a remarkable sermon (see Acts 2), and several thousand people were baptized.

When we read the narrative sections of the Bible, we must avoid what I call the "Where's Waldo?" approach. The Where's Waldo? series of books contains pictures of large numbers of people, and somewhere in the crowd is this little fellow Waldo (or Wally, as I think he was originally called by the English creator). He is wearing a red-and-white-striped sweater and a hat. The whole point of the books, the only point of the books, is to try to find Waldo in the crowd—in the city, on the beach, or wherever he happens to be.

I suspect that many Christians read the narratives in the Gospels, and perhaps in Acts, as though they are looking for Waldo. And in this case, Waldo is themselves. In other words, they are looking for themselves in the narrative. The most important question for them, and perhaps almost the only question, is: "Where am I in this passage? Am I there in Nicodemus, or in Bartimaeus, or in Simon Peter, or in whomever?"

Of course, these passages of Scripture do *apply* to us, but they are not first and foremost *about* us. In the Gospels and Acts, our first focus shouldn't really be on "find me" but on "find Jesus." Who is He? What is He like? What is He doing? We first ask, "Who is Jesus here, and what is He doing?" And only then do we ask, "How, then, does that apply to me?"

I say this because many Christians today seem to focus so much on their own experience that they tend to miss something that is fairly obvious. If they are asked what Peter's sermon on the day of Pentecost is all about, they'll say, "Well, obviously it's about how you can get the baptism with the Holy Spirit."

But if you read the passage carefully and thoughtfully, I think you'll give another answer to that question. What is Peter's Pentecost sermon really about? Peter is telling us what these strange phenomena mean. And his answer is that they are telling us something about the Lord Jesus Christ. It's as though Peter were saying, "If you're going to understand the meaning of this event, I need to tell you what has happened to Jesus." His whole sermon is what people today would call an evangelistic sermon about Jesus Christ. It's Jesus he preaches, not the Spirit.

Of course, that is just how the Spirit wants it to be. When the Spirit came, the people were pointed to Jesus, and we need to remember that.

2

Seeing through the Lens of Scripture

YESTERDAY, I INTRODUCED THE IDEA THAT when we think about Pentecost, we need to think about what Jesus was doing. If we were to ask most Christians what Pentecost is about, they'd tend to say that it's about the Holy Spirit. Of course, they are not totally wrong. But that is not the whole story. At least, Simon Peter didn't think so, judging by the sermon he preached. He spoke to answer the question that people were asking: "What is all this about—these strange sounds, this preaching of the gospel in different languages?"

When Peter answers that question in his sermon, he first demolishes the cynics in the crowd who accuse them of being drunk. He points out that it's only the third hour of the day, which is nine o'clock in the morning. Peter says that these men were not filled with intoxicating liquor; rather, what was occurring was the fulfillment of the prophecy of Joel 2.

God promised through the prophet Joel that in the last days, the Spirit of God would be poured out on all flesh, with sons and daughters prophesying, young men having visions, and old men dreaming dreams. Peter essentially tells the crowd, "What this means is that the future is now; it's happening today." We could almost use the words of Jesus in the Nazareth synagogue when He said, "Today this Scripture has been fulfilled in your hearing" (Luke 4:21).

Pentecost is much more than just an amazing personal experience that people had. Notice how Peter's mind is working here. It's worth pausing on this because Peter thinks biblically about what's happened. And if you think about it, that is a huge change in Simon Peter. Typically in the Gospels, he doesn't think very biblically. He just thinks the way he thinks himself, and he thinks he is right.

We would find it faintly amusing, I think, if Peter had explained what was happening on the day of Pentecost by saying, "Well, the way I like to think about what's happening is this," and then maybe said, "John, Andrew, do you have anything you'd like to share with the people here about how you think about it?" I know I'm painting a caricature, but some Christians do speak that way.

Simon Peter doesn't say, "Well, here's how I think about it." No, he is seeing these events through eyeglasses that have been crafted to a biblical prescription, and the optometrist who has helped him is the Lord Jesus. Those seminars between the resurrection and the ascension had radically transformed the way he thought. There is a tremendously important lesson here for us to learn, too. Peter now thinks about everything through the eyeglasses that are prescribed by the teaching of Scripture.

As we discussed in earlier weeks, one of Eve's cardinal mistakes when she was tempted by the serpent was to see things through her own eyes and not through ears that listened to God's Word. Eve forgot one of the most basic spiritual principles of all: the saints of God seek to see and understand things through the lens of God's Word.

That may seem far removed from our discussion of the day of Pentecost, but it's important for us to begin to develop this new instinct that Peter now had, the instinct that he revealed on the day of Pentecost, an instinct that he had been taught by Jesus Himself. Peter's tendency to see everything through his own eyes was receding into the background, and he was learning to live as Jesus did—on every word that came from the mouth of God. His new instinct was to ask, "What does Scripture have to say about this situation?"

That is a great lesson for all of us to learn, but we can learn it only if we soak our hearts and our minds in God's Word. If the statistics about Christians are correct, then those of us who profess to be evangelicals may well be the most Scripture-ignorant generation of evangelical Christians since the time of the Reformation.

So what Peter learned is enormously and desperately important for us. We need to get back to our Bibles because we can't have a multiweek seminar with the Lord Jesus in any other way.

We'll need to think more about Pentecost tomorrow.

3

Welcome to the Last Days

JERUSALEM MUST HAVE BEEN AN AMAZING PLACE at Pentecost, with people from all over the world there for the feast—all kinds of colors, facial features, languages, and accents. Then around nine o'clock in the morning, something happens. People hear a strange sound, maybe even tornado-like. Then the group of Jesus' disciples are speaking to them in all their own different languages. No wonder they were asking the question, "What on earth does this mean?"

The spokesman of the little disciple band, Simon Peter, stands up and preaches a sermon. He even has a text from the second chapter of Joel. "These events," he says, "are exactly what Joel was talking about when he said that in the last days the Spirit of God would be poured out on all flesh, and sons and daughters would prophesy." So he says, "You need to realize that this means that the last days have begun."

Don't you love it when someone asks you, "Do you think we're living in the last days?" Because if you know your Bible, you say, "Yes, we're definitely living in the last days." When people ask that question, they are usually thinking: "There is global warming; there is conflict all over the world; there is some dictator who might be the antichrist. Maybe the end is near. Will there be a great tribulation? When will Jesus return? Are we living in the last days? Is the resurrection about to take place?" But that is not quite how the Bible sees things. That last question—When will the resurrection take place?—actually brings us to the heart of the matter because it's the resurrection that ushers in the last days.

That is what Peter is talking about here. The resurrection has taken place in the resurrection of Jesus. Paul will later say that Christ's resurrection, ascension, and enthronement has inaugurated the last days. His resurrection that inaugurates the last days is the firstfruits of the resurrection that will take place on the final day. The last days, therefore, have already begun.

Peter also says that the outpouring of the Spirit on the day of Pentecost is a visible sign that something has happened that divides history into two ages: the earlier days and the last days. That which from the Old Testament point of view was always "the future" has become "the now."

Before Pentecost, God's people were looking forward to the day of resurrection. Now God's people are living in light of that resurrection. As Paul puts it, "The old has passed away; behold, the new has come" (2 Cor. 5:17). A new creation has been inaugurated within the world that is dominated by the old creation. When we become Christians, we become part of that new creation, yet we still live in the context of the old one dominated by the world, the flesh, and the devil. The difference is that now we are living in the power of the risen Christ.

Pentecost, therefore, was a monumental occasion that leads Christians to see themselves, the world, and everything else in a monumentally different way. If you're a Christian, welcome to the last days! And so live today, knowing that you belong to the new creation that has been inaugurated in Christ.

The old has passed away; the new has come. As Paul says, if anyone is in Christ, then he or she is part of the new creation. When you begin to see your life through the lenses of Pentecost, even with the challenges you face, your life will have a wholly different atmosphere to it. When that is true of you, then there will be people who ask, as they asked on the day of Pentecost, "What's the explanation for this?"

And of course, our answer is the same as Simon Peter's—ultimately, it's Jesus.

4

The Promise of the Holy Spirit

IN PETER'S SERMON ON THE DAY OF PENTECOST, apart from the words he quotes from Joel 2, he mentions the Holy Spirit only once. Why is this the case? The answer is that his sermon is not so much about what the Spirit is doing, but about the fact that what the Spirit is doing tells us something about the Lord Jesus. That, of course, is consistent with Jesus' words in the upper room when He said, "[When the Spirit comes,] he will glorify me, for he will take what is mine and declare it to you" (John 16:14).

But there is another promise Jesus gave the Apostles in the upper room that is very relevant here. He said in John 14:16–17, "I will ask the Father, and he will give you another Helper, to be with you forever, even the Spirit of truth, whom the world cannot receive." Jesus was telling them that He was leaving them and going back to the Father. They were crestfallen. The prospect of His sending another Helper to be with them forever didn't really thrill them because what they wanted was Jesus Himself to be with them forever.

I wonder if you've ever reflected on Jesus' words here: "I will ask the Father, and he will give you another Helper." I suspect we don't think about them as much as we should in connection with the day of Pentecost, but clearly Simon Peter did. These words of Jesus lie behind something he says in his Pentecost sermon that I suspect we don't think enough about either. He says: "This Jesus God raised up, and of that we are all witnesses. Being therefore exalted at the right hand of God, *and having received from the Father the promise of the Holy Spirit*, he has poured out this that you yourselves are seeing and hearing" (Acts 2:32–33, emphasis added).

I wonder if you see what this means. Peter is saying: "What you can see and hear—the coming of the Holy Spirit—is actually evidence of something that you can't see or hear. It's evidence of a transaction that has taken place invisibly and inaudibly in heaven."

Try to imagine the scene: Jesus has ascended. He has finished His work. He has returned to the presence of His Father, and He is saying something. What's He saying? "Father, I promised them that I would ask You for something." And the Father says, "My Son, because of what You have done, You can ask Me for anything." The Lord Jesus says: "Father, You sent the Holy Spirit to be with Me throughout My life and ministry. He empowered Me. He sustained Me. I was resurrected by His power. I'm asking You if He may now be sent to be with My disciples because that was Our plan, wasn't it?"

Perhaps here we can imagine Jesus as referring to Psalm 2: "Ask of me, and I will make the nations your heritage" (v. 8). "Father, if the nations are to be My inheritance, Your Spirit needs to be poured out on all flesh. Abba, Father, let's send the Spirit."

And this is what happened on the day of Pentecost. The very same Spirit who had superintended the life of Jesus—His conception, His growth in the womb, His birth, His nurturing, His baptism, His temptations, His public ministry, His atoning work, His triumph over sin and death—is the Spirit He is now asking the Father to send to us.

That is the marvel of the day of Pentecost. Yes, there were external signs because it was a major event, but the really important thing was the internal reality. Jesus was not sending a different Holy Spirit from the One who had superintended His life, nor was He sending three thousand different Holy Spirits to those who professed His name. Rather, He asked the Father that the same Holy Spirit He had known—His Holy Spirit—would be sent to the church. And that is the wonder of Pentecost: that the same Holy Spirit that Jesus knew, we come to know.

There is a little-known hymn that has a line worth thinking about in this regard: "Think what Spirit dwells within thee." I suspect we don't think about that nearly often enough.

5

The Glory of Pentecost

WHAT DOES THE DAY OF PENTECOST MEAN? We've been seeking to answer that question all week, though we've only begun to scratch the surface. Today, I want to point out just one more dimension to Peter's answer to that question.

We've already seen that Peter's sermon quotes Joel 2:28–29: "And it shall come to pass afterward, that I will pour out my Spirit on all flesh; your sons and your daughters shall prophesy, your old men shall dream dreams, and your young men shall see visions. Even on the male and female servants in those days I will pour out my Spirit."

Is Peter saying here that the real indication that the Spirit has come in a person is that he or she prophesies? In a sense, the answer is both yes and no. Joel is saying that in the last days, something will be different from the days in which he wrote. In the last days—the days of the new covenant—things will be different from the days of the old covenant.

In the old covenant, prophesying, seeing visions, and dreaming dreams were typical ways in which God revealed Himself and His will to His people.

But we see in the Old Testament that this immediate, firsthand knowledge was not something that everyone had. In fact, it came in different forms, mediated through three specific roles or offices in the old covenant. Only a small number of men held these roles: the priest, the king, and the prophet. It was through these three ministries that

God made His Word, His forgiveness, and His rule known to His people. Amos 3:7 is helpful here: "For the Lord GOD does nothing without revealing his secret to his servants the prophets."

Not every old covenant believer had immediate access to the Lord's secret. In fact, only the prophet and those to whom he revealed it would have the secret. Prophesying, having dreams, seeing visions—that means having access to God's secret. In the old covenant, that was the firsthand experience of a very small number of people, who then mediated that secret to all the people. We might say that the knowledge of God and His will that people had under the old covenant was always secondhand; it was always mediated.

But now in Jesus Christ, all that has changed because He is the Prophet, the Priest, and the King. In fact, He is the secret. Doesn't the Apostle Paul speak about the fact that in Him the mystery (or "secret," as we might translate it) has been made known to us all? Now that Christ has come, now that Christ has worked, now that Christ has been exalted, we no longer need these other mediators to say to us, "Know the Lord," because through the gift of the Holy Spirit, we've all come to know Him, from the least to the greatest.

That is what Joel's words were looking forward to. He was describing the knowledge of the Lord that, in old covenant terms, came through prophecy, dreams, and visions, and saying that in the new covenant—in the one Prophet, Priest, and King, our Lord Jesus—by His Spirit, we all know the Lord immediately.

Peter understood that the coming of the Spirit of God to bring us immediately to Jesus and to faith and union with Him meant that we would know Him in this wonderful, firsthand, personal way. We would all have intimate access to Him, and we would all experience the forgiveness of sins, not by the pictures of sacrifices but by the knowledge of Jesus Christ crucified.

That, chiefly, was the wonder and glory of Pentecost. It meant that all believers—no matter their gender, social status, or country of origin—brought to Christ by the Spirit immediately and equally are brought into the knowledge of the Lord. And that isn't just restricted to the Jewish people; the Spirit was poured out on all flesh. Everyone was hearing the good news in their own language. And this was all because the Father had promised His Son, "Ask of me, and I will make the nations your heritage" (Ps. 2:8).

On the day of Pentecost, that internationalizing of the knowledge of God in Jesus Christ by the Holy Spirit was beginning.

No wonder we celebrate the day of Pentecost.

WEEK 23

The Person and Nature of Christ

1

Thinking about Jesus

MORE THAN ANY OTHER CULTURE IN HISTORY, ours has made it increasingly difficult for Christians to clear their minds of the noises and voices that crowd in on us. We've become a generation of people who possess vast amounts of fairly detached pieces of information.

One thing that has changed is that we used to learn things by researching books, which meant that the information we read was usually in its proper context. If you had a question about George Washington, you had to find a book on the American Colonies in the eighteenth century, and then find the sections that dealt with George Washington. Two things happened as a result. The first was that in that process, you learned more than you had set out to learn.

And second, you would find what you were looking for in its proper context. You didn't just type in your question and get a specific one-paragraph answer that was isolated from everything else that you might know.

I was a bit slow on the uptake in terms of technology. It was only by reading the work of some of my seminary students that I realized I could do what they were doing. Instead of going to my bookshelves to gain information, I could just type in my question, and presto, the answer would appear on the screen. But then it dawned on me that I was collecting fragments of a picture, but I didn't really know where and how those fragments fit into the frame.

The point I'm trying to make is that this bombardment of instant and often disconnected information has actually made it more difficult for us to be able to stop and reflect—even for a few minutes—on the person of the Lord Jesus Christ. It has made it harder for us to do what Hebrews 12 tells us to do: to look to Jesus and to consider Him.

Can you sit down and think for five uninterrupted minutes about the Lord Jesus and how great He is? Or is it the case that we can't concentrate on the Savior for a few minutes without our minds either being distracted and bouncing around to other things, or just shutting down because the effort seems to be beyond us? If that is the case, this is a worrying situation.

My purpose here is not to be harsh about our failures. That would just discourage us instead of encourage us and lift us up. But unless we recognize that we're struggling in this area, we won't make much progress. The first step to making progress is usually recognizing how weak we are and that we need help if things are to change.

So I want to spend this week thinking about the Lord Jesus Christ— or perhaps, more accurately, thinking about how we can think about Him. What we need is not to make up our own thoughts about Jesus. Rather, we need truths about Him to be brought to bear on our minds and our spirits that will lead us and help us think about Him. And that will happen only when our minds are informed and filled with the truth about Him.

One thing that always helps us think clearly is having a framework or an outline for our thoughts. So here's a simple framework that Christians have long used for meditating on the Lord Jesus: He is one person, and He has two natures.

This week, we'll try to fill in that outline a little.

2

The Person of the Son

I'VE NEVER HEARD ANYONE SAY THAT they suffer from "Christological attention deficit syndrome," but maybe you share my suspicion that many of us who are Christians experience this problem. We find it difficult to reflect on the Lord Jesus for even a few minutes at a time. If we're honest, we'd probably admit that one reason for this is that we don't actually know enough about the Lord Jesus to sustain prolonged meditation.

In minds that are often full of unconnected and disconnected pieces of information, and in a world full of many voices, what we need is for our minds to be better stocked with the knowledge of Christ: who He is and what He has done. That process of stocking up knowledge and retaining it is facilitated by having structures in our thinking that serve as foundation stones we can build on.

I remember a woman once telling me very sweetly (with the intention of encouraging me) that she'd listened five times to a recording of a sermon I'd preached, and every time she learned something new. I thanked her for her encouragement, and I meant it. But I also thought to myself, "If she had known something like the Shorter Catechism, she probably could have taken all that in by listening perhaps only twice."

The problem was not that she wasn't a keen Christian; it was that she didn't have what I think of as the Velcro strips of basic Christian doctrine. So in a sense, there was nowhere for most of the message to stick.

So here's a first Velcro strip to help us grow in our ability to reflect on the Lord Jesus Christ: He is a divine person. If we focus on that fact, we might be amazed at how—just like a pebble thrown into a pool—ripples of reflection might be created in our minds from Scripture. And before we know it, we begin to reflect on Him in wonder and worship.

Think, for example, about the dramatic way that Jesus is introduced in the gospel of John: He is the Word (1:1). It's interesting that John doesn't give the identity of this Word or tell us that it's Jesus until verse 17. But by the time he tells us, he has given us plenty of food for thought to reflect on and adore. Jesus was with God, face-to-face with God.

As Gregory of Nazianzus eloquently said, the moment that we think about the one person, we realize we must think about all three, and the moment we think about the three persons, we are carried back in our minds to think of the one God. Gregory said, "My sight is filled to the brim, yet the greater part of what I am thinking eludes me." Thinking about Jesus is an endless endeavor.

John's gospel more or less ends with that wonderful confession of doubting Thomas: "My Lord and my God!" (20:28). Between John 1 and John 21, we learn what it means that "the Word became flesh and dwelt among us, and we have seen his glory, glory as of the only Son from the Father" (1:14) and "from his fullness we have all received, grace upon grace" (v. 16).

Christ is the divine Creator. Through Him all things were made. But He became flesh so that through Him we might be remade. Only the Creator can fix things, and the Creator is God the Son. But things need to be fixed from within, so He became flesh so that through Him, by the Spirit's rebirth, we might be restored to the Father's family and might again have fellowship with God as His children.

That prompts us to begin to leaf through John's gospel in our minds, or perhaps to leaf through its pages with our fingers. As we do, we see in every chapter this divine person, the incarnate Son of God, entering the broken life, the blind life, or the confused life of a man or a woman—from the high-born and rich like Nicodemus and Joseph of Arimathea, to the quintuple-husbanded woman at the well, to the beggar at the pool of Bethesda, to the anonymous blind man whose sight He restored, to His dear friend Lazarus whom He raised from the dead, to the beloved disciples with whom He was so amazingly patient.

As those ripples begin to appear on the pool of our minds, we're beginning to spend time in the presence of Jesus. It makes us want to sing, "Who is He in yonder stall?" or "in deep distress?" or "on yonder tree?" We want to sing: "'Tis the Lord, O wondrous story! 'Tis the Lord, the King of glory! At His feet we humbly fall, crown Him, crown Him, Lord of all!"

3

Truly God and Truly Man

THIS WEEK, WE ARE THINKING TOGETHER ABOUT what helps us to meditate lovingly on our Lord Jesus Christ. On Monday, I suggested that some Christians have long found that there are basic building blocks that help us. Christ is one divine person with two natures—a divine nature and a human nature—united in one person. Yesterday, we were thinking about our Lord's divine person. Today, I want to think with you about the fact that He has two natures.

The Son has always had a divine nature. He has all the qualities of God. He is, as the Shorter Catechism says, "infinite, eternal, and unchangeable in his being, wisdom, power, holiness, justice, goodness, and truth." He is the Lord of creation. He is the Lord of providence and history. As the divine Son, He has always enjoyed perfect union and communion with the Father and the Spirit, face-to-face with God, dwelling in unimaginably great mutual love and joy together.

Knowing this makes John's statement at the beginning of his gospel so utterly amazing to us: "The Word became flesh and dwelt among us" (1:14). The eternal Word took on a human nature, conceived as a male child in the womb of a young virgin named Mary, in the remote region of the Roman Empire that had been renamed the province of Palestine.

In one sense, you can almost sympathize with the early Christian apologist Tertullian when he wrote, "I believe this because it's incredible," although he should have said that he believed it although it was incomprehensible. We can say it and believe it, we can describe it, but we can't fully comprehend it, far less explain it. And then we remember that God is God and we are not God, so this is hardly surprising.

It's also not surprising that the early Christian theologians had to work pretty hard to put all this into words. When they did so, they knew that they were not giving an *explanation* of the incarnation. Rather, they were giving a *description* and *exposition* of what happened that would help protect Christians from taking false steps in how they thought about or described the Lord Jesus.

Think about it this way: You don't like people wrongly describing your spouse, your parents, your children, or your friends, do you? These great Christian thinkers wanted to prevent us from misdescribing the Lord Jesus. In what's called the Definition of Chalcedon, written in AD 451, a group of Christian thinkers tried to summarize the biblical teaching. This is what they wrote:

> Following, then, the holy fathers, we all unanimously teach that our Lord Jesus Christ is to us one and the same Son, the self-same perfect in Godhead, the self-same perfect in manhood; truly God and truly man; the self-same of a rational soul and body; co-essential with the Father according to the Godhead, the self-same co-essential with us according to the

manhood; like us in all things, sin apart; before the ages begotten of the Father as to the Godhead, but in the last days, the self-same, for us and for our salvation born of Mary the Virgin *theotokos* as to the manhood; one and the same Christ, Son, Lord, only-begotten; acknowledged in two natures unconfusedly, unchangeably, indivisibly, inseparably; the difference of the natures being in no way removed because of the union, but rather the properties of each nature being preserved, and both concurring into one person and one hypostasis; not as though He were parted or divided into two persons, but one and the self-same Son and only-begotten God, Word, Lord, Jesus Christ; even as from the beginning the prophets have taught concerning Him, and as the Lord Jesus Christ Himself hath taught us, and as the symbol of the fathers hath handed down to us.

That is a stunning statement, and I know it's a mouthful. But perhaps one or two of those phrases grab you and lead you to respond, "I need to think more about that."

4

Coessential with the Father

AS WE SAW YESTERDAY, THE DEFINITION of Chalcedon was carefully worded to help us think clearly and deeply about Christ. Christians can be a bit impatient with that kind of detailed thinking, can't we? But if we were musicians, we wouldn't be impatient with those funny squiggles that Beethoven made on pieces of paper. We wouldn't say, "Oh, it's all just far too complex and dense," if we were listening to the *Moonlight Sonata* or his Sixth Symphony.

Neither should we think about the dense words of the great theological statements as too complicated. They give us a beautiful, detailed description of our Lord and Savior, Jesus Christ. These theologians weren't just being theoretical. They were concerned about ways of thinking about Jesus that are not really faithful to Scripture.

That is why the Definition of Chalcedon is still helpful to us: it can save us from false ways of thinking about Jesus. We will look at four of these false ways of thinking—two today, and the other two tomorrow. They are all associated with particular historical individuals, although the views they expressed were, and still are, not limited to these individuals.

Chalcedon says that Christ is "perfect in Godhead, . . . co-essential with the Father." The writers were responding here to Arianism, a view associated with the fourth-century cleric Arius. He was resisted by the great Athanasius, who was frequently exiled because of his faithfulness to Scripture and to Christ. Arius and those he influenced held that the Son was the greatest of all of God's creation but was not Himself God. The beliefs of Arius are alive and well today in Jehovah's Witnesses and in many Unitarians.

Why is this so important? The greatest thinkers in the Christian church have always had one question at the back of their minds when they've thought about our Lord Jesus Christ: "Could this Christ I am describing actually be qualified to be my Savior? If not, then I must be describing Him wrongly."

The problem, then, with Arianism is that if Jesus isn't truly God, then He can't reconcile us to God. Only God can reconcile us to God. If you're alienated from someone, I can perhaps *facilitate* a reconciliation, but only that other person can *effect* the reconciliation. This is the wonderful truth of the gospel that Paul expresses in 2 Corinthians 5:19: "In Christ God was reconciling the world to himself, not counting their trespasses against them."

Chalcedon went on to say that the Son is also "co-essential with us according to the manhood." Here, they were thinking about the false teaching of Apollinarianism. Apollinaris lived at the end of the fourth century and was a strong opponent of Arianism. Apollinaris, however, emphasized the full deity of Jesus by saying that the divine Logos took the place of the *nous*, or the rational soul, in the incarnation of the Lord.

What's the problem with that? Well, if Jesus' *nous*, His mind, was not human but instead was replaced by something divine, then the Lord Jesus isn't really coessential with us; He is not truly human. And if He is not truly human, He is not really one of us. In fact, He would be a kind of superhuman. And if that is the case, He can't really represent us. He can't be obedient in our place. The fact that He is not truly human disqualifies Him from being the substitute for our sins and securing our salvation (see Heb. 2:5–18).

What Chalcedon is really saying to us is this: We have a great Savior who is truly one of us. He is truly like us—except in regard to sin—and that is what qualifies Him to be our Savior. He is God, and that is what qualifies Him to reconcile us to God. That is the message of Chalcedon. The more you think about it, the more it will help you to think clearly about the Lord Jesus.

And the more you think clearly about the Lord Jesus, the more you'll love Him.

5

One Person, Two Natures

THIS WEEK, WE HAVE THOUGHT ABOUT Jesus in relationship to His true deity and His true humanity. We will conclude our reflections this week by looking at another statement in the Definition of Chalcedon. It says that Jesus Christ, the God-man, is "acknowledged in two natures unconfusedly, unchangeably, indivisibly, inseparably; the difference of the natures being in no way removed because of the union, but rather the properties of each nature being preserved, and both concurring into one person and one hypostasis; not as though He were parted or divided into two persons, but one and the self-same Son and only-begotten God, Word, Lord, Jesus Christ."

The Chalcedonian theologians had a couple of errors in mind when they penned these words. One is called Eutychianism, named after Eutyches, who taught in Constantinople in the first half of the fifth century. Eutyches held that Christ was *of* two natures but not *in* two natures. That view is sometimes called the Monophysite heresy. It held that in the incarnation, the divine nature and the human nature were combined in the Lord Jesus. In other words, He had a kind of new nature, a third kind of nature, a God man nature without the hyphen.

The Chalcedonian theologians were also reacting against another deviant view associated with Nestorius, who was briefly the patriarch of Constantinople. There have been questions about exactly what Nestorius taught, but the view named after him held that in Jesus, we have not only two natures, human and divine, but also a human person and a divine person. Nestorius objected to calling Mary *theotokos*, the God-bearer. Instead, he wanted to call her *Christotokos*, the Christ-bearer, as though there were two persons.

This is why Chalcedon says that Christ possesses His human and divine natures "indivisibly, inseparably; the difference of the natures being in no way removed because of the union, but rather the properties of each nature being preserved, and both concurring into one person and one hypostasis; not as though He were parted or divided into two persons, but one and the self-same Son and only-begotten God, Word, Lord, Jesus Christ."

The reason that this is all so important is that we want to describe our Lord Jesus properly and accurately because we love Him. The touchstone is always this: If this is true of the Lord Jesus Christ, is He really qualified to be the Savior of human sinners? If He is two persons and not one person, then as Nestorius's critics saw, it's impossible to see how there was a real incarnation at all. I don't think Nestorius intended that implication, but the law of unintended consequences operates in theology as well as in daily life.

When they wrote the Definition of Chalcedon, these early theologians were trying to correct false views of Christ because they were concerned with thinking and speaking properly about Him.

I'm reminded of a weekend when Dr. R.C. Sproul spoke at the church where Derek Thomas and I served. One Sunday morning, he preached a fine message on the person of Christ that was full of this great Christology. Afterward, at the door, a man shook hands with Derek and said to him vigorously, "It's about time somebody was teaching some theology to us in this church!"

I used to love telling R.C. that story. After all, Derek and I were both professors of theology. Weren't we doing that? I still smile at this. But the man made an important point: without theology, without great Christology, without patiently thinking things through, we don't really have a very good foundation on which to build our Christian lives. So it's worth the hard thinking.

Until next week, I hope you can think as deeply as you can about the Lord Jesus.

WEEK 24

The Work of Christ

1

Every Spiritual Blessing in Christ

LAST WEEK, WE LOOKED AT ONE of the most wonderful (and also one of the most intellectually challenging) topics we could ever discuss: the person of the Lord Jesus Christ. The Apostle Paul put it this way: "Great . . . is the mystery of godliness: He was manifested in the flesh" (1 Tim. 3:16). Thinking about the person of Christ brings us again and again to the point where we say: "Lord, You are too great and high for me, and You stooped so low in taking my humanity. I want to confess the mystery of Your person. I want to know You and trust You and love You better." Therefore, this week we will continue thinking about Jesus, but we will discuss His *work* rather than His *person*.

Yet we need to avoid a misstep as we do so. We often talk about the person *and* the work of Jesus Christ, and our theology textbooks tend to do the same thing. In one sense, it's a very natural division. His divine person, in two natures, is a huge topic to study. And what He came to accomplish, His work, is another huge topic to reflect on. Yet we must never separate Christ's work from Christ's person. His work occurred in space and time in human history, but it didn't take place outside Him. We speak about His person *and* His work, but we can't abstract His work from Him, as though it were something separate from or outside Christ Himself. In a sense, His work is embodied in Him. That is why He took a body.

We see this in the words of Hebrews 10:5–7, in which Jesus is quoted as saying: "Sacrifices and offerings you have not desired, but a body have you prepared for me. . . . 'Behold, I have come to do your will, O God.' " All of Christ's work for us took place in and through the body that He assumed and possessed—and perhaps, just as amazingly, still possesses in the presence of His Father.

Sometimes the gospel has been sincerely and earnestly preached as though when we come to believe in Christ, there are specific things— almost like commodities—that He transfers to you. It's as though He has something you don't have, and He gives it to you so that you now have it and He does not. I suspect that sometimes people think this way when a preacher tells them to come to Christ for justification, or for reconciliation, or for adoption.

But there is a potential danger in that way of thinking. It can lead people to think that they can have these blessings apart from Jesus Christ Himself, or that they can have Christ's salvation without Christ's lordship. But the New Testament makes clear that you can't do that; you can have only Jesus Christ. And when you have Him, you have everything in Him. When that dawns on us, it's a great protection against seeking blessings instead of seeking and trusting the Lord Jesus Himself, in whom these blessings are found, and in whom they are experienced.

That is one of the big points in Paul's lyrical passage in Ephesians 1:3-14. Every spiritual blessing—redemption, pardon, adoption, sanctification—is to be found in Jesus Christ and only in Jesus Christ. As Paul puts it very succinctly to the Corinthians: "[Christ] became to us wisdom from God, righteousness and sanctification and redemption" (1 Cor. 1:30).

We'll look at some of these specific blessings this week, but before doing so, it was important to first make sure that we avoid this mistake of seeking or wanting blessings but not looking to the Lord Jesus Himself. That was one of the mistakes that led people into the muddle-headedness of thinking that a person can trust Christ as Savior without having Him as Lord, as though one could have salvation but not sanctification, or forgiveness but not holiness.

No, we can have only Jesus Christ Himself, and He is both Savior and Lord. And gloriously, when we have Him, then all these blessings are ours in Him as well.

2

The Propitiation for Our Sins

THE AUTHOR OF HEBREWS TELLS US that Christ is able to save us completely (Heb. 7:25). But if this is true, then what Christ has done for us (what we often refer to as His work) must meet our needs. But here we should pause. Some people assume they know what their needs are. And the danger of that assumption is that we then begin to assess Christ's work in terms of our understanding of our own needs.

We actually need to turn things around and assess our needs in light of what Christ has done. Because we really understand our needs only when we see what He had to do in order to meet them. And so for the rest of the week, we will think about four New Testament words that help us to understand our needs and Christ's work.

The first word is *propitiation*. Paul uses it in Romans 3:25 when he says that God put Christ forward "as a propitiation by his blood, to be received by faith." John uses it in 1 John 2:2: "He is the propitiation for our sins, and not for ours only but also for the sins of the whole world."

But what does *propitiation* mean? It's not a word that we use much today. It refers to the idea of doing something that averts or exhausts the anger or wrath of another. When Paul and John speak about the Lord Jesus as a propitiation, they are thinking back to the temple sacrifices of the Old Testament. These sacrifices were made in the recognition that because of human sin and rebellion, the people were exposed to the wrath of God, and a sacrifice needed to be made.

Maybe that is the reason we don't speak much today about propitiation. We don't like thinking about the wrath of God, and we like even less thinking that we are under that wrath. When people are awakened to the dangerous condition they are in, they tend to say things like, "I need to do better." But even if they were to be perfect from that point on, they'd still not escape the wrath of God. Why? Because, as Paul says, it's revealed against *all* ungodliness and unrighteousness (see Rom. 1:18). We can't compensate for our past sins by putting new obedience on the scales to try to balance it. We deserve the wrath of God for all our sin.

There is another reason we don't speak much about propitiation today. We don't like to think of God as so perfectly holy that He can't look on our sin, or to think that anything unholy entering His presence would be undone by it, just as the prophet Isaiah experienced, crying out because he felt he was disintegrating in the presence of God.

But the place where we see what sin really is and deserves is not in the temple with Isaiah but at the cross of Calvary with the Lord Jesus.

If we want to understand what the wrath of God is, then we need to see and hear Jesus bearing it. When God's wrath was poured out, God's beloved Son, supported by the Holy Spirit, cried out "My God, my God, why have you forsaken me?" (Matt. 27:46) out of a sense of absolute God-forsakenness. The world outside had grown dark during the hours of His passion. But the world within, the world He inhabited, was one of pain and deep darkness. And His deepest pain was that sense of divine abandonment.

As Simon Peter came to see, Jesus carried our sins in His own body to the tree (see 1 Peter 2:24). That is where we see the wrath of God. That is what we deserve because of our sins. It's because He bore our sins in our place that He has become the propitiation for our sins.

Many modern scholars think that the Greek word Paul uses here, *hilastērion*, should actually be translated "mercy seat," partly because it's the word used for the mercy seat in the Septuagint, the Greek translation of the Old Testament that Paul used. Whether that is correct or not, certainly the mercy seat helps us grasp something about Christ's propitiation. Paul says that God the Father put forth Jesus as a *hilastērion*, and that is both the horror and the wonder of the mercy of God in Christ. The horror is God's wrath against our sin. The wonder is God's love that He provides mercy in the propitiatory sacrifice of His Son.

In the hymn "Beneath the Cross of Jesus," Elizabeth Clephane speaks about the cross as the trysting place where heaven's love and heaven's justice meet. That is why we thank God that Jesus Christ is the propitiation for our sins.

3

God Justifies the Ungodly

YESTERDAY, WE WERE THINKING ABOUT THE word *propitiation*. That is a word that belongs to the temple and to the sacrifices that avert the wrath of God. Today, we will move from the temple to the law court, because in Jesus Christ we discover not only the propitiation for our sins, but also that in Jesus Christ there is *justification*. That is a huge and glorious subject—far too much to talk about in a brief devotional. But let me underline a few things that are helpful to us about being counted righteous in God's sight, which is what *justification* means.

The first is this: what the gospel teaches us is the staggering truth that God justifies those who in themselves are ungodly. As long as we think of ourselves as partly godly, or more or less godly, or just as godly as the next person, we're never going to understand the gospel, and we're never going to be justified.

In telling the parable of the tax collector and the Pharisee, Jesus asked: "Which of them went home from the temple justified? The tax collector or the Pharisee?" Every evangelical knows the answer: the tax collector was justified. But what if we retitled the parable as the tax collector and the evangelical? That would be a bit of a shock. But isn't there still a tendency in many of us who are evangelicals to thank God that we are not like others, to think that there are all kinds of good things that we do, and even to think, "I thank You, God, that I'm not like him or her"?

The great spiritual physicians have always recognized how easy it is for us to fall back into thinking that we are justified because of our sanctification. In other words, we can think that we are justified because we've become the kind of person that God would justify. But our real Christian joy rests in this: that it's not the godly or the becoming godly whom God justifies, but the ungodly. Some might say: "Well, that is a dangerous doctrine to teach. Preach that, and people will live any way they please." That is exactly the charge that was leveled against Paul's preaching on the doctrine of justification. And that is why he showed how wrong that complaint was in his letter to the Romans.

The second thing to emphasize is this: justification—being counted righteous because of Christ's righteousness and not our own—takes place at the very beginning of the Christian life when we come to trust in Christ. Because it's Christ's righteousness that is counted to us, that righteousness is perfect. It's complete; it's final; and it's absolutely irreversible. Every true Christian is therefore justified from the beginning of their Christian life with the same righteousness of Jesus Christ.

Let's try to bring out just how stunning this is by way of illustration. Imagine there are two women reading this book. The first is Sarah Jones. Sarah is seventy-five. She has been a Christian since she was fifteen. She spent forty years serving as a nurse on the mission field, and now back home, she is probably the most respected and loved person in the whole church. The second is Sarah Smith. She just became a Christian three Sundays ago, also at age fifteen. Listen to this: seventy-five-year-old sanctified Sarah Jones is no more justified than fifteen-year-old new believer Sarah Smith. And Sarah Smith is no less justified than Sarah Jones.

There can be two different responses to that statement. One is, "Yes, absolutely right." And the other is this: "There is something about that that makes me feel uncomfortable. It can't be right to say that a girl of fifteen who has just become a Christian can be as justified as a seventy-five-year-old saint." Well, the truth is that the person who is justified by faith can never be more justified than he was the moment he came to faith, because he is not justified with his own righteousness; he is justified with Christ's righteousness. He can never add to that. And the wonderful news is that it's not only perfect; it's final, and it's irreversible.

There is much more to say about justification, but this is one thing that makes justification so wonderful, so liberating, so joy-producing, so life-changing.

I hope you're finding that to be true.

4

Redemption through His Blood

A THIRD WORD THAT HELPS US understand the work of Christ is *redemption*. It's a word drawn from the world of slavery, which was common in the Roman Empire in which Jesus and the Apostles lived. Some scholars suggest that maybe a third of the population of Rome were slaves. The empire depended on slaves. Some were treated very harshly, but others were more like employees. Slavery also existed among the people of God in the Old Testament. In some instances, it was a way to get out of debt.

But unlike in our society, in which a person for all practical purposes sells forty hours in their week to someone else, and that person or company "owns" those hours of their life, every hour of every day of a slave's life belonged to his or her master. The master's will was the law that governed the slave's life.

It was possible, both in Rome and in Judaism, for a slave to purchase his or her freedom and be set free by the payment of a price—the redemption price. The New Testament uses that language to describe what Jesus has done for us. Through His death, He has redeemed us. He has paid the redemption price needed to set us free. Paul says that we are "justified by his grace as a gift, through the redemption that is in Christ Jesus" (Rom. 3:24). Jesus put it this way: "Truly, truly, I say to you, everyone who practices sin is a slave to sin," but "if the Son sets you free, you will be free indeed" (John 8:34, 36).

Most people don't think of themselves as being slaves to sin. But that is partly because they have a very selective and superficial view of what sin is. Remember the rich young ruler? He might not have been perfect in his own eyes, but he kept the commandments (at least externally), and he certainly didn't think of himself as a sinner, much less a slave. But when Jesus put His finger on the young man's wealth, it turned out that he was enslaved to it. Not only was that the case, but the young man wasn't able to free himself from it. And so he turned his back on Jesus.

Not every sinful bondage is a bondage to the obvious sins. The dark truth is that by nature we follow the ways of the prince of the power of the air and the course of this world. We walk in all kinds of sinfulness. We are dead, and therefore powerless, and therefore enslaved to sin. We need to be redeemed.

The good news is that Jesus Christ is a Redeemer. In the Old Testament, a relative, a kinsman, could redeem a family member. Christ, therefore, has become our kinsman, taking our human nature so that He might die in our place and redeem us. He has done everything needed to set us free from our bondage to sin, death, and Satan.

How has Jesus done that? By dealing with the guilt that led to the bondage. He has done it by setting us free from the dominion of sin over us because, in His death, He died to sin once for all in order that we might die to sin in Him and be liberated from its dominion. There is full redemption in Jesus Christ.

But we need to remember that redemption isn't a commodity that Jesus hands over to us; it's a reality that we experience when we're united to Him. We have redemption *in* Jesus Christ. It's found only in Him. It's not given to us as an item we can get without having Jesus Christ Himself.

I hope you have found that you, too, are in Christ and that He is your Redeemer.

5

Reconciliation in Christ

THIS WEEK, WE'VE DISCUSSED HOW JESUS provides for us a *propitiation* that saves us from God's wrath, a *justification* that saves us from our guilt, and a *redemption* that sets us free from our bondage to sin. So in a sense, we've visited the temple, the law court, and the slave market. But now there is a fourth word to think about. It's the word *reconciliation*, and it has to do with personal relationships.

Of these four words, perhaps *reconciliation* has the most contemporary ring to it. It implies that there has been alienation. We've become increasingly familiar with the idea of alienation in personal relationships: husbands alienated from their wives, children alienated from their parents. And in the world of the individual, there is a new psychological vocabulary that has developed: an individual being alienated from himself or herself. There are all kinds of ways that this idea has taken root today. We have entire organizations and specialists in all kinds of fields whose goal or expertise is to bring about reconciliation or a new integration, because alienation involves disintegration.

What the Bible teaches us is that all these alienations, these disintegrations, have a single root. Every human alienation is rooted in our alienation from God. We are at enmity with Him because of our sin, and He is at enmity with us in our sinfulness. Only when reconciliation takes place will our lives begin to be reintegrated. Only when our alienation from God, caused by our sin, is dealt with can these secondary alienations begin to find a resolution.

In 2 Corinthians 5, Paul tells us that God has provided the reconciliation we need in Jesus Christ. The root of the Greek word for *reconciliation* is actually "change" or "exchange," and that is what we find in Christ. In Christ, God has made what the Reformers used to love to call the great or wonderful exchange. God was, in Christ, reconciling the world to Himself in this way: "For our sake he made [Jesus] to be sin who knew no sin, so that in him we might become the righteousness of God" (2 Cor. 5:21). Jesus has made an exchange. He has changed places with us. He takes our sin, and in Him, we are counted righteous with His righteousness.

Jesus is the Suffering Servant about whom Isaiah 53 speaks: He was wounded for our transgressions. He was crushed for our iniquities. Upon Him was the chastisement that brought us peace, and with His stripes, we are healed. All we like sheep have gone astray. We have turned to our own way. And the Lord has laid on Him the iniquity of us all. It's exchange, exchange, exchange.

But Paul also tells us that when we receive this exchange, this reconciliation in Christ, there is a series of exchanges that begin to take place in our lives. Yes, we exchange enmity with God for His friendship. But we also exchange the life of the old creation for that of the new: "If anyone is in Christ, he is a new creation," or literally, "If any in Christ—new creation" (2 Cor. 5:17). We exchange the old way of thinking about other people. We usually see them according to merely human perspectives, but now we exchange all that. We have new eyes to see them in the light of the judgment seat of Christ, and we have compassion on them.

And there is another exchange, Paul says. We no longer live for ourselves as we used to do, but for the Lord Jesus, who has reconciled us to God. We no longer run from Him as our enemy; we run toward Him as our friend and Savior. We live for ourselves no longer but for Christ, who died for us and rose again.

Jesus has done everything we need to live the reconciled life. Propitiation, justification, redemption, reconciliation—it's all ours in Jesus Christ. And if we are in Christ, then it really is all ours.

No wonder we've been taught to sing, "Hallelujah! what a Savior!"

WEEK 25

The Holy Spirit

1

Knowing the Holy Spirit

IN OUR STUDY THIS WEEK, we will reflect on something invisible. Or to be more accurate, *Someone* invisible. We're going to look at the ministry of the Holy Spirit. John 3 records Jesus' famous words to Nicodemus, in which He compared the work of the Spirit to the wind. In both Hebrew and Greek, the same words are used for *wind* and *spirit*. Jesus is saying here that the Spirit's work is like the wind in the sense that you can't actually see Him, but you know He is there because of His effects on people.

In my early days as a Christian, it seemed as though everyone who spoke on the subject of the Holy Spirit had all read the same book, because they usually began by saying, "The Holy Spirit is the forgotten person of the Godhead." When that was said often enough, it started to sound believable. I'm not sure whether I believed it, but in my teens, I was too young to know any better.

The more I heard this statement, the more I realized that what they were really talking about was the so-called charismatic gifts of the Spirit. It slowly became clear to me that much of this kind of talk was actually about power, about unusual gifts, and not really about the person of the Holy Spirit Himself. It was about having powers, not about knowing a person.

This isn't surprising, because often the same thing happens with both the Father and the Son. We focus attention on what They can give us and what we can get from Them, and much less attention on who They are and how we can know Them. It's easy for us to focus on the blessings that God gives to us without actually growing in the knowledge of our benefactor. Maybe it seems more relevant (and easier) to talk about these blessings rather than talk about who Jesus is as one divine person in two natures; or about Jesus exercising His threefold ministry as Prophet, Priest, and King; or about His two states of humiliation and exaltation. That all sounds very complicated until we realize that as we think about these things, we get to know Him better.

The same is true of the Holy Spirit. If we focus only on the blessings that He gives us, we are a bit like a husband who enjoys eating the meal his wife has made but hardly ever reflects on the wife who prepared it. If that is true of the Father and the Son, then I suspect it's even more so when it comes to the Holy Spirit, because *Father* and *Son* are words that naturally have a deep resonance with us by way of human experience. In light of Jesus' words in John 14:9, "Whoever has seen me has seen the Father," we've got some very visible evidence recorded in the Scriptures about the Father and the Son, how they relate to one another, and how they relate to us. But when we say "Holy Spirit," there seems to be something remote, distant, and opaque about who

He is. Perhaps it's not surprising, then, that we sometimes hear Christians refer to Him as an "it"—not a person but an impersonal force or power, just like the wind.

Scripture tells us about the work of the Holy Spirit in part to help us know Him better, and it's on getting to know Him that we will focus our attention this week. So even though we will talk about what He does for us and in us, I want to encourage you to ask yourself this question: "What does this tell me about Him?" Of course, we need the light of Scripture to help us think about this—not only what the Spirit does but who the Spirit is who does it.

It's sometimes said that the one thing we know about the Spirit is that He glorifies Christ and not Himself; therefore, we shouldn't focus attention on Him. But that is a muddleheaded statement. The fact that He doesn't glorify Himself doesn't mean that we shouldn't glorify Him. The Nicene Creed states, "We believe in the Holy Spirit, the Lord and Giver of Life; who proceeds from the Father and the Son; who with the Father and the Son together is worshiped and glorified; who spoke by the prophets."

These words are a kind of litmus test of our knowledge of and our relationship to the Holy Spirit. As we close today, it's worth asking yourself this question: "Do I worship and glorify the Spirit together with the Father and the Son?"

To do that, we need to get to know Him better.

2

Another Helper

THIS WEEK, WE'RE THINKING ABOUT THE person of the Holy Spirit. And like everything else in the Christian life, we can't just sit down and say, "I'm going to think about the Holy Spirit." We don't think up what we think. In some ways, it would be more accurate to say that our thinking needs to come down to us. In other words, the knowledge of the Holy Spirit needs to flow down into our minds from the mountain of Scripture and its teaching. But where do we begin?

We could turn to Genesis 1 and work our way forward in Scripture. That would certainly make for a great Bible study, but it would be a lengthy one and fairly slow, especially if you're a new Christian. Often, the best place to start with teaching that is either new or difficult to accept is to ask this question: "What did the Lord Jesus believe and teach about this?" Especially if we find something difficult to accept, asking this question can help us to get over the emotional hurdles we sometimes feel. Because if Jesus believed something, then we want to believe it, too, if we're Christians. If it was important to Him, then it's important to us. And if we're His disciples, we want to try to understand it and believe it.

The Lord Jesus spoke to His disciples about the Holy Spirit on a number of occasions. He assured them that the Father wanted to give them the gift of the Spirit. But it seems that it was only in the last hours of His life that He taught them more fully. So perhaps the place to look for His fullest teaching is John 14–16, which records what Jesus said in the upper room in those last hours before He went out to be arrested and then crucified.

What did Jesus tell His disciples about the Spirit? The first thing He tells them about the Spirit is this: "I will ask the Father, and he will give you another Helper, to be with you forever, even the Spirit of truth, whom the world cannot receive, because it neither sees him nor knows him. You know him, for he dwells with you and will be in you" (John 14:16–17). The Greek word for "helper" is *paraklētos*, from which we derive the English word *paraclete*.

Notice that Jesus says "another Helper." In Greek, there are two different words that can be translated "another." Our English word *another* can mean "another of the same kind." For example, if your little boy eats a cookie and says, "May I have another?," he means that he wants another cookie of the same kind. But *another* can also mean "another of a different kind." Maybe your little boy takes a bite of the cookie and says: "I don't like chocolate chip cookies. May I have another one?" He means another one of a different kind. The Greek language usually, although not always, uses different words in these two different situations. And in John 14:16, the word "another" in "another Helper" is the word *allos*, which means "another of the same kind."

Jesus tells the disciples here that He is going to ask the Father to give them another Helper, One who is just like the Helper they already have—that is, the same kind of Helper as Jesus Himself. They won't have Jesus with them in the way He was with them in the upper room, but the One who will be sent to them will be another just like Jesus. The Holy Spirit will be everything to them that Jesus had been to them.

Later, in John 16:7, Jesus says something further that must have staggered the disciples. It still staggers us today. He said that it was to the disciples' advantage that He was going away, because otherwise the Spirit, the other Helper, wouldn't come to them. Perhaps these words are the best litmus test of how well we know the Spirit. Because most of us, like the disciples, would surely be inclined to say, "Jesus, I'd far rather have You with me the way You were present in the upper room than have the Holy Spirit."

Imagine being able to hear Jesus' voice, to see His gesticulations, to listen to His words, to gaze at His face, to feel His presence. Imagine what the beloved disciple, who was reclining at table close to Jesus, must have felt when he heard these words. Nothing could substitute for Jesus. How could Jesus leaving and another Helper coming possibly be to his advantage?

Of course, the answer is that the Spirit is another just like Jesus.

We'll return to this tomorrow. But in the meantime, remember that if you are a Christian, the other Helper who is just like Jesus is with you.

And as we'll see, He is more than just with you.

3

The Indwelling of the Holy Spirit

WHICH WOULD YOU RATHER HAVE: Jesus or the Holy Spirit? Most of us would probably say Jesus. But we'll never really get to know the Holy Spirit unless we get to the bottom of Jesus' words in John 16:7 ("It is to your advantage that I go away, for if I do not go away, the Helper will not come to you."). The key to understanding them is found in His earlier words, where He said that the world can't receive the Spirit because it doesn't see Him or know Him. But then He added, "You know him, for he dwells with you and will be in you" (John 14:17).

These words are often understood as if the Lord Jesus was meaning something like this: "In the old covenant, the Spirit was *with* God's people. But in the new covenant, He is going to be *in* God's people." In other words, people understand this as though Jesus was answering the question of the difference between the old covenant experience of the Spirit and the new covenant experience—and His answer was that the Spirit was *with* people in the old, but He is *in* people in the new.

I want to suggest that we think about these words in a different way, because I believe that what our Lord is actually saying is this: "Unlike the world that doesn't know the Spirit, you *already* know the Spirit I'm going to send to you *because you've seen Him in Me*. You've seen Him dwelling in My life these past three years. He has been with you *in Me*. And it's that very same Spirit who has been with you in Me, indwelling Me these years—*He* is the Holy Spirit I'm going to ask the Father to send to you."

In Numbers 11, the Lord took the Spirit who had been on Moses and shared that same Spirit with the seventy elders, and they started prophesying and praising God. The same thing happened to two other men, Eldad and Medad, and someone complained: "They shouldn't be prophesying. They shouldn't have the Spirit." Moses responded:

"I wish all the Lord's people were like that. I wish the Lord would give all His people the Spirit He has given to me and the seventy elders." Now what Jesus is saying is this: "What Moses and the law couldn't do, I'm going to do because you're all going to receive the very same Spirit you have seen and known in Me."

Some weeks ago, we noticed the often-overlooked words of Simon Peter in his Pentecost sermon. He said, "Being therefore exalted at the right hand of God, and having received from the Father the promise of the Holy Spirit, he has poured out this that you yourselves are seeing and hearing" (Acts 2:33). In other words, the Lord Jesus ascended to heaven and said: "Father, You promised Me something, and it's time for that promise to be fulfilled. You promised that I could send the very same Holy Spirit who dwelt in Me to dwell in My dear friends, My disciples, and then in all Christians."

Do you see what this means? It means that the Holy Spirit who was in the life of Jesus from the moment of His conception until the end of His life, when by the power of the eternal Spirit He offered Himself as a sacrifice to the Father, is the same Spirit that the Lord Jesus was promising to give to His disciples. Not another spirit, but the Spirit of the Lord Jesus.

It's not surprising that the disciples couldn't take this in. But this is why the Spirit is another Helper just like Jesus: because He *is* the Spirit who was dwelling in the life of Jesus those thirty-three years. And that is the Spirit He promised to send to the disciples.

The implications of this are too wonderful for words. Jesus Himself in His flesh could not indwell His disciples, but He can do that by His Spirit.

We can think about it this way: How many Holy Spirits are there? Is there the Holy Spirit who dwelt in Jesus, and then another Holy Spirit who came to indwell the disciples, and perhaps a multitude of Holy Spirits who come to indwell each of us? No. Is there one Holy Spirit who dwelt in Jesus and another Holy Spirit who dwells in all disciples? No. There is only one Holy Spirit—the very same Holy Spirit who indwelt the Lord Jesus throughout the whole course of His life. And when *He* comes to indwell a believer, then we understand why it's to our advantage that Jesus has gone to the Father and asked the Father if He could send His own Holy Spirit to every single one of His disciples.

It's because each Christian is indwelt by one and the same Spirit of the Lord Jesus that we are so wonderfully united, first of all, to the Lord Jesus Himself, and then to each other.

It's no wonder that the Apostle Paul says that Christ indwelling us by the Holy Spirit is the hope of glory. We'll think more about that tomorrow.

4

The Spirit of Christ

YESTERDAY, WE DISCUSSED JESUS' WELL-KNOWN words to His disciples in John 14:17, in which He tells them that the Spirit they had seen in Jesus was now going to indwell them. I suggested that Jesus' words here are not about the difference between an Old Testament believer and a New Testament believer but rather about the difference between seeing the Spirit in Jesus and then experiencing the very same Spirit of Jesus in our own lives.

It's wonderful to think about that because it helps us appreciate our Savior all the more. It also helps us to appreciate the Spirit more when we think that the Spirit—who is, as the older writers used to say, the bond of love between the Father and the Son—actually comes to indwell every single believer.

I want to draw attention to this because it's the reason that the Spirit is called the "Spirit of Christ."

In the gospel of Luke, we read Mary's response to the angel who tells her that she will conceive a son: "'How will this be, since I am a virgin?' And the angel answered her, 'The Holy Spirit will come upon you, and the power of the Most High will overshadow you; therefore the child to be born will be called holy'" (Luke 1:34–35). The gospel of Matthew records Joseph's interaction with an angel: "Joseph, son of David, do not fear to take Mary as your wife, for that which is conceived in her is from the Holy Spirit" (Matt. 1:20). From the very moment of Jesus' conception, the Holy Spirit was engaged in His life.

When Luke tells us in chapter 2 that Jesus increased in wisdom and in favor with God, He is actually reminding us that this was prophesied about the Messiah in Isaiah 11:2. He would be full of the Spirit and therefore full of wisdom.

Then at Jesus' baptism, the Spirit came upon Him to anoint Him for His public ministry. Immediately after that, full of the Spirit, Jesus was led by the Spirit into the wilderness to be tempted by the devil. Mark actually uses even stronger language in his gospel: he says that the Spirit *drove* Jesus into the wilderness. It's a striking picture of the way in which the Holy Spirit directed Jesus as He fulfilled His Father's plan.

In the Nazareth synagogue, Jesus said that He fulfilled the ancient prophecy from Isaiah: "The Spirit of the Lord is upon me, because he has anointed me to proclaim good news to the poor" (Luke 4:18).

When He was accused of being in league with the devil, He demolished that criticism and said that He cast out demons by the finger of God. In His human nature, He was enabled to exercise that power because He was trusting in the Holy Spirit's power.

And so Matthew tells us that in His healings and in His grace, Jesus fulfilled the wonderful prophecy of Isaiah about the coming Servant of the Lord on whom God would put His Holy Spirit.

What becomes clear is that in everything Jesus did for us, He was relying on the Spirit's presence and power. He wasn't injecting a measure of deity into His human nature to enable Him to be a superman. Remember that the two natures of Christ are never mixed or confused in that way, but each acts in accordance with its own character.

Although much is left unsaid in the New Testament, Hebrews 9:14 seems to suggest that the Lord Jesus was enabled—despite all the weakness of His crucifixion—to offer Himself as a sacrifice for our sins because He was undergirded and strengthened by the Holy Spirit.

Then, as Paul says in the opening words of Romans, Jesus was "descended from David according to the flesh," entering our weakness, bearing our sin, and "was declared to be the Son of God in power according to the Spirit of holiness by his resurrection from the dead" (Rom. 1:3–4).

Why mention all these verses about the Lord Jesus when we're talking about the Holy Spirit? Simply to make the point that from womb to tomb, and eventually to the throne, the Lord Jesus was indwelt by the very Holy Spirit that He promised to give to His disciples. That is mind-stretching, isn't it? But it's also heartwarming. The very same Spirit who was there for thirty-three years in the life of the Lord Jesus is the Spirit about whom Jesus spoke to the Father when He said, "Father, the time has come for Us to send the Holy Spirit to My disciples."

And the day of Pentecost was the very first day that Christians experienced what it meant to be indwelt by "another," who is just like Jesus Himself, because He was there, present with Jesus those thirty-three years.

You may remember the hymn that has this line in it: "Think what Spirit dwells within thee, what a Father's smile is thine." And that is one of the great things that Jesus was teaching the disciples in the upper room.

5

The Spirit of the Father

JUST AS WE GET TO KNOW the Father through the revelation of the Lord Jesus, the same is true of the Holy Spirit. And so our main focus this week has been getting to know and love the Holy Spirit through His relationship to the Lord Jesus because He is the Spirit of the Lord Jesus Christ. But He is also the Spirit of the Father.

Jesus told His disciples that when they were persecuted or brought to trial, the Spirit of the Father would help them to speak (Matt. 10:20). Jesus explained this more fully in His final teaching session with the disciples before His crucifixion. He said that He would ask the Father, and the Father would give the Holy Spirit to the disciples because He is indeed the Spirit of the Father (John 14:16). Later, in John 15:26, Jesus says that the Holy Spirit He sends will be the Spirit who comes to them from the Father.

So who sends the Holy Spirit to us? The Father or the Son? It's not one or the other, but both together.

Jesus says that the Spirit "proceeds from the Father" (John 15:29). He goes out from the Father. What Jesus means is that there has always been this wonderful relationship between the Father and the Spirit in all eternity. And now the Spirit who has gone out from the Father will be sent by the Father to the disciples.

This is mysterious beyond our understanding. It stretches our minds. But that is a good thing. We can't put the Holy Spirit in a box. And Jesus, in these last hours, is apparently giving what He sees to be very practical teaching to the disciples. If they understand who the Holy Spirit is, they'll have a wonderful sense of the sheer privilege of being a Christian. They'll be strengthened in every difficult situation, no matter how bleak it seems.

Jesus wanted the disciples to know that the Spirit who would come from Him came right from the very heart of the Father. Just as the Son of God was eternally in the heart of the Father (John 1:18), so the Spirit was eternally proceeding from the Father. Jesus had said to Philip: "Have I been with you so long, and you still do not know me, Philip? Whoever has seen me has seen the Father" (14:9). In other words, we see what the Father is like by watching Jesus. There is nothing in the Father that is unlike Jesus. And we've already seen that there is nothing in the Spirit that is unlike Jesus.

That explains what Paul says in Romans 8 and in Galatians 4. When the Holy Spirit comes to us, we not only say that "Jesus is Lord" by the Spirit (1 Cor. 12:3), but also cry "Abba! Father!" by the Spirit of the Father. Paul is saying that no one can instinctively cry out to God "Abba! Father!" unless they are indwelt by the Spirit of the Father and the Son (Rom. 8:15; Gal. 4:6). When we receive the Spirit, we come to confess Jesus as Lord, and we come to know God as our dear heavenly Father. We are able to address Him the way Jesus addressed Him, as "Abba! Father!"

I think this is a real test of whether someone is a genuine Christian. Unbelievers can say the words of the Our Father, the Lord's Prayer. But what I've noticed is this: in a crisis, when they really feel themselves pressed against the wall, the cry that emerges from their lips is, "O God," at best, and never "Abba! Father!" Because unless we've been born again by the Spirit of the Lord Jesus, we don't have the instincts of God's true children.

In a way, this is our first privilege, our simplest privilege, and also our highest privilege when we are given the gift of the Father's Spirit, who is also the Spirit of the Son. We call Jesus "Lord," and we call the Father "Abba, dear Father." There is nothing more reassuring or marvelous than that. But it does leave this lingering question: "Have you ever called God 'Abba! Father!'?" In order to do that, you need to be able to call the Lord Jesus Lord and Savior.

I hope you're able to do that today.

WEEK 26

The Providence of God

1

All Things Work Together

IT'S A HEARTWARMING THING TO REMEMBER that the same Spirit of the Lord Jesus indwells every single believer. It reminds us that we are bound together with every other Christian, even if we never meet each other. We are indeed, as the Apostle Paul indicates, united in the Spirit.

We experience that in remarkable ways. Speaking about church discipline, Paul writes to the Corinthians, saying, "When you are assembled in the name of the Lord Jesus and my spirit is present" (1 Cor. 5:4). What he means in saying that is that they are so bound together in the one body by the Holy Spirit that he wants to share in what they are going to do. Later in the same letter, he says that when one member suffers, the whole body suffers because we are all indwelt in the same way by the same Spirit.

What's the point here? It's this: We share in each other's lives in the fellowship of Jesus Christ, and the Lord is working in our lives to make us more like Christ. But we need to remember that for all the unity we share, the Lord doesn't work in the same way at the same time in every single one of us. Rather, He paints on the canvas of our lives with many different colors and shades. The colors He is painting into your life just now may be very bright, but the shade He is using in someone else's life may be very dark. Yes, He is bringing all of us to glory, but He polishes our graces in very different ways. And so sometimes we find ourselves asking the question, "Why is this happening to me?"

Another word for it would be *providence*.

This week, we will reflect on one of the great illustrations of God's providence in Scripture. But first, we must answer a question: "What do we mean by *providence*?" Here's a wonderful answer from the Heidelberg Catechism, written in 1563:

> Providence is the almighty and ever present power of God by which God upholds, as with his hand, heaven and earth and all creatures, and so rules them that leaf and blade, rain and drought, fruitful and lean years, food and drink, health and sickness, prosperity and poverty—all things, in fact, come to us not by chance but by his fatherly hand. (Q&A 27)

That is a beautiful statement of providence, isn't it? It may remind you of the wonderful first question and answer in the same Heidelberg Catechism:

> Q. What is your only comfort in life and in death?
> A. That I am not my own, but belong—body and soul, in life and in death—to my faithful Savior, Jesus Christ. He has fully paid for all my sins with his precious blood, and has delivered me from the tyranny of the devil. He also watches over me in such a way that not a hair can fall from my head without the will of my Father in heaven; in fact, all things must work together for my salvation.

That is why we love Romans 8:28, with its teaching that all things work together for good for those who love God and are called according to His purpose. We know that Paul isn't saying, "Everything will work itself out OK for everybody." Rather, he is saying that despite everything, God will work together all the varied pieces of the jigsaw puzzle of our lives as believers in order to do us ultimate good—namely, to fulfill His purpose in our lives.

We mustn't think that we are left to define what that "good" is because Paul goes on to define it himself. He says in the very next verse that God's purpose is to conform us to the image of His Son, to make us like the Lord Jesus. And that is the goal He has in every step He takes in His providence in our lives.

But it's important to remember the words of Asaph in Psalm 77:19. As he reflected on God's ways with His people in His providence, he wrote, "Your way was through the sea, your path through the great waters; yet your footprints were unseen."

That is the challenge to faith, isn't it? God is working providentially in our lives, but we are not always able to see His footprints. Sometimes it feels that we are in the storm, and we've no idea what direction He is taking. That is why William Cowper wrote:

> God moves in a mysterious way
> His wonders to perform;
> He plants his footsteps in the sea,
> And rides upon the storm.

But then Cowper—who knew a great deal of pain and struggle in his life and must often have asked, "God, why is this happening to me?"—goes on to say:

> Ye fearful saints, fresh courage take;
> The clouds ye so much dread
> Are big with mercy, and shall break
> In blessings on your head.

2

God Meant It for Good

THE BIBLE IS ACTUALLY A BOOK ABOUT the providence of God. From Genesis 3:15 onward, it tells the story of how God works to provide salvation for His people in Jesus Christ, and governs all things to achieve this purpose.

I've probably had a sense of providence since I was a very small boy, although it was some time before I really began to understand the gospel itself. Our family didn't go to church, and we had only a few shelves of books in our home. But one of them was my maternal grandmother's old Bible. It was small, thick, and bound in black leather, and it had really small print. Since we didn't have any central heating in the house in those days, in the winter months I used to get into my parents' bed once they'd gotten up and enjoy the warmth they had left behind, and I would read my grandmother's Bible.

There were two stories that I read all the time. One was the story of Daniel, which took me quite a while to find because it was so far on in the Bible. The other one was a bit elusive, too, since the hero didn't have a Bible book named after him. He was tucked away in the last quarter of the book of Genesis: yes, it was the story of Joseph.

When I look back, I think maybe this was one way that God was preparing me to be a minister. Because one of the big questions in Joseph's life must have been the very question that people often ask their ministers: "Why is this happening to me? Where is God, and what is He doing?" It's worth reflecting again on the story and pausing here and there to ask that same question: "What is God doing?"

The story of Joseph really begins with Jacob's making the same mistake of favoritism that his own father and mother had made. Genesis 37 says, "Now Israel loved Joseph more than any other of his sons" (v. 3).

Not only that, but Jacob made it obvious by making the special robe for Joseph. It isn't at all surprising that Genesis goes on to say, "But when his brothers saw that their father loved him more than all his brothers, they hated him" (v. 4). To make matters worse, when Joseph had his dreams, he seems to have been naive enough, and maybe even self-absorbed enough, to actually tell his family about them.

I can hardly imagine what would've happened if, at the age of seventeen, I had said to my parents and brother while we were eating breakfast, "By the way, I had this dream last night about four sheaves in a field, and your sheaves gathered around my sheaf and bowed down to it." And then the next morning, if I had said, "I had a dream about the sun and the moon and a star last night, and all three were bowing down to me."

Notice how Jacob had repeated his own parents' sin of favoritism. There is an echo in this story of his deceitfulness too. Jacob had deceived his father, Isaac, in order to get his brother's blessing. Jacob's sons repeated that father-deceiving sin, so that now Jacob is being deceived. What a mess it all seems.

But here's the curious thing, something beyond wonderful: when you turn to the end of the book of Genesis to see how all this ends, Joseph himself tells us that even though what happened in their family was sinful and harmful, "God meant it for good" (Gen. 50:20).

That doesn't really fit our logic. It's surely one or the other: our sin or God's purpose for good. We might think that God doesn't use a mess like this; after all, He is a God of order. But God works everything together for the good of His people (and it sure takes a lot of working!). It takes divine wisdom. It takes divine power. And it takes time. But think about the story of Joseph this way: Joseph would never have ended up as prime minister of Egypt and preserver of nations in the ancient Near East had it not been for this mess in which they were all involved.

The older Christian writers used to illustrate the way God's providence sometimes works by thinking about the mechanical clocks with which they were familiar. The cogwheels moved in opposite directions in order to drive the hands of the clock around the clockface to tell the right time. That is surely how God sometimes works and how He advances His purposes. So William Cowper was right:

> Judge not the Lord by feeble sense,
> But trust him for his grace;
> Behind a frowning providence
> He hides a smiling face.

And that is part of the mystery of God's gracious providence.

3

The Mystery of Providence

YESTERDAY'S READING ENDED WITH WORDS ABOUT the mystery of providence. That expression might be familiar to you because it's the title of a well-known and wonderfully helpful book written by John Flavel. He was a minister on the south coast of England in the seventeenth century, and he knew a great deal of suffering.

If you've ever read any of his works—there are actually six large volumes of them—I think you'll agree that it must have been a tremendous blessing to have had John Flavel as your minister. Like many of his colleagues in the seventeenth century, he went through very difficult times, yet they were God's investments in his ministry. So perhaps it's not surprising that he was able to write a wonderful book on the providence of God.

Flavel describes God's providence in a very clever and helpful way. He wrote that the providences of God are like Hebrew words: they can be read only backward. Unlike English, which is written from left to right,

Hebrew is written from right to left. God's providence is sometimes like that. In terms of the way we think, it sometimes seems back to front.

We can't second-guess God's providences in our lives—although most of us try to do that at some point. The Lord leads us to do something, and we tend to assume that certain things will follow. But that is not always the case. His ways are not our ways. His thoughts are not our thoughts. Sometimes, indeed, we assume that if we are obedient, then everything will kind of turn out toward fulfilling our own expectations. And then, sometimes, it seems as though life crumbles in our hands. God's providence is a very great mystery, and we can't always understand what He is doing.

That was certainly true of Joseph's story. Yesterday, we noted Jacob's responsibility for the mess he introduced into his own family life. We saw something of the deceitfulness of his own sons. And yet all of that seemed to be part of God's ways of undeceiving Jacob. At first, he wasn't completely untwisted. But God was working in him through these messy circumstances to transform his life, to make him a person of integrity, and to bring about a reconciliation with his family.

Jacob deceived his father, and then his sons deceived him about selling Joseph into slavery. Interestingly, they dipped Joseph's colored coat in goat's blood—just as Jacob had deceived his own father by the way in which he covered himself (in goatskins), so his sons were deceiving their father in turn. But not even this really transformed Jacob, because clearly Benjamin then became the favorite.

As the plotline unfolds, we notice something remarkable that takes place. To receive back the son that he has lost (Joseph), Jacob has to be willing to lose the son that he now cherishes most of all (Benjamin). Jacob doesn't want to let Benjamin out of his sight. We can't help but wonder if Joseph, who insisted that his brothers bring Benjamin to see him, sensed that God wanted him to be the instrument that would help break this family behavior pattern of favoritism. And what resulted was a beautiful family reconciliation.

That is wonderful, isn't it? But because we can read the whole story of Joseph in under an hour, it's easy to forget that these events unfolded in Jacob's life over a decade and a half. Not only are God's thoughts and ways not ours, God's sense of timing isn't ours either. It's only because we can look back over many years that we see how various strands of God's purposes were being woven together. As Flavel said, like Hebrew words the providence of God makes ultimate sense only when we read it backward.

The doctrine of the providence of God doesn't relieve us from going through difficult times and seasons in which we wonder what God is doing. But the doctrine of providence does reassure us that God knows what He is doing. We can't pre-guess God's purposes, and we don't understand the whole of God's purposes either. One reason for this is that He works in His providence in our lives not only for our lives, but because of what He plans to do in the lives of others.

Therefore, the answer to the question, "Lord, why is this happening to me?" may well be: "My child, My purposes in you are not simply for you. I work in you in order to work through you in the lives of others." That was wonderfully true of Joseph's life. Yes, in God's providence he was being chastised, but God had a purpose in that to do good to others.

And so as we yield to the Lord's providence in our lives, we also learn to ask Him to make that providence work in and through us, not only for His glory, but also for the blessing of others.

4

Instruments of God's Providence

A FEW WEEKS AGO, I SUGGESTED that the reason Satan tempted Eve before he tempted Adam was that the strongest leverage the devil has is often found in manipulating God's best gifts. That is what makes him so hateful. He doesn't use discarded trash; he uses the best to try to bring about the worst. Think about marriage. How is it that two people who couldn't bear to be apart from each other a few years later can't stand being in the same house and get divorced? The old Roman proverb is right: *corruptio optimi pessima est*—the worst is the corruption of the best.

One of God's very best gifts is family. That is exactly why Satan seeks to corrupt and to destroy families. The dysfunctional family life that has become so characteristic of the twenty-first century is surely one of the devil's greatest triumphs. And this week, we're thinking about a biblical illustration of a dysfunctional family in the story of Jacob's family and the story of Joseph in Genesis 37–50.

What a mess: an unwise father, a naive and apparently self-centered youngest son, and jealous brothers—a potent cocktail of sinful tendencies that led to a great deal of misery for all of them. Yet in His providence, God transformed it.

Yesterday, we looked at the way in which God's providence unraveled and began to untwist Jacob. Today, we will reflect on how God did the same thing in Joseph's brothers.

Joseph's brothers were jealous of him and angry with him, so they sold him into slavery. They then deceived their father into believing that Joseph had been killed. Then, no doubt, they tried their hardest to forget about him—"out of sight, out of mind."

But while they tried to forget, God was working. And because of a providential need that affected the ancient Near East, they found themselves—all unknown to them—standing in the presence of their brother but not recognizing him. Neither they nor Joseph himself could imagine that their past circumstances were going to be the instruments of God's providence to transform them. It looks as though Joseph realized that he had come to the kingdom—Pharaoh's kingdom, but also God's kingdom—"for such a time as this" (see Est. 4:14), and he does some very significant things.

First, Joseph tells his brothers to bring their youngest brother, Benjamin, down to Egypt with them to prove that they are innocent and not spies. In a way, he must have known that this would break his father's heart, but also that his father's heart needed to be broken.

The brothers' response is fascinating. They say to one another, "In truth we are guilty concerning our brother, in that we saw the distress of his soul"—speaking about Joseph—"when he begged us and we did not listen" (Gen. 42:21). After all these years, their consciences are being pricked and bursting open. And at last, they confess their sin and their guilt.

When they brought Benjamin down, Joseph arranged for them to be seated at the table in the order of their birth. If you're good at probability calculations, you'll know how unlikely it is that this would happen by accident. The brothers were astounded. They must have felt that something totally supernatural had happened. If someone knew the order of their birth, then could it be that "Someone" had been watching them all along? No wonder they were amazed. They must have had some sense that God was watching them and that something was afoot.

Then Joseph tightened the screw in a very interesting way. They all got food from Joseph's own table, but Benjamin was served a portion five times the size of any of the others. I think that is what you might call favoritism!—but that is the point, isn't it? Joseph was turning out to be God's providential instrument of testing the brothers to see whether the work of grace that had begun in them had now delivered them from jealousy and hatred of their youngest brother.

Then Joseph had his own silver cup placed in Benjamin's sack. When it was found, the brothers were all dragged back to Egypt. What would happen to Benjamin? Judah pleaded with Joseph for mercy, not just because of Benjamin, but because of his concern over what it would do to his father, Jacob, if Benjamin didn't return home. This is a marvelous illustration of a transformation in his heart. They now really care about the father they had once deceived.

The brothers eventually found themselves being embraced by Joseph and embracing him in return, and bringing Jacob and the whole family to Egypt, just as God had promised to Abraham would happen one day to his descendants (Gen. 15:12–16).

What does this part of the story teach us? It teaches us that God keeps His promises, but it also teaches us that He gives wisdom to His children to help them understand their role in His purposes.

Perhaps in the midst of the confusion and sin of the world around us, instead of just complaining about it, we should be asking the Lord for wisdom to be an instrument of His providence, to bring healing and reconciliation.

And yes, perhaps even to lead people to faith.

5

The Glory of God's Providence

WE'VE BEEN THINKING ALL THIS WEEK about the mystery of God's providence and trying to draw out some of the lessons that emerge from the story of Joseph in Genesis 37–50.

This whole section is introduced by the words, "These are the generations of Jacob" (37:2). We've been watching the way in which the Lord worked providentially and graciously in Jacob and in Joseph's brothers. But before the week ends, we need to say something more about Joseph himself.

We find wonderful words toward the end of the book of Genesis when Joseph tells his brothers, "As for you, you meant evil against me, but God meant it for good" (50:20). He was really expanding on what he'd said earlier when his brothers discovered, to their horror, that he was the prime minister of Egypt: "And now do not be distressed or angry with yourselves because you sold me here, for God sent me before you to preserve life" (45:5).

It probably didn't feel like that to Joseph when he was down in the pit, or when he was sold as a slave in Egypt, or when his success in Egypt was destroyed by Potiphar's wife, or when his hopes were dashed when the cupbearer whose dream he'd interpreted forgot him and he was left in jail. This isn't a story about how God's providence means that God's people always enjoy health, wealth, and happiness. But it is a story about how God sovereignly works things out for His own glory.

I think we can see that in several ways.

For one thing, God brought Joseph to the right place at the right time. God's timing is significant. There is a very interesting hint about this in the time markers in Genesis 37–50. Joseph is seventeen when the story begins, and he is thirty when he becomes prime minister of Egypt. That is fourteen years by inclusive reckoning. That time marker isn't accidental. When Joseph interprets Pharaoh's dream, he tells him that there will be seven years of plenty and then seven years of famine. Seven plus seven makes fourteen. There is a theology in these numbers, isn't there? Fourteen long years of preparation for fourteen years of great wisdom.

There is a tremendous lesson for us to learn here. We tend to think that a little polishing up for a few days will equip us to serve the Lord. Maybe seven days, seven weeks, or seven months. Surely that would be quite enough to prepare us for many years of service. How naive and self-assured we can be! God's transforming work does not happen overnight. It's not done by one experience.

Thinking about Joseph reminds me of what I call "God's cul-de-sac principle."

Some people I've known who have had real gifts and a desire to serve the Lord Jesus seem to be shunted down a kind of dead-end street, exactly the way Joseph must have felt. Yet the marvelous thing is that what God is really doing is taking them out of the traffic that they are in so that He can put them back into the traffic where He intends to use them most for His glory. We can see that in the life of Joseph. God wants him to be in the right place at the right time, and this cul-de-sac principle works marvelously.

There is something else here, because clearly Joseph is not simply in the *right place* at the *right time*. God has also been preparing him to be the *right man*. What we notice about Joseph when he is seventeen is that he is impatient, he is unwise, and he seems a little self-centered. But through these years, the Lord turns him out from himself, and he becomes God-centered. God gives him wisdom for his folly and, amazingly, gives him patience.

There is something else you can't avoid in the Joseph story. It's a principle that emerges finally in the Lord Jesus. In his sermon on the day of Pentecost, Peter said that although Jesus was crucified at the hands of wicked men, it was God's purpose that others would be brought to salvation through that event. Joseph's life is a little picture of that: "God meant it for good, to bring it about that many people should be kept alive" (Gen. 50:20). It's almost as though, in His providence, God wanted to make Joseph more like Jesus.

That is the truth, isn't it? We're not all going to have the dramatic experiences of a Joseph. We're certainly not all going to end up as prime ministers or as presidents. But here's one thing that is true in God's providence in our lives: by His grace, each one of us who is a Christian is going to be conformed to the image of His Son. He is going to make us just like Jesus.

And then we will see that all the providences of God in our lives were worthwhile.

WEEK 27

Places That Matter to Me

1

A Little Pulpit in Scotland

GEORGE WHITEFIELD WAS AN ENGLISHMAN WHO was instrumental in the First Great Awakening in eighteenth-century America. Whenever he went back to the University of Oxford in England where he'd been a student, he kissed the spot where he remembered his early experience of God's saving grace. It wasn't that Whitefield believed that some places or spaces are more holy than others. But it's true that some places are special to us and have been sanctified to us by God because of what happened there.

This week, I'd like to reflect on some of the places in my own life that are like that. I don't do this because my life is so important that you need to hear about it! Rather, I hope my reflections will stimulate you to look back and to be filled with a sense of gratitude to God for what He has done for you, perhaps in certain particular places. In that way, we can do what the old hymn says to do: "Count your blessings, name them one by one; and it will surprise you what the Lord has done"— because we do so easily forget.

At one time, the screen saver on my computer was a photograph of the old pulpit that once stood in St. George's Tron Church in Glasgow, Scotland. It's no longer there, but it was significant to me. The pulpit itself was unusual. It was white, stood maybe twenty feet high, and was reached by a spiral staircase. The pulpit itself was just a small circle. Perhaps two people could stand in it if they didn't need a lot of private space. It was surrounded by a gallery on three sides, and some of the seats were near enough that the people sitting in them could almost hit the preacher if they'd carried a long stick.

When I was almost fifteen, I came to faith in Jesus Christ sitting in a seat on the south side of that gallery listening to a sermon on John 8:12. The one thing my conversion has in common with John Wesley's is that I think it was somewhere between eight o'clock and nine o'clock in the evening.

Years later when I finished my theological studies, I was appointed assistant minister in that congregation and had the privilege several times every month of preaching from that pulpit. I later became the senior minister of the church. Often when I was preaching, especially in the evening, I'd look over to the place where I'd been sitting and wonder if there was another young fourteen-year-old sitting there who was being drawn to Christ.

As I mentioned, that pulpit isn't there any longer, nor is the congregation still in that building. They felt they could no longer remain in the denomination, and so they had to sacrifice the building. I have no idea where the pulpit is. For all I know, it's an ornament somewhere, or maybe it's broken down and gone forever. But it will always remain a special memory for me because from it the gospel was preached to me and to thousands of others. And from it, I was able to preach the gospel.

I'm grateful to God for that, and I honor those who preached to me from that pulpit. I can recall sermons that others preached from it and their memorable impact on my Christian life. But the one I remember most of all was the first one I heard there as a fourteen-year-old. The minister spoke on these words from Jesus: "I am the light of the world. Whoever follows me will not walk in darkness, but will have the light of life." Although the pulpit is gone, the words I heard from it that night have remained. And they've been true to me, for the Lord Jesus is the same yesterday, today, and forever. I'm so grateful that there, sitting in the gallery, looking at the high white pulpit, I heard Jesus' voice calling me to follow Him. I often think of the lovely hymn by Horatius Bonar:

I heard the voice of Jesus say,
"I am this dark world's Light;
Look unto me, thy morn shall rise,
And all thy days be bright."
I looked to Jesus, and I found
In him my Star, my Sun;
And in that light of life I'll walk,
Till trav'ling days are done.

All so wonderfully true for me.

I hope my story stimulates you to think of your story and to be thankful again for the place where you first came to faith in the Lord Jesus and became His disciple, and for the people who pointed you to Him. Or if you've listened to sermons from the pulpit in your own church and perhaps never come to Christ, why not take hold of this promise that meant so much to me, from John 8:12? Jesus is the Light of the World, and those who trust Him as their Savior and Lord will walk in the light.

If you take hold of Jesus and that promise, then He reassures you that you will never walk in darkness.

2

Room C.3.7

YESTERDAY, I TALKED ABOUT A PULPIT, and today I want to talk about the study bedroom I occupied for a year when I was eighteen. In college and university residences in the United Kingdom, students usually have a study bedroom of their own with perhaps some shared facilities with other students. My room was numbered C.3.7, block C in the residence, third floor, room 7. I haven't been back in that room since I was a student, and I'm sure they don't have a plaque that says, "Sinclair Ferguson once studied and slept here." But the memory of that room is sacred to me because of several life-changing things that happened in that small space.

I was eighteen and in my second year at university, studying philosophy and psychology. I think I was reading Martin Luther's comment that Romans is a key to the whole Bible when the thought struck me that if that is true, it means that while the whole Bible is inspired by God, there are some parts of it, some books in it, that function like a set of keys that open up all the other books.

Although I'd been reading the Bible for about ten years at that time, I realized for the first time that what I needed to do was to give special attention to those key books, to spend more time studying and mastering them—or more accurately, letting them master me and the way I think, felt, and acted.

And so that was what I did. One of the memories that makes me smile was that later in the academic year, I went to the local Christian bookshop with some prize money I'd received from the philosophy department. I spent it not on Plato, Aristotle, Immanuel Kant, or even the Scottish philosopher David Hume, but on Christian books that would help me to pursue this new idea: studying the Bible and getting hold of the key books. I remember one of the books I bought—with a smile, as I wondered what my philosophy professors would think about it. It was Professor John Murray's commentary on Romans.

The second thought that came to me in that room was prompted by the first. I thought, "I wonder if what is true of Scripture is also true of other books." There was no course in a Scottish university on the great books of Western civilization. But it wasn't those books I was thinking about; it was Christian books. And I made a decision that I would try to read some of the great Christian books. Even if I felt a little embarrassed talking with fellow students who were discussing the latest Christian paperback, I'd be prepared to say, "I'm sorry,

I haven't read that," and I would try to read the great books that had transformed the church.

Don't misunderstand me. I'm not saying not to read the latest Christian books. But I did learn a lesson in those teenage years: if you do read Christian books, make sure you read some of the ones that have lasted through the years and made a lasting impact on Christians for generations. You'll maybe not be surprised to learn that it was that same year that I bought not only John Murray on Romans, but John Calvin's great work, *The Institutes of the Christian Religion*. Looking back, I really believe that purchasing and reading those books has repaid itself many times over because they were books that not only instructed me, but modeled for me how to think in a biblical way.

If you're a young student or young Christian, maybe those thoughts could be life-changing for you as well. I certainly hope so.

3

A Seminary in Philadelphia

WE'VE BEEN THINKING THIS WEEK ABOUT places that God has sanctified to us because of what happened there, and I've been mentioning some in my own life in the hope that it will encourage you to count your blessings as well.

My study bedroom as a college teenager also has a part to play in this next memory. I think I had just turned eighteen and was sitting in it in a meeting with a group of fellow students from our InterVarsity group. We were discussing the teaching syllabus for the next academic year. Our president said, "Professor John Murray is retiring from Westminster Seminary, and we can ask him to speak next session." I still recall my reaction: "Who on earth is Professor John Murray? And where on earth is Westminster Theological Seminary?"

Fast-forward another fifteen years, and I found myself standing exactly where Professor Murray had stood, lecturing on the same subjects he had taught, and belonging to a theological faculty in which half the members had studied under him. It was one of the most difficult decisions of my life to accept this invitation to join the faculty because it was in the United States and not in Scotland. It meant leaving the place and the people I called home. It had taken about a year and a half from the president's first approach to me for us eventually to arrive in Philadelphia, and that wasn't the end of God's strange providences in our lives.

After I heard Professor Murray when I was still a student, I remember thinking, "It would be amazing to study at Westminster Seminary." The books written by the faculty had been enormously helpful to me. There seemed to be giants in that land in those days, gifted scholars who were also valiant for the faith of Jesus Christ—men who had made great personal sacrifices and had shaped an institution that was now shaping many others.

But as a student, I was as likely to go to the United States to study theology at Westminster Seminary as to go to the moon to purchase green cheese. So you can understand that finding myself there fifteen years later—and as a faculty member—was absolutely astonishing to me. Looking back, I sometimes pinch myself and think, "How did that happen?"

I am profoundly grateful for the privilege of being taken on board, befriended, and in the fellowship of men whose ability far exceeded my own. The fellowship and shared ministry of faculty and staff, and the many shared hours with intelligent and highly motivated students from all over the world, made that day in that room a very sacred memory to me, as well as made the campus a special place to me later on. One thing that made it easy for me to make relationships with some of the students—relationships that lasted into later life—was that when I started teaching, I was about the average age of the students, so it wasn't difficult to be mistaken for one. In many ways, we grew up together.

Perhaps like me, you, too, are grateful for the special continuing bonds that were created during your earlier years. I think especially in Christian ministry, these bonds are absolutely essential. Often in the history of the church, it's those bands of brothers that the Lord has used to sustain one another and to advance His kingdom. Although I was a faculty member, I was also a student learning side by side with fellow students. As iron sharpens iron, as a professor I was being shaped even as I sought to be an instrument shaping others.

Looking back, the most important thing is the bonds that were created. Sometimes men would come to my office and ask, "Will you mentor me?" or "Will you disciple me?" I've always had reservations about some mentorship or discipleship programs because they seem to be too heavy on a kind of official teacher-student dynamic and light on what I think is actually central in the New Testament. And so I would say: "No, I won't mentor you, and there are several reasons for that. But here's what I will do: I'll be your friend." Apart from all that I learned academically in my years at the seminary, the thing that I really value more than anything else, the thing that made the place a sacred space to me with memories of God's presence and God's blessing, was this: friends. There God gave me friends.

That reminds me of something significant that Jesus said to the disciples at the end of His ministry: "I have called you friends" (John 15:15).

Isn't it interesting how much *friends* meant to Jesus and not just *disciples*? I hope that today, you can be very thankful for the friends the Lord has given you.

4

Home

THIS PRACTICE OF THINKING ABOUT the people, places, and moments in which the Lord has met with us is something that our spiritual fore-fathers thought was important for our spiritual well-being. We all have different places and different events that have been spiritually signifi-cant in our lives.

There is one place, however, I hope you can put on your list: home. Some of us may have moved so often that we find it difficult to answer the question, "Where do you call home?" Over the years, our family has lived in about a dozen different houses that you could have called "home," at least in the sense that they've been the place where we've returned at the end of the day. But they haven't all felt the same way in terms of "This is our home."

There is a difference between a house's being where you return at the end of the day and where you feel is really home. Home is where you sense that you belong, where your roots are, where the people you feel you belong to live. In many ways, the old adage is true: "Home is where the heart is," where you have a sense of ease and comfort. This isn't just physical comfort with familiar things but comfort with people.

But what makes a house a home? It's not the things in it, but the people who share it. In that sense, I've had two homes. I was brought up in a small family: my dad, mom, and a brother about three years older than me. I can't really put into words my parents' commitment to their two sons. Plus, they were amazingly patient with the younger son (me). I don't think either of my parents had any schooling past about the age of thirteen or fourteen, but my mother especially was resolutely committed to our education. She taught us the basics herself when we were small. She made learning—reading, writing, spelling, and arithmetic—fun. She didn't leave me any choice about whether I would study Latin at school. When I look back, I owe them more than I realized, and I wish I could tell them that now.

My brother and my father died within a short space of each other in the 1970s, and my mother died a decade later. What I owe to them is perhaps best measured by the fact that I still feel an overwhelming sense of loss at times, powerful enough to bring tears to my eyes. But then God gave me a second home: first, the girl I fell in love with from the moment we first met (although you understand that there are two sides to every love story), and then our children and grandchildren. "God settles the solitary in a home," David says in Psalm 68:6, and I couldn't have been more blessed in that respect.

But I know this isn't every Christian's experience. So the reason I wanted to mention it is that it reminds me not only of the importance of our natural home and family life, which is obviously one of God's fundamental and most wonderful gifts to us. It's because that is not ultimately the family to which we belong. Yes, those families are important. But the wonderful thing about the grace of God is that He brings us into an older family. He brings us into a bigger family. He brings us into a happier family. He brings us into a worldwide family and an eternity-long family.

We are reflecting on that because I want to remind us that family is the basic biblical way of thinking about the fellowship of the church. Here, we are given spiritual fathers and mothers, brothers and sisters, aunts and uncles, sons and daughters, grandchildren, and even great-grandchildren. And here, no matter how dysfunctional a family we may have come from, we've been brought into a family that is beginning to be functional.

One of the tragedies of our time is that governments and institutions are spending billions of dollars seeking to improve people's sense of self and sense of self-identity. But they can never provide what the church of Jesus Christ can provide: a Savior who gives our lives significance, and brothers and sisters in Christ who love us and with whom we will spend eternity.

Whether your own natural family life has been wonderfully blessed or perhaps, sadly, tremendously dysfunctional, reflect with me today and into the future on the blessings of belonging to the family of God that stretches to the ends of the earth, and into the mists of eternity.

Count your blessings, name them one by one, and it will surprise you what the Lord has done.

5

A Marble Pulpit in South Carolina

I BEGAN THE WEEK BY THINKING about the significance of the pulpit from which I first heard a sermon from John 8:12 that brought me to faith in Christ, and from which I later had the privilege of preaching frequently when I became the church's minister. So it's a good and fitting way to end the week with another pulpit, thirty-eight hundred miles away as the crow flies: the sacred space and place for me of the pulpit in First Presbyterian Church in Columbia, S.C.

Like the pulpit in Scotland that I spoke about, this one, too, is white. But unlike the Scottish one, this pulpit is an enormous marble block. Sometimes men in the congregation who had served in the FBI or other agencies would express to me their concern about my safety if anything untoward were to happen in a service. I'd enjoy pointing out to them that with this solid-marble protection, I was probably in the safest place in the whole building.

As I look back on preaching God's Word and seeking to feed and serve God's people from that particular pulpit, I think of it as a priceless privilege God gave me. This was so not primarily because of the preaching, but because of the privilege of loving the people of God and sensing the love and affection of God's people in return.

Many of them were like Barnabases to me. Barnabas is a disciple of Christ in the New Testament whose name means "son of encouragement." I've sometimes known people that I call *Sabanrab*—that is actually *Barnabas* backward—because they've been the very reverse of encouragers. I wish every minister received the kind of encouragement, love, and affection that I still feel from the congregation I served in Columbia.

I reflect now on the fact that I left the church and retired (or at least, kind of retired). Why would a minister do that? Of course, there are always going to be several dimensions to the answer, but I thought it might interest you to know one of them. A pastor is part of a spiritual relay race and team. He enters into the labors of others, and his task, in a way, is to serve his people well so that he can help prepare them for the next ministry. At least in my own case, I felt that the Lord had given the congregation the next ministry and the next minister who would give them a sense of continuity and progress. I'm talking about my then-colleague and longtime friend Derek Thomas.

In a sense, every pastor comes to a congregation because he wants to love them, and he needs to learn to leave them because he wants someone else to love them. I wish every pastor had the blessing of knowing he could leave the people he loves with a person he knows also loves them, with that person already being there.

I say that not in an ultra-pious way, as though love for a congregation is a special minister's virtue. It's actually part of what's given to a minister if he is really called by the Lord. Of course, he is to work hard at loving, maybe especially loving some of the members, but it's much less of a virtue and much more a gift from God that is part and parcel of his call to minister to the congregation.

A pastor's love for his people isn't so much worked up as it's sent down. He is like the servant in Jesus' parable in Luke 17 who says he was only doing what servants do. That is how you feel as a pastor in loving the flock. You're simply using what God has given you. Yes, sometimes it's a challenge to express that love and sometimes a challenge to express it to particular people. And I know that can be more difficult in some settings and in some people's lives than it is in others. It can be a challenge to love, but it's first of all a gift from heaven.

When I think of that great white pulpit, it's not my own sermons I think about. It's loving the people to whom I preached the sermons. It's loving to serve them with food from God's Word, and to worship and serve with them, knowing I could never repay the love that I received in return. That great marble pulpit is also a special place for me because of the people who surrounded it.

So I began this week with a pulpit, and I end it with another pulpit to remind me of the sacred places that have brought so much blessing to me and for which I'm thankful. And the central blessing is the blessing of belonging to the family of God, to the church.

I hope that your church family is a sacred place for you as well—where you've met with God, where you're fed on His Word, where you've loved and been loved. And next week, we're going to think together about exactly that: the church.

WEEK 28

Pictures of the Church

1

The Body of Christ

I WAS SLOW TO APPRECIATE CLASSICAL MUSIC. One of the first pieces I enjoyed was *Pictures at an Exhibition* by the Russian composer Modest Mussorgsky. It's a suite of ten piano pieces with a recurring melody that conveys the sense of walking from one picture to another. It's a clever idea to try to convey the theme of a picture gallery through music, because it makes an appeal to the imagination.

The Bible also uses pictures that appeal to our imagination and help us to see what God intends the church to be.

In the book *Images of the Church*, the author, Paul Minear, suggests that there are over ninety images or pictures of the church in the New Testament. That number is probably squeezing out every last drop of juice, but certainly, there are several pictures in the New Testament that help us to admire and meditate on the wonder of the church.

What picture first comes to your mind? If you were to ask that question of every Christian in the past two thousand years, the central answer would probably be that the church is the body of Christ. We're all familiar with the way the Apostle Paul uses that phrase, perhaps especially his statement in 1 Corinthians 12:27: "You are the body of Christ and individually members of it." More essays and books have been written on this picture of the church than any other, I suspect, and scholars today still discuss where Paul got the idea.

I remember being in a Latin class as a schoolboy and reading an account by the Roman historian Livy, who told how the Roman consul

Agrippa Menenius tried to quell a revolt of the plebeians by telling them that society worked like a body—some just happened to be important parts, and others were minor parts; each one needed to fulfill its proper role. In some ways, he was pulling the wool over their eyes, as though to say: "If you are complaining about not getting enough food, quit your moaning, because you are not the stomach. Get back to where you belong and get on with it."

That wasn't what Paul had in mind when he spoke about the church as the body. Perhaps the idea arose, as some people think, from his conversations with Luke, who was a physician. Perhaps in Paul's mind the picture had something to do with the Lord's Supper and sharing in the one bread that Jesus spoke about as "my body" (e.g., Matt. 26:26). Or perhaps it was because Jesus told Saul that when he was persecuting Christians, he was actually persecuting Jesus Himself, as though they were one body. Whatever the origin of the picture Paul uses, it teaches us some very important lessons about the church.

First, it teaches us that the Lord Jesus is the head of the body. He directs it. He owns it. He is the Lord of the body. It's Jesus' church, not my church or the minister's church. It's not even *our* church; it's *His* church. We need to remember that because often when things go wrong in churches, it's because we've forgotten this. Those who are elders or have spiritual oversight in any way need to put this at the top of the agenda sheet: Jesus is head. It's His church, not ours.

Another important aspect of this picture is that it reminds us that the members of the body are all different, but each member has a part to play. They are all needed if the body is to function properly.

Paul puts it this way in Ephesians 4:15–16: "Rather, speaking the truth in love, we are to grow up in every way into him who is the head, into Christ, from whom the whole body, joined and held together by every joint with which it is equipped, when each part is working properly, makes the body grow so that it builds itself up in love." Only when each part is working properly does the body build itself up in love.

What a marvelous picture that is to help us understand how much we all need each other and how much we need to love each other.

Third, it's interesting that Paul uses the picture of the body to make a completely different point from the one Menenius Agrippa made. Paul says that in the body of Christ, we treat the parts that seem less honorable with greatest honor. We give special attention to those who are weakest and have the greatest need. We especially honor the people who seem to lack honor (1 Cor. 12:22–26). His point is exactly the countercultural and counter-sinful lifestyle that characterizes a real church family. Unlike the plebeians being put in their place to serve those of a more noble family, the truth of the life of the church is that the church of Jesus Christ is the place where the apparently least honorable are given the greatest honor.

That is a great picture, isn't it? It makes us rejoice in this wonderful privilege.

And perhaps it challenges us, too.

2

The Flock of God

THIS WEEK, WE ARE LOOKING ONE BY ONE at some of the biblical pictures of the church to help us understand what it means to belong to a specifically Christian community. We saw yesterday that the church is the body of Christ. Today, we'll explore how the New Testament tells us that the church is the flock of God.

That is a very much-loved picture, isn't it? I suspect it has a stronger emotional pull on us than the picture of the body, but perhaps that is more true of people who live in rural areas like much of my home country of Scotland. As you drive, you see fields filled with sheep, and it's amazing to see how much time they spend eating. That is very interesting when we think about the metaphor of a flock for the church.

Many of us love the picture of the church as a flock because we are familiar with some of the great passages in the Scriptures. Perhaps we love to sing Psalm 100: "All people that on earth do dwell, sing to the Lord with cheerful voice. . . . We are his flock, he doth us feed, and for his sheep he doth us take." And surely we love the words, "The LORD is my shepherd; I shall not want" (Ps. 23:1).

Or perhaps we are strengthened by Psalm 77, written by the melancholic Asaph. He strengthened his soul in God with wonderful words that reassured him that the God of Israel's past will be the God of Israel's present and the God of his own present: "You led your people like a flock by the hand of Moses and Aaron" (v. 20). The thought is this: if God can lead the giant flock of the exodus people and take them through the desert and provide for them, then He can surely do the same for us as a community and for me as an individual.

This picture of the church as a flock comes straight out of the Old Testament. But even more significantly, it also comes straight from the lips of the Lord Jesus. He said, "I am the good shepherd" (John 10:11). We are His flock.

I sometimes wonder if any of the Bethlehem shepherds who visited Jesus on the night that He was born brought any of their favorite sheep with them—or maybe a sheep that especially needed to be looked after. And I wonder if Mary ever told Jesus afterward, "You know, You were surrounded by sheep the very day You came out of my womb, and You've been surrounded by sheep ever since."

The great thing about the Good Shepherd is that He knows the needs of the whole flock. He knows each and every one of His sheep by name, and He calls us by name. It's one of the signs that we really belong to the church, that we really are Jesus' sheep, that we've heard His voice in the gospel and have begun to follow Him.

Here's something else: when the sheep respond to the Shepherd's voice, they inevitably come not only nearer to Him; they come nearer to each other as well. We all have one and the same loving Shepherd. We belong together only because He has called us together. And although we may not have common interests in life, we have heard the same voice. We recognize the same need for the same Shepherd to guard us, and we know that we have one Shepherd who will feed us and lead us. It's the fact that we all depend on Him that makes us sensitive to and understanding of each other.

But this picture of the church as a flock also reminds us that like sheep, we are prone to wander. It's very easy for us to be critical and judgmental when we see a fellow believer wander off, isn't it? There is the tittle-tattle, the gossip, and the criticism. And we Christians can say some fairly ghastly things about our fellow believers' failures. But the thing about the Good Shepherd is that He goes after His sheep and brings the wandering ones home. We need to learn to do that as well. Of course, it's also clear in the Gospels that the Lord Jesus recognized that there are false sheep, wolves in sheep's clothing, and He treated them accordingly. But it's amazing the lengths He said He would go to make sure that none of His true sheep would ever be lost—and what that cost Him.

I often think of the words of an old song that is based on Jesus' parable about the Good Shepherd's finding His lost sheep: "But none of the ransomed ever knew how deep were the waters crossed; nor how dark was the night that the Lord passed thro' ere he found his sheep that was lost. Out in the desert he heard its cry—sick and helpless, and ready to die."

If you think about the church as a flock that is made up of sheep like that, every single one of us needing to be found by the Good Shepherd, you will begin to see and to treat fellow members in a very different and a much more loving way.

Reflect on that today. The Lord is not only your Shepherd; He is the Shepherd of the whole church. He is the Shepherd of *your* church, and He is the Shepherd of *everyone* in it.

3

The Bride of Christ

SO FAR, WE'VE DISCUSSED THE CHURCH as the body of Christ and as the Lord's flock. Today, it's time to mention the bride of Christ. Like the picture of a flock, the picture of a bride is one that was used for ancient Israel. In Ezekiel 16, God describes His relationship with His people. They were nothing. They were like a baby that had been discarded on the side of the road, her body unwashed, no swaddling clothes wrapping her at all. And then He gave her life and caused her to flourish.

Then Ezekiel, speaking on God's behalf, changes the metaphor. Israel is no longer an infant but has grown into young womanhood and is ready for love and marriage. So the Lord married her and adorned her. But then, sadly, she trusted in her beauty and in the riches the Lord had given and prostituted them. Reminiscent of the story of Hosea, isn't it? We remember the Lord's words in Hosea 11: "How can I give you up, O Ephraim? How can I hand you over, O Israel?" (v. 8).

That picture of a faithful God and the church as God's bride comes to its fulfillment in the Lord Jesus. The church is the bride of Christ. Paul says in Ephesians 5 that this picture is actually embedded in the original creation of mankind as male and female, a man and a woman made for each other. The marriage in Eden and our marriages, too, are intended to be a picture of the relationship between the Lord Jesus and His people. It's a picture of His amazing love for us. As the hymn puts it, "From heav'n he came and sought her to be his holy bride; with his own blood he bought her, and for her life he died."

This is a picture that has many lessons to teach us, but here's one of the most important: Paul says that one day the church will be presented to the Lord in splendor, "without spot or wrinkle or any such thing, that she might be holy and without blemish" (Eph. 5:27).

Think about that when you reflect on your own church fellowship.

Paul implies that there are spots on our faces. We have wrinkles. The Lord Jesus isn't blind to them, but He is a loving, gentle, and patient divine beautician. The Spirit is determined that the Lord Jesus will have a beautiful bride in glory, and that requires not just the work of a beautician. It requires the work of a reconstructive surgeon.

If that is the case, we need to learn to be very patient with one another. Some Christians want to see change overnight. Sometimes younger ministers can make the same mistake. But that is not usually God's timing, is it? He works patiently because He loves us. Generally speaking, He does things slowly because that is the best way.

One of our children is a pediatric surgeon. He has been one for more than a quarter of a century now. He has operated on a lot of children and met not a few anxious parents, so he needs to be very patient. Some time ago, I said to him, "I suppose now you must get through your list of operations much more quickly." He gave an interesting, and I thought impressive, reply. He said, "Actually, Dad, I work more slowly now just because I want to be careful to do the very best job I can for every one of these children."

I was moved by that, of course because he is our son, but also because it made me reflect on the fact that every operation he performs is on someone else's son or daughter. It made me think: "If my son works carefully that way, making sure he does the best job even if it takes more time, then surely that is all the more true of the Lord Jesus as He patiently removes the spots and wrinkles and all such things from the church. He is getting the bride ready for the wedding day."

This is a word to some of us who have become impatient with the spots and wrinkles in our own church family. Remember, the church is not *your* bride; she is Christ's bride. And remember that His love for her means He wants to do the very best job in removing those spots and wrinkles, and it's His purpose to do that patiently. You and I need to be patient and wait for the Lord to work in others, and also patient to learn to wait for Him to work fully in us.

When that happens in our fellowship, we become increasingly Christlike, and people begin to notice.

4

The Temple of God

HOW DO YOU THINK ABOUT THE CHURCH as a whole, and how do you think about your church in particular? That is the question we've been reflecting on this week as we look at some of the pictures that are used in the New Testament: body, flock, and bride. Here's a fourth one: the church is a temple.

What was a temple? It was a place where God made His presence known and met with His people.

Biblical scholars have become much more conscious in recent years that the garden of Eden is actually described in temple-like terms. That is why, for example, later in Israel's story the role of the priests is described in the language that was used of Adam in Eden (e.g., Gen. 2:15; Num. 3:7–8). The garden, the tabernacle, and the temple were all special spaces and places where God met with man and where man experienced the presence and the revelation of God.

When Jesus was crucified, the great temple curtain in Jerusalem was torn from the top to the bottom. On that curtain were emblems of cherubim, the angels of God who, with flaming swords that turned in every direction, guarded the entrance to the garden of Eden. What a picture that was.

Why did the curtain in the temple tear upon Jesus' death? It signified two things. One was that the way into God's presence was now opened through Jesus. But the other was that the temple was now being deconsecrated by God Himself. The place where God meets with men and women is no longer a specific geographical building built for one particular nation. Now that temple is the person of the Lord Jesus Christ.

As the Apostle Peter put it, Christians are like living stones being built together into a spiritual house in which spiritual—rather than animal—sacrifices are offered to the Lord (see 1 Peter 2:5). These spiritual sacrifices are praise, obedience, and a community offering itself to the Lord in worship. Now the temple is being built not in one location, but throughout the earth as its stones are shaped, chiseled, and fit together in Jesus Christ. They begin to sparkle in their multicolored beauty as they do what the old tabernacle and temple were designed to do: reflect the praiseworthiness and excellencies of our God.

That is a wonderful and important picture of the church, but it's also a good lens for us to view our own churches through. We are part of this great temple of living stones that belong to the Lord Jesus. The divine stonemason, the Holy Spirit, is chiseling us into shape so that we fit in with each other. That is something to think about, isn't it? When we find that there is friction between or among our members, we need to remember that the Lord is chiseling us. He is a master stonemason. He is working in our lives to make us fit better into His plan and fit better with these other living stones who are our brothers and sisters.

If stones could speak when they are being chiseled, they'd probably be saying, "Ouch, that hurts!" Therefore, it shouldn't surprise us if our own lives are punctuated by a series of "Ouch, Lord, that hurts!" when He builds us into His church. It's no easy task to fit together stones of so many different shapes and sizes, especially if they are resistant to being reshaped or being stuck beside a stone they don't really care for much. But what makes the difference is knowing and trusting who is doing the chiseling and why He is doing it. Our master mason is working to make our church a place where we live together in such a way that the multifaceted grace and glory of our Lord Jesus will become visible among us, not just in isolated individuals, but in what we are as a fellowship.

You may be familiar with the first question and answer in the Westminster Shorter Catechism. But have you ever thought what the first question and answer in a church catechism might be? I think you'll agree that it should be this: "What is the chief end of the church as the temple of God?" Answer: "The chief end of the church as the temple of God is to glorify God, and to enjoy him forever."

I hope that has begun to take place in your church.

5

The Family of God

IT'S IMPORTANT FOR US TO THINK ABOUT the nature of the church in general because it helps us to think more clearly about our own local churches. Just as important, it should help transform our churches so that we become the kind of fellowships that our Lord Jesus intends us to be. After all, it is not we but the Lord Jesus Himself who is building this church.

We looked this week at four pictures the New Testament employs in describing the church: body, bride, flock, and temple. Which of these do you think is the most important picture of the church in the New Testament? It's a bit of a trick question, because I don't think it's any of these. In fact, the most important picture isn't ultimately a picture at all; it's the reality. Body, bride, flock, temple—all these are metaphors. When the Bible uses them, it's saying that the church is like this in many respects. These are pictures.

So what is the most important picture that isn't a picture at all, but the reality itself? It's this: the church is the family of God. Here, *family* isn't a picture. It's not a metaphor. It's the reality. In fact, we might say that it's the human family that is actually the metaphor. God's family is the real thing. God has given us rebirth through His Spirit. We've been adopted into His family. We're His sons and daughters. We've received the Spirit of adoption, and we call Him "Abba! Father!" We are therefore brothers and sisters, fathers and mothers, sons and daughters spiritually. That is how Paul tells Timothy we are to treat each other as Christians (1 Tim. 5:1–2).

But there is even more, although I don't think we meditate on it nearly enough.

God created two branches to His family: there is an earthly branch to which we belong, and there is a heavenly branch to which the angels and archangels, the seraphim and the cherubim belong. Amazingly, wonderfully, through His death and resurrection, the Lord Jesus has brought us together into one family united under one head—the branch of the family in heaven, and the branch of the family now on earth. And so besides brothers and sisters, fathers and mothers, sons and daughters, you might say we also have a large number of heavenly cousins.

What's stunning is that the letter to the Hebrews hints that when we come to worship as a church, we're not only experiencing a weekly reunion of the earthly family in our Father's presence; it's more like a Scottish clan gathering. The whole clan is present from everywhere. The way Hebrews puts it is that we join "innumerable angels in festal gathering" (Heb. 12:22), as well as "the spirits of the righteous made perfect" (v. 23), and best of all, Jesus Himself, "the mediator of a new covenant" (v. 24). What a family!

In that family, the Lord Jesus is our Elder Brother, into whose image we are being transformed. The Spirit is the Spirit of adoption, who assures us inwardly of all the family blessings that are ours and helps us to grow more and more like our Elder Brother. This isn't a picture; it isn't wishful thinking. It's what Hebrews 12:18–24 tells us is already true.

There are some important lessons we can learn here. One is that this explains why we're told not to neglect meeting together (Heb.

10:25). If we understand what is truly happening when we meet, who would be foolish enough to miss it if they could possibly be present? This also helps to explain why true worship is such a blessed experience, because we've gone to a far better attended worship service than we realized.

There is one more lesson. If this is what church is, if this is what worship is, don't you think it would transform both our worship and our church life to realize that we are family?

This is important today. We're living in a culture full of dysfunctional families and a world full of young people who, as a result, have no idea who they are or where they belong. They are told to make themselves up. But when our churches become expressions of this wonderful reality that we are family, then all kinds of people, young and old, are able to look at our church family and think: "That looks like how life was meant to be. Look at how these Christians love one another. How on earth has that happened?" And the answer is: "This is the family of God. This is the church that Jesus is building. And in that church, you are welcome, and you will be loved for Jesus' sake."

So make sure you enter the church through Jesus, the door. After all, it's His church.

WEEK 29

Old Testament Passages That Shaped Jesus

1

Meeting Christ in the Old Testament

SOMETHING HAS HAPPENED IN THE LAST few decades in some evangelical preaching, as well as in the training of younger men and women to read and teach the Bible. What is it? We hear a lot more about "finding Christ in the Old Testament" or "preaching Christ from the Old Testament." The key verse is almost always Luke 24:27, in which Cleopas and his companion meet Jesus on the road to Emmaus and do not recognize Him at first. We're told that "beginning with Moses and all the Prophets, [Jesus] interpreted to them in all the Scriptures the things concerning himself."

At pastors' conferences, in training programs on Bible reading, and in the preaching of many younger ministers, there has developed a huge emphasis on what I would call "getting to Christ" or "preaching Christ" from the Old Testament. That is not a new idea. People have been doing that for a long, long time. And I'm all for preaching Christ from the Old Testament because it does point to Him.

But I have to confess that sometimes I'm left with the feeling that it's being done today in a very mechanical way. There are actually books that will tell you the five, or the seven, or the ten ways to do it, so that after listening to a number of sermons, you can begin to guess which way the preacher is going to connect the text to Christ. It can end up sounding more formulaic than organic, more like applying a system than talking about a real, living flesh-and-blood person. It doesn't sound as though Jesus is someone who is loved so much as

Jesus is someone who solves a problem in the incomplete story of the Hebrew Bible.

One of the inadequacies in all this is that when some preachers have shown you how to get to Jesus from the Old Testament passage, they just stop. They don't actually present the incarnate Lord Jesus as the wonderful person He is—full of perfect love, wisdom, kindness, grace, patience, and humanity. It feels more like someone's finding the answer to the final clue in the daily crossword puzzle than finding the living, breathing, loving Savior.

In addition, sometimes next to nothing is said about the personal, psychological realities that are being described in the Old Testament passage that is being preached. I've also noticed that preachers who have learned a method of preaching Christ from the Old Testament and who follow that method every time they come to the Old Testament don't always connect passages in the New Testament to the Lord Jesus.

Why do I say all this? My concern here is to underline that a significant difference exists between reading and teaching the Bible as a piece of literature using certain principles of interpretation, and meeting with the living Lord Jesus to whom the Bible points. He is not Himself a piece of literature, but a living person.

What we need is to meet Jesus through His Word, not to confuse Him with the pages of the Bible that point us to Him. This is critical because only then does reading or preaching the Bible pass the litmus test that Cleopas and his companion experienced. When the Old Testament points us to *this* Christ, our hearts burn within us.

The reason I wanted to mention this is that I want to focus our attention this week on four passages in the Old Testament that very clearly point to Christ because the New Testament itself makes it clear that they do.

When Luke tells us that Jesus showed Cleopas and his companion things about Himself in all the Scriptures, I don't think He began with

Genesis 1:1 and went through the Bible verse by verse. But I am sure He would have mentioned the four passages we're going to focus on the rest of this week. I think He might have said to them: "Don't you see now how the person described in these verses was Me? Do you see how they promised that I would suffer and then be glorified?"

What do you think these passages might be? Here's a clue: they all belong to the same section of the same book of the Bible. Are you intrigued? Do you know the answer?

We'll unfold the answers this week.

2

A Bruised Reed He Will Not Break

WE NEED TO THINK CAREFULLY ABOUT how the Old Testament points to the Lord Jesus. This week, we will look at four Old Testament passages that the New Testament makes clear would have been in Jesus' own mind during His lifetime, as well as in His post-resurrection teaching about the things in the Bible that concerned Himself. I wonder if you guessed that the passages are all in the second half of Isaiah, in what we call the Servant Songs. You'll find them in chapters 42, 49, 50, and 52:13–53:12.

Isaiah foresaw that since the people of God had breached His covenant, they were destined for judgment. As He had promised, God would send them into a far country into exile. But as he looks into the future, Isaiah sees deliverance and restoration to the promised land on the horizon. Remarkably, it would come through Cyrus, the pagan king of Persia. That is why Isaiah 40 begins with the words that we are familiar with from Handel's *Messiah*: "Comfort, comfort my people, says your God" (v. 1).

In chapter 6, Isaiah describes his experience of becoming profoundly aware of his own sinfulness. He then becomes equally profoundly aware of the fact that the people's geographical exile was simply a reflection of a much more sinister exile. And so he knew that political deliverance was not an adequate solution to their real problem, which was spiritual: their sin. What the people really needed was deliverance from their deeper bondage to sin and their exile from God.

God gave Isaiah insight into how He would bring that deliverance. The Lord would use His servant Cyrus to bring about political restoration, but it would take a different kind of Servant to rescue Israel from the power and consequences of sin. And so over the horizon, a shadowy figure begins to appear. His presence is announced in these words in Isaiah 42:1: "Behold my servant, whom I uphold . . . ; I have put my Spirit upon him."

That poem is worth meditating on. Let's look more closely at just one of Isaiah 42's amazing statements, which is quoted in Matthew 12:18–20 and refers there specifically to the Lord Jesus: "He will not cry aloud or lift up his voice, or make it heard in the street; a bruised reed he will not break, and a faintly burning wick he will not quench" (Isa. 42:2–3).

That is such a beautiful description of the Lord Jesus, isn't it? I love that Isaiah's poem begins with the words, "*Behold* my servant." In other words, "Look at Him." I hope you can find time to do that today—not just to see the words but to actually consider Jesus in these words and focus on the One to whom the words point, admiring and loving Him. It's the lack of doing this that tends to weaken our Christian lives.

Think about these two descriptions of Jesus. If I were walking through a field and came across a slender reed that had been damaged, my instinct would be to do what I would've done as a boy: pull it up, break it off completely, and throw it away—just finish the job. It's had its day; it's done.

But Jesus doesn't do that.

Then think of the other picture: a dimly burning wick. Where we live in Scotland, storms sometimes cause power outages, and occasionally we have to resort to using candles. Eventually they burn down, the light begins to flicker, and there is smoke. What do I do? Well, I just snuff out the candle. It's useless now, and I discard it.

But what if the bruised reeds and the dimly burning wicks are people? Weak people, frail people, people whom life has damaged, even people we don't see any use for any longer? Does Jesus ignore them or snuff them out? After all, they are just dimly burning wicks.

Truth to tell, we're all bruised reeds and dimly burning wicks in the Lord's sight, but He doesn't throw us away or snuff us out.

I've met Christians who live in fear that Jesus is going to do exactly that to them. That is why this word *behold* is so important. *Behold* Jesus. Look. See what He is really like. He is a gracious, kind, tenderhearted, and patient Savior to His people. He doesn't break bruised reeds or snuff out dimly burning wicks. Instead, He mends them and fans them into life.

A couple of verses later in this passage, the Servant is described in this way: "He will not grow faint or be discouraged" (Isa. 42:4). These words actually echo what was said earlier about Jesus. The Lord Jesus is able to help bruised reeds and dimly burning wicks because He was victorious when His heel was bruised (Gen. 3:15). And although the darkness sought to extinguish the light, the Light of the World still shines (John 8:12).

That is what makes Him exactly the kind of Savior we all need. So let's make sure we behold Him today.

3

A Light for the Nations

THIS WEEK, WE'RE LOOKING AT A remarkable series of prophetic poems, or songs, in the second half of the prophecy of Isaiah. We call them the Servant Songs, and we saw the first one yesterday in Isaiah 42.

Today's song is in Isaiah 49, and it's a little different. In the first song, it's God the Father who says, "Behold my servant" (Isa. 42:1). But in the second song, the Servant Himself begins to speak. At one point, He even dialogues with the Father, who says to Him, "You are my servant" (49:3).

Then amazingly, the Servant is described as "the LORD," even when He is talking about Himself as honored by the Lord His God (v. 5). In the Gospels, we read about the religious leaders trying to trap Jesus by asking Him trick questions that they think He won't or can't answer. At one point, He challenges them in return. He says in effect, "OK, tell Me this: Explain Psalm 110:1."

These leaders had been rightly taught that the Messiah would be the Son of David. Jesus asks, "How is it then that David, in the Spirit, calls him Lord, saying, 'The Lord said to [David's] Lord, "Sit at my right hand, until I put your enemies under your feet?'" If then David calls him Lord, how is he his son?" (Matt. 22:43–45).

You can see the point Jesus is making. You don't call your son "Lord." If anything, it's the other way around. The only answer to Jesus' question is this: Psalm 110:1 must mean that the Messiah would be born in David's line, but He would be the very Son of God. These words in Psalm 110 can mean only one thing: the Lord God would become incarnate. He would take human nature from the family of David.

In Isaiah 49, the Servant of the Lord, the Messiah, is also being presented as divine. But what's so amazing about this passage is that in the very same context—in which the Servant is clearly the Lord God Himself—He is equally clearly clothed in the weakness of our flesh and exposed to humiliation. The passage speaks about the Servant's feeling He has spent His strength in vain. There seems to be no fruit.

The Gospels tell us that everyone deserted Jesus, and at the end, He cried out, "My God, my God, why have you forsaken me?" (Matt.

27:46). This passage in Isaiah 49 answers that question. The Lord God replies that because His Servant has been willing to experience all this, God's people will be accepted and welcomed back. His sense of alienation is the root of our sense of welcome.

He goes on to say that this will not be limited to bringing back the elect or the preserved of Israel: "I will make you as a light for the nations, that my salvation may reach to the end of the earth" (Isa. 49:6). This reminds us of the promise the Father gives to the Son in Psalm 2:8: "Ask of me, and I will make the nations your heritage." Christ's path of suffering was to be His path to glory. This is the very point He made to the two disciples on the Emmaus Road. His salvation will reach to the ends of the earth.

We're living in days when this prophecy is being fulfilled. That is true despite all the doom and gloom we hear about the church. It's true that we haven't yet fully fulfilled the Great Commission, and the church often fails. But God's promise to His Son that He will give Him the nations for His inheritance has not failed, and it will not fail.

I remember teaching a one-week intensive course in seminary with around fifty wonderful students from all over the world. They came from Latin America, from India, from the Far East, from Nepal, from Uganda, from the United States, and from Canada. And there I was in the middle of them as someone from Scotland. We were not only a group of students together, but also a visible expression of the way these words in Isaiah are being fulfilled today.

So let's not lose heart. As the hymn says, "Jesus shall reign where'er the sun does his successive journeys run; his kingdom stretch from shore to shore, till moons shall wax and wane no more."

He has promised it, and so it will be.

4

The Savior's Open Ear

WE KNOW FROM THE NEW TESTAMENT that both the Lord Jesus Himself and the Apostles saw the Servant Songs in Isaiah as prophecies of Jesus' ministry that give clues to His character and significance. Today, we will reflect on the third of these songs in Isaiah 50:4–9. If this is the first time you can remember reading Isaiah 50:4–9, I hope you'll read it again and again. It's not only one of the most beautiful descriptions of the Lord Jesus in the Old Testament, but also one of the most instructive. So let's look at a few points from it today.

First, in this poem the Servant Himself speaks and picks up what was said of Him earlier in the first Servant Song. He is able "to sustain with a word him who is weary" (Isa. 50:4). If you're Anglican, you'll be familiar with the words of the prayer book communion service, which introduces Jesus' words from Matthew 11:28: "Hear what comfortable words our Saviour Christ saith unto all that truly turn to him: 'Come to me, all you who labor and are heavy laden, and I will give you rest.'" These words in Isaiah are the explanation for Jesus' words in Matthew's gospel. He is the One who gives rest to the weary.

Isaiah 50 goes on to explain why the Lord Jesus is able to do this. Listen to what the Servant says: "Morning by morning he awakens; he awakens my ear to hear as those who are taught" (v. 4). He wakes up in the morning and says to His Father, "Speak, Lord, for Your Servant is listening."

What was Jesus listening to? How did His heavenly Father communicate with Him in His humanity? There is an element of mystery here. But sometimes when we talk about reading our Bibles, we speak about the ministry of the Spirit in illuminating the Scriptures. He brings insight and understanding to us, and we say, "Oh, now I see it," or, "Now I see how it applies." Perhaps it was something like that with Jesus.

He wouldn't have owned His own Bible. That is a thought, isn't it? He couldn't have afforded a Hebrew Bible of His own, but He had memorized it thoroughly, perhaps every single word of it. In fact, He knew it so well that when He was tempted, He was able to quote Deuteronomy 8:3, 6:13, and 6:16. Most of us can't do that, no matter how many Bibles we own.

I wonder if there were mornings when Jesus woke up and these very passages in Isaiah 42, 49, and 50 were already on His mind, as though His Father had quietly placed them in His ear. And when Jesus woke up, He would reflect on how He might fulfill them that very day.

But there is more here. The Father not only *awakened* the Servant's ear; He also *opened* it. The Servant not only heard what the Father said; He listened in the sense of taking it in, working it out, applying it to Himself, and being obedient to His heavenly Father. Remember how He said that He lived by every word that proceeds from the mouth of God? Think of it: every word. And in His case, that led in only one direction: to the cross.

Listen to what He goes on to say here: "I was not rebellious. . . . I gave my back to those who strike, and my cheeks to those who pull out the beard; I hid not my face from disgrace and spitting" (Isa. 50:5–6). We read the fulfillment of these words in the passion narratives of the Gospels. Our Lord knew that His loving obedience to the Father's plan would lead to being humiliated and crucified.

But He also knew from this passage that His Father would be with Him and help Him. The disgrace and the shame would not last beyond the garden tomb and the resurrection because although He would be treated as guilty and condemned, He was actually innocent. And all His enemies, human and supernatural, would not be able to keep this good man down. In fact, He says here that they will all be like a piece of clothing that a moth has eaten up—one touch from God and death will fall to pieces before Him.

This is surely worth meditating on today so that our love for the Lord Jesus grows and grows. If this picture of the Savior doesn't make us want to sing, "Hallelujah! what a Savior," I'm honestly not sure what will.

5

The Gospel according to Isaiah

WE'VE BEEN THINKING THIS WEEK ABOUT the Servant Songs that the prophet Isaiah wrote about the Messiah. But if someone had asked Isaiah who it was he was writing about, he'd have had to say he didn't really know. He certainly didn't know exactly who He was or when He would come. Peter reminds us of this in 1 Peter 1:10–12.

The prophets wrote about the grace that others would experience in the future. God especially enabled Isaiah to write about how the Messiah would suffer before He entered His glory, even if he didn't know who He would be or exactly when or how He would come.

Today, I want to draw attention to the fourth song. It's the best-known one. Most of us think about it as the Suffering Servant song of Isaiah 53. But the song actually doesn't begin at Isaiah 53:1; it begins at Isaiah 52:13.

It begins with the same words as the first Servant Song: "Behold, my servant" (v. 13). The opening stanza in the song speaks first about the exaltation of the Servant: "He shall be high and lifted up" (v. 13), and then it goes on to speak about His humiliation: "His appearance was so marred, beyond human semblance" (v. 14). It then goes on to speak about the effect of the Servant's work: "So shall he sprinkle many nations" (v. 15). That surely refers to His saving work. Even kings will become silent one day in His presence (v. 15).

But then the song goes into the details with which most of us are more familiar. Chapter 53 explains why He will be so highly exalted:

it's because He was so profoundly humiliated for our sakes. These verses not only fill out the picture of His sufferings, but also explain it. They tell us that the reason for those sufferings was our sin, that He was wounded for our transgressions and bruised for our iniquities, that He died under the judgment of God. But it was our judgment He was taking, and because of that, He was raised up and exalted.

Almost every time I read these verses, I remember a morning assembly in my final year in high school. One of my friends stood up to read the Bible lesson for the day. It was just an ordinary state school (times have really changed!). The passage for the day was Isaiah 53, and my friend introduced it with these words: "The reading this morning is from the gospel according to Isaiah." I still remember my instinctive reaction: "Oh, Hugh, Isaiah isn't a gospel; it's a prophecy." I'm sure he knew that, and it was just a slip of the tongue.

But later on, I thought: "Hugh, you are absolutely right. You couldn't be more right about Isaiah 53. It's the gospel according to Isaiah. It's the gospel of Jesus, the gospel of the Suffering Servant. It's the gospel that the Holy Spirit enabled Isaiah to write, even if he wasn't able to understand what he was writing."

So centuries before our Lord Jesus came into the world, the pattern of His life was there in the Bible.

Earlier in the week, we heard the Servant say to the Father, "You waken my ear each morning and open My ear to listen, and I commit Myself to You and to this plan of salvation" (see Isa. 50:4). How wonderful it is to think that the Lord Jesus must have learned Isaiah 53 by heart when He was probably the same age I was, and perhaps even younger. He increasingly understood that this passage was speaking about Him and was telling Him what the Servant of the Lord was to be.

How wonderful that He committed Himself to doing the will of His Father, knowing that this would entail so much suffering, and that He did that out of love for His Father and love for us. That surely makes us want to sing:

Died he for me, who caused his pain? . . .
Amazing love! How can it be
That thou, my God, shouldst die for me?

Or maybe we want to sing:

See, from his head, his hands, his feet,
Sorrow and love flow mingled down:
Did e'er such love and sorrow meet,
Or thorns compose so rich a crown?

Or perhaps this is what we should be singing today:

Were the whole realm of nature mine,
That were a present far too small;
Love so amazing, so divine,
Demands [and shall have] my soul, my life, my all.

I hope you feel that way, too, today.

WEEK 30

The Temptations of Jesus

1

He Was Tempted As We Are

LAST WEEK, WE LOOKED AT A SERIES of passages from Isaiah that shaped the life of our Lord Jesus. This week, we will continue our focus on Jesus, this time looking at His temptations.

When someone mentions the temptations of Christ, most of us probably instinctively think of the forty days at the beginning of Jesus' ministry. But Jesus also spoke about His whole life as being a time of testing. Toward the end of His life, He said to the Apostles, "You are those who have stayed with me in my trials" (Luke 22:28). The book of Hebrews emphasizes that throughout His whole life, Jesus was tempted in every way, just as we are (Heb. 4:15).

How can that be, and what does that mean? After all, the Scriptures teach us that Jesus is the Son of God; He is divine. And the book of James says that God does not tempt and that He cannot be tempted (James 1:13). So how could Jesus really be tempted?

This is where our Christology helps us. R.C. Sproul wrote a book with a fascinating title: *Everyone's a Theologian*. We are all theologians, and the point of that book is that we need to learn to be good ones. If we are not clear on our theology (and in this case, our Christology), if we haven't seen how the biblical teaching about Jesus fits together, then we'll be confused about what the Bible is saying here in regard to Jesus' temptation.

How could God the Son be tempted? It's because He was truly man as well as truly God. He was as truly human as you and I are. He had flesh and bones and blood. He grew physically. He grew mentally. He felt pain. He needed sleep. He had emotions. At times, He was filled with joy. Other times, He was deeply distressed.

The Chalcedonian Definition of AD 451, which we've mentioned before, helps us here. It explains that Scripture teaches that Jesus is a divine person and therefore has a divine nature. He also assumed our human nature. But these two natures were never mixed or confused. There was no point in Jesus' life when His human nature was given a little injection from His divine nature so that it, for example, could withstand special pressures or be immune to temptation. No, our Lord Jesus knows what it's like for human nature to be tempted.

And since Jesus always withstood that temptation in ways that we don't, He knows what it's like to be tempted to the extreme. When Hebrews says that God's Son was tempted in all points as we are, obviously it doesn't mean that He experienced every single temptation in every situation of the sum total of Christians who have ever lived. Rather, it means that there is no dimension of temptation and testing that He didn't experience to the full.

Of course, there is a very important difference between the Lord Jesus and us. Without this difference, Jesus could never have become our Savior. There are temptations that come to us from outside ourselves—from the world and from the evil one—and Jesus experienced these in full. He never gave in. He experienced their force to the maximum.

But there are also temptations that are sourced from within us. They may be heightened by the world and the devil, but they are rooted in our own fallen and sinful nature, in our flesh. That was never true of Jesus. You remember how He once said: "The ruler of this world is coming. He has no claim on me" (John 14:30). What Jesus meant was this: "There is nothing in Me that Satan can land on, no loose thread of sin that he can pull on to unravel Me."

If Jesus had been tempted by His own desires, it would mean that

He had sinful desires; He wouldn't be holy and undefiled and separated from sinners. He would never have been able to act as our sinless substitute and sacrifice, and He could never clothe us in His own perfect righteousness.

Not only that, He'd need help Himself, too. Someone who has failed can't really give us the help we need.

We need someone who has never failed. Only such a person can help us not to fail. And Jesus is exactly that kind of Savior because He faced temptation and overcame it.

2

Christ's Victory in the Wilderness

FOR THE NEXT FEW DAYS, WE WILL THINK about the temptations of Christ in the wilderness, which are recorded in the Synoptic Gospels. After His baptism and an extended period of fasting, Jesus was confronted by the devil. Satan faced Jesus with three specific temptations. These accounts of the wilderness temptations are not recorded to tell us how to resist temptation. They may help us to do that, but they aren't primarily about our temptations. They are about Jesus' temptations.

I sometimes refer to what I call the "Where's Waldo?" (or "Wally" in the United Kingdom) approach to reading the Gospels. The whole point of the Where's Waldo? books is to find Waldo in a crowd of people. When I first saw those books, I thought: "That is how some of us read the Gospels, with ourselves as Waldo. We're looking for ourselves in the story. Am I there as Nicodemus, or Zacchaeus, or Simon Peter?" The problem with that approach is twofold. First, we weren't there. Second, and perhaps even more important, it can divert us from looking at Jesus in the story and discovering more about who He is and what He is like.

When we read the temptation narrative, we can make the mistake of thinking, "The most important question here is, How does this passage help *me* to deal with temptation?" While it does that, the point of the passage is not so much to help *me* deal with temptation. It's about how *Jesus* dealt with these very special temptations because He is our Savior. This is about Him, not about me. It's about what He has done for me, not what I need to do for Him.

There is something right at the beginning of the temptation narrative that underlines this for us. Each of the first three Gospels says it in one form or another. Matthew puts it this way: "Then Jesus was *led up* by the Spirit into the wilderness to be tempted by the devil" (4:1, emphasis added). Mark says, "The Spirit immediately *drove* [Jesus] out into the wilderness" to be tempted (1:12, emphasis added). And Luke notes, "Jesus, full of the Holy Spirit, returned from the Jordan and was *led* by the Spirit in the wilderness for forty days, being tempted by the devil" (4:1–2, emphasis added).

Do you see the point? There is a military strategy here. Satan is the prince of this world. He has usurped the authority and dominion that God originally gave to Adam. In Genesis 1:26–28, we are told that God made man in His image and gave him dominion. And now the divine director of military operations, the Holy Spirit, is leading out the great general, Jesus Christ, into the field of combat to regain that dominion.

The Holy Spirit is the connecting link between the heavenly operations center and the battlefront. What we have here—to borrow language from World War II—is the beginning of D-Day. Something is going to happen here for the first time in human history. The man, Christ Jesus, the new Adam, is going to enter enemy-occupied territory—a garden that has been turned into a wilderness by the enemy—and He is going to face him down, withstand his fiercest attacks, and conquer him.

And so the temptation narrative is really all about Genesis 3:15 coming to pass. The seed of the woman is beginning to crush the head of the serpent. That is what caused Martin Luther to sing:

But for us fights the proper Man
whom God himself hath bidden.
Ask ye, who is this same?
Christ Jesus is his name . . .

And He will win the battle. In the desert, the Lord Jesus began to fight that battle in earnest and won it. Of course, there were more battles to come before the war was over, but this was a significant one. And because of that, we can be more than conquerors through Him who loved us.

Tomorrow, we will think more about what it means that Jesus has conquered the enemy.

3

Not by Bread Alone

WE'VE SEEN SO FAR THIS WEEK that the Gospel writers' purpose in describing Jesus' temptations was not to set Jesus before us simply as an example. Rather, they are telling us that Jesus is, in a sense, returning to the scene of Adam's failure. But now He is not in a garden surrounded by tame animals who meekly accept the names He gives them because He is their King (contrast Gen. 2:19). Instead, He is in the wilderness, and Mark tells us that He is with wild animals (1:13). He is in a fallen world, and He has been led there by the divine strategist, the Holy Spirit. He has entered enemy-occupied territory, and He is going to win back dominion.

Jesus is confronted with three temptations. They are described in detail by both Matthew and Luke, and both tell us that the first temptation was, "If you are the Son of God, command these stones to become loaves of bread" (Matt. 4:3; see Luke 4:3).

We needn't be rocket scientists or technical theologians to figure out the motive behind this temptation. Jesus has been fasting. He is no doubt weak. He is hungry. So Satan says to Him, "Jesus, if You are the Son of God, do a miracle and feed Yourself."

The words "if You are the Son of God" could mean one of two things. Satan could be saying: "If it really is true that You're God's Son, then You would be able to do this. I'll challenge You. I'll bet You can't." Or it could mean: "Since it's true that You are God's Son, You shouldn't be starving. Your Father wouldn't want that, would He? So Jesus, what harm would there be in turning these stones into bread?"

Jesus knew that He was God's Son, and Satan obviously knew it, too. Therefore, I'm personally inclined to take the second view here. If that is the case, then we notice several features about this temptation that are reminiscent of Satan's temptation in the garden of Eden.

First, Satan uses a similar technique. He tempts Eve by saying, in effect: "You know, God's really mean. Did He really say that you couldn't have any of this gorgeous fruit of these trees?" He says to Jesus: "Look, Jesus, you're God's Son. You have all this power. Your Father has led You here by the Spirit, and He is not giving You any food. Don't you think that is mean? Turn these stones into bread."

Later, Jesus turned a few loaves and fish into food for thousands. So what could possibly be wrong with turning a few stones into a few bread rolls for one person, especially since He is the Son of God? Surely it was OK to stave off His hunger; otherwise, He was in danger of dying.

But there is a great gulf fixed between these two things. Jesus fed the multitude because of their need and because He loved them. But here in the wilderness, He recognized that Satan was tempting Him to be diverted from His Father's will, to doubt His goodness, and to take matters into His own hands.

That is why Jesus replied, "Man shall not live by bread alone, but by every word that comes from the mouth of God" (Matt. 4:4). That was exactly what Adam and Eve failed to do. But this man—the second man and the last Adam—was going to resist when the tempter said to Him what he had first said to Adam and Eve: "Why don't you just eat?"

It's wonderful that Jesus lived not by bread alone but by every word from God's mouth, because the mistake that Adam and Eve made was to live according to the fruit they saw on the tree and not according to the words that came from God's mouth. What Jesus did here is expressed in the hymn "Praise to the Holiest in the Height":

> O wisest love! that flesh and blood,
> Which did in Adam fail,
> Should strive afresh against the foe,
> Should strive and should prevail.

I wonder if that morning, when Jesus woke from whatever sleep He'd been able to have, He remembered the words that we were thinking about last week:

> Morning by morning . . .
>   he awakens my ear. . . .
> The Lord GOD has opened my ear,
>   and I was not rebellious;
>   I turned not backward. (Isa. 50:4–5)

That is certainly what happened in these wilderness temptations.

What a strong Savior the Lord Jesus is. He is the victorious second man. That is actually why He is also called the *last* Adam, because nobody now will ever need to do what He did for us. Hallelujah! what a Savior!

4

The Pinnacle of the Temple

MATTHEW AND LUKE DESCRIBE THE three temptations of Jesus in detail, but they record them in different orders.

In Matthew, the order is (1) turning stones into bread, (2) throwing Himself down from the temple, and (3) receiving the kingdoms of this world in exchange for worshiping Satan.

But in Luke, the order is (1) turning stones into bread, (2) receiving the kingdoms of this world in exchange for worshiping Satan, and (3) throwing Himself down from the temple.

To some Bible readers, that seems very puzzling. But there is almost certainly a straightforward explanation. These two Gospel writers are each recording the three temptations in terms of what they want to communicate to us about the Lord Jesus. Today, we'll look at Luke's ordering of these events.

Luke's climax is with the temptation for Jesus to throw Himself down from the temple. Satan said, "If you are the Son of God, throw yourself down from here, for it is written, 'He will command his angels concerning you, to guard you,' and 'On their hands they will bear you up, lest you strike your foot against a stone'" (Luke 4:9–11).

It's interesting that in this temptation, the devil actually quotes Scripture. To be specific, he quotes from Psalm 91:11–12.

In the earlier temptations, it was Jesus who was quoting Scripture. Now it's as if the devil is trying to throw the Bible back in Jesus' face. He quotes these promises that were given to believers in general, and he challenges Jesus by essentially saying: "Since You're the Son of God, prove that these promises hold good by giving a spectacular demonstration that they work. Go on, Jesus. Test God to see if His promises are true, and then people will flock to You." It is worth remembering that the devil uses (or more accurately, misuses) the Bible.

How did Jesus respond? He demonstrates that He knows and uses Scripture better than the devil does. He answers this false use of Scripture with true and authentic biblical teaching, saying, "You shall not put the LORD your God to the test" (Deut. 6:16). With these words, He unmasks Satan. Jesus has come to fulfill the purposes of God, not to tell God that He needs to prove His Word to Him. And God's purpose was that the Lord Jesus would be crucified for our sins. And as Jesus Himself would later make clear, His disciples would then take up their cross and follow Him.

It's interesting that Jesus is being tempted here to gather disciples by another way altogether—by a spectacular action. The devil knows that people love spectacular events and are impressed by them. But Jesus recognizes that it's unbelief that says, "I'd believe in Jesus if He did something spectacular." Jesus didn't come to win converts by parading spectacular powers; He came to save sinners by suffering and dying on the cross for them, and only then rising victorious over sin, death, hell, and Satan.

That is why He resisted the temptation to leap from the temple. He certainly would have created a stir that way, but He couldn't save sinners from the wrath of God that way. And that is what He came to do.

I'm so glad that He refused to be diverted, and I hope you are, too.

5

All the Kingdoms of the World

TODAY, WE'RE CONCLUDING OUR WEEK OF REFLECTIONS on the wilderness temptations of our Lord Jesus. We noted that Luke and Matthew arranged the temptations in a different order. So far, we have reflected on the temptations to turn stones into bread and to leap down from the temple. These are the first and the last ones in Luke's gospel. The middle one—Satan's bargain—is the climactic temptation in Matthew's gospel. If Jesus will bow down and worship Satan just once, then He can have all the kingdoms of this world.

First, let's explain Matthew's order. One of the themes at the beginning and at the end of his gospel is that while Jesus came from among the Jews, He came to save people of every nation. So at the beginning of Matthew's gospel, wise men come from the east to worship Jesus, and at the end, His disciples are sent into the world with the good news about Jesus. Therefore, it would be natural for Matthew to climax his description with a temptation that concerned all the nations or all the kingdoms of this world.

But there is something else here, and the best way to explore it is by asking this question: "Why was this really a temptation?" I ask that question for a fairly obvious reason. If this were you, would it be such a great temptation? I suspect many of us would think the whole thing was ridiculous. Who did Satan think he was, offering Jesus the kingdoms of this world? He doesn't have any right to do that, does he?

But Jesus understood that He was being offered exactly what was lost by the fall.

Adam and Eve were created to have dominion, to extend the kingdom of God to the ends of the earth. But Satan had usurped that dominion. He became the prince of this world. And I think that is the reason that this is the climactic temptation in Matthew's gospel. All the kingdoms of the world are on offer. Satan is prepared to part with them if Jesus will just worship him once. And apparently, Satan did have the ability to make that offer.

What made this a very real temptation—and I think this is why Matthew sees this as the climactic temptation—is that this is exactly what Jesus came into the world to regain. Satan knew exactly why this temptation might be attractive to Jesus. He is the second man. He is the last Adam. He has come to regain what Adam lost, to restore what might have been, to gain dominion over the earth, and to purchase people for God from every tongue and tribe and people and nation. In a sense, Satan is offering Jesus the very thing that God sent Him into the world to regain, and He is offering it to Him without the pain of the coming years and their terrible climax in His cruel death on the cross.

There is even more here. It looks as though Satan is prepared to give up his own hard-won dominion for the sake of getting back at God by diverting Jesus from God's will. That is why our Lord's response here is so important. Where Adam failed, Jesus succeeded. Where Adam and Eve listened to the serpent and disobeyed God, Jesus listened to the voice of God and obeyed Him in our place.

We noted at the beginning of the week that when we read the temptation narrative, we shouldn't first be asking, "How does this help *me* overcome temptation?" because the passage is about Him, who He is, what He came to do, and what He has done. It's not about us.

But perhaps we should end the week on this note. Here's how Jesus resisted temptation, and here's what will enable us to resist temptation, too: trusting in the One who has overcome Satan and learning to say, "I will worship the Lord my God, and Him only will I serve." Satan cannot withstand the soul that is resolutely committed to the Lord Jesus and has experienced His salvation.

I hope you have that resolution, and I hope you've experienced His amazing salvation. Hallelujah, indeed, what a Savior!

WEEK 31

Soul Shapes

1

The Shape of the Soul

THIS WEEK, WE WILL BE EXPLORING what I call "soul shapes." You could look through many volumes of systematic theology and not find a section titled "soul shapes"—you could probably look through every Christian book you own and still not find a reference to "soul shapes"! So what do I mean by this phrase?

It's a slightly idiosyncratic way of thinking about ourselves and the challenges we face as individuals—challenges that we don't even recognize. The idea came to me one day as I was thinking about one of our children, who works in the field of forensic psychiatry. Of course, she doesn't talk to me about her patients, some of whom seem to be very sick physically and mentally, and some of whom have been profoundly abused and come from very deprived backgrounds.

When our daughter was young, she was a great doodler. If she hadn't become a physician, she might have gotten a job as a syndicated cartoonist. This gave me a rather whimsical idea: maybe we could write a book together on spiritual conditions titled *Soul Shapes and How God Reshapes Them.* She could draw a series of illustrations of souls that are bent out of shape—sick and distorted—to make the point as visually vivid as possible. And then we could write on how the gospel reshapes us to the new norm—namely, our Lord Jesus Christ.

So soul shapes is our theme this week. But before we look at soul shapes, we need to think about what is meant by the term "soul."

Genesis 2:7 says, "The LORD God formed man of the dust of the ground, and breathed into his nostrils the breath of life; and man became a living soul" (KJV). In the Hebrew text, this is the very same language that is used in Genesis 1:24 of the animals that God created. Thus, when Genesis speaks about man becoming a living *soul*, it doesn't mean that he has some mysterious extra part to him that the animals don't have. Genesis uses the same language about the animals and about men and women; they are both living creatures, living souls.

What distinguishes humans from the animals, then, is not that we have souls and they don't. We're all God's living creatures. The difference is that we have been made in the image of God. That is who we are and what we are made to be. That is how we are intended to function. That is the specific soul shape that we have. That is the specific kind of living being we are. The animals certainly reflect God's creative genius, but they are not shaped the same way that we are, as His image and likeness.

The word that is used here in the Hebrew Bible for both animals and humans, *nephesh*, simply underlines our creatureliness. It carries with it the idea of being dependent on God for life and for all good things. We didn't create ourselves. We don't sustain ourselves. Every day, every hour, every moment, we are dependent on our loving and caring God for everything. We're meant to know this, to acknowledge it, to enjoy it, and to sense the privilege that it is.

"Soul" is not so much something we *have*; it's the privilege of what we *are*. We are shaped, as it were, in His image. We're meant to be a kind of miniature reflection of who He is. And because that is so, we have the very special potential to have fellowship with Him. That is what we were made for. That is why our souls have been fashioned the way they are.

Have you ever used a tool to do something it was never designed to do, and then, to your horror, damaged both the thing that you were trying to use it on as well as the tool itself? As a result, neither can now function as it was originally designed to do. The thing you were trying to fix gets bent out of shape, and the tool you were trying to use seems no longer useful. That is a kind of parable of what happened to our humanity in the garden of Eden.

In fact, one of the Hebrew words for *sin* has as its root meaning the idea of being twisted. As Paul says in Romans 1, we have exchanged the truth about God—and therefore the truth in our own lives as His image bearers, the truth of what we were meant to be—for the lie, not for neutrality. The result is that we've forfeited the glory of God for shame.

What Scripture teaches us is that we are all, by nature, souls that have been bent out of shape. What we need is for our true soul shape to be restored.

And the good news of the gospel is that Jesus Christ can effect that restoration.

2

Turned In on Ourselves

WE ARE MADE IN GOD'S IMAGE. We are meant to be like Him, to reflect His glory, and to glorify and enjoy Him forever. But we have sinned. We have distorted that likeness. We are bent out of shape. We are twisted. It's a bit like what happens when, instead of putting our car into drive (or first gear), we make the mistake of going into reverse. That is our basic problem. That is what sin does. It distorts the shape of what the Old Testament calls our *nephesh*, our soul. We're living in reverse gear!

Today, we'll begin looking at a few of the most common soul shapes. The first one may ring a bell with some of us. It's been known about for centuries, and it even has a Latin name. Martin Luther diagnosed it in the early sixteenth century. This soul shape—or perhaps more accurately, soul misshape—is what he called being *incurvatus in se*, being turned in on ourselves.

This is what Augustine meant when he said that there are two ultimate loves: love of God and love of self. We can love ourselves in the proper biblical sense only when we see ourselves as created by God as His image bearers and we live as His likeness and for His glory. When we turn away from that in our sin, we fall short of His glory. Something becomes distorted. We focus on ourselves, and everything we do, either obviously or subtly, becomes part of a new liturgy of self-centeredness.

As the English archbishop William Temple said so well, our sin means that we make ourselves, in a thousand different ways, the center of the universe. But when we do that, our soul is bent over and turned in on itself. It separates itself from the source of true life and nourishment and eventually starves itself of spiritual oxygen, shrivels up, becomes hard, and dies.

In C.S. Lewis' imaginative book *The Great Divorce*, he portrays a bus full of people coming from hell to heaven for a short visit. He describes how they cut their feet on the grass of heaven because it's too substantial for them to walk on. While shrunken souls can create their own very substantial-looking exterior self, the soul that lives for itself—however carefully disguised—cannot remain hidden forever. Its godlessness, its shrunkenness, will become manifest.

The question is: "Is there a remedy for this sickness? Is there a divine pharmaceutical? Can we be saved from it?" The answer, of course, is yes. There is restoration, healing, and transformation for souls curved in on themselves, and it's available to us in Jesus Christ. His lordship over our lives and our submission to Him as our Savior begins the marvelous reshaping of our souls. That is why the Son of God came from heaven.

The remedy for the bent soul shape is found in the way that the Lord Jesus came into the world that we have distorted. He lived a life of perfect soul shape, took the judgment of God against all our sinful distortions, and then by His grace gives us not only forgiveness but the beginnings of new life.

As He calls us to trust Him, He gives us the ability to repent, which really means the beginning of the turning back from the old sinful way, the turning outward to the Lord, and the reshaping of our souls in the likeness of the Lord Jesus, who is Himself the image of God.

It's significant that Martin Luther, who spoke about this basic problem of a bent soul shape as being *incurvatus in se*, also wrote in the very first of his famous Ninety-Five Theses, "When our Lord Jesus Christ said, 'Repent,' He meant that the whole of the Christian life should be repentance."

Yes, the whole Christian life is a process of souls that have been sinfully bent out of shape being bent back into shape by grace. That can be a painful process, but it's gloriously worth it. This is a word for all of us because this soul-shape distortion has affected every single one of us.

Thank God that Jesus can bend us back.

3

The Big-Headed Soul

I WONDER IF YOU'VE EVER THOUGHT the following: "I might never have been." After all, we did nothing to bring ourselves into being. More than that, this world might never have been. Our existence, the fact that we have life, we owe entirely to God. Because that is true, it's logical (and was originally instinctive) for us to love Him, to live for Him, to want to please Him, and to enjoy Him.

This reveals how sinful our sin really is because it even blinds us to these basic realities. We don't see God clearly, we don't see the world clearly, and we don't see ourselves clearly. What fools we are to make ourselves the center of the universe when, compared to our glorious Creator, we are no bigger than ants crawling across the ground. But we strut about so full of ourselves. We need to be reminded of Paul's words in Romans 9: "Who are you, O man, to answer back to God?" (v. 20).

Therefore, one way that our sin distorts our soul shape is that it causes our heads to inflate with pride and self-sufficiency. We are big-headed souls, and that is not a pretty sight.

The big-headed soul comes in various forms, but its basic form is that its mind is not willing to subordinate itself to Scripture, which is simply another way of saying that it's not willing to subordinate itself to God and to His mind. Paul puts it this way in Romans 8:7–8: "The mind that is set on the flesh is hostile to God, for it does not submit to God's law; indeed, it cannot. Those who are in the flesh cannot please God."

The diagnostic test of the inflated head is its reaction to that word "cannot." It's one thing to say that you *do not*. It's a step further to say that you *cannot*. "Do not" is a statement about a behavior pattern. "Cannot" is a statement about the very core of your being, about who you are as a person, about your total inability to do something. You are spiritually sick, mortally sick, and you cannot heal yourself. That is the problem of the soul that has an inflated head.

Acknowledging that you're sick is the first step to a cure. Refusing the diagnosis or believing that you can deal with it yourself and no one will tell you what you're not capable of doing—that is the road that leads to spiritual disaster, and it's actually the symptom of having this inflated-head soul. You're exalting your mind above God's Word, which reveals His mind. It's your word against the Word of the Great Physician. And unlike your mind, His mind understands the truth of the matter.

There are many manifestations of this head-enlarged soul. Alas, some of them remain after the renewal of regeneration has begun. We don't go straight to glory. There can be pride in the rightness of our own views, and that rears its ugly head from time to time. This isn't limited to times when our views are wrong and muddleheaded. It can also be the case when our views are right, which can be even more dangerous. We hold the right view but with an inflated-head soul. We hold the right view in the wrong way and in the wrong spirit. It manifests itself in the way that we speak to or about others, and it leaves a very distasteful impression on them.

Being biblical is not just a matter of getting things right; it's about *being* right. That means holding the truth in the spirit of the truth, in the atmosphere that is consistent with the truth. John 1:17 tells us that Jesus is full of grace and truth. When that is true of us, then our misshapen, big-headed souls begin to shrink to normal size again.

What's the remedy for the soul-shape distortion of big-headedness? Paul writes the prescription in Philippians 2:5–11. It flows out of our union to the Lord Jesus: "Have this mind among yourselves, which is yours in Christ Jesus, who, though he was in the form of God, did not count equality with God a thing to be grasped, but emptied himself, by taking the form of a servant, being born in the likeness of men" (vv. 5–7).

Jesus humbled Himself for our sakes. He took the servant form in human likeness. His thinking was conformed to the thinking of His heavenly Father. His mind was submitted to the revelation of His will. He was meek and lowly in heart. His soul shape was full of grace and truth. And here on earth, John and his fellow Apostles felt that they not only heard propositional truth from His lips; they experienced and saw truth in the grace and humility of His life and in His very atmosphere.

Jesus said that the Spirit would take what belonged to Him and show it to us (see John 16:14). That is what He wants to do now. And more than showing it to us, He wants to heal us, to reshape us to be more like our Lord Jesus.

It's both a relief and a blessing to read that there is medicine for our sick souls, and it lies here in these words of Philippians: "Have this mind among yourselves, which is yours in Christ Jesus."

4

Solutions for Distorted Souls

AS A YOUNGSTER, I WAS HELPED BY a comment written in the personal diary of Robert Murray M'Cheyne, a young Scottish minister in the first half of the nineteenth century. He wrote to this effect: "I have discovered that in me lie the seeds of every known sin."

We mustn't forget that.

But it's also true that each of us can be fertile soil for particular sins. Our souls can be bent out of shape in very individual and personal ways. I suspect that may be the reason that some of the letters in the New Testament have fairly lengthy lists of the sins of the flesh—or, as we might say, distortions of our soul shape.

The Apostle Paul gives one of these lists in Galatians 5:19–21: "Now the works of the flesh are evident: sexual immorality, impurity, sensuality, idolatry, sorcery, enmity, strife, jealousy, fits of anger, rivalries, dissensions, divisions, envy, drunkenness, orgies, and things like these." Some of these ugly soul shapes are more subtle than others. They include not only the obvious sins of the flesh, such as sexual immorality, but also what the late Jerry Bridges called "respectable" sins, such as strife, enmity, and jealousy. The other New Testament lists are rather similar.

It's interesting that we sometimes speak about a person's being "eaten up" with jealousy. What a picture that is of a soul shape: a person who sees something that someone else has and wants it. They begin to eat themselves away. A person who's jealous of someone else, in every moment of that jealousy, is eating themselves away in a process of self-destruction.

I wonder if you've ever met a Christian who gets irritated or angry and says, "I don't suffer fools gladly." It sounds as though they regard that as a virtue, but they don't realize that it's destroying them. They are suffering from a clogging up of their spiritual arteries, and the love and patience of the Lord Jesus isn't able to pulsate through them, enabling them to pity and love sinners.

After all, Jesus was willing to suffer fools to save and transform them. Jesus was full of compassion for foolish, wandering sheep. But this person thinks that such people deserve everything that he metes out to them in the way he dismisses them. He breaks bruised reeds and extinguishes dimly burning wicks. He doesn't realize how un-Jesus-like his soul is shaped.

The list of misshapen, distorted, disintegrating soul shapes could go on and on. And here's the challenging thing: we often don't notice it in ourselves. That is a real problem, but it is one for which the Lord provides courses of treatment that will help us.

Let me mention two of them briefly.

The first is friendships—Christian friends who know us, care about us, and are trustworthy. They love us enough to wound us if it's necessary. It's a terrible thing to be wounded in the house of your friends, but there is a Scripture that says, "Faithful are the wounds of a friend" (Prov. 27:6). Incidentally, that is one thing the gift of marriage is for: to help us know ourselves better and to be encouraged to grow in grace.

Here's another element of the treatment that goes along with the first. It's a remedy provided for us even if we're not married and even if we don't have really close friends, because every Christian has a friend who sticks closer than a brother (Prov. 18:24).

How does Jesus help us? He helps us through the regular preaching of His Word. I hope you've often discovered that under the faithful preaching of the Word, the Lord Jesus is speaking to you in a way no one else could—speaking about things in your life that, as far as you know, no one else could possibly know about.

He is like a physician who has a very special diagnostic gift, and as His Word is preached in the grace of the Spirit, we sense that the Lord Jesus is speaking to us personally. It's almost as though we hear God's voice saying the same words He said to the disciples on the Mount of Transfiguration: "This is my beloved Son ...; listen to him" (Matt. 17:5).

This may be why Paul told Timothy to preach the Word in a way that was consistent with its purpose: to teach, to reprove, and to *correct*. That word "correct" was used in the first century in the context of the practice of medicine. It's used of healing something that has been broken or distorted. There is a reshaping of our souls that takes place through the ministry of the Word.

I hope you have such a ministry. I hope you pray for it. And if you have it, please don't neglect it, because it will reshape your soul into the image of our Lord Jesus Christ.

5

Shaped by Grace

HAVE YOU EVER HEARD SOMEONE SAY, "Something seems to have bent him out of shape today"? It may be because that person is irritated and irritating, or because he is moody and uncommunicative. The effects are obvious. But what isn't so obvious about being bent out of shape is why it's happened. We see the effects, but we don't always know the cause. That is what I mean by a person's soul shape: it's the inner distortion that takes place invisibly in our hearts. It manifests itself either quickly or slowly in patterns of life that are un-Christlike.

Earlier this week, I mentioned how helpful a statement from Robert Murray M'Cheyne's diary has been to me: "The seeds of every known sin are in my heart." Yet at the same time, we are individuals, and sinful distortions manifest themselves in particular ways in particular people. We share a common disease and the same basic distortion, but it shapes itself individually.

When I was growing up, toothpaste used to come in metallic-type tubes. Sometimes little nicks or holes would appear, and as you squeezed the toothpaste, it would come out one of these little nicks in the side. When you put your finger on that nick to try to prevent the toothpaste from coming out, the toothpaste seemed to find another little nick from which to emerge!

That is a parable of the way sin works in our lives. Our sinfulness manifests itself at particular points of our spiritual weakness, and we try to cover that point up. But then it just reappears in another form. Sin will always out. And the fact that it appears in one way in my life and another way in your life doesn't mean that you have conquered sin in the area that I haven't; it just means it's manifesting itself at your lowest point of resistance, wherever you happen to be weak and easily tempted.

So much more could be said about different soul shapes, but I want to end this week by sharing something that has been helpful to me personally. I think it helps to protect Christians who are serious about sanctification from falling into the temptation to be judgmental about the frailties and weaknesses of others.

Around the time I was helped by those words of Robert Murray M'Cheyne, I was also helped by some words of the great seventeenth-century writer John Owen. He said that you don't measure someone's spiritual growth by the height that they seem to have attained but by the distance they've had to travel and the obstacles they've had to overcome to arrive where they are today.

I often think about that. I see people who really don't seem to be very tall spiritually, at least certainly not when compared with others. Some of them seem to be in so much need at times. They need encouragement. They almost seem to limp along, while others walk easily or even run. But then you discover their background—the damage that has been inflicted on them by others, the few advantages they've had.

They seem to us to be the little people, but we've not taken into account the tremendous obstacles they've experienced and overcome. The truth may be that they have grown far more than we have, even if to all appearances they have not reached the height that we think we have attained. But nothing is hidden from the eyes of our Savior. And He sees, hidden in the inner soul shape of these so-called little people, a development of spiritual graces that is far greater than ours, perhaps, because by His grace, they've overcome tremendous obstacles.

What I want us to avoid is knowing about soul shapes and then being critical of the shapes of others. That is why I mention this as something to bear in mind.

So don't measure someone else's soul shape or spiritual growth by how tall they seem to be. Rather, learn the obstacles they've overcome, and then you'll really begin to appreciate them. That is something to bear in mind when you're at church this coming Lord's Day. It'll make you a more appreciative member of whatever church you belong to.

WEEK 32

People Who Have Helped Me

1

Our Hidden Helpers

HAVE YOU EVER NOTICED THAT THE Apostle Paul mentions a remarkable number of fellow Christians in his letters? There are dozens and dozens of them, and we wouldn't know of their existence apart from these little cameos that he paints. They give us hints of what these people were like, what they meant to him, and how some of them helped him.

The name that often pops up in my mind is one that Paul mentions in Romans 16:13. He refers to a man named Rufus, and he describes him as "chosen in the Lord." But if all Christians are chosen in the Lord, why would Paul say that particularly about Rufus? I suspect it was because this was the Rufus who had a remarkable connection to the Lord Jesus. He was probably the Rufus mentioned in Mark 15:21, the son of Simon of Cyrene. Simon, if you remember, was the man who carried Jesus' cross to the place of His crucifixion. Mark would have mentioned Rufus and his brother Alexander in his gospel only if they were well known to the church. Paul also mentions Rufus's mother at the end of his letter to the Romans. He says this lovely thing about her: "[She] has been a mother to me as well." Isn't that beautiful?

I wonder if this kind of feature in the Bible—appreciation of an otherwise unknown woman who had obviously been such a blessing to Paul—has the same effect on you as it does me. It makes me think about individuals who have helped me in my own Christian life, but most people don't know much about them. I'd like to tell you about some of those people this week, not to draw attention to myself, but to think about people who are hidden away in our lives, just as Rufus's mother would have been hidden away in Paul's life. We wouldn't know anything about her if he hadn't devoted a sentence to her in Romans.

I hope this will encourage you to reflect with gratitude on the hidden people who have been a help and blessing to you as well.

In his letter to the Philippians, Paul says, "What you have learned and received and heard and seen in me—practice these things, and the God of peace will be with you" (4:9). That was part of his special role as an Apostle—to model the Christian life. But he also tells us to honor those who similarly follow Christ faithfully. That is because Christian faith and life are not merely matters of book learning, as though being a Christian were basically a matter of opening the Bible, studying it, and asking, "So what do I need to do to make a success of this?"

The Christian life is not only about *knowing* but about *being*. It's not merely about what we know but about what we become because of what we know. The ultimate purpose of biblical instruction is not only the renewal of our minds but what flows from that—as Romans 12:1–2 makes clear—namely, being transformed into the likeness of the Lord Jesus. Being a Christian can be something that is caught from others as well as taught. It's about a new way of living, about a style, about an atmosphere, about a manner of life that is worthy of Jesus. And we often learn that through the people who have helped us.

Think this week about the people in your own life as I share with you some reflections of the people who have helped me. I suspect that if you start doing that, you'll soon feel that you're in the same boat as the author of the letter to the Hebrews. He says toward the end of his list of the heroes of the faith in Hebrews 11 that time would fail to tell of all the people who came to mind.

I don't think I'm alone in feeling that what I am as a Christian and who I am as a Christian is in very large measure the fruit of other people's loving investment in my own life. Probably most of them have very little idea how much they've done to help me, and I suspect they wouldn't be able to take it in if I tried to tell them, as I've sometimes done. I've breathed in the atmosphere of the grace of Christ that they breathed out, and it's been a tremendous help to me.

This week, I'll mention a few people who helped me from my days as a young teenage Christian around the age of fifteen to the day I became a minister when I was twenty-three. And I suspect that each day this week, I'm going to feel even more grateful for their influence. The people I want to mention are not the well-known Christians who have influenced me, but the hidden people that you'll never meet—until perhaps you meet them in glory.

But today, you could start thinking with gratitude of the people who are hidden away in your own life and have been major blessings to you.

2

The Man in Black

I'M GOING TO CALL THE FIRST PERSON who helped me "the man in black." It's not Johnny Cash, the American singer who always dressed in black. This is a man I met only once in my life, but I've never forgotten him.

I was fourteen and had come under conviction of sin. Maybe people today would say I was a "seeker." Although we were not a churchgoing family, I'd started going to church morning and evening. One Sunday night in the dead of winter, I was walking down the hill to our home. There had been snow the previous week, and it had turned to ice. At one point, I felt my feet slide on the ice and just managed to regain my balance and stop.

As I stopped, I saw a shortish man standing right beside me. He was dressed in black from head to toe. If I remember rightly, he even had a black hat on his head. Men wore hats in those far-off days. I vividly remember seeing his eyes look at mine and glance down momentarily at the Bible I was carrying. Then he said to me out of the blue: "Are you saved, son? Are you saved?" Looking back, I can still remember tears coming unwillingly into my eyes. I said to him: "I don't know, but I want to be. I want to be more than anything else in the world." And he told me to go home and ask the Lord Jesus into my heart.

We parted, and five minutes later when I was home, I tried to do what he told me. And strange though it may sound, somehow I knew I wasn't succeeding. It felt too mechanical. More than that, I had a sense that I actually *couldn't do it*. But then four weeks later, I came to faith in Jesus Christ through a sermon on John 8:12: "I am the light of the world. Whoever follows me will not walk in darkness, but will have the light of life."

When you hear this story, you might think that this stranger shouldn't have told me to ask Jesus into my heart, but rather to repent and believe. But even if he had put it that way, I don't think that itself would have made any difference. In God's economy, he might have said the same words to another young person who went home and became a Christian that very night.

I suspect that in God's sovereign purposes, I needed to discover that I wasn't able to do the one thing I knew I needed to do. I was dead in my trespasses and sins. And if the gospel invitation was, "Behold, I stand at the door and knock. If anyone hears my voice and opens the door, I will come in to him and eat with him, and he with me" (Rev. 3:20), then I had to learn that I was lying helpless inside the room and couldn't get to the door. I was beginning to hear the voice, but I wasn't able to get up.

God's ways with us are both individual and mysterious, and I'm sure that in doing this the Lord was preparing me for future service. But this dear man who spoke to me, prompted by the Spirit, was a stepping stone on the pathway that would soon bring me to living faith in Christ. So although I met "the man in black" for no more than a few minutes and never saw him again, I've been grateful to him ever since.

One day years later, I was sitting with a group of men, and we were sharing our spiritual-pilgrimage stories. One of them asked me a little more about where and when this had happened to me. Then he said, "You know, I think that might have been my father." If it was, the son had discovered something about the way the Lord had used his father. And there is a wonderful lesson there, too, about faithfulness.

Your man in black might actually be a woman in white, a mom, a dad, a friend, or a colleague. It might be somebody you never really knew, who passed through your life only briefly. But as they did, you might have sensed—perhaps without realizing it at the time—that the aroma of Christ was present in their life, and something stirred within you.

Almost all of us have somebody to be grateful for when we look back to the beginnings of our Christian life. It's wonderful how God weaves together His purposes and people to bring us to Christ.

3

An Older Friend in the Faith

ANOTHER PERSON WHO WAS A SPECIAL gift of God to me had the very Scottish name of Hamish. I met him through some friends at the church I attended as a teenager. They were all slightly older than I was, and they took me to various Christian meetings and introduced me to their Christian friends. Some of them prayed for me to become a believer. I'm grateful for the way that they introduced me to the wonder of Christian fellowship because, like all young Christians, I was a little like the pilgrim in John Bunyan's *The Pilgrim's Progress*. I needed older companions and their wisdom—people who were already on the way. And one of these was Hamish.

I was still in my mid-teens and a relatively young Christian. At the time, I had no idea what age Hamish was. When you're fifteen or sixteen, anyone who's working five days a week and drawing a salary is, by definition, almost ancient. But Hamish took an interest in me and talked to me about spiritual things, as I'm sure he did to others.

I don't think he would've minded if I said he was an unusual person. He wasn't a Presbyterian. He belonged to a nondenominational church. I don't know if he'd ever heard the expression *Reformed theology*. He encouraged me to read books that were popular among some groups of Christians in those days—books that, to be honest, are different from the books I tend to recommend to younger people.

But what struck me was his evident love for Christ and his zeal for the gospel. He knew so many more Christians than I did, and he wanted to introduce them to me because he wanted to encourage me. It all seemed so natural, so organic. It wasn't a formal mentoring. It wasn't a program. He wasn't telling me to take a course in anything. He was my friend. Perhaps my experiences of people like him are the reason that when people ask me, "Would you be a mentor to me?,"

I've always said, "No, but I will be your friend," because that is what Hamish was to me.

When I left home and went to university, I lost touch with Hamish. But years later, I met him again. He'd been involved in a horrific automobile accident. His recovery was painstakingly slow. Physically, he struggled. He was no longer the man he once was. He no longer had the same powers. But two things about Hamish struck me, and they remain with me. The first was the way that, struggling through his physical weakness, there was the same sense of love and zeal for the Lord Jesus Christ.

The second thing was this (and it staggers me a bit to think about it): he used to come to hear me preach. I don't know if you can imagine what that meant to me—that someone who had seemed so far ahead of me, so much older in every way, would come and sit under my ministry of the Word. Hamish had a way of looking at you. He was hungry for the Bread of Life. He wanted to be fed from the Word of God, and it still moves me to think about him.

When I first came to the United States to teach in a theological seminary, I made it one of my aims that whenever a student I didn't know came to see me, I tried to find the answer to this question: "Who has invested themselves in this young man's life?" Sometimes the answers made me think that perhaps what I thought was just normal—the organic occurrence of an older Christian showing genuine Christian friendship to a younger person without strings attached—wasn't so normal after all. I began to wonder if I'd had something special. But these types of friendships *should* be normal. And so it saddened me to think that there might be men going into the ministry who had never known that "normal" that I'd known. So I'm tremendously thankful for Hamish and for his friendship.

Perhaps you have a Hamish to be thankful for today. But whether that is true or not, maybe the lesson Hamish teaches us all is best summed up in Jesus' words at the end of the parable of the good

Samaritan: "You go, and do likewise" (Luke 10:37). You become a Hamish to somebody else.

May the Lord help us all to be such men and women.

4

A Christian's Enduring Influence

ALL THE PEOPLE I'M TELLING YOU about this week belong to my early days, and they are all hidden people. It's quite possible that nobody who reads this book will ever have known them, apart from my sharing with you about them. Like you, I appreciate well-known preachers who minister to us. But it's the hidden people who usually mean the most to us, isn't it? They are the Lord's special gifts to us.

I went off to university when I was seventeen. I belonged to a Bible reading society called the Scripture Union, which had a great influence among young Christians in Britain and in the old British Commonwealth countries. Those were the days of badges, a sign that you belonged to something bigger than yourself. The Scripture Union badge was a lamp on a green background, reminding us that God's Word is a lamp to our feet and a light to our path. I wore it on my lapel.

In my very first week on campus, I was going up the stairs in the residence I lived in when an older student passed me on the way down. I later discovered that his name was Dennis. As he passed me by, he paused, pointed to the badge on my lapel, and said, "You'll find another badge like that in room . . ." and he mentioned a room number and kept on walking down the stairs.

We all had our own separate study bedrooms in the residence. And so later on, I climbed the stairs and knocked a little nervously on the door of the room he had mentioned. It was opened by a tall, older student wearing a black graduate's gown. We undergraduates wore red togas, believe it or not, although there was a kind of code that dictated that you showed your seniority by wearing it farther back on your shoulders. I can still see him coming to the door as I said, somewhat nervously, "One of the other students told me I'd find a badge like this"—pointing to my badge—"in your room." "Come in," he said warmly.

I know it sounds like the beginning of a spy movie or something out of the days of the early church when Christians are said to have drawn fish on the ground as a sign to others that they were Christians— all very cloak-and-dagger. But in a university of about three thousand students with just a few dozen students in the InterVarsity group, it was my introduction to some of the longest-standing Christian friends I've had.

Dennis graduated at the end of that year. He went back to the northeast of England where he lived, and I never saw him again or heard about him. I have no idea if he ever heard any news of me either. We were like ships passing in the night in one sense. But we weren't passing in the night. For a few months, we were passengers on the same ship, on the same journey, until he needed to sail on to his next port of call. And so I was never able to tell him how I looked back later on those early months at university with tremendous appreciation for his investment in my life.

There is something else I'm grateful to Dennis for. We were talking about prayer one day, and I said to him, "You know, Dennis, I've never found prayer easier than I'm finding it just now." He said to me in his enthusiastic Northeast England accent, "Well, enjoy it while it lasts." That might not have been the encouragement I was looking for, but it was actually full of wisdom. The Christian life, of which prayer is a kind of miniature of the whole, has seasons when the road seems level, smooth, brightly lit, and full of joy. But Dennis was simply reminding me that at other times, it can be mountainous and dark.

It's interesting that after all these years, I can still remember the big lessons that Dennis taught me. The first is this: when you meet a young person about whose faith you know very little, be sensitive and take things step by step. It's easy to do harm by being a spiritual bull in a china shop. And here's the second lesson: when life is full of blessing and relative ease, then do enjoy it—just don't make the mistake of thinking that it's always going to be like that, because you're not home yet.

As I think about these amazing hidden people who have helped me, I also realize that some fellow believers who are reading this may never have had friends like that. But if so, there is still a real lesson to learn from them. Even if you've never had such a friend, you can be such a friend to somebody else.

I hope you'll pray about that and that it will bear fruit in your life.

5

The Legacy of a Godly Life

THE FINAL FRIEND I'VE CHOSEN TO SHARE about this week was a man named Bill. I first saw Bill and his family at the church I attended as a student. Later that year, I met him again in a Hebrew class I took as an undergraduate. He was older than I was, and he had several children. As it happened, in the providence of God we ended up in the same year in our theology degree at university. We were different, not only in age, but also very much in personality. But I cannot adequately express the impact that his wonderfully human, personal godliness made on me.

He'd been a skilled market gardener, and the Lord had called him into the ministry. His life was full of the rich, heavenly fruit of the Spirit—especially patience. He and his wife, Marion, with their children, probably survived on a pittance. But what they had, they shared with me and treated me like a member of their family. I treasure the memory of my student days with them.

Our theological education was by no means all conservative. I'm not quite sure how much I learned from lectures—with some notable exceptions—but I learned a great deal from Bill and his family and their love for Christ. His life was one of humble godliness and seriousness without lugubriousness. It was weighty with grace without being heavy with dullness. He had a level of loving devotion to the Lord that made me feel glad and at ease in his presence, even though I felt then—and still do now—that I would never grow spiritually tall enough to be the same height that he was.

One thing in particular that Bill told me has left an indelible stamp on me, especially as a minister. For a reason I can't quite remember, I was invited to come one summer Sunday evening from my home city to the city where we attended the divinity school to preach in the church that Bill's family attended year-round. As it happened, I preached on Christ the Suffering Servant from Isaiah 52:13–53:12. Bill came to greet me after the service. We hadn't seen each other for a number of weeks. He mentioned the sermon, and then he added these simple words: "The Holy Spirit loves to exalt the Lord Jesus in preaching."

It may sound strange, but I'd never actually heard anyone say that before. Of course, what Bill said was rooted in Jesus' words: "When the Spirit of truth comes, he will guide you into all the truth, for he will not speak on his own authority, but whatever he hears he will speak, and he will declare to you the things that are to come. He will glorify me, for he will take what is mine and declare it to you" (John 16:13–14). I knew these words well enough, but it was the way that Bill so graciously, so deliberately applied them to preaching that stuck with me. It was not only the words he said; it was *how* he said them. It became a guiding light to me in the years that followed.

Bill was later the human instrument in bringing me to the first congregation I served as its minister. All the years I knew him, he remained the same constant Christian. He was never the minister of a large congregation. He never seemed to speak at conferences or conventions. He never wrote a book. I don't know if he ever set foot outside the British Isles. But none of that matters to me. What does matter is that he was one of the godliest men I've ever met, and I've often thought that I was never worthy to tie his shoelaces. He is with the Lord now in glory. What he was here on earth, as a relatively hidden person, is no longer hidden. I'm sure heard he the Lord Jesus say to him: "Well done, good and faithful servant. . . . Enter into the joy of your master" (Matt. 25:23).

Bill came from an area of Scotland near where Robert Murray M'Cheyne was a minister. He had a very elderly aunt who, as a young girl, had a very elderly friend who'd been in M'Cheyne's congregation in the 1840s—absolutely amazing. We both loved the words of M'Cheyne's hymn "When This Passing World Is Done." It contains these words:

Then, Lord, shall I fully know,
Not till then, how much I owe.

Bill knows now. But I also wonder if the Lord Jesus will have shown my dear friend how much I owe him for the way he befriended me, the way he nurtured me, the way he encouraged me, the way he shared his devotion to Christ with me, and the way he pointed me to this great secret that the Holy Spirit loves to honor Christ in preaching.

So I'm thankful this week for the man in black; for my friend Hamish; for Dennis, the student I knew in my first year at university; and for my dear friend Bill. These are just a few of the many who have helped and blessed me along the way. I've mentioned them in the hope that it might stimulate you to think of people who have helped to shape your life.

I hope you can give thanks for similar friends. And I also want to challenge all of us, whether we ourselves have had such friends or not, to become that kind of friend—the kind of Christlike friend who sticks closer than a brother.

WEEK 33

The Emotions of Jesus

1

The Personal Jesus

THE LONGER I'VE GONE ON IN the Christian life, the more this question has become important to me: What was, and is, Jesus really like?

Perhaps you're familiar with the pop song "Personal Jesus," written and recorded by the band Depeche Mode in the early 1990s. I first heard the Johnny Cash version. Perhaps Johnny Cash thought the song had a Christian meaning, in the sense that people speak of Jesus as their "personal Savior."

But I think the song is actually about how one person can be a Jesus-like figure to another—someone to hear your prayers and to be there for you. That is who "your own personal Jesus" is—in distinction from the actual Jesus of the Christian faith.

Over the years, I've noticed that sometimes Christians do make up their own personal Jesus. They'll say things like, "The way I like to think about Jesus is . . ." But that is a muddleheaded way of thinking about the Lord Jesus. How I like to think about Jesus is irrelevant. What's important and relevant is what Jesus is actually like. To say it a different way, I'm not the one who decides what Jesus is like. He is the One who decides what He is like. He doesn't fit into the way I like to think about Him. Rather, I need to learn to fit into the way He really is.

Of course, the place to find out who He really is and what He is really like is the Bible. This is especially true of the Gospels. By saturating ourselves in what we read in the Gospels, we get to know who Jesus really is and what He is really like. And since the Christian life involves our progressive transformation in becoming more and more like Jesus, it's essential that we know what He is like.

But there is another reason for asking this question in light of a trend in evangelical preaching over the past fifty years or so. Before that time, preachers preached Christ and Christ crucified, as Charles Spurgeon did. No matter where they began their sermons, they would get to Christ. They did that because their hearts, souls, and minds were centered on the person of the Lord Jesus. By and large, they didn't do it by any particular formula. They did it because they were full of Christ. As a result, they not only communicated the truth about Christ, but also communicated all the affections that Christ has for His people.

Sometimes today, I feel as though I'm standing on the banks of the river Jordan, listening to John the Baptist saying, "Behold, the Lamb of God, who takes away the sin of the world," but I'm not actually being helped to behold Him as the loving Savior He is, as the personal Jesus.

One of my friends, who was a professor of psychiatry, once described this to me as "substitutionary atonement lite." In other words, the message about Jesus—"He died for our sins"—is abstracted from Jesus' incarnate person in flesh and blood. But that is the Jesus my heart is hungry for—the Jesus who was kind to sinners, who touched lepers, who cared for lonely people, who was tired and hungry and thirsty, who was demeaned and shamed. It's the affectionate Jesus I want to know, not just "substitutionary atonement lite." I want to know the Jesus who loved me and gave Himself for me (see Gal. 2:20). I want to know that personal Jesus.

That is where the challenge lies for all of us. It's easier to think of a formulaic Jesus, to use words like *atonement* and *justification* and *reconciliation* to describe what He does—and they are hugely important—but we mustn't abstract them from Jesus Christ Himself. Christ *Himself* is our peace. *He* is our righteousness. *He* is our sanctification. *He* is our redemption.

The challenge about presenting the personal Jesus is that we can do it well only when we know Him well and love Him well, too. As the author of Hebrews puts it, we must fix our eyes on Jesus (see Heb. 12:2). We'll think more about this tomorrow.

2

He Grew in Favor with God

I SAID YESTERDAY THAT WE NEED TO HEAR more preaching and reflect more on the way in which the New Testament focuses on who Jesus is—His person and what He is really like.

I don't think anyone who knows me would misunderstand what I'm trying to say here. I love great works of biblical exegesis and biblical theology, and I really love systematic theology. But none of these became incarnate. None of these was crucified for me. It's Jesus Christ Himself I need and want.

There is a good litmus test that indicates whether we have a healthy biblical view of Jesus and whether He is truly real to us. It's found in a single verse in the Gospels: "And Jesus increased in wisdom and in stature and in favor with God and man" (Luke 2:52). It's obvious that Jesus must have grown in stature. He was a baby small enough to fit into a manger. He became a boy. Luke's words cover His teenage years, at least. Jesus grew in height. No doubt as He worked in Joseph's carpenter shop and elsewhere, He became stronger. He grew in stature.

We can also understand that Jesus grew in favor with men and women as they got to know Him. It was only later in His ministry that people seemed to turn against Him and He fell into disfavor. So we see how Jesus grew both in physical stature and in favor with people.

But then there is another statement: "Jesus increased in wisdom." If He worked with Joseph the woodworker, and if He learned a trade, then from that point of view, He grew in wisdom. He didn't have all of Joseph's skills when He was a three-year-old. He learned the tricks of the trade—how to get two pieces of wood to hold together, how to shape the wood, how to build a house or a piece of furniture. So surely we can grant that He grew in that kind of wisdom.

But what about spiritual wisdom? Didn't Jesus already have all wisdom because He was God? Luke is saying here that if Jesus was truly incarnate in our humanity, He must have needed to grow, to learn, to advance in spiritual wisdom and understanding. He must have grown, for example, by reflecting on the wisdom in the Old Testament. If we take seriously what Luke wrote here, then we'll develop a new sense of wonder that Jesus learned more and more wisdom the older He got. He was truly human as well as truly divine.

But it's the last statement that is the real litmus test. Let me put it this way: Did the Jesus whom you trust grow in favor with God as well as with man? That is a staggering statement. Is that your personal Jesus, or is that just a step too far? You see, if you have reservations about Jesus growing in favor with God, then somehow or another you've gotten caught up in a false theology. Underneath your view of Jesus lies some false thinking that is not consistent with Scripture.

How can this be?

While the two natures of our Lord are united in His one person—His deity and His humanity united in His divine person—they are never mixed, and they are never confused with each other. Each nature retains and exercises the properties appropriate to that nature. That is what Luke is saying here. The tests and temptations that Jesus experienced increased in severity as He grew from infancy, to childhood, to adolescence, to manhood. More demanding obedience was called for; more personal sacrifice was required. As He became ultimately obedient to death, even to the horrible death of crucifixion, His Father's favor toward Him increased correspondingly. There was more reason for the Father to favor His Son because His Son's obedience expanded to the point where He was willing to die on the cross in obedience to His Father.

I've often said that when Jesus took the ultimate step of obedience in His death on the cross, we can imagine the heavenly Father singing quietly through His tears, as it were:

My Jesus, I love thee,
I know thou art mine;
. . . .
If ever I loved thee,
My Jesus, 'tis now.

It's not that the Father didn't always love the incarnate Son perfectly; it's that the incarnate Son gave Him more and more specific reasons to have favor toward Him.

The Christian church has often struggled with these verses, but I think you can see what Luke is saying. Jesus is not an imitation man, not a pretend man, not half a man and half a God, nor is His human nature a composite of some parts human and some parts divine. No, He is truly man. His nature is the same as ours, apart from sin.

This is the repeated message of the book of Hebrews. Jesus Christ is perfectly suited to be our Savior and our friend because He really and truly came among us and bound His flesh to our flesh in the same bundle of life.

As the Christmas hymn puts it, "Day by day like us He grew." But that is why the hymn can go on to say, "And He feeleth for our sadness, and He shareth in our gladness."

We'll think more about this tomorrow.

3

Rest for Our Souls

WHAT IS JESUS REALLY LIKE? IT'S critical for us to ask that question. Otherwise, Jesus is little more than a figment of our imagination, a "personal Jesus" invented in our own minds who doesn't bear much resemblance to the person described in the New Testament. That is where we need to go, where we need to soak our minds and affections, if we want to know the real Jesus. So where do we begin?

Of course, we can start at the beginning, and we got close to that yesterday. We looked at what Luke tells us about Jesus when He was twelve years old. But here's another place to begin: with what Jesus said about Himself. And of all the things He said about Himself, perhaps Matthew 11:25–30 is the most obvious place to look.

In this passage, Jesus identifies Himself as the Son of God, the only One who knows God fully, the only One who can reveal the Father to us. He says, "No one knows the Father except the Son and anyone to whom the Son chooses to reveal him" (v. 27). Then He adds these words: "Come to me, all who labor and are heavy laden, and I will give you rest. Take my yoke upon you, and learn from me, for I am gentle and lowly in heart, and you will find rest for your souls" (vv. 28–29).

The old Anglican prayer book describes these as the "comfortable words" of our Lord Jesus Christ. It doesn't mean that they wrap us in soft wool. The word *comfort* comes from the Latin *cum forte*, "with strength." That is what Jesus offers to us here. He invites those who are conscious of their weakness and their sin to come to Him and find rest. The real Jesus understands our human condition. He knows all about our weakness and our need.

He also invites us to wear His yoke, and He promises that when we do, we will find rest. There is an old tradition that says that the sign outside Joseph's carpenter shop in Nazareth read, "Our yokes fit well."

It's a lovely picture, isn't it? We are burdened; we are weighed down with our weakness and our weariness, with our sin and with our guilt. And there is a kind of yoke of conscience that says, "You need to do better." But what we need to be is united, or yoked, to the Lord Jesus. Then we will discover rest for our souls.

That is what the real personal Jesus is like. He is a Savior whose yoke will fit well on us as we yield to Him. He is a Savior who brings to us all the blessings that God has stored up for us. And Jesus describes that as "rest."

If we can listen to that promise the way the original hearers probably did, it will become even more marvelous to us, because what was lost in the fall was "rest."

Think, for example, of Noah's time. What was longed for when Noah's parents gave him his name was—rest. They seemed to have hoped that he would be the man promised in Genesis 3:15 who would bring deliverance from the evil one and, at last, give spiritual rest. That is why they gave him the name *Noah*, because it sounds like the Hebrew word for "rest." In a sense, they were given some rest, but not the ultimate rest they needed. Later, God's people were given another picture of rest—rest in the promised land—but it was only a picture.

So now at last, Jesus is saying, "The rest that people have longed for throughout the ages, the peace of mind and heart that they crave, the rest that can be found only in coming to Me and trusting in Me and leaving behind and turning away from everything else—that rest is now being offered to you, and it's being offered to you by Me, and you'll find it in Me."

I'm reminded of the words of one of my favorite hymn writers, Horatius Bonar:

I heard the voice of Jesus say,
"Come unto me and rest;
Lay down, O weary one, lay down

Your head upon my breast."
I came to Jesus as I was,
Weary and worn and sad;
I found in him a resting place,
And he has made me glad.

That puts in a nutshell what we most need, doesn't it? *Rest.* And when you know and trust the real Jesus, who speaks to you in Matthew 11:25–30, you find that peace and that rest. So today, let's come again to this Lord Jesus.

Perhaps you need to come to Him for the very first time and discover that He is meek and lowly in heart, and He invites you Himself to come to Him. Come, then; let's trust Him and find rest.

4

Christ, a Man of Feeling

SOME TIME AGO, I WAS READING a once well-known book by an older Scottish professor of theology named James Stalker. It's called *Imago Christi*, the "image of Christ." The book has chapters on such topics as Christ as a friend, Christ as a man of prayer, Christ as a student of Scripture, Christ as a sufferer, and so on.

It's a little different from most books on Christ that are written today, but there is value in the chapter titles alone. They make us think about the Lord Jesus not in terms of categories but in terms of personal descriptions, in terms of what He was really like in our humanity. And because we know that "Jesus Christ is the same yesterday and today and forever" (Heb. 13:8), He is the same today as He was during those days described in the Gospels.

Toward the end of Professor Stalker's book, there is a chapter title that really arrested my attention. It's "Christ as a Man of Feeling." That is a subject that has interested and fascinated me for a long time—it's what the American theologian B.B. Warfield called "the emotional life of our Lord." Professor Stalker approaches this chapter in a very simple way by looking at the gospel narrative of the raising of Jairus's daughter.

This passage comes at the end of a section in Mark 4:35–5:43. In this section, Jesus reveals His authority in a series of ways. He calms the storm in Galilee and shows His power over nature. He exorcises the demons from a man and shows His power over the kingdom of darkness. He heals the woman with the issue of blood and shows His power over disease. And He raises Jairus's daughter and shows His power over death.

All that is true and right, but what does it tell you about Jesus? It tells you that Jesus is very powerful indeed. But what does it not necessarily tell you? It doesn't necessarily tell you that His power was exercised not just for its own sake or just for what it could do, but in a way that gave expression to the feelings, affections, and emotions of the Lord Jesus.

And so, focusing on the raising of Jairus's daughter, Stalker points out how the following qualities are evident in the Lord Jesus: compassion, sensitiveness, indignation, delicacy, modesty. That is more than mere power, isn't it? These are beautiful personal qualities in the Lord Jesus. And it's because He is like that that we are drawn to Him to trust Him and love Him and tell Him about ourselves and our need. And that surely must have meant a tremendous amount to Jairus and his wife.

Listen to the fine way in which Professor Stalker finishes his chapter:

Such was the heart of Christ as it is laid bare in a single story. By taking a wider sweep we might have accumulated more illustrations. But the clue, once seized, can be easily followed in the Gospels, where the notices of how He felt in the different situations in which He was placed are far more numerous than anyone whose attention has not been specifically directed to them would believe.

Then he concludes:

Nor would it be difficult to trace the refining influence which intercourse with Him had on His disciples—how they learned to feel about things as He did. There is no other influence so refining as genuine religion. Where the Gospel is faithfully preached and affectionately believed, there is gradually wrought into the very features of people the stamp of the Son of man. The friendship of Jesus breeds the gentle heart.

That is worth thinking about for the rest of the day. Let's pray that we will be helped to know that Jesus is like this.

5

The Anger of Jesus

YESTERDAY, I MENTIONED AN ESSAY TITLED "The Emotional Life of Our Lord." It was written by the great American theologian B.B. Warfield. In his essay, Warfield points out the emotion that is most frequently attributed to Jesus. I wonder if you can guess what it is.

The answer is *compassion*.

I imagine many of us might be able to guess that. But then Warfield singles out an element in Jesus' emotional makeup that I suspect we don't think about nearly as often: anger and indignation.

This anger and indignation appear early in Mark's gospel. Jesus is angry with the Pharisees because of their lack of compassion for a man with a withered hand (Mark 3:1–6). Later on, He is indignant about the way that His own disciples are hindering little children and infants from being brought to Him for His blessing (10:14).

But the most impressive place where we see this aspect of our Lord Jesus is at the grave of Lazarus, when He saw Mary and some of the Jews wailing with grief. We're told that "he was deeply moved in his spirit and greatly troubled," and this language is repeated just a few verses later (John 11:33, 38). The older versions say that Jesus "groaned in the spirit," and Warfield points out that the Revised Version suggests "moved with indignation" as an alternative translation, which he prefers.

At the grave of Lazarus, Jesus was in a state not of uncontrollable grief, but of unrepressed anger. Yes, Jesus wept. But, Warfield writes, "the emotion which tore His breast and clamored for attention and utterance was just rage." Jesus was burning with rage against Satan, against death, against the deception of Adam and Eve.

Why?

Jesus came not only to save us from the penalty of sin, but from its horrible effects in bondage and in death. He came to "destroy the works of the devil" (1 John 3:8). And of those works, He saw death as the most terrible. That is exactly why He became incarnate. It was out of the most wonderful love. But in a sense, it was also out of hatred. We might even say that the only pure hatred that has ever been is Jesus' hatred of Satan and all the destruction and sorrow and separation he has produced.

I wonder if this is difficult for some of us to grasp. The loving Jesus was also an angry Jesus, an indignant Jesus, a Jesus who hated as well as loved. Does that make you tremble a little? It's natural that it would, because perfect holiness does make us tremble. When we see this in Jesus, we begin to recognize how He is absolutely committed to destroying everything that would prevent our salvation.

He hates death, and He hates it because of the way it seizes and separates His own blood-bought people from one another. He hates the sin that lies behind it. His emotions of indignation and hatred are actually emotions of love. They are as healthy as they are necessary. It's altogether appropriate that the Lord Jesus should hate every false way simply because He loves us so much. His love and His hatred are really two sides of the same coin.

We need to remember that the love the Lord Jesus has for us is a profoundly jealous love, and that is why it can give rise to such indignation and hatred. It can't be otherwise. These are two sides of the same coin of the Lord's covenant devotion toward us.

Perhaps this is why the love of Jesus can sometimes make us tremble—because it's a fierce love, a determined love, an uncompromising love. It is a holy love that is committed to having the whole of my life without reservation because He knows that otherwise, I can never really be happy.

Alas, at times, it seems we rest content with a love that reassures us occasionally rather than a love that possesses us entirely. But the real Jesus wants to have all of us.

I wonder if that is the Jesus you know and trust. I hope so.

WEEK 34

Sanctification

1

Set Apart for God

MOST OF US HAVE MET CHRISTIANS who don't like it when we mention the word "doctrine" or get irritated when we use a word like "justification." Strangely enough, these same people sometimes also get upset if we don't know what a "bunt" is in baseball or don't understand the difference between a "birdie" and an "eagle" on the golf course. If they are interested in soccer, they are upset that we don't understand the "offside" rule, or if it's cricket, they are upset if we don't know the difference between fielding at "silly mid off" and fielding in the "gully."

Every branch of life, every aspect of human knowledge, has its own vocabulary and terms to convey essential information, sometimes in a kind of shorthand. Big words, in that sense, really are important in the Christian life. I say this to prepare you for this week's theme. It's one big theological word: *sanctification*.

Strictly speaking, the noun *sanctification* isn't used all that often in the Bible, but the verb *to sanctify* is used about 150 times in one form or another. And the result of being sanctified—*being holy*—is used another hundred times, meaning "something or someone that has been sanctified."

The Hebrew and Greek verbs used in the Bible for *sanctify* both mean "to set something apart." In a negative sense, it means being set apart from an ordinary, common, day-to-day use. But it also has a positive sense: being set apart for a special use, being set apart for something or someone in particular.

Imagine walking into a furniture store and seeing exactly what you need. It will fit right in with your other furniture and furnishings. You want to buy it. But then as you look more closely, you see there is a card on it that says, "Reserved for Mrs. Smith." You can't have it. That is what *sanctify* means in the Bible. It means to be reserved. It means to be set apart for God. It means being dedicated to His use so that nobody and nothing else can have us. Being holy, being sanctified, means that the Lord has put His "reserved" sticker on our lives.

This is why, if you think about it, being sanctified—being a saint—is not something that is true only of special Christians. You actually can't be a Christian at all without being a saint—someone who has been set apart for the Lord, or sanctified. That is why Paul quite often greets the recipients of his letters as "the saints" who live in one place or another. The Lord has claimed them. The Lord has reserved them for Himself. The Lord has set them apart from the world.

I still remember how thrilled I was as a young Christian to learn that I was actually a saint. I think before that I felt a bit like the ugly duckling in the Hans Christian Andersen tale.

If you're of my generation, maybe you remember Danny Kaye singing the song in the movie *Hans Christian Andersen* about the ugly duckling whose feathers were all stubby and brown, "and the other birds said in so many words, 'Get out of town! Get out, get out, get out of town.' And he went with a quack and a waddle and a quack in a flurry of eiderdown."

The poor creature got very depressed, and all through the winter, he hid himself away. He was ashamed to show his face, afraid of what others might say. Then a group of swans saw him and told him that he wasn't an ugly duckling at all. He had been a cygnet (a baby swan). The swans "spied him there and very soon agreed, 'You're a very fine swan indeed,'" says the song. And then he takes a look in the lake and he sees his reflection: "I am a swan! Whee! I'm not such an ugly duckling." And the song ends:

> Not a quack, not a quack, not a waddle or a quack
> But a glide and a whistle and a snowy white back
> And a head so noble and high
> Say, who's an ugly duckling?
> Not I!
> Not I!

I've often thought of that song as a picture of how some of us feel as Christians.

It's so easy to forget who we really are as Christians and what that means right down at the roots of our being. And we certainly live in a world that often seems to despise Christians and makes us feel small, as though we're no better than ugly ducklings in the world's eyes. But if God has put His hand on you, if He has set you apart, if He has said of you, "You are reserved for My Son, the Lord Jesus Christ," then you're not an ugly duckling. You're a saint. And when you know that you're a saint set apart for God, it can make all the difference in the world.

So remind yourself of that today. If you're a Christian, you're a saint, and it should make you want to sing.

2

The Fruit of Sanctification

SANCTIFICATION IS NOT JUST A MATTER OF being separated from sin, although that is definitely part of it. Sanctification—being a saint—is true of all Christians because sanctification means that our life is now reserved for the Lord. In other words, it means belonging to the Lord Jesus, living with and for Him. And since we become like those with whom we live, it means becoming like the Lord Jesus. As Paul says in Romans 8:29, that is God's purpose for us: to become like His Son.

Seeing holiness in these terms helps us. It can protect us from some of the false ideas about sanctification that we encounter. For instance, we know that holy people will do holy things. But this personal dimension—being like Jesus—means that being holy isn't just a matter of doing the right things or performing in the right ways. That can be very mechanical and even metallic. It can turn you into a rather cold fish of a Christian. You might not realize it, but when you're in the presence of others, instead of warming to you, people stiffen up and feel uncomfortable.

I remember hearing that the famous Scottish minister Alexander Whyte once said, "There is such a thing as sanctification by vinegar."

It hardens you, and it's not very attractive. It has a sharp odor, and that odor repels. When people have fallen short or messed up, they don't want to share their heart with a vinegary Christian. But they would with somebody who is really like the Lord Jesus.

Here's something else about sanctification: it saves us from confusing gifts with graces. The graces—the fruit of the Spirit that Paul mentions in Galatians 5:22–23—grow in us only because of God's grace. And in that sense, they are gifts, too. But having special gifts—the gifts that the New Testament talks about—is not the same thing as the fruit of the Spirit.

The Bible stresses this because we can be deceived into thinking that because someone has special gifts—and the more special, the better—they must be particularly holy. And some people trade on that. But remember, Jesus said that it's not by people's gifts, but by the fruit that is produced in their lives that real holiness is seen.

Toward the end of the Sermon on the Mount, Jesus said that many would stand before Him, telling Him about the mighty gifts they had and the marvelous things they did in His name. Yet He will say, "I never knew you; depart from me" (Matt. 7:23). Those words are intriguing. Jesus doesn't deny that they did things in His name. What He denies is that He knew them. Or to put it another way, He says: "There was no real relationship between us. You were all about performance, all about what you did. But you never said, 'I want to be like the Lord Jesus and known by Him.'"

That is why if you want to know what holiness looks like, what it means to be a saint, it would be best to avoid the current trend in the evangelical subculture of focusing on well-known preachers. In these public spheres, what you see is usually people's gifts—or people who think they have gifts. It's not so easy to see or hear or sense whether they have the graces that the New Testament calls the fruit of the Spirit. Instead, focus on the believers who belong to your own church family. Look at some of them, and see how the fruit of sanctification is evident in their lives.

Please don't misunderstand me. I'm certainly privileged to have friends who are well-known preachers with great gifts, and I've seen the grace of the Lord Jesus in them. But it is usually from the hidden people in the churches that I belong to that I've learned most about what it actually means to be a saint, to be sanctified, to become more and more like Jesus. And at the end of the day, that is the only thing about us that is going to last forever. Only what reflects the Lord Jesus is going to last through all eternity.

So let's never forget how important sanctification is. But let's also never forget that it means becoming like the Lord Jesus Himself.

3

A More Excellent Way

THIS WEEK, WE'RE LOOKING AT HOW SANCTIFICATION—being holy, being a saint—is a matter of becoming more and more like the Lord Jesus. Today, we'll consider what that might look like. The Apostle Paul addresses this question in his letter to the church in Corinth. This church was experiencing a number of problems. One was that some people were emphasizing their spiritual gifts, but doing that in a very un-Christlike way. Gifts without real holiness can be very dangerous indeed. It's a mystery how this occurs—gifts without grace. But it does.

At one point in his letter to the Corinthians, Paul gives a longish list of spiritual gifts. Then he says, "Earnestly desire the higher gifts" (1 Cor. 12:31). You can imagine some of the Corinthians saying: "Wow, let's go for it. We are really into the higher gifts here. Prophecy, speaking in tongues, working miracles—we're all for the higher gifts in Corinth." But then Paul lets the Corinthians down with a bump. He says, "And I will show you a still more excellent way."

Here's a question for you: "What words come next in this passage in 1 Corinthians?" They are words with which we're familiar: "If I speak in the tongues of men and of angels, but have not love, I am a noisy gong or a clanging cymbal. And if I have prophetic powers, and understand all mysteries and all knowledge, and if I have all faith, so as to remove mountains, but have not love, I am nothing. If I give away all I have, and if I deliver up my body to be burned, but have not love, I gain nothing" (1 Cor. 13:1–3). That is the more excellent way.

All the things that Paul lists here, which can apparently be present when love is absent, are things we do or accomplish. But none of them describes who we really are or what we're really like. And that is the point: gifts are not the same as grace. Accomplishments are not necessarily indicators of love. But love is an essential indicator of holiness, of sanctification, of being a saint.

Paul goes on in great detail to describe what love is like. One thing you might do is to read through 1 Corinthians 13 out loud, and every time the word "love" appears, replace it with a different word. Replace it with the word "Jesus." I think that will make 1 Corinthians 13 come alive to you.

If you want to know what love looks like, then look at Jesus. If you want to know what it means to be Jesus-like, to be someone who grows in Christlikeness, then look at the way Paul describes what he calls the "more excellent way."

Jesus is patient and kind; Jesus does not envy or boast; Jesus is not arrogant or rude. Jesus does not insist on His own way; Jesus is not irritable or resentful; Jesus does not rejoice at wrongdoing, but rejoices with the truth. Jesus bears all things, believes all things, hopes all things. Jesus endures all things.

Sometime today, you will probably be in situations where one of these statements will come to mind—situations in which we or others might envy or boast, or be arrogant or rude, or insist on our way, or be irritable or resentful, or be secretly pleased when someone does something wrong. But this passage teaches us that sanctification, becoming like the Lord Jesus, is all about these nitty-gritty situations in daily life. That can be very humbling, because it's so often there that we fail.

But remember this, too: it's in these very ordinary things in life that Christlikeness appears in us. And as we grow in grace and love in a Jesus-like way, that is how we grow in sanctification. And perhaps some of the people we know who don't know the Lord Jesus will be able to catch a glimpse of Christ in us and through us and begin to seek Him for themselves.

Let's pray that this will be so.

4

Sanctification Summarized

WE'VE SEEN THIS WEEK THAT THE basic meaning of sanctification is that we are now reserved for the Lord Jesus. We now belong to Him in order to be transformed by His Spirit into His likeness. Yes, we still remain ourselves; we don't lose our individual personalities. But in those personalities, we become more and more like Him. Yesterday, we saw what that looks like in practical terms. It means the life of love that is described in 1 Corinthians 13.

Today, we'll look at this from a different perspective. What happens to people like us—people who were once dead in trespasses and sins—to turn us into saints? A verse that helps answer that is Galatians 2:20: "I have been crucified with Christ. It is no longer I who live, but Christ who lives in me. And the life I now live in the flesh I live by faith in the Son of God, who loved me and gave himself for me." These words give us sanctification in four prepositions. Let's look at each one briefly.

The first preposition to notice is the word "for": Christ loved me and gave himself *for* me. That is the foundation of everything, isn't it? Christ died in my place, the just for the unjust to bring me to God (see

1 Peter 3:18, KJV). Later in his writings, Paul says that there are several dimensions to this death of Christ. He died for the guilt of sin.

Notice the second preposition: I have been crucified *with* Christ. By faith, I'm united to Christ. I come to share in the death that He died. He died for my sin, and so in Him, I'm free from its guilt. But Christ also died *to* sin—to the reign of sin, as Paul says in Romans 6:10. And so because I'm united to Him, I share not only in the freedom that I have from guilt, but in deliverance from my bondage because I share in Christ's death to sin. In Christ, I, too, died to sin and was raised to newness of life. So as Paul says, sin no longer has dominion over me; Jesus does. I'm no longer under the authority of King Sin, but King Jesus. I've been delivered from the kingdom of sin so that I can be set free from its lifestyle and live in the kingdom of Christ and in the lifestyle of the kingdom of God. Sin no longer governs me, but holiness and Christlikeness govern me (Rom. 6:1–14).

Here's the third preposition in Paul's words: Christ now lives *in* me. Think about it this way: it's one thing to be given a new nationality, to come from one kingdom to another kingdom. But it's another thing to be able to speak the language of that new kingdom fluently. That takes time.

How do we get the resources and power that we need to live a life of holiness? The Lord Jesus Christ by His Holy Spirit comes to indwell our hearts and lives. That is staggering, isn't it? No wonder Satan often tries to hide this from us and make us lose sight of or forget this. But those who know that the Lord Jesus indwells them know where the strength to live for Him really comes from.

Then there is a fourth preposition: we live *by* faith in the Son of God. The Spirit of Christ indwells us and works in us, but He doesn't push us out of the way, as though to say: "I'm here now. I'll do it all. You just sit down there, say nothing, and do nothing." No. When holiness becomes real, then you and I actually become holy. We begin to think holy thoughts and have holy desires and do holy things and live holy lives. That is to say, we actually become more like Jesus because His Spirit indwells us and works in and through us.

Sanctification isn't a matter of the Spirit's turning us into an automaton. It's the reverse. And that is why Paul says, "The life I now live . . . I live *by* faith in the Son of God, who loved me and gave himself for me." Sanctification becomes ours by faith—not by faith as a single act, as a kind of crisis moment, but by living day by day, hour by hour, trusting in the Lord.

So here are four prepositions that summarize the way of holiness. Christ died *for* us—that is the foundation. And because of that, we died *with* Christ, Christ lives *in* us, and we live *by* faith. But the thing is, it takes our whole lives to learn how to live that way.

So let's remember Galatians 2:20, and let's live by faith in Christ today.

5

Principles for Holiness

LET'S END THIS WEEK BY MENTIONING two important principles of sanctification, two important principles of becoming like Jesus. We'll reflect on these principles through the eyes of two great Christians who commented on them.

The first is the great seventeenth-century theologian and pastor John Owen. Let me remind you again of what he says—I am paraphrasing him: You measure growth in holiness not by the height someone seems to have reached or the place to which they seem to have arrived but by the distance a person has traveled to get where they've arrived, and especially by the obstacles they've overcome in order to get there.

Now, it's no more wise spiritually for a Christian to be constantly taking his or her own spiritual pulse than it is to be doing that with your physical pulse, at least unless you're under medical care. Looking inward all the time can tend to a kind of spiritual self-absorption, which at the end of the day is profoundly unhelpful.

But I've found what Owen says here tremendously helpful in recognizing growth and holiness in other Christians. Imagine a Christian who seems to have it all together. She seems so far ahead of that second woman in the church who so often appears to be struggling. It's surely that first woman who's really grown in sanctification and holiness. It seems obvious. But is it? If you think of the second woman in terms of the difficulties she has had to face, the obstacles that she has overcome, the disadvantages that she has had (and maybe she hasn't had many advantages), perhaps that is a better measure of her progress. And the wonderful thing is this: you don't need to appreciate the first woman any less to be able to appreciate that the other woman has actually made tremendous progress, against all the odds. And when you see that, you begin to love, appreciate, and admire both of them.

These words of Owen are worth repeating again and again because they help us to understand how to live in holy fellowship with one another. We begin to see other people through Christ's eyes and to love them in a Christlike way.

The second principle is beautifully expressed in words by the famous eighteenth-century Anglican minister Charles Simeon. His ministry had a massive influence not only in Cambridge, where he was a pastor, but also throughout the United Kingdom, even to the present day. One of his students was a brilliant young man by the name of Henry Martyn. You may know his name because he became a missionary in India and Persia, and he died when he was thirty-one. Simeon said something about Martyn when the latter was still a young man that has always impressed me. He said that the striking thing about Martyn was not only that he manifested the fruit of the Spirit but that all the fruit seemed to be in perfect proportion in his life.

I wonder if you know someone who has the fruit of self-control and is very self-disciplined. They are not only firm; they are almost hard on themselves. But they are also hard on others. In this case, the fruit has gotten out of proportion. It's not balanced by the fruit of gentleness. Their self-control is more intimidating than it is attractive. And perhaps, even sadly, it goes along with just a little touch of superiority or an assumption that everyone should be like them. Your life of self-control, if that is true of you, is actually leaving an unpleasant aroma in the room when you leave it.

Paul speaks about the *works* of the flesh, plural, but about the *fruit* of the Spirit, a collective singular. The works of the flesh are the marks of a life that is actually disintegrating. The fruit of the Spirit marks the life that is being reintegrated.

I once saw an interview with a Japanese master creator of bonsai trees. I know nothing about bonsai, so I found something he said really interesting. He said all bonsai trees are shaped in the form of a triangle. I'd actually never noticed that, although it's fairly obvious. They are perfectly proportioned miniatures. But he said that if you look, you'll see that the triangle shape isn't necessarily at the same angle on every tree.

When he said that, I thought, "That is a terrific metaphor for our sanctification." Holiness, Christlikeness, becomes evident in our lives when the fruit of the Spirit is increasingly well proportioned in us and has a Christlike shape. But the angle that that same shape will take in each person's life will be slightly different from every other Christian you meet.

Here, then, is a wonderful thing to think about today: that we are all being reshaped in the image of Christ, and yet each one in a slightly different way.

WEEK 35

Baptism

1

The Promise of Baptism

THIS WEEK, WE'RE GOING TO LOOK AT the sacrament of baptism. It's important to note from the start that if we think of baptism first and foremost as a controversy rather than as a gift from the Lord Jesus, we've got hold of the wrong end of the stick. Baptism is a gift from the Lord Jesus to help us all live for His glory. Though there are aspects of baptism that different denominations disagree on, we will reflect on something more fundamental.

Whatever our views pertaining to baptism, believers aren't always particularly good at appreciating why Christ gave it to us, what it means, and the impact it's meant to have on our daily Christian living. Baptism isn't just something that happened once and is over and done with. If you read the New Testament, you notice that its significance is meant to last through the whole course of our Christian life.

The first question to ask is this: What is baptism? What kind of event is it, and why do we do it?

I suspect that we tend to view baptism through a close-up lens and forget to think about it in terms of its place in the whole story of the Bible. If we do, we'll forget that baptism is actually only one of a whole series of rites that God gave to His people throughout the various epochs of His self-revelation.

Right from the very beginning, God always added some kind of physical sign to His covenant word of promise. We're all familiar with the promise to Noah that God would never flood the earth again. Is

God's promise enough for us? Well, yes. He is God, after all, and He doesn't lie. Will He ever break His promise? No, He won't. He can't. Why, then, does He tell Noah that the rainbow will be a sign to him that He will remember His promise? It's not because God needs the reminder. It's because He knows Noah needs to be reminded that God remembers!—and to experience the reassurance that comes from that.

Some years ago, the snow in the mountains around our village in the Grampian Highlands of Scotland melted, and there was also a downpour of rain. The river that runs through the village burst its banks. Half the village was flooded, and people were out of their homes for months. It was a once-in-a-century-size flood and a terrible time for the village. And now, whenever the snow melts, the rain falls, and the river rises, what do you think is the first thing on people's minds? Yes—floods.

If that is true in our village, what must Noah have felt when it started raining again? But in His kindness, the Lord gave him a sign to confirm His promise: "Just in case you forget it, Noah, whenever you see the rainbow in the sky, you can be sure I see it, too, and that I am remembering My promise to you."

In each of the great covenants that God went on to make with His people, He did something similar: He gave them His word of promise; then He added to it a visible sign to reassure them of the meaning of His promise and that He would keep that promise.

This happened in the promise that God gave to Abraham in the sign of circumcision. The Apostle Paul says that it was a sign and seal of the God-given righteousness that faith receives.

So when we fast-forward to the new covenant in Christ, it's not really a surprise that God adds two signs to His promise: the sign of baptism and the sign of the Lord's Supper. And both of them, in different ways, are given to us to confirm the promise of the gospel.

The first function of these signs is to point to what *God* has promised to be and to do. They don't, first of all, point us to what *we* have done or what *we* are to do.

That is very important to get clear in our minds if we're going to benefit from our baptism. But it's something that many Christians can get confused about because sometimes it's our response to Christ that has been emphasized more than Christ Himself, or our response to the gospel rather than the content of the gospel.

Baptism points us to what Christ has done. But many of us tend to think that baptism points to us and to our faith. But in fact it is a sign of God's gospel promise. It points us to Christ and to the way in which God's promises are all fulfilled in Him. So if someone asks you about the meaning of baptism and your answer begins by describing something you have done, then you're really turning its meaning upside down.

These signs don't work that way. Baptism points to and confirms to us what Christ has done. It says, "Fix your eyes on Jesus and trust in Him, repenting of your sin." It's not a sign of what we have done, but a sign and reassurance of what He has done for us.

We'll think more about that tomorrow.

2

The Meaning of Baptism

YESTERDAY, I HINTED THAT TOO MANY CHRISTIANS think about baptism the wrong way around. If you ask them what baptism means, the first thing they do is talk about themselves rather than talk about Jesus Christ. But the central meaning of baptism is that it points us to the Lord Jesus first, not to ourselves. Like the gospel of which it's a sign, it's about Him first and foremost. And that is true of all the biblical signs that we sometimes call sacraments. First and foremost, they are reassurances to us of what the Lord has done.

You are probably familiar with that famous optical illusion in which you see either an old hag or a beautiful young woman. Many people, if they see the old hag in the picture, seem to find it very difficult to find the beautiful woman. Sometimes it's a little bit like that with baptism. Some of us look at it and see only ourselves and our faith decision. Forgive me for putting it this way, but if we think baptism is about ourselves, then we are perhaps more likely to be looking at the old hag! After all, we are sinners.

But baptism presupposes that we are sinners and that we need to be cleansed. That is why it points us not to ourselves first, but to Christ. It points us, as sinners, to the promise of cleansing and renewal there is in Jesus Christ, and that is why it gives us such daily reassurance. It's not so much a message about our faith, but a sign that calls us to live by faith. So we need to see something quite different in the picture that baptism portrays. Not ourselves—the old hags, the sinners—but the beautiful woman, or to put it in real-life terms, the beautiful Savior.

Think about it this way: baptism is a sign of the gospel. But how does the gospel work? Not by pointing to me and what I do. In fact, the gospel presupposes my sinfulness and points me to the One who alone can save me. It reminds me that I have no resources in myself and I can't contribute to my salvation. I'm spiritually dead and in spiritual bondage, and I need to look away from myself to Jesus Christ and His resources. That is how the gospel functions. And if that is how the gospel functions, it shouldn't surprise us that it's also the way the signs of the gospel function—and baptism functions that way. It's given *to* us; it's never done *by* us. It points us to what Christ has done, and it's Christ who gives us the sign.

If our view of baptism is that it's a sign of something we've done, then it just points us back to what we have done. What we really need is to be pointed away from ourselves and what we've done and toward the Lord Jesus and every spiritual blessing that we are given in Him. In Him we have forgiveness of sin, redemption from sin, and adoption into the family of God—all those spiritual blessings that the Apostle Paul enunciates in Ephesians 1.

That is why, famously, when Martin Luther found himself discouraged and under stress, he used to say to himself, "*Baptizatus sum*—I'm a baptized man." Why did that help him? Because it lifted his eyes away from his own sinfulness, and from the difficulties and stresses he faced, to the Lord Jesus Christ and His all-sufficiency. It reminded him that all the promises of God are yes in Jesus Christ.

Think of the way a husband, momentarily tempted to be unfaithful, might touch his wedding band and be reminded of his wife's love and faithfulness to him. He is strengthened by that to resist temptation by saying: "This is the sign and seal my wife placed on my finger the day we were married. She loves me, and I will not betray that love, nor will I deny her faithfulness to me." And so he is strengthened to resist. In the same way, the Christian finds that the sign of baptism is a reminder and confirmation of what the Lord Jesus has done to set us free and to cleanse us from sin. And so the gospel message of baptism strengthens us to remain faithful to the One who loved us with a Calvary love.

That is what the older writers used to describe as *improving* baptism. They didn't mean making it better; they meant proving day by day that its message really works in our Christian lives. It wasn't given to us just for the experience of the moment; it's for every single day of our Christian lives.

Here's a question for you to consider: "When was the last time the fact that you were baptized made any practical difference to your life as a Christian?" That is what it was given to you for—yet some of us haven't thought about our baptism for weeks, perhaps even for years.

That is something worth pondering.

3

Why Was Jesus Baptized?

BAPTISM IS A SIGN THAT POINTS US away from ourselves and to the Lord Jesus Christ. We'll miss its real power and usefulness in our lives if we think that its chief message is to point us to what we ourselves have done rather than to what Jesus has done for us. Everything Jesus did was for us. He had no need to do it for Himself. When He was baptized, it was for us.

Think back to Jesus' baptism. John the Baptist was baptizing vast numbers of people at the Jordan River, summoning them to repent of their sins. When he saw Jesus coming, he cried out, "Behold, the Lamb of God, who takes away the sin of the world!" (John 1:29). Sacrificial lambs, of course, needed to be without spot or blemish or any such thing. So it's not surprising that when Jesus came to John to be baptized, John resisted Him. John was the sinner needing to be baptized, not Jesus.

So why did Jesus insist on being baptized? That was the question that John himself struggled to answer. But if we think about the scene, perhaps its significance will become clear to us. Great crowds have come to the river Jordan to be baptized, confessing their sins. In your mind's eye, watch what happens.

Do you see what John is doing? He is symbolically washing the sins off the people and into the river Jordan. Then Jesus comes to John. What does John do next? He baptizes Jesus with the very water into which those sins have been symbolically washed.

There is a profound gospel message in this scene, and it's profoundly theological, too. It's a picture of the gospel—sinners washing away their sins into the water, but then Jesus Himself being baptized with that sin-polluted water. It's as though the sins that have *washed off* these sinners have now *washed over* the person of the Lord Jesus. A staggering reversal of position is taking place here—what the Reformers used to call the "wonderful exchange." Jesus is being baptized into our sin so that we might be baptized into His righteousness. Sin-filled water pours over Him; cleansing grace flows over us.

Jesus viewed His baptism at the hands of John as the initial stage that would lead to His full and final baptism on the cross. He later said, "I have a baptism to be baptized with, and how great is my distress until it is accomplished!" (Luke 12:50). His baptism with water was a sign, a pointer, a confirmation, a seal, of the baptism with blood that would be administered to Him on the cross.

At the heart of baptism lies the fact that it symbolizes our union with Jesus Christ, in which He was made to be sin for us—although He personally knew no sin—so that we might become in Him the righteousness of God (see 2 Cor. 5:21). He would be cursed so that the blessing promised to Abraham might come to us (Gal. 3:13). He would be wounded for our transgressions and bruised for our iniquities. With His stripes, we would be made whole. He has been baptized into our sin that we might be baptized into His righteousness.

And so our baptism carries this message for us: "Behold, the Lamb of God, who takes away the sin of the world!" (John 1:29). Therefore, trust Him and repent, because in the reality to which the baptism of Jesus points you will discover what it is to be justified and adopted. In a sense, the message of our baptism is also that God says to us in Christ, "You are My beloved son in whom I am well pleased, and I adopt you into My family." That is the message contained in baptism, and it calls us to believe the message.

So baptism is an ordinance of the gospel. It operates like the gospel. It proclaims, by means of a visible sign that we see with our eyes, the very same message that the gospel proclaims to us in words that we hear. And like the gospel it symbolizes, it is a permanent call to us to trust in the Lord Jesus Christ and to repent of our sins.

This is one of the reasons that it helps us to understand that baptism isn't first of all a sign of what we do but of what Christ has done for us. But then it's a sign that calls us to do something—to come to Christ, to live for Christ. And when we see that our baptism reflects Christ's baptism—first in the river Jordan and then on the cross of Calvary—then every time we're at a baptism, the gospel is being preached to us in order that every day of our lives we might live as baptized Christians.

That is why baptism is given to us right at the beginning of the Christian life and stays with us right to the end.

4

Baptized: A New Identity

AS WE CONSIDER BAPTISM THIS WEEK, I've tried to avoid the usual controversies that arise—whether believers only or believers and their children should be baptized, whether baptism should be by immersion or pouring or sprinkling. I've done that not just to avoid stirring up controversy but because discussing these things rarely helps us do what our spiritual forefathers urged us to do—namely, to *improve* our baptism by making good use of it in an ongoing way in our own Christian life.

Even our spiritual forefathers who used that term sometimes felt they were fighting a bit of a losing battle. The Westminster divines, who wrote the Shorter and Larger Catechisms, called improving our baptism a "needful but much neglected duty" (WLC 167). So here are some questions we should ask ourselves: "When did I last think about my own baptism? When did I last try to improve it? When did I last think, 'This really makes a difference to my Christian life, knowing that I was baptized'?"

Today and tomorrow, we'll look at two ways in which we can all improve—or make the best spiritual and practical use of—our baptism. And it's possible that they may challenge us to adjust our focus a little bit.

Sometimes when we talk about baptism, we focus all our attention on what we are baptized *with* and ignore what we are baptized *into*. We're baptized with water. Water is the instrument and the means that we use to baptize. But despite all our discussions about the amount of water we use, that is not really the chief focus of what we are baptized into. Paul says in Romans 6:3: "Do you not know that all of us who have been *baptized into Christ Jesus* were baptized into his death?" (emphasis added). He uses similar language in Galatians 3:27. We are baptized with the element of water, but we are baptized into fellowship with a person, the Lord Jesus Christ.

Perhaps an analogy might help. You've been at weddings and watched the groom place a wedding band on the bride's ring finger and say: "With this ring, I thee wed. With all my worldly goods, I thee endow." Did you know that neither the words nor the ring is essential to their marriage? The words and the ring are a sign and seal of it. They are a visible representation of the marriage bond. The big thing is not the ring but what the ring represents. The ring isn't the commitment, but it expresses the commitment in this moving, visual way.

Baptism is like that: it's the visible expression of Christ's commitment to us in our union with Him. It's like the wedding band placed once for all on the ring finger. Our once-for-all baptism with water is a permanent reminder of the new identity that belongs to all those who trust in Christ. We're no longer our own; we belong to another. And in belonging to Jesus Christ, we are endowed with all that He has done for us through His death and resurrection.

Paul goes on to explain what this means. In union with Christ, not only are our sins forgiven, but the dominion and reign of sin over us has been broken. We're not yet free from sin's presence or its influence, but we're no longer under its reign. We've been given a new identity. We belong to a new kingdom altogether. Jesus reigns over us. Paul goes on to say that because we are in Christ, sin will no longer have dominion over us. Therefore, we're now called to give ourselves without reservation to Him (see Rom. 6:4–14).

Let me put it this way: baptism is actually a naming ceremony. We are named for the Father and the Son and the Holy Spirit. It doesn't in itself do anything *in us*, but it does something permanently *to us*. It names us for God.

In many countries and states, the last time a bride signs her name the way she had always done is on the marriage papers. I know there are people who object to women's changing their name to their husband's name when they get married, but we shouldn't object if we're Christians, because we understand Paul's words about marriage. Its deepest meaning lies in the way it points to Christ. And when we're united to Christ, we're given a new name. We take our Savior's name. We become *Christians*.

Paul expresses this powerfully in Romans 6 when he says that the symbolism of baptism begins to be realized in our lives when we understand that we are a new category of person altogether—a person who has a new identity, a person whose identity is that he or she has died to sin and been raised to newness of life. And so we no longer live the way we used to live.

When we grasp that, when baptism makes that impact on us, then we've begun to "improve" our baptism.

5

Named in Baptism

BAPTISM ISN'T JUST SOMETHING THAT HAPPENED to us once in the past and has no relevance to us in the present. It's more like an engagement ring or a wedding band that provides a constant reminder to us of who we are now in Christ.

I'm fairly sure that I'm not the only one who thinks that when we engage in controversy over baptism, we are very rarely improving our own. Sometimes those controversies actually divert us from what's really most significant about our baptism. So I want to bring our week-long reflections to a close by mentioning something that has often puzzled me. In the sermons I've heard on baptism, I've sometimes heard infant baptism defended or believers' baptism argued for. I've heard immersion emphasized or pouring justified. But I'm not sure I've ever heard a sermon on what is actually central to baptism.

Maybe your experience is different. But before you respond that it is, maybe it's wise to ask the question, "What actually is most important about baptism?" Jesus gives us the answer when He says: "All authority in heaven and on earth has been given to me. Go therefore and make disciples of all nations, baptizing them in[to] the name of the Father and of the Son and of the Holy Spirit" (Matt. 28:18–19). What's central and most important to baptism is the name into which we've been baptized. The name that reveals the One into whom we've been baptized, the name of God the Trinity, the single name of the three-person God— the Father, the Son, and the Holy Spirit.

I'm sure there must be many ministers who have preached at baptismal services on the Trinity and our fellowship with each person in the Trinity. But I don't think I've ever heard one. I suppose, sadly, it's an indication that we preachers tend to have a particular view of baptism, and we feel we need to defend it (or maybe even attack the opposing view). It's possible to do all that and yet fail to focus on what is central—to miss the baptism forest because of the controversy trees, as it were.

At the heart of the visible sign is Jesus' interpretation that the reality to which it points is nothing less than our fellowship with the Father who loved us, the Son who died for us, and the Spirit who transforms us. This means something very important, and it's helpful for us to reflect on it in terms of an Old Testament passage.

Do you remember the Aaronic blessing in Numbers 6:24–26? That is the blessing we often use in church:

> The LORD bless you and keep you;
> the LORD make his face to shine upon you . . . ;
> the LORD lift up his countenance upon you and give you peace.

You notice that it has a kind of Trinitarian ring ("The LORD . . . the LORD . . . the LORD"). But I wonder if you remember the words that follow it. God says, "So shall they put my name upon the people of Israel" (Num. 6:27). That benediction is pointing forward to our baptism. That is what baptism is. It's the Lord, the Lord, the Lord—the Lord who is Father, the Lord who is Son, the Lord who is Holy Spirit—putting His name on us.

That doesn't do anything *within* us, but in fact, it does do something *to* us.

When the city registrar asked my parents, "Who is this child?," they said, "We are putting this name on him: Sinclair Buchanan Ferguson." That did absolutely nothing *within me*, but it did do something *to me*. It meant that this was the name to which I would respond for the rest of my life. Yes, I could repudiate it, just as the Israelites could repudiate that Aaronic blessing, and just as people do repudiate their baptism. But nevertheless, that name marks us for the rest of our lives because it summons us to believe in the Trinity, to trust in the Savior, and to live in fellowship with God.

In other words, as we've seen, baptism preaches the whole gospel of God to us, and it calls us to respond to Him. We've been named for the Trinity, and our baptism calls us to respond to the Trinity. It points us to the way that the entire Trinity—all three persons equally and together—has conspired to work for our salvation. And that is a daily call to us to live moment by moment, hour by hour, trusting in the Father, believing in the Son, and with the help of the Holy Spirit, living a new life devoted to God.

That is why we can daily be strengthened by saying with Martin Luther, "*Baptizatus sum*," or, if you're a woman, "*Baptizata sum*."

So let your baptism remind you of what the Lord has done for you and of the name that you've been given. And let it remind you not only of who you are but of what you are called to be.

WEEK 36

The Questions of Romans 8

1

Beloved Bible Verses

WHAT'S YOUR FAVORITE PASSAGE IN THE BIBLE? If we took a poll, I'm fairly sure that some or all of Romans 8:28–39 would be near the top of the list. This week, we'll reflect on one specific feature of this portion of Scripture.

By any stretch of the imagination, it's an amazing passage. My church history professor once noted in a lecture that if we want to be convinced of the inspiration of the New Testament—what makes it different from other books—we just need to read the writings of the Christians who came after the biblical authors. The difference is unmistakable. When we read Romans 8, we're bound to think, "There is nothing in human literature just like this."

Do you ever read the Bible out loud to yourself? Until at least the time of Augustine, people used to read everything out loud. If you think about it, the Bible was actually written to be read out loud. It was the only way that people who couldn't possibly have afforded a copy of the Bible had access to it. And because it was written to be read out loud, I think we sometimes benefit most from it when we read it out loud to ourselves.

So I suggest that we read these verses out loud now:

And we know that for those who love God all things work together for good, for those who are called according to his purpose. For those whom he foreknew he also predestined to be conformed to the image of his Son, in order that he might be the firstborn among many brothers. And those whom he predestined he also called, and those whom he called he also justified, and those whom he justified he also glorified.

What then shall we say to these things? If God is for us, who can be against us? He who did not spare his own Son but gave him up for us all, how will he not also with him graciously give us all things? Who shall bring any charge against God's elect? It is God who justifies. Who is to condemn? Christ Jesus is the one who died—more than that, who was raised—who is at the right hand of God, who indeed is interceding for us. Who shall separate us from the love of Christ? Shall tribulation, or distress, or persecution, or famine, or nakedness, or danger, or sword? As it is written,

"For your sake we are being killed all the day long;
we are regarded as sheep to be slaughtered."

No, in all these things we are more than conquerors through him who loved us. For I am sure that neither death nor life, nor angels nor rulers, nor things present nor things to come, nor powers, nor height nor depth, nor anything else in all creation, will be able to separate us from the love of God in Christ Jesus our Lord.

There is a feature in verses 31–35 that is rather unusual. When you see it for the first time, you can't avoid noticing it every time you read it thereafter. What is this feature?

We'll answer that question tomorrow!

2

Who Can Be against Us?

WHAT IS THE RATHER UNUSUAL FEATURE OF Romans 8:28–39 that I referred to yesterday? It's the fact that this series of verses is framed by a rapid-fire series of questions: If God is for us, who can be against us? Who shall bring any charge against God's elect? Who is to condemn? Who shall separate us from the love of Christ?

It's not just the simple fact of this rapid-fire series of questions that strikes me as significant here. Of course, we get the sense that Paul has tremendous confidence that nothing can withstand the purposes of God or the power of the gospel. But what's significant is that all these questions begin with the same interrogative pronoun. More specifically, the interrogative pronoun used on each occasion is a *personal* pronoun.

Paul doesn't ask "What . . . ?" but "Who . . . ?" It's not "What can be against us?" or "What can constitute a charge against us?" or "What can condemn us?" or "What shall separate us?" It's "Who? Who? Who? Who?" Surely that can't be accidental. After all, when he asks his fourth question, he goes on to give a list of potential separators—tribulation, distress, persecution, famine, nakedness, danger, and sword. All these things are "its," but Paul doesn't ask, "*What* shall separate us?"

So there must be a reason why Paul uses the personal pronoun *who* and not the impersonal pronoun *what*. Perhaps you've already guessed the answer. It's because all opposition to the Christian and to his or her relationship with the Lord Jesus is not ultimately rooted in things, events, or circumstances—in *whats*. It's rooted in someone, a *who*— namely, the evil one. This is the one whom the book of Revelation calls the "ancient serpent, who is called the devil and Satan, the deceiver of the whole world—. . . the accuser of our brothers" (Rev. 12:9–10).

Paul's first question is, "If God is for us, who can be against us?" (Rom. 8:31). Clearly, he doesn't expect the answer to be "Nobody." He certainly faced plenty of opposition, as do we. But his logic is this: If God is for us, then ultimately, nothing and no one who stands against us can ever be successful. Nobody who is against us can ever prevail. Satan can't ultimately prevail.

It is true, as Peter wrote in his first letter, that the one who is against us—our adversary the devil—goes around like a roaring lion, seeking to devour us (see 1 Peter 5:8). But God is greater than our enemy. And if He is for us, then all of the devil's efforts to oppose us and destroy us will fail. He may harass us, harm us, or hurt us, but he cannot overcome us if God is for us.

Paul's words raise an important question: "How do we know that God is for us, especially when we're facing all kinds of opposition from people or circumstances, and Satan seems to be shooting his fiery darts at us?" If those darts hit the mark, they cause panic in our hearts and destabilize us. We had assumed that God was for us and that He loves us, but now we're not so sure.

In some ways, the importance of the original question Paul was asking—"*Who* is against us?"—is that it leads us to this other question. And even more importantly, it leads us to the answer. That answer is not—despite what some Christians seem to think—"Well, I know God is for me because so many good things are happening in my life." If my assurance that God is for me is based on good things happening in my life, how am I going to handle things when everything seems to go wrong and life begins to crumble? You can't imagine the Apostle Paul saying, "I know God is for me because everything is going swimmingly in my life"—because usually, it wasn't.

So what is the answer? What gives us this deep, unshakable conviction that God is for us is this: He did not spare His own Son, but gave Him up for us all. If that is true, if He did that for me, then I can be absolutely certain He will give me everything necessary to keep my soul safe and to bring me home to Himself.

That is the irrefutable Apostolic logic of the cross of Christ, and I hope you're learning to use it day by day.

3

Who Shall Bring Any Charge?

I CAN'T REMEMBER WHEN OR HOW IT STRUCK me that the famous series of questions Paul asks in Romans 8:31–35 all begin with the personal interrogative pronoun *who*, despite the fact that everything in his list is a *what* and not a *who*. But now I can't read these great verses without reflecting on this striking feature of this amazing passage. There is no variation in it. He keeps asking the question, "Who?"

We've seen that the *who* refers to Satan. That is who Paul has in mind when he asks, "Who can be against us?" (Rom. 8:31). It's also who he has in mind when he asks, "Who shall bring any charge against God's elect?" (v. 33).

The fact is that many people did bring charges against Christians—the book of Acts makes that clear enough. There were several occasions when the Apostles were brought before the religious or civil authorities to face accusations. But that is not what Paul is ultimately talking about here, and his answers seem to make that clear.

The accusations that Paul is talking about here are the ones the devil brings against us. Scripture tells us that these charges are made in the courtroom of heaven. According to Revelation 12:10, the devil is the accuser of the brothers and "accuses them day and night before our God." There is something mysterious about this because it isn't something that we see or hear directly.

Elsewhere in Scripture, we learn about this activity of the devil. Jesus said to Peter: "Simon, Simon, behold, Satan demanded to have you, that he might sift you like wheat, but I have prayed for you that your faith may not fail" (Luke 22:31–32). And of course, in the opening chapters of the book of Job, we're told how the devil accused Job before God, saying: "Does Job fear God for no reason? Have you not put a hedge around him and his house and all that he has, on every side? You have blessed the work of his hands, and his possessions have increased in the land. But stretch out your hand and touch all that he has, and he will curse you to your face" (Job 1:9–11).

There is also that amazing scene in Zechariah 3. The prophet has a vision of Joshua, the high priest, standing in the presence of God, and Satan is standing at his right hand to accuse him. What makes the picture so dramatic is that Joshua is wearing dirty clothes that represent his sinfulness. He is standing before God's judgment throne. Satan is accusing him before God, saying: "He has no right to be here. He deserves to be excluded from heaven and sent into the outer darkness that will match the dark stains on the clothing he is wearing."

But then something wonderful happens. The angel of the Lord speaks. He says, "Behold, I have taken your iniquity away from you, and I will clothe you with pure vestments" (Zech. 3:4). He commands the filthy garments to be taken off Joshua and then has him robed from head to toe in clean vestments.

That is surely a wonderful picture of the gospel and of the

believer's justification. The Lord Jesus takes our filthy garments of sin and swaps them for His pure garments of perfect righteousness. When that happens, none of the adversary's charges of sin and guilt before our God can ever stick to us. And that is what Paul is talking about in Romans 8:33: "Who shall bring any charge against God's elect?"

We know the answer—Satan brings those charges—but we also know that his accusations cannot stick because the One in whose court these charges are brought is none other than the God who justifies sinners in and through Jesus Christ. God the Son, the One who could condemn us, is the One who actually saves us. As the book of Revelation tells us, the saints overcome the accuser of the brethren not because of their own righteousness, but by the blood of the Lamb (see Rev. 12:11).

John Newton teaches us to sing in his wonderful hymn:

Approach, my soul, the mercy seat
Where Jesus answers pray'r. . . .

Be Thou my shield and hiding place,
That, sheltered near Thy side,
I may my fierce accuser face
And tell him, Christ has died.

We saw yesterday that the death of Christ is the basis for the logic that nothing can ultimately be against us. We see today that the basis of our assurance that Satan's accusations against us will not stick is that we wear the garments of Christ's righteousness. Isn't that glorious?

What a wonderful relief the gospel brings to our consciences. I hope you'll taste that today.

4

Who Is to Condemn?

TODAY, WE'LL LOOK AT THE THIRD QUESTION Paul asks in Romans 8: "Who is to condemn?" (v. 34). At first sight, we might think that Paul is simply repeating himself. After all, there doesn't seem to be much difference between an accusation of guilt and condemnation. Many of us feel condemned the moment anyone accuses us.

But there is a difference.

An accusation is brought when someone thinks that we are guilty of something. The condemnation is the *result* of being found guilty. It's about the sentence that follows the verdict. It's about the imprisonment that results from being found guilty. This is intriguing, because if Paul has already said that no accusation against us can stick when God has justified us in Christ, why does he need to bother talking about condemnation?

Here's the answer, I think: logically that may seem to be true, but spiritually it isn't always like that, precisely because our "adversary the devil prowls around like a roaring lion, seeking someone to devour" (1 Peter 5:8). We saw yesterday that he fails to bring in a verdict of guilty in the court of heaven because God has justified us in Christ. We have complete righteousness in Christ. But the fact is that we still stumble and fall in our Christian lives. We may be justified before God, but we're not fully sanctified. In fact, we're still very conscious of our sin and guilt.

Some of us are very easily drawn by the evil one to focus on that sin and guilt. He delights to stimulate us to feel that we are failures. And when that begins to happen, he comes to accuse us. But this time it is not in heaven. He accuses us here on earth in our own consciences. What then happens is that some of us become paralyzed and lose our joy, and we begin to lose sight of the amazing love of our heavenly

Father for us. So it's not just a matter of accusation; it's a matter of feeling that we are undergoing a kind of prison sentence because of our sin.

I often think that is exactly how Simon Peter must have felt when, weeping bitterly, he ran into the darkness of the Jerusalem night after he had denied the Lord Jesus. He had not just failed Jesus; he'd actually sworn that he didn't know Him and that he wasn't one of His disciples. Jesus had said that Simon Peter was clean; he was justified. But Peter must have felt as though the devil was shouting in his ear, "Condemned, condemned, condemned!" All the joy was gone, with nothing but recriminations left. Satan was telling him, "There is no way back for you this time." He was undergoing the sentence—the condemnation—that followed the verdict for his sin.

Does Paul have an answer to this? He certainly does. It's the answer Peter needed, and it's the answer we need. In fact, it summarizes some great truths that Paul has already laid out in Romans. Paul gives this answer to the question, "Who is to condemn?": "Christ has died for you so that there would be no condemnation for those who are in Christ Jesus. Not only is this true, but the Christ who died for your sins has been raised for your justification. And more than that, He is even now at the right hand of God, and He is interceding for you. He will never let you go. You can never be condemned" (see Rom. 8:34).

I think that is why so many of us love the relatively recent resurrection of the old hymn "Before the Throne of God Above"—because it contains this verse:

When Satan tempts me to despair
And tells me of the guilt within,
Upward I look and see him there,
Who made an end of all my sin.
Because the sinless Savior died,
My sinful soul is counted free;

For God, the just, is satisfied

To look on him and pardon me.

You see, we not only need the finished work of Christ for us on Calvary; we need the ongoing work of Christ interceding for us in heaven. Then we will know, as Simon Peter must surely have discovered that terrible night, that even though Satan has desired to sift us like wheat, the Lord Jesus Christ is praying for us.

Who, then, could ever condemn us?

5

Who Shall Separate Us?

TODAY, WE COME TO PAUL'S FOURTH QUESTION in the closing verses of Romans 8: "Who shall separate us from the love of Christ?" (v. 35). The first items in this long list of potential separators are, interestingly, all impersonal: tribulation, distress, persecution, famine, nakedness, danger, and sword. As his list continues—death and life, things present, things to come, height and depth—it becomes obvious that Paul is really thinking about powerful personal forces, the devil and his angels, who are against us. How can we be so sure that we are secure against such opposition as this?

Paul doesn't give the kind of specific answer he gave to his three previous questions. Now all he says is that "we are more than conquerors through him who loved us" (v. 37) and that nothing can "separate us from the love of God in Christ Jesus our Lord" (v. 39).

These seem to be statements more than arguments, confessions more than logical explanations. But there is a powerful logic at work here, too.

Paul is picking up the threads of what he'd said earlier. We conquer through the love of God because that love is demonstrated to us in Christ. The Apostle is now bringing together everything he'd said earlier and weaving it into a threefold cord that can't easily be broken.

Let's look at what he said in Romans 8:28–30, where he laid the foundations for these verses.

First, he stressed that God's power is perfect. He emphasized that all things work together for good for those who love God—but only because God Himself works them together. He works *all things* together—no exceptions, no limitations. In other words, nothing can happen to the Christian believer unless it is ultimately for his or her good.

Second, in verse 29, he indicated exactly what that good is. It's our being conformed to the likeness of God's Son, Jesus Christ. The Spirit of God employs every event in our lives to bring this to pass. Whether encouraging or discouraging events, whether joyful or sad events, they are all employed in the hands of the heavenly potter to make us like the Lord Jesus. The very things that seem to threaten our security in Christ can be used by Him to make us more like Him.

Then in verse 30, Paul indicates that the One whose power is said to be perfect in verse 28, and whose plan is seen as perfect in verse 29, is also the One whose purposes are perfect. Those He predestined, He called; those He called, He justified; those He justified, He also glorified. Nothing can stand in the way of the God of sovereign grace as He fulfills His plan and purposes for His people—the people for whom His Son died and whose Spirit transforms into His likeness.

That is why we can sing the words of Augustus Montague Toplady's hymn "A Debtor to Mercy Alone":

My name from the palms of his hand
Eternity will not erase;
Impressed on his heart it remains,
In marks of indelible grace.

Yes, I to the end shall endure,
As sure as the earnest is giv'n;
More happy, but not more secure,
The glorified spirits in heav'n.

WEEK 37

Reflections on Preaching

1

How Important Is Preaching?

THIS WEEK, WE'RE GOING TO REFLECT on the subject of preaching. This topic is relevant to all of us, whether we are preachers or listeners. No doubt, we all have our own opinions about preaching and about the preaching that we regularly listen to. Therefore, it's important that we don't merely react to preaching in an "I like it; I don't like it" way. Rather, we should consider what preaching is and what it should be. That can help us do what Paul asked the Ephesian church to do: to pray for the preaching of the mystery of the gospel (Eph. 6:18–20).

Someone once asked me, "How important is preaching?" Question 89 of the Westminster Shorter Catechism asks the same question in different words: "How is the Word of God made effectual to salvation?" That is, how does it point us to Christ and then transform our lives? The answer is striking: "The Spirit of God maketh the reading, but especially the preaching, of the Word, an effectual means of convincing and converting sinners, and of building them up in holiness and comfort, through faith, unto salvation."

Many Christians today seem to think that their own Bible reading or home group makes a far bigger impact on their Christian lives than preaching does. As a result, those things are far more important to them than the sermons they hear.

Were the men who wrote the catechism wrong, or were they just living in a different time? Was that true in their day, whereas we live in a technological day when things have changed? Was preaching so much more important in their yesterday than it is in our today? Christians who draw these conclusions do so almost entirely on the basis of their own experience. But the fact that someone gets more out of the neighborhood Bible study than they do out of the preaching they hear doesn't mean that that is how it should be.

Jesus told us that we need to take heed what we hear. He also said that we need to take heed how we hear as well as what we hear. So we need to probe a little deeper. What if the problem is in the preaching we hear? Or what if it's in the way that we are listening (or not listening, for that matter)? What if it's in the way we are praying or not praying? In that case, it wouldn't be surprising if we thought that preaching was, at best, secondary to our spiritual growth, or hardly important at all.

Muddleheaded views about preaching seem to come around every decade or so. Some time ago, there was a lot of talk stating that what we need is not more sermons, but more dialogue. In fact, some preachers started having dialogues in their pulpits instead of sermons. When I first heard this, it made me think that the people who say this kind of thing have never heard true preaching. Because when you hear true preaching in the Spirit of Christ, you find yourself entering into the most intense dialogue of soul that is possible. True preaching takes you to levels of dialogue with God that nothing else can.

Then there was a call for drama. Since people love dramatic gifts, it was said that we should have less preaching and more drama. If that weren't so muddleheaded, it would be amusing. Don't these people know that the Apostle Paul, the preacher, lived in the age of Greek drama? Don't they know that the great Puritan preachers of the sixteenth and seventeenth centuries lived at the high point of English drama, in the age of Shakespeare?

And then there were those who said that people don't want to listen to preaching anymore, so we needed to devise new methods of communicating the gospel. Of course, there are new methods of communicating the gospel, and they can be rightly employed. But it's muddleheaded to think that people's telling us they don't want to listen to preaching is a modern reaction. Not at all. Paul told Timothy that he would experience a time when people didn't want to listen to preaching. What was Paul's counsel? What was Timothy to do when people didn't want to listen to biblical preaching? Paul's answer was this: "Preach the word." The way to respond when people don't want to hear preaching is by preaching (see 2 Tim. 4:1–5).

We noted at the beginning of today's reflection that Paul asked the Ephesian church to pray for the preaching of the mystery of the gospel. Before we think more about preaching tomorrow, consider this question:

"When did you last pray about the preaching that you hear?"

2

What Is Wrong with Preaching Today?

OUR SPIRITUAL FOREFATHERS BELIEVED THAT preaching was the chief means of conversion and spiritual growth. But it seems that many Christians don't think that way any longer. Instead, they consider that the sermon is an added extra to their own Bible study, home group, or other Bible study program. Why, then, did Jesus and the Apostles do so much preaching? Could it be that we're looking at things the wrong way around? What if preaching is still meant to be the chief means of converting people and building them up in their most holy faith? And if it is, why, then, isn't some preaching doing that?

I once saw a fascinating interview with the late John R.W. Stott, the distinguished Anglican evangelical preacher. He was asked what he thought of the state of preaching today. I can still hear his answer ringing in my ears, articulated in the beautifully modulated accent of an upper-class graduate of the University of Cambridge. He replied with one word: "Miserable." That really hurts if you're a preacher! But if Dr. Stott was right—and he certainly believed in the centrality of preaching—then the problem today is not so much preaching but preachers. And we need to think seriously about that. Wherein lies the problem?

We can all think of possible answers. You might think that the answer is that there are men who preach who shouldn't. They want to serve the Lord, and preaching is one of the most obvious ways to do that, so they become ministers. But they are not actually gifted to preach. And so when they become preachers, the fact that they can't preach ends up being balanced by people's saying, "But he is really a very nice man."

So how do we recognize a preacher? The threefold ingredients of a call to preach are these: first, gifts for preaching; second, a desire to serve by using them; and third, the recognition by others of God's call and God's gifts in a person's life. Sometimes, however, there is simply a kind of passive acceptance that if someone wants to become a preacher and he is a keen Christian, then he should. Sometimes the church blames the seminary or the theological college for poor preaching. Sometimes the seminaries and theological colleges blame the church for not sending better candidates for them to train.

In one sense, all this is understandable. It may not always be equally clear that a person has particular gifts. And it's not always clear that what appear to be gifts are really being fed by spiritual graces.

The people who make the decisions in this area can vary from "hard-liners"—not all of whom exude the fruit of the Spirit themselves—to the "softhearted" who, because they don't want to hurt anyone and are conscious of their own weaknesses, are very reluctant to ask the important questions about a call to preach. We all need help in this area.

But while that is true, there is something else that is really important to say. While I can't be dogmatic about it, I have a sense that one answer to the question, "What is wrong with preaching today?" is found in the words of James 4:2: "You do not have, because you do not ask."

We closed yesterday with the question, "When did you last pray about preaching?" I really do wonder if we pray for preachers only when we happen to be looking for a new one in our own congregation. But preachers don't just suddenly emerge full-grown when congregations need them. If Martin Luther was right that it's prayer, meditation, and testing that make a man a preacher, then preachers are long in the making. Therefore, this should be a constant prayer burden for us.

There is something else we should remember. In a sense, congregations make preachers. I don't mean during their ministry, although there is a lot of truth in that. I mean that when young people are being nurtured and nourished in your congregation, that is where they are being prepared—not by experts in exegesis and theology, but by the care, nurture, example, counsel, and love of older fellow believers. Congregations make preachers especially when they pray that already, in their own fellowship, God would prepare, call, and equip the preachers who will preach to their grandchildren.

So Jesus' call in Matthew 9:38 to "pray earnestly to the Lord of the harvest to send out laborers into his harvest" isn't just about overseas missionaries. It's about praying for preachers.

3

The Effects of Preaching

THERE ARE FADS IN PREACHING, just as there are about almost everything in church life. If you live long enough, you begin to realize that is exactly what they are: fads. Often, they are the result of cloning. Someone does something different. It looks as though it works, so then others follow. The result is that we lose sight of what is fundamental and ought to be unchangeable in the way we think about preaching.

What should be fundamental? Clearly, the exposition of the Scriptures in the power of the Holy Spirit is foundational, especially the kind of exposition that leads to the hearers being bowed down before the Lord in faith, worship, surrender, and obedience.

That is surely part of what Jonathan Edwards had in mind when he spoke in defense of what he believed was the true preaching of the gospel during the First Great Awakening in the eighteenth century. This preaching was being criticized because of some of its effects on people. Here's what Edwards wrote: "I don't think ministers are to be blamed for raising the affections of their hearers too high, if that which they are affected with be only that which is worthy of affection, and their affections are not raised beyond a proportion to their importance, or worthiness of affection."

Then he says this: "I should think myself in the way of my duty to raise the affections of my hearers as high as possibly I can, provided that they are affected with nothing but truth, and with affections that are not disagreeable to the nature of what they are affected with."

That is a very illuminating way of talking about preaching, especially when we remember that Edwards is widely acknowledged as one of the greatest intellects in North American history. But he wanted his preaching to raise the affections of his hearers as high as possible, in a way that was consistent with the truth.

I've had the privilege of listening to a great deal of preaching just like that, and it contrasts with a kind of preaching that tells hearers how they ought to feel. The result is that even when what is said is in the indicative mood—that is, stating the facts of the gospel—in emotional tone, it's in the imperative mood. It always seems to be coming down on the hearers instead of lifting them up. They feel they are being crushed, not encouraged and uplifted; knocked down, but not built up.

So what's the difference with the kind of preaching that Edwards wrote about? It's this: whether the teaching is in indicative sentences describing what God has done, or in imperative sentences telling us what we are to do, the preaching raises the affections. As a whole, it doesn't hammer the hearers into the dust but gets underneath them and lifts them up to God. This kind of preaching is not constantly telling us what we are to do or feel. It's enabling us to do it, and it makes us feel it. That is part of what Paul must have meant when he wrote to the Thessalonians about the fact that the Word itself is "at work" in people when it's preached in the power of the Holy Spirit (see 1 Thess. 2:13).

C.S. Lewis used to advise young writers never to tell their readers how they should feel about anything but rather to describe it so that readers would feel it. That is what happens in true preaching. There is an unhelpful preaching that always seems to be pressing us down. But there is a fruitful preaching that through the power of the Spirit seems to get under us with the Word and lift us up to God—or in Edwards' words, to raise our affections on high in admiration and adoration of our glorious God and Savior. That happens even when the preached Word convicts us of sin. It convicts us of sin to lead us to Him.

I wonder if that is your experience in church.

One of the telltale signs that something has gone wrong here is when ministers or "worship leaders," as they are called today, tell us at the beginning of a service that there will be half an hour of worship, and then so-and-so will come to teach or to preach from God's Word. What's wrong with that? Simply this: the chief effect of hearing the preaching of the Word is meant to be . . . worship. The response to the kind of preaching that Edwards talked about is always a sense of awe and reverence, of wonder and praise, before the grace, glory, majesty, holiness, and love of our God. And that is what worship is.

The Apostle Paul told the Corinthians that it was this kind of preaching that would expose hearts and cause even unbelievers to bow down before the Lord Jesus Christ, not the novel, the spectacular, or the apparently impressive (see 1 Cor. 14:24–25).

That is worth thinking about and praying about.

4

Different Kinds of Preachers

IT'S IMPORTANT TO REFLECT ON THE SUBJECT of preaching because Jesus urged us to take heed to both how we hear and what we hear. It's also important because we are to heed Paul's appeal in Ephesians 6:18–20. Right after his teaching on the Christian's spiritual armor, he urges the Ephesians to pray for preachers and to pray for their preaching.

When students begin courses on preaching in seminary or in theological college, their teachers often give them a preaching grid by which they can assess each other as they listen. It may ask questions such as these: Was the main point clear? Were the illustrations appropriate and helpful? Was the introduction attention-grabbing? Was the conclusion well handled? Was the length of the sermon appropriate? This might help you imagine the ordeal a student can go through if he doesn't think more highly about himself than he ought to. Who is really sufficient for these things?

I have to confess that my own theological education didn't include any teaching on preaching, and we were never given a preaching grid. Actually, I used to think that preaching grids were probably evil inventions of American professors used to make their students feel completely inadequate. Perhaps they were, yet in some ways, that is important, too! But they also do have a practical point: they provide a framework of reference for students, helping them to see what's important, and perhaps helping them to correct some of their mistakes.

On the other hand—and this may just be a personal view—I've sometimes felt that when a teacher of preaching insists on his students following his own pattern, perhaps saying, "No, John, we do it this way," the great danger is that everyone gets squeezed into the same mold. Inevitably, some will end up like David wearing Saul's armor. It just doesn't fit. The sad thing is, this can squash the gifts that a young preacher has by insisting that he use gifts that he doesn't have.

I've sometimes seen that happen, and the result is that it can take years for a man to untangle his true preaching self. I'm convinced that Ezekiel could never have preached one of Isaiah's sermons, nor could Paul have preached the sermons of the Apostle John. Phillips Brooks was surely right and biblical when he said that preaching is characterized by truth coming through personality.

This helps us to avoid the cult of preacher personality, which is probably as bad (if not worse) today as it was among the Corinthians. After all, they had only Peter, Paul, and Apollos to compare. But we have YouTube, Vimeo, and a multitude of other ways that we can listen to endless numbers of preachers. I've even seen lists of "the ten best preachers" and so on. We often hear people say, "My favorite preacher is so-and-so." So how can we avoid that cult of the favorite or the best preacher?

Here's something that I found very helpful when I first read it as a teenager. In one of his letters, our friend John Newton, whom we've already mentioned in these pages, answers a question that he'd been asked: "Why is it that one man's preaching helps me more than another's?"

How can we answer that question without creating a ranking of preachers? Newton's answer was this: Remember that God shapes individual men not only with different gifts but with different burdens, emphases, and personal characteristics. And you, too, have your own particular needs. Therefore, it shouldn't surprise us that one man's ministry may be especially helpful to us at a particular time, or that another man's preaching would minister to us in a special way. Sameness would mean that everyone was wearing Saul's armor, and it doesn't fit everybody. It's not a "one size fits all."

So instead of comparing, we should rejoice in the fact that there are different shapes, sizes, hues, and burdens in different men's preaching. Comparisons are odious, but thanksgiving for each is altogether appropriate.

Perhaps I can underline this with a couple of personal comments. I've had the privilege of hearing and knowing most of the men that many of us regard as the finest biblical preachers from the 1960s to the 2020s. Two things strike me. One is that although they were all faithful to Scripture, their preaching styles were very different from each other's, and the burdens you could sense in their preaching varied. The second—and I say this about the man whose preaching made the most impact in shaping my own life and ministry—is that nobody should have regarded his style as a model for themselves. If he'd gone to preaching school, every single preaching teacher under the sun would have tried to change him!

So here, I think, is a great lesson: learn to feed on the good food of the Word no matter who is preaching it to me. I hope that you think the same way.

5

The Power of the Spirit in Preaching

WE'VE THOUGHT ABOUT PREACHING THIS WEEK, chiefly to encourage us all to pray for those who preach and to pray for ourselves as we receive preaching. Yesterday, we reflected on how God gifts our preachers differently from each other.

That reminds me of some words written by an English merchant who, on a visit to Scotland in the seventeenth century, heard three of Scotland's greatest preachers: David Dickson, Robert Blair, and Samuel Rutherford.

He wrote that he had sat under the ministry of "a well-favored" old man with a long beard "who showed me all my heart." That was David Dickson. Then he said he heard a sweet, majestic-looking man "who showed me the majesty of God." That was Robert Blair. And then he heard a little fair man "who showed me the loveliness of Christ." That was Samuel Rutherford. Three great preachers, but very different men with different burdens from the Lord. And that is it, isn't it? The same Spirit but a diversity of operations (1 Cor. 12:4–6). And like that merchant, we should rejoice in it.

But with the diversity, there is a common thread. This thread ought to be more than the fact that a preacher's sermon meets the standards of his preaching professor's preaching grid. I remember Dr. Martyn Lloyd-Jones saying that he felt he could forgive almost any failure in a preacher as long as the preaching brought him into the presence of God. How does that occur? The answer, at least in part, is what our forefathers used to call *unction*.

Unction is the work of the Holy Spirit on a preacher as he preaches that has the effect of bringing us before the face of God and into His presence. Another great Scottish preacher, John Livingston, put it this way: "There is sometime somewhat in preaching that cannot be ascribed either to the matter or expression, and cannot be described what it is, or from whence it cometh; but with a sweet violence it pierceth into the heart and affections, and comes immediately from the Lord. But if there be any way to attain to any such thing, it is by a heavenly disposition of the speaker."

I think it's fairly obvious that unless you've experienced this, it's not really possible to know what Livingston is talking about. And even as one who had experienced this in a remarkable way, Livingston knew that it's not easily defined.

In our own time, there has been almost a campaign in some quarters to deny or even demean this element of unction in preaching. There is a reason that that is a mistake, though: the Lord Jesus Himself needed unction to preach. Remember His famous words in His home synagogue in Nazareth? He was given the scroll of Isaiah, and He read Isaiah 61:1–2: "The Spirit of the Lord is upon me, because he has anointed me to proclaim good news to the poor [and] liberty to the captives and recovering of sight to the blind, . . . to proclaim the year of the Lord's favor." Then Jesus said, "Today this Scripture has been fulfilled in your hearing" (Luke 4:16–21).

Thomas Goodwin once wrote that God had only one Son, and He made Him a preacher. And if our Lord Jesus Christ needed the anointing of the Holy Spirit to preach with authority (and as John says, He received this Spirit without measure), don't you think that preachers today need the presence and power of the Holy Spirit and His anointing if their words are to have an effect greater than ordinary human speech? Isn't that what enabled Paul to say in 1 Corinthians 2:4–5 that despite his own personal weakness and fear, his preaching was not in plausible words of wisdom to make up for his own inadequacies, but in demonstration of the Spirit and of power, so that our faith might rest not in the wisdom of men but in the power of God?

Let me appeal to you once again to pray about the preaching that you hear, to pray about the preaching you'll hear this coming Lord's Day, and to pray for your preachers. I'm sure we don't do that as often as we should or as much as we need to.

So let's pray for the coming of the Holy Spirit, lest James's words be true, that we have not because we ask not.

WEEK 38

Texts That Shaped Me

1

Come to Christ for Eternal Life

HAVE YOU SEEN THOSE JOIN-THE-DOT PUZZLES in which you try to guess the person or object as you connect dots that seem to be randomly placed on the page? Sometimes life is like that—full of apparently isolated dots. But as Christians, we know that they are not accidental or random. The dots will eventually all make sense, even if it's not clear what that final picture is going to be.

Passages of Scripture can be like those dots. One way in which we sometimes catch a glimpse of God's plan and pattern in our lives is to think of the specific verses or passages in Scripture that have made a special impression on us. We can view these passages as divinely placed dots and watch them being connected to give shape to our life.

Looking back, I think I can see (at least in part) how God has "joined up the dots" to give my own life shape. This week, we'll reflect on some of those passages, not because there is anything special about my own experience, but because this may be a way of encouraging you to do the same—to trace the Lord's ways with you.

Both Scripture and the old masters of the spiritual life tell us that it's important to remember God's ways with us. Because when we remember His providential dealings with us, it helps us praise Him for His watching over our lives, and it helps us to trust Him when we're not exactly sure what He is doing with us. It helps us sing, "'Tis grace has brought me safe thus far, and grace will lead me home."

Our first passage this week is John 5:39–40.

I began to read the Bible when I was eight or nine. My family didn't go to church, but I was sent to the local Sunday school. One of my teachers, a man named Jimmy Stewart, encouraged me to join a Bible reading society called the Scripture Union. It had a program for reading through the Bible every three years or so. I probably read the Bible twice by the time I was fifteen. About four months before my fifteenth birthday, I was reading in John 5, and some words seemed to leap off the page to me. I suppose I'd been a bit like the young Samuel—God was speaking through His Word, but I wasn't really recognizing His voice. But then the words of Jesus that I was reading seemed to walk off the page, as though the Lord Himself was addressing me and saying, "Sinclair Ferguson, what I was saying to these people during My earthly ministry, I'm now saying to you as well."

Here are the words: "You search the Scriptures because you think that in them you have eternal life; and it is they that bear witness about me, yet you refuse to come to me that you may have life."

That was exactly what I'd been doing: searching the Scriptures. In fact, I thought that was what it meant to be a Christian. I thought that reading the Bible and trying to do good things would perhaps balance any failures in my life.

It wasn't that the message of the Bible was obscure; it was that I was spiritually blind. I'd done exactly what those contemporaries of Jesus had done, even if not as intensively. I had repeated their mistake. I thought that reading and studying the Bible was how one qualified for eternal life. I knew about the Savior, but I'd never come to Him. I was actually spiritually dead.

It wasn't that I doubted any of the articles of the Apostles' Creed. What I needed was not more Bible study notes, even if they were helpful. What I needed was to come to Christ and trust in Him. And now He was speaking to me through His Word. In some ways, these two verses changed everything. Of course, they were surrounded by much else in my life. Looking back, I realize that there were people praying for me, and that the Lord was working in my heart and in other ways, too. He was, as it felt, closing in on me.

The Bible's teaching on God's sovereign grace seemed to be written on my story from the beginning. I felt as though, somehow, He had been pursuing me and drawing me when I wasn't really pursuing Him, and certainly not seeing Him. I still had not trusted Christ, and that is why the words of Jesus in John 5:39–40 arrested me and showed me what was missing. And in my mind, it marks the beginning of everything that has followed in my life since.

It's altogether possible that someone reading this might be in the same situation that I was back then. If that is true of you, I hope you'll hear the Lord Jesus saying through these very same words, "Friend, you're missing the point."

That can be a hard thing to hear because it's humbling, but listen to the words of the Lord Jesus: "What you need to do is to come to Me and find eternal life."

2

Following the Light of the World

I HOPE THAT YOU'VE ALREADY STARTED THINKING about passages that have shaped your own life. The texts I'm thinking of are great texts, and that is another reason I want to share them. It just so happens that they've meant a lot to me in particular.

Yesterday, we were reflecting on the first words that seemed to leap off the pages of the Bible to me: John 5:39–40. Today, it's another verse from John's gospel. It was the text of the sermon to which I look back as marking the point of my coming to faith in Christ.

The verse is John 8:12: "Again Jesus spoke to them, saying, 'I am the light of the world. Whoever follows me will not walk in darkness, but will have the light of life.'"

I'd been what our forefathers would have called "awakened" but not yet converted. I hadn't been seeking after Christ, but now I was. And as those same forefathers would have said, I'd come under conviction of sin. In essence, what happened was this: I knew I wasn't perfect. I knew that I did specific things that were wrong and failed in various ways. Yet I was doing my best to keep the commandments from my youth up, as the rich young ruler had done.

To put it another way, I knew that I sinned sometimes, but I didn't think of myself as a sinner. I shared the natural person's view, assuming that the divine report card probably read something like this: "Basically more or less satisfactory, but could try harder and do better." But now I was discovering not just that I *did* sinful things, but that I *was* a sinner. In other words, the sin wasn't just in my actions; it was woven into the warp and woof of my life. A sinner was what I *was*. Basically, before God, I wasn't satisfactory at all.

If you know and have experienced what I'm talking about here, you'll understand what I'm about to say. Having read the Bible since I was eight or nine and seeking to live a decent life, thinking that is what it meant to be a Christian, the discovery that I was actually a sinner by nature—not just someone who occasionally lapsed—came as a tremendous shock to me, and it shook me to the foundations. That is the only way I can express it.

I began to realize that I'd seen myself entirely from the wrong point of view—my point of view, not God's point of view. I was seeing myself in terms of whether I was as good as the next person. I wasn't thinking about myself *coram Deo*, standing before the face of the holy God. And now I was having a kind of miniature version of the experience Isaiah described in Isaiah 6. I was only fourteen going on fifteen, but I really felt undone. And I now realized, to use Jesus' words, that the light I thought was in me was actually darkness (Matt. 6:23).

It was then that some older friends suggested I go to a Saturday night service at a city-center church in Glasgow, and I did. During the sermon, Christ was presented to this fourteen-year-old boy who was conscious that he was in spiritual darkness, and Jesus Christ spoke to me again: "I am the Light of the World. Follow Me, and you'll no longer walk in the darkness." I came to understand why Charles Wesley wrote as he did in his own conversion hymn:

And can it be that I should gain
An int'rest in the Savior's blood? . . .

Long my imprisoned spirit lay
Fast bound in sin and nature's night;
Thine eye diffused a quick'ning ray;
I woke, the dungeon flamed with light;
My chains fell off, my heart was free;
I rose, went forth, and followed thee.

I don't think that the Lord Jesus meant that we'd never experience any dark days in life if we're Christians. You couldn't read the rest of His teaching or the teaching of the Apostles and think that, could you? He wasn't promising that life would be plain sailing. He meant what David discovered: that even when we walk through the valley of deep darkness, He is with us, so it's never totally dark. There is always light. We may not even be able to see as far as the end of the tunnel, but we can see Jesus. And He has promised to be the light of life to us and guide us through the darkness. For He alone has gone into the outer darkness of the cross for our sins and dispelled total, final darkness from our lives.

And so, as Charles Wesley says, and millions of others can say, "I rose, went forth, and followed Christ." I hope you have, too. He'll never leave you. He'll never forsake you. He is the Light of the World.

So make sure you've come to Him and that you're trusting Him as your Savior and following Him as your Lord. And if you are, look back with thanksgiving today for the way He brought you, too, to come to trust Him.

3

Servants for Jesus' Sake

THIS WEEK, WE'RE THINKING ABOUT VERSES that have shaped me. I hope this doesn't seem self-centered, because these verses do contain wonderful biblical truths. But we're reflecting on them in this way to encourage ourselves to think of God's Word working in our own life, both in the past and in the present.

The third text is 2 Corinthians 4:1–6:

Therefore, having this ministry by the mercy of God, we do not lose heart. But we have renounced disgraceful, underhanded ways. We refuse to practice cunning or to tamper with God's word, but by the open statement of the truth we would commend ourselves to everyone's conscience in the sight of God. And even if our gospel is veiled, it is veiled to those who are perishing. In their case the god of this world has blinded the minds of the unbelievers, to keep them from seeing the light of the gospel of the glory of Christ, who is the image of God. For what we proclaim is not ourselves, but Jesus Christ as Lord, with ourselves as your servants for Jesus' sake. For God, who said, "Let light shine out of darkness," has shone in our hearts to give the light of the knowledge of the glory of God in the face of Jesus Christ.

The reason I mention this passage is that I was privileged to have the late Eric Alexander preach at my ordination. He was, without a doubt, one of the finest and most eloquent preachers of his generation, and he chose these opening verses of 2 Corinthians 4 as his text. Perhaps even more than he could have imagined that night, this passage has helped shape my thinking about what it means to serve the Lord Jesus. You can guess why it would make an impact on a young man who was called to preach. But these words also help us all to understand, care for, and pray for our own pastors, and they include general encouragements for all of us not to lose heart.

First, Paul stresses how he resisted the temptations that arise in the ministry to be successful according to worldly standards. He knew that there were men who became successful in people's eyes by asking the question, "What works? And as long as it works, let's do it." But Paul saw that not as a recommendation but as a temptation—and it still is. We love success, and we can be envious of the success of others and seek it for ourselves. This envious spirit can be so twisted into us that some people produce videos and podcasts with the main, if not sole, aim to pull other ministers down. It's all done under the guise of guarding the flock. But here's the giveaway: they never seem to build up the flock. They only pull down. And alas, a person can get a following that way, and some of these people are now a "success."

There are various success models for ministry that are "alive and well" in the present century. Sadly, destroying other people's success can sometimes prove almost as successful. What a mess our sinful hearts can create—yes, even when we are in the ministry. I remember a friend telling me that his seminary president used to say to them, "There are two chief sins in the ministry: laziness and pride." You can tell from 2 Corinthians 4:1–6 that Paul resisted both, and pastors and preachers need help to do that today, too.

Second, Paul described his preaching as "the open statement of the truth" (v. 2). He uses the word *phanerōsis*, which means "a manifestation, a revelation, a disclosure." It's a great word to describe what we're seeking to do when we preach: to unfold, to manifest what's actually there in the text of Scripture. I love what the Scottish Old Testament professor John "Rabbi" Duncan said about Jonathan Edwards' preaching: "His doctrine is all application and his application is all doctrine." He meant that in Edwards' preaching, there was a kind of double *phanerōsis*: God's Word was exposed and made plain, and as a result, people's hearts were exposed and God dealt with them. And that is certainly what we need in the preaching of the Word.

Third, Paul says that he doesn't preach himself: "But [we preach] Jesus Christ as Lord, with ourselves as your servants for Jesus' sake" (v. 5). Doesn't that strike you as odd? After he says, "We preach Christ, not ourselves," why does he then finish the sentence by talking about himself again? What Paul is saying is that when he preaches Jesus Christ as Lord, he does that as a bondslave of the Lord Jesus, but also as a bondslave of his hearers—in this case, the Corinthians. He is on his knees, as it were, before them. He is serving them, not lording it over them. As he wrote to the Thessalonians, Paul not only presents the gospel, but offers himself to them as their servant as he preaches the gospel (see 1 Thess. 2:8).

That is a good reason to keep using the word *minister* and not just the word *pastor*, because *minister* is Latin for "servant." *Doulos*, the Greek word that is used by Paul in 2 Corinthians 4:5, also means "bondservant." You can tell, can't you, when God's Word is being preached in that kind of spirit?

I'm sure you can see some of the reasons that these verses in 2 Corinthians 4:1–6 have power to shape any minister. They've certainly shaped me.

Let us pray that they'll shape more and more young ministers in our own time, because that is so vital for the health of the church.

4

Dead to Sin's Dominion

THINKING ABOUT PASSAGES OF SCRIPTURE THAT have shaped our lives is a wonderful exercise that helps us to see how God's Word has been at work in us, as Paul puts it in 1 Thessalonians 2:13.

I almost hesitate to mention the fourth passage today because it has fourteen verses, and it's not the easiest passage to understand. Not many of us read it and immediately think, "Yes, I've got it." It's Romans 6:1–14.

I first became conscious of this passage's importance through a book someone gave me when I was sixteen. The book taught what used to be called the "Higher Life," and one element in its teaching, which appealed to these verses in Romans 6, was that there was a new level of sanctification possible that could be experienced by a particular act of faith. I read and reread the book, but to be honest, I just didn't "get it." I felt as though I were being asked to leap onto the top of a table from a standing start, and so I put the book to one side. But a year or so later, when I was in my first year at university, I heard an address that touched on Romans 6, and I realized that I needed to give more serious attention to studying that passage, and so I did. To tell the truth, I don't think I've preached on it all that often considering how important it's been to me, but the truth it teaches has been like background music in my life ever since I was a late teenager.

So what's the big deal in Romans 6? Well, just that it is a big deal. The great Welsh preacher Dr. Martyn Lloyd-Jones, who preached on Romans for about fourteen years in London, recorded that a well-known individual came to see him once to ask him when he was going to begin a series of expositions on Romans. Lloyd-Jones replied, "When I can understand Romans 6!" The great Scottish churchman and theologian

Thomas Chalmers thought that this was perhaps the most interesting chapter on the Christian life in the whole Bible. So it is a big deal. This chapter is important because Paul suggests to the Romans that there is something every Christian should know, but he suspects that maybe the Roman Christians don't understand it. The reason that they should know it is that it's part of the meaning of their baptism.

What is it? It's that through the work of the Spirit, faith unites us to Jesus Christ. You remember how the New Testament puts it: we believe not only *in* Christ but *into* Christ, so that we can be said to be now "in Christ." And if we're united to Christ, that means that we are united to Him in His death and resurrection. Paul says: "Do you not know that all of us who have been baptized into Christ Jesus were baptized into his death? We were buried therefore with him by baptism into death, in order that, just as Christ was raised from the dead by the glory of the Father, we too might walk in newness of life" (Rom. 6:3–4). He goes on to say, "For the death he [Christ] died he died to sin"—that is, to the dominion or reign of sin (v. 10). So if we are united to Him, then we, too, have died to the dominion of sin and been raised into newness of life. We've been set free.

That is why Paul asks this question at the beginning of the chapter: "How can we who died to sin still live in it?" (v. 2). If that is the case, then as he says at the end of the passage: "Don't let sin, whose reign over you has been broken, re-establish that reign. Don't let your bodies become instruments or weapons for sin to use. Remember, you've died to sin's dominion. You've been raised to a new life in another kingdom altogether, the kingdom of Jesus Christ."

What I discovered in my studies in those now-far-off early days of my Christian life was this: Paul uses a particular form of speech in Romans 6:2. I think we could express it like this. He says: "We belong to the category of people whose very identity as Christians is as follows: we are those who have died to sin. How can such people go on living in sin?"

A massive transition takes place when we come to faith in Jesus Christ. We have a new identity. We have died to the dominion of sin. And so to go on living in sin would be a contradiction of who we really are. It would involve identity amnesia. We would be forgetting what it means to be in Christ.

There is a lot more than this in Romans 6, and the same teaching is expounded elsewhere in Paul's writings. But here's one of the reasons that this teaching on union with Christ is so important in our current day. It's crucial for us to grasp this understanding of our union with Christ, especially if we are younger people or younger Christians, because we live in a time when identity is at the top of the agenda. This is an epoch of profound identity crisis in the Western world, so knowing who you really are is a wonderful blessing.

If I'm a believer, I am "in Christ"—that is my identity. I'm no longer a citizen of the kingdom where sin reigns both over me and in me. I'm a member of a new kingdom. I have a new family, a new citizenship, a new identity altogether. I'm someone who is in Christ, and I belong to Him.

Discover this, and it helps to transform life, and it gives us both stability and dignity. And that is surely what we need today, don't you think?

5

The Same Yesterday, Today, and Forever

TODAY, WE COME TO THE LAST OF what I've called "texts that have shaped me." We are closing the week with words probably familiar to all of us: "Jesus Christ is the same yesterday and today and forever" (Heb. 13:8).

The author of Hebrews has been inviting his readers to think about those who had been their leaders. Just as he had done after reminding them of the great heroes of the faith in Hebrews 11, he tells them, "You've got to fix your eyes on Jesus." He points them away from all others to the person of the Lord Jesus Christ. Leaders come and go, but Jesus is the same yesterday and today and forever.

I suspect that these words are often read as more or less the equivalent of saying that Jesus is eternally the same. But there is more to the words "yesterday and today and forever" than that. "Yesterday" here doesn't just mean "the day before today." It's referring to yesterday from the point of view of the writer, to what he had called earlier in Hebrews "the days of his [Christ's] flesh" (Heb. 5:7). In other words, he is talking about what Jesus was like during those years—Jesus as we read about Him in the Gospels. This is the Jesus who preaches the kingdom of God, who calls men and women to repentance and faith, who shows the power of His kingdom in works of grace and transformation, who reveals Himself as full of grace and truth. This is the loving Jesus who cared for the needy, the poor, and the sick. This is the Jesus who was the friend of sinners, the Jesus who said: "Come to me, all who labor and are heavy laden, and I will give you rest. . . . Learn from me, for I am gentle and lowly . . . , and you will find rest for your souls" (Matt. 11:28–29). This is the Jesus who said: "I am the light of the world. Whoever follows me will not walk in darkness, but will have the light of life" (John 8:12).

If that is when "yesterday" was, then it follows that "today" is not just "the day after yesterday"—it is all the days after the "yesterday" when the Son of God walked this earth. It's what the author calls "today," meaning any day, week, month, or year until Christ returns (see Heb. 4:7–8). He is telling us that the Lord Jesus is "today" and He will be "forever"—the same wonderful person He was "yesterday." It's not just that He is *like* the Jesus of the Gospels. He still *is* that Jesus. It's true that He is now exalted at God's right hand in glory, but nevertheless, He is the same "today" and will be "forever" as He was in that "yesterday" of His ministry on earth.

Why has this verse shaped my life? First, it taught me how to read and apply the Gospels and how to get to know the Lord Jesus better.

I've mentioned before what I call the "Where's Waldo [or Wally]?" approach to reading the Gospels, in which people try to identify themselves with one of the characters—maybe Nicodemus, or Zacchaeus, or Mary, or Martha. But the Gospels were written *so that we would find and see Jesus Himself in them*—who He is, what He is like, what He came to do for us, and what He has accomplished for our salvation. And He is that same Jesus for us today. That is what Hebrews 13:8 is telling us.

Do you see Jesus in the Gospels? He is still that same Jesus for you today. Not only that, He is going to be that same Jesus *every* today until He comes again. And He is always going to be like that because that is who He is.

Do you read the Gospels that way? If you're a preacher, do you preach the Gospels that way? There is a lot of emphasis these days on how to preach Christ from the Old Testament. But there is something more important than that: it's learning how to preach Jesus from the Gospels, because that is where we learn who He still is and what He is still like today. That is the Jesus we all need to get to know better and love more—the real flesh-and-blood Jesus.

It's fascinating to me that this is actually one of the central emphases of the entire book of Hebrews. I suspect that is why the author wrote these words toward the end of his exhortation. It is not surprising that they have come to mean a great deal to me. I hope their truth will mean a great deal to you. "Jesus Christ is the same yesterday and today and forever." That is not only a great text; it's great good news.

If you're a believer, you, too, will have particular texts and passages that have shaped you. And as we have been thinking this week, it would be worthwhile taking a few minutes to reflect on them this weekend and to appreciate once more all that the Lord has done for you and how He has shaped and molded you through His Word.

As the old song says, "Count your blessings," we might say instead, "Count your texts, name them one by one, and it will surprise you what the Lord has done."

WEEK 39

Take Heed

1

Take Heed How You Hear

DURING HIS EARTHLY MINISTRY, Jesus not only said, "Pay attention to *what* you hear" (Mark 4:24, emphasis added). He also said, "Take care then *how* you hear" (Luke 8:18, emphasis added). He then added this intriguing comment: "For to the one who has, more will be given, and from the one who has not, even what he thinks that he has will be taken away."

Do you see what Jesus is saying? Hearing God's Word rightly is what increases our capacity to rightly hear God's Word. There is a kind of exponential growth. On the other hand, not hearing it rightly isn't a neutral thing. It actually makes it even more difficult to hear it rightly the next time. Not only that, the person who doesn't hear God's Word rightly may not even know it. He may think that he has all he really needs already. "But," Jesus says, "even that will be taken from him." It's really a very sobering statement.

Christians desire to hear good preaching. We know it's vital for our own spiritual health and for the spiritual health of our church family. But I wonder if we give as much attention to *how* we hear what we hear as we give to *what* we hear.

Two weeks ago, I mentioned the preaching grids that professors love to give budding preachers. But the wisest preachers also had hearers' grids. Perhaps the most famous of them is found in a book by the sixteenth-century English Puritan William Perkins titled *The Art of Prophesying*. In it, Perkins shares his own "hearers' grid" with us. He suggests that at any given time, there may be seven different kinds of hearers in the congregation. He wrote about that because he wanted to help preachers address the people who were in the congregation, not people who existed only in the preacher's imagination.

We need to ask ourselves, "What kind of hearer am I?" And we should ask it not just once, but again and again. It's easy to simply assume that we are good hearers of the Word of God, perhaps failing to recognize that we are beginning to lose our ability to hear His voice. We listen, but we're detached. We assess, but we don't take in. We don't chew on the message. We don't digest it. And the more that happens, the more it's going to happen.

I've met people who have been wonderfully faithful to their church, even when the pulpit has stopped feeding them. They find themselves eking out spiritual nourishment, maybe on their own, or maybe in a small Bible study group. Slowly, they get used to not being fed by preaching. Eventually, they conclude, "Well, it is what it is." Then, perhaps, they come with a friend to a church where the Word is faithfully ministered in the grace of the Spirit, and they realize that they are being starved Sunday after Sunday. But now they scarcely notice it because the impoverished diet of preaching they were hearing has damaged their appetite, and they badly need to get it back.

If we don't take heed to *what* we hear, we will slowly cease to take heed to *how* we hear. But the fact is, we can sit under a living biblical ministry, and because of our own detachment, we can similarly be starving ourselves by not digesting the food that is being served.

That is also a sobering thought, but it's a wake-up call as well.

2

Hardened Hearers

THIS WEEK, WE'RE EXPLORING THE THEME of taking heed how we hear. Yesterday, we mentioned in passing the "hearers' grid" that the English preacher-theologian William Perkins employed. But One greater than William Perkins also had a hearers' grid, didn't He? And you may be familiar with it already: it's the parable of the sower.

Jesus' story about the farmer, the seed, and the soils is told in each of the first three Gospels. He hints that it's really "the parable of parables." He says in Mark 4:13 that if the disciples didn't understand this parable, they'd never understand the other ones. It's as if He were saying: "This parable is the key. If you can't follow it and apply it, then it's clear that you're not yet hearing properly."

The parable portrays a common scene in the rural Holy Land in the time of our Lord Jesus. It's seed-sowing time. The farmer goes out into his field with his basket of seed, and he starts sowing. The same farmer uses the same quality of seed, but the results vary considerably. And as Jesus explains, this is a picture of the Word of God being sown by Jesus in His preaching, and then in the preaching of His disciples. Same preachers, same Word preached, but significant differences in what happens next. The differences are all related to the condition of the soil into which the same quality of seed has been sown—that is, the spiritual condition of those who hear the Word of God.

In Jesus' hearers' grid, there are four different kinds of soil, which describe four different kinds of hearers of the Word of God. The first one is pictured by the pathway. Some seed fell on it, and then the birds appeared. The seed had hardly touched the ground before the birds swooped down for their effortless fast-food meal. I imagine every minister has experienced preaching his heart out to his congregation, and then as he shakes hands at the door, he meets someone who makes it obvious that his or her heart and mind were elsewhere during the sermon.

Sometimes that was already clear to the preacher. It's surprising how many people forget that if they can see the preacher, the preacher can see them! A picture that sometimes comes to my mind is of the church doors opening just before the service ends, and birds flying in to steal the seed of the Word of God that has been expounded. It doesn't even last long enough to get out of the church door. It makes no difference to some hearers.

There is often a kind of subversive element in Jesus' parables. For this particular parable, we might ask: "Wasn't the pathway the part of the field where the sower would have walked again and again, carrying his seed? Was that what had hardened the soil?" Since the seed had not penetrated the soil, every time the farmer went sowing, that ground was getting harder and harder until it became virtually impenetrable. It wasn't that the farmer wasn't there; it was that the farmer often walked there.

I suspect that is true of some people. It's not *never* hearing faithful preaching from the Bible that leads to complacency and indifference. It's our detachment from the truth of God that leads us to being distant from, or perhaps even defending ourselves against, the truth and its life-changing power. We have often heard the Word of God, but instead of responding to it and applying it to our lives, we've resisted it. And now resisting it is of such second nature to us that it takes no effort at all.

So this parable is about hearing the Word of God. But it's also part of the Word of God. I wonder, "Are you a frequent listener to God's Word, but one whose heart is like the pathway?" If so, there needs to be some plowing done.

We need to ask the Lord to break up that hard soil before it's too late and even what we do have disappears.

3

The Kind of Faith That Falls Away

THE PARABLE OF THE SOWER DESCRIBES in vivid terms what happens when God's Word is preached. Some of the seed fell on the pathway and soon disappeared. But then Jesus says that some fell on rocky soil.

Years ago, my wife and I were able to watch our home in Scotland being built. I remember going along before they put down the lawn at the rear of the house and being horrified to see that the soil was chockablock with rocks of various sizes. Fortunately for me, none were really too large. But despite all my efforts, I suspect not a few of those rocks are still there under the grass.

Perhaps that is what we envisage when we read about this rocky soil. But Jesus' picture is probably quite different. He is picturing soil that is lying on a rocky substratum, so the soil isn't very deep. And as the seed coat cracks open, the embryo can't put down very deep roots. As a result, the shoot that springs up quickly, and apparently successfully, doesn't receive enough nourishment, and it soon dies.

It's easy to be critical of the disciples for having to ask Jesus what this parable was all about, but we should probably be glad that this happened. Our Lord's explanation is far better than our own guesswork, and it's very illuminating. He says that rocky-ground hearers are the ones who, when they hear the Word, immediately receive it with joy. But they have no root in themselves, and they endure only for a while. Then if things get difficult, they immediately fall away.

If you've been a Christian for some time, you probably know exactly what Jesus is talking about here. This is someone who responds wonderfully to the gospel. Notice Jesus' words: "[They] receive it with joy" (Mark 4:16). People are thrilled about their conversion and their testimony, and they seem to have a tremendous appetite for spiritual things. But then, just as suddenly as they seemed to be converted, they disappear from view. Perhaps even as I say that, it reminds you of someone you once knew. This is an exact description of some of the most apparently impactful conversions of people I've known. And it's sometimes hard for us to take in what happened: What went wrong?

How can that be? These people seem to have had such joy in the Lord.

But Jesus tells us that it can happen. And more than that, He explains why it happens. Notice what's emphasized in this apparent conversion:

immediate joy. But it's what is absent that is significant. There is joy mentioned, but there is no mention of sorrow. There is no lasting breaking up of the soil. There is something underneath that allows for the immediate joy, but not for the deeper sorrow of repentance.

Certainly, every person's conversion to Christ has a unique shape, and it's often specially related to the womb of providences in which they've been spiritually conceived. But if there is no sense of sorrow for our sin—if there is only the joy of a kind of psychological relief—then there will be no lasting transformation of life. Because when the gospel seed is planted in good soil, it breaks open in our lives in conversion and repentance as well as faith. There is always going to be some sense of sorrow for sin, and repentance as well as faith, when we see that what we really needed was a Savior from sin.

Of course, Jesus doesn't give us proportions, does He? All that really matters is that we see our need of Christ because we see that we're sinners. The theologian-pastor John Owen once commented that if you can lance a boil with a pin, you don't need to use a sword to do it. But Jesus does imply that one without the other—joy without sorrow for sin—is not going to survive. So in whatever proportion they are present, they will both be present in a genuine conversion, and they'll both keep on growing throughout the whole course of our Christian lives. And that is what makes for a plant that has been truly planted by the Lord. That is how the good seed of the Word of God bears fruit. We will think more about that good seed later this week.

4

Choked by the Cares of This World

WE'VE BEEN THINKING ABOUT HOW JESUS' parable of the farmer, his seed, and the soils helps us to think about *how* we hear. The parable also analyzes how we do that in four different ways: some seed fell on the path, some fell on soil with a rocky substratum, and then some seed fell in thorny soil. The thorns grew up and choked it so that it yielded no grain. There was nothing to show at harvest time.

It's a really interesting parable because, among other things, it makes us ask questions that the parable itself doesn't quite answer. Here's one of them: Are we supposed to envisage the farmer as sowing his seed on ground where thorns were already evident, or is it only afterward that those thorns have sprouted up?

Perhaps when the farmer sows his seed, it's inevitable that some of it falls on ground where there are thorns, and that those thorns will choke its growth. Jesus and His disciples do something similar when they preach His Word. The gospel is to be preached to everyone, not just to the elect or to people who look as though they might be elect! That's part of what we mean when we speak about the free offer of the gospel—it's offered to all. Its effects are varied, of course.

But what Jesus is saying here is that the seed is sometimes sown in thorny soil, and it sprouts. That is to say, the gospel has an effect on someone's life. But then something destructive happens. This time, it's not that the roots hit a rocky substratum and wither and die immediately. Rather, Jesus says that over time, the cares of this world and the deceitfulness of riches and the desire for other things enter in like weeds and choke the Word, and it proves unfruitful.

What's this all about? I think we can say that this is a picture of someone who responds to the gospel and seems to be a real Christian, yet there is something missing. At first, it isn't obvious. Maybe someone with considerable spiritual discernment might pick it up, but the person himself or herself might not realize what's happening. Because it isn't so much what *is* happening as what *isn't* happening that is the problem. There is no weeding of the soil. The person isn't dealing with the weeds in their heart.

Jesus says these weeds come in several varieties. Our minds seem to be more taken up with our concerns in this world than thinking about Christ.

In one congregation in which I served, part of the hiring process for ministry positions included my participating as part of a small group of people who would interview candidates. There was a question I often asked—at least until I discovered that other members of our staff would forewarn the candidates, telling them I was almost bound to ask this question!

Intrigued? What was the question? It was this: "What do you tend to think about when you've got nothing special to think about?"

I found that the answer to that question—where your mind tends to drift when nothing is demanding your attention—often indicates what's important to you. Do we tend to drift downward to the cares that burden us, or do we daydream about money and how we would spend it, or possessions that we would like to have, or things that we don't have? These are the "other things" (Mark 4:19) that push out our love for and our meditation on the Lord Jesus Christ. Then it's just one further push, and He is squeezed out of mind altogether. The thing is, it doesn't need to be sinful things that dampen affection for the Lord Jesus, just these *other* things. And the result? Spiritually unfruitful lives.

Perhaps you've seen this happen, too. I know I have. We often say that weeds grow naturally, but having a good lawn doesn't. That needs care and attention. It requires discipline. And here, it means dealing properly with our hearts, and it will certainly mean putting sin to death.

Our Lord's analysis of our spiritual condition is really very searching: three different kinds of soil in which the Word isn't bearing fruit. Jesus wants us to ask ourselves: Are we like the pathway? Are we like the rocky soil? Are we like the thorny soil? Perhaps what we most need today is Christ's help to break up the hardness in our hearts or break down the rocky substratum that is lying below the surface, or the Spirit's help to do the necessary weeding.

There is a feature in Jesus' parables that is usually called "end stress." The "punchline" comes at the end. The point to which the whole parable is leading is the last thing that is said. In the case of the parable of the sower, it's also the most encouraging part of the parable, and we'll think about that tomorrow.

Meanwhile, let us pray that today will be a day when the Word of God bears some fruit in our lives.

5

The Hundredfold Harvest of God's Word

WHEN YOU TELL A STORY, YOU don't put the conclusion in the middle. If you tell a joke, you don't give away the punchline before the end. If you do, you'll ruin it and nobody will laugh, unless perhaps they are laughing at you. Likewise, in Jesus' parable of the sower, the seed, and the soils, not only is there searching analysis of our spiritual condition, but there is also good news right at the end. The good seed of God's Word falls on good soil, and it yields a harvest—thirtyfold, sixtyfold, or even a hundredfold. That is pretty amazing, isn't it?

But what is good soil? What Jesus means here is soil that has been well prepared. It could be hardened soil that has been broken up. It could be rocky soil where the substratum has been cracked open. It could be weed-infested soil where serious weeding has been done and weed killer has been applied. Then we can look forward to a great harvest. You can see the spiritual parallel here. This is the wonder of the gospel.

The gospel seed may not look like very much when we first see it. But when it's planted in good soil, its wonderful effects begin to appear, and it yields an abundant crop at the harvest. When instead of the cares of this world, or a desire for material well-being, or the pursuit of ambition opposing the influence of the Word of God we yield our lives to Him—yes, faults and all—we will become fruitful. Because Jesus Christ is no one's debtor.

A personal example comes to mind. When I was on the verge of becoming a Christian, I thought that I might lose some friends in the process. But as I look back now, I'm amazed at the hundredfold harvest of new Christian friends—and not just the size of the harvest, but the quality of it. These are amazing friends who are a privilege and joy to know, who are brothers and sisters to me, believers to whom I owe so much. And these friendships have been, for me, part of the thirtyfold, sixtyfold, and, yes, hundredfold yield of the good seed of God's Word.

Yes, there is plowing, and yes, there is also weeding to be done as we receive the Word of God and as we take heed how we hear. But remember the promise of Isaiah 55:

> As the rain and the snow come down from heaven
>   and do not return there but water the earth,
> making it bring forth and sprout,
>   giving seed to the sower and bread to the eater,
> so shall my word be that goes out from my mouth;
>   it shall not return to me empty,
> but it shall accomplish that which I purpose,
>   and shall succeed in the thing for which I sent it.

> For you shall go out in joy
>   and be led forth in peace;
> the mountains and the hills before you
>   shall break forth into singing,
>   and all the trees of the field shall clap their hands.

> Instead of the thorn shall come up the cypress;
>   instead of the brier shall come up the myrtle;

and it shall make a name for the LORD,

    an everlasting sign that shall not be cut off. (Isa. 55:10–13)

That is surely a great note on which to end this week of thinking about the parable of the sower and the way in which the Word of God transforms our lives. So let's do what Paul said the Thessalonians did: receive the Word of God not as the word of man, but as it really is, the Word of God, which is at work in believers (1 Thess. 2:13).

And let's also take heed this coming Lord's Day not only to *what* we hear but to *how* we hear, praying that the seed that is sown will have a wonderful harvest in our lives.

WEEK 40

The Grammar of the Gospel

1

Learning Gospel Grammar

THIS WEEK, WE ARE GOING TO REFLECT ON a subject that may have bored you in elementary school. Perhaps it still bores you today, but it's an enormously important one in the school of Jesus Christ. It is the rules of grammar.

What is grammar? Here's how the multivolume *Oxford English Dictionary* defines it: "that department of the study of a language which deals with its inflectional forms or other means of indicating the relation of words in the sentence and with the rules for employing these in accordance with established usage." This somewhat technical definition can be simply put in this way: grammar is about how the language we use actually works.

If you've ever had to learn a foreign language, you'll know that every language has its own grammar. One of the first challenges for us may be discovering that the way the foreign language works is different from the way our own language works. So to speak it properly and to make sense, we must follow the rules of its grammar.

Most of us first learn grammar not from textbooks but from listening to others speak the language as we grow and develop in our early years. The same is true in the Christian life. The Christian gospel has its own grammar, but it's a foreign language to the natural man. By nature, we speak another language and use a different grammar. And the more we use it, the more natural and right it seems to us. As a result, we're not able to understand the language of the gospel.

The Apostle Paul said exactly this to the Corinthian church, which was overly impressed by this world's language and wisdom: "The natural person does not accept the things of the Spirit of God, for they are folly to him, and he is not able to understand them because they are spiritually discerned" (1 Cor. 2:14). By contrast, he says that the gospel comes "in words not taught by human wisdom but taught by the Spirit, interpreting spiritual truths to those who are spiritual" (v. 13). Paul isn't saying here that the gospel can't be expressed in English. He is saying that the gospel's grammar is different from the grammar of the natural man, and so the natural man has difficulty understanding it. It's like a foreign language to him.

The story of Nicodemus's interview with Jesus is a powerful illustration of this truth. Nicodemus would have had no difficulty understanding Jesus' words in the sense that they both knew and spoke in the same language. But by his own admission, Nicodemus didn't understand what Jesus was saying. He was trying to understand Jesus according to the grammar of a natural fallen man. And Jesus told him that unless he was born again, he couldn't see or understand the kingdom of God. Nicodemus had no problem understanding the actual words Jesus was speaking, but he admitted he couldn't understand what Jesus was saying: "How can a man be born when he is old? Can he enter a second time into his mother's womb and be born?" (John 3:4).

You see, Jesus was telling him something he couldn't understand. And paradoxically, Nicodemus was telling Jesus that he couldn't understand it. He could follow the words that Jesus was using, but he didn't understand their "grammar." He couldn't see the logic of the gospel. Why was that? It was because the rules of grammar that he knew had taught him that the way into the kingdom of God was by circumcision, by being a Jew, by reading the Torah, and by keeping the commandments—and this dear man took that with all seriousness. There is something quite admirable about him. He was a Pharisee. In fact, Jesus calls him *the* teacher in Israel—the great theology professor, we might say. And Nicodemus seems to have been modest enough and thoughtful enough to come secretly to talk to Jesus.

We read later on in John's gospel that Nicodemus helped his friend Joseph of Arimathea anoint Jesus' body and lay it in the garden tomb. In a way, you can't help loving this dear man. And yet when we first meet him in John 3, the grammar of the gospel was a complete mystery to him. He needed to go back to gospel grammar school.

When we hear great sports stars speak, they'll often talk about making sure that their fundamentals are in place. Because if they are not, things are bound to go wrong. It's the same with gospel grammar. That is why it's so important to make sure that we understand it well, and that will be our aim this week.

2

Gospel Indicatives and Imperatives

WE REFLECTED YESTERDAY ON THE NEW TESTAMENT'S teaching that by nature we speak a different language with a different grammar from the language of the gospel of grace. What is in the gospel grammar? We'll begin with looking at what are called "moods."

The mood of a verb is just a sophisticated way of talking about its quality or tone. There are several verbal moods, but we'll focus on the two that we call *indicatives* and *imperatives*. An *indicative* is a statement of fact, such as "God loves you." An *imperative* is a statement of command, such as "Love the Lord your God with all your heart, mind, soul, and strength."

Here's the important point in gospel grammar: God's indicatives are always the basis for God's imperatives. This is why we often find the word *therefore* in the New Testament. It's because of who God is and what He has done for us in Christ that we should *therefore* respond in a certain way. What God does in His grace (the indicative) is the foundation for what we do in our response of faith and obedience—responding to His imperative.

Here is another example from 2 Corinthians 5:19. First, the indicative statement of God's grace is, "In Christ God was reconciling the world to himself." Then there is the connection in verse 20, "Therefore," followed by God's imperative: "be reconciled to God." The imperative is rooted in the indicative.

The message of the gospel is that in Jesus Christ, God has righteously laid aside His enmity toward sinners. That is the reason that we, in turn, are called to lay down our arms, to abandon our hostility, to come in repentance and faith, and to receive the reconciliation.

The problem is that the natural man, who doesn't understand the grammar of the gospel, always reverses the indicative and the imperative. He thinks, "I know I'm not perfect, but I will make compensation by doing better in the future, and then God will be reconciled to me." But the truth of the gospel and the only way of salvation is actually the other way around.

Most people think something like this: "I've been a decent person. I've tried to obey the commandments. I'm as good as the next man (and probably better). I've tried to compensate for anything wrong I've done by the good things I've achieved, and I think I've probably accomplished enough. Therefore, God will accept me."

In fact, it's even common that when people are convicted of their sin but still don't grasp the grammar of the gospel, they respond with a new determination to do better, to turn over a new leaf, to start again, to try harder. Indeed, sometimes when a Christian explains the gospel to them, that is exactly how they respond. They are presented with indicatives: "We are sinners. Christ died for sinners." But what they hear is: "You need to be better. You need to try harder."

Their understanding of the grammar of the gospel is so deformed that they hear the indicatives as though they were actually imperatives. The language of the gospel of the free grace of God in Jesus Christ is actually a foreign language to them. That is why it takes the ministry of the Holy Spirit to help people understand spiritual things. Only He can get the gospel to "click" in people's understanding.

But here's something worth noting: sometimes, even when we've been born again and come to faith in Christ, we can still lapse back into the old grammar again. We make our acceptance with the heavenly Father dependent on how we are doing spiritually or how we think we're doing: Did we have our quiet time? Did we do this? Have we stopped doing that? Now, these things are not unimportant in the Christian life. But as John Owen says, we mustn't confuse the foundation of the building with the superstructure.

So it's always important for us as Christians to refresh our grasp of gospel grammar to make sure that our lives are resting on the foundation of what God has done in the Lord Jesus. Because when that is true—when the mighty indicatives of God's grace in Christ are in place—then we know that there is in Christ all the grace and help we need to fulfill the all-embracing, all-demanding, life-transforming imperatives of the gospel.

So let's keep going back to visit the grammar school of the gospel.

3

Already and Not Yet

YESTERDAY, WE LOOKED AT THE INDICATIVE and imperative moods of the verbs in which the gospel is expressed. That is what gives the gospel shape and expresses its tone of grace. But there is more to verbs than moods. Verbs also come in different *tenses*. There are basically three tenses, although they come in different forms: past, present, and future. The gospel comes in all three, and the New Testament teaches us to live the Christian life in relationship to them.

Perhaps the simplest way to summarize its teaching is this: the gospel teaches us to live today conscious that we are living *now* between the *already* and the *not yet*. We live now in light of what God did in the past in Christ, but also looking to the future when Christ will come again. We live between the *already*—what Christ has done—looking forward to the *not yet*—what He is still to do. And that helps us realize that while our experience of God's grace in Christ is real, it is as yet incomplete. Already in the past, Christ has become incarnate, lived, died, risen, and ascended, and He is now reigning, still the same incarnate Savior. But He has not yet brought about the consummation that will occur when He returns in majesty and glory.

The European theologian Oscar Cullmann famously used events

in World War II to illustrate this. We celebrate the Normandy land-ings on June 6, 1944, as D-Day—the day when, in a sense, the decisive events that would end World War II took place. But the war was not ended until the unconditional surrender of the German forces in May 1945 and of the Japanese forces in August 1945. Those days are often referred to as V-Day (Victory Day), V-E Day (Victory in Europe Day), and V-J Day (Victory in Japan Day). But in the year or so between D-Day and V-Day, there was still conflict, suffering, and loss of life. The decisive events took place in the past in 1944, but their full impli-cations would not be worked out until the future, the following year, in 1945.

You can see the point of Cullmann's illustration. In His incarnation, death, resurrection, and ascension, Christ has done everything that is decisive for our salvation. He has revealed God to us. He died for our sins. In His death, He has broken the dominion of sin and death, and He has crushed the head of Satan, the serpent. He triumphed over him on the cross, as Paul says in Colossians 2:15. But all the implications of that are not yet fully worked out, either in the world, or in the church, or in ourselves as individuals. Sin is still present in the world. People still rebel against God. Satan may be wounded, but he is still active. And we still stumble. Only when Christ returns will all His enemies become a stool for His feet. But here is what the New Testament wants us to grasp: the D-Day of Christ's death, resurrection, and ascension has been so decisive that it guarantees that V-Day will come.

What's the point of this? It's that we need to realize that the big thing has already been accomplished by the Lord Jesus, and it guar-antees that however painful the mopping-up operations may be, His final victory is certain. And so we live between two moments, looking back in faith to D-Day and all that Jesus has done, and looking forward in expectation to V-Day and the consummation of His victory, when the earth will be full of the knowledge of the glory of the Lord as the waters cover the sea.

But there is something else here. It's that this macro-story is reflected in the micro-narrative of our own lives as Christians. There is already a D-Day, and there will be a V-Day. There is a *not yet* about the Christian life. We live now by faith, *already* united to Christ, with our sins forgiven and set free from sin's dominion, but we are *not yet* set free from sin's presence. We still live in a fallen world. And although we've been delivered from the realm of darkness, Satan continues to tempt and accuse us.

So we're still in a battle between D-Day and V-Day. It can be tough going. We may experience suffering and loss. We'll certainly experience opposition. We'll have to fight against indwelling sin. But the important thing to remember from the grammar of the gospel is this: the decisive battle and victory has already been won by the Lord Jesus in our lives, too. And one day, He will come again in glory, and we will enjoy Victory Day in a marvelous way when we see Him face-to-face. We are already more than conquerors through Him who loved us.

So let's thank God that we know the grammar of the gospel.

4

Positive and Negative Steps in the Christian Walk

TODAY, WE COME TO ANOTHER GRAMMAR LESSON in the school of the Lord Jesus. When we use verbs, we employ them in both positive and negative senses. We do some things, but there are other things we don't do.

In his letter to the Ephesians, Paul several times describes the Christian life as a walk: we are to walk in a manner worthy of our calling. We are to walk in love. We are to walk as children of light. We are to walk as wise people. But Paul teaches us that *walking worthy* in this way also means that we *don't walk* in ways that are unworthy of Christ.

Walking in love means that we don't walk in sexual immorality or impurity. Walking wisely means that we don't walk in foolish ignorance of God's will. We don't walk like drunk men controlled by wine, but as people who are filled with the Holy Spirit who walk in ways that encourage each other and are marked by thankful hearts. There is always both positive and negative, and the gospel produces both in us. It's really important to see that and to look out for it when you're reading the Scriptures. Because once you begin to notice it, you'll find this principle throughout. And if you've never noticed it before, you'll wonder how you could have missed it.

Most of us by nature tend to emphasize one or the other—the positive or the negative. Some of us do something similar physically when we walk. The stress goes out on our lead foot, and it takes more pressure than the other one. And in the same way, some of us are naturally drawn to stressing the positive aspects of spiritual growth—love, joy, peace, and so on—while others of us have a natural tendency to be drawn more to focus on how we can deal with our sin. None of us is as yet perfectly balanced. So we need to be conscious of the particular ways in which we as individuals tend to lose our balance.

In our day, you've probably noticed that what people call *negativity* is "out" and *positivity* is "in." But if our lives are going to give expression to the gospel—if we're going to speak the gospel's grammar—then we need both. Living the Christian life on only positives is never going to work. Trying to live it on only negatives is going to lead us to confuse dealing with sin with the whole reality of sanctification. Saying no to sin is essential, but it's only one element in sanctification. There also needs to be the other, the positive, the putting on of the Lord Jesus Christ, positively growing to be like Him and walking as He walked.

There are passages in Scripture that help us toward this balanced Christian lifestyle and help us to grasp the marvels of gospel grammar.

The most extensive is Colossians 3:1–17. Here, Paul seems to combine several elements of gospel grammar. "The indicatives and the imperatives" are there, "the *alreadys* and the *not yets*" are there, and "the negatives and the positives" are there.

First, Paul presents us with glorious indicatives. In verses 1–4, he reminds us of our new identity in Christ: we have died with Him and have been raised with Him. In fact, our lives are hidden with Christ in the presence of God. That is all true *already*. And then comes the *not yet*: when Christ appears, we are going to appear with Him in glory. Then comes a flood of powerful imperatives in verses 5–17. They come first in a series of negatives in verses 5–11, where Paul tells us what we need to put off. Then there is an equally vigorous series of positives in verses 12–17 of what we need to put on, and they are all the attractive characteristics that the Lord Jesus manifested.

There is a beautiful harmony here in the picture that Paul paints of the Christian life. It's as though He is saying, "Here is what it means to live according to the grammar of the gospel and for our lives to speak clearly of the Lord Jesus Christ—indicatives and imperatives, *alreadys* and *not yets*, negatives and positives."

Let me commend reading and reflecting on Colossians 3:1–17. It's a marvelous crash course in using the grammar of the gospel.

5

What It Means to Be in Christ

THIS WEEK, WE'VE HAD A SHORT refresher course on how the gospel works. As with the English language, the grammar in which the gospel speaks has indicatives and imperatives; past, present, and future tenses; and positive and negative verbs. And today, we'll think about prepositions.

A preposition is a word that enables us to understand the relationships between things. Most but not all are short words such as *to* or *from* or *with*. All these prepositions I've just mentioned play an important part in the grammar of the gospel, but today we'll focus on the preposition *in*.

So far, we've focused on verbs, which are "doing" words—God's doing and our doing. But when we talk about prepositions, we're thinking about relationships. In that context, no preposition is more important to gospel grammar than the preposition *in*, especially when it appears in the phrase *in Christ* or one of its several variations in the New Testament: *in Him* or *in the Lord*. These various ways of saying the same thing appear scores of times in the New Testament.

Perhaps we can highlight the importance of the expression *in Christ* in this somewhat provocative way: there is no evidence that the Apostle Paul ever thought of or spoke about himself as a Christian. If you think about it, the word *Christian* is used only three times in the entire Bible. New Testament believers do not seem to have described themselves that way. In fact, it may well have been a term of abuse, like the word *fundamentalist*. The New Testament way of answering the question, "Who are you, believer?" is by this prepositional phrase: "I am a person who is *in Christ*."

I started reading the Bible when I was about nine, but it was years before this truth dawned on me. I remember puzzling over Paul's words in 2 Corinthians 12:2 that he had known "a man in Christ" who, fourteen years before, had a remarkable experience of being caught up into the third heaven. I wondered who this anonymous man was, and then eventually it dawned on me: "Of course, Paul was speaking about himself." This was how he characteristically thought of himself: he was now a man *in Christ*.

He explains this in Romans 5:12–21. We were by nature in Adam. He was the head of the original humanity, of which we are part. He acted for us as our representative when he sinned, and then his sinful nature was passed on to us through natural generation. But now by faith, we are no longer in Adam. We have been translated and are now in Christ. All that Christ did, He did as our representative and substitute. He lived our life, and He died our death. He did this for our salvation. And now by the ministry of the Spirit, He unites us to Himself by faith, and we come to share in all the benefits and blessings of His work. All that He has done for us is now ours, and we receive it all because we are in Christ. This is who we are now. This is our new identity. We are men and women and young people who are in Christ.

Paul tells us in Ephesians 1:3–14 what it means to be in Christ. We receive every spiritual blessing in Him because we've been chosen in Him. We've been predestined in Him. We've been redeemed in Him. We've been pardoned in Him. We experience illumination in Him. We are given adoption in Him. We are brought to sanctification in Him. And all this is to the praise of His glorious grace.

This is who I am if I'm a Christian. The gospel grammar gives me a way of identifying myself. It gives me a way to think about myself and who I am. And that is important, because how we live is the result of who we believe ourselves to be.

What's the importance, then, of this phrase "in Christ" in the grammar of the gospel? It's this: it's possible for a Christian to suffer from identity theft and then identity loss, and it can be very difficult to regain. The result is, to use an expression of our forefathers, that we end up living below the level of our privileges. We don't realize who we are—that is, who we are in Christ. We don't realize that in Christ, everything that is in Him is now ours. And if we are in Christ, then He wants everything that is His to become ours, too.

That is how the grammar of the gospel structures our thinking so that we can live the Christian life with our heads held high because we know who we are. Nobody in all the world is more privileged or has a more glorious identity than the man or the woman or the young person who can say, "I am in Christ—that is who I am."

It's clear in Ephesians 1:3–14 that Paul regarded this element in the grammar of the gospel as one of the most thrilling aspects of being a Christian. In fact, these verses are so marvelous that the American theologian B.B. Warfield is said to have believed they should never be read; they should only be sung! To know that you are in Christ puts melody into your soul and music into your life.

I hope you can rejoice in that today, and I hope you'll continue to reflect on these various aspects of the grammar of the gospel that we've been thinking about this week.

It is truly a glorious thing to be in Christ, to be a Christian. So enjoy being one this weekend.

WEEK 41

The Lord's Supper

1

The Lord's Supper: A Proclamation

A FEW WEEKS AGO, WE DISCUSSED the subject of baptism. This week, we'll think about the Lord's Supper. After all, we are baptized once, but we come to the Lord's Table frequently. But even though we partake of it regularly, I sometimes wonder, "If someone gave us a 3×5 card after we received the Lord's Supper and asked us to write down what it meant and what we were thinking about, what would we say?" We might be surprised by some of the answers.

This week, then, we'll reflect on five things to think about when we come to the Lord's Supper. And because simplicity is of the essence of the supper, we'll focus each day on just one word.

Today's word is *proclamation*. Paul writes in 1 Corinthians 11:26, "As often as you eat this bread and drink the cup, you proclaim the Lord's death." I've sometimes heard it said that we shouldn't take the Lord's Supper without a sermon because of what Paul is teaching here. It's surely right to have an exposition of biblical teaching when we come to the table, however short it is. But that is not the kind of proclamation Paul is thinking about here.

He is not saying there needs to be the Lord's Supper *plus* a sermon. Rather, he is saying that the Lord's Supper *is* the sermon. The Lord's Supper itself is the proclamation. In other words, the supper is the gospel in dramatic form. Yes, we need words to interpret what's happening. But when we understand the biblical teaching on the supper, we realize that it's a visible dramatization of the message of the gospel. The broken bread portrays Christ's body, sacrificed on the cross for us. The poured-out wine portrays His blood, shed for the forgiveness of our sins.

A miniature drama is being enacted at the table. We might even borrow Paul's words in Galatians 3:1 and say that before our eyes at the supper, Christ is "publicly portrayed as crucified." Then these symbols of His body and blood are offered to us. We're invited to receive them, to eat and to drink, and to take them to ourselves, just as the risen Christ is carried to us in the proclamation of the gospel and offered to us, and we're urged to receive Him and to feed on Him. Following the pattern of the first Lord's Supper, we then offer each other the bread and the wine. We pass it to the person sitting beside us so that in this drama, each of us receives Christ in the gospel and offers Christ in the gospel by means of these signs.

Here's something to have fixed in our minds as we are offered the bread and the wine: Jesus is being publicly portrayed before my eyes as the One who was crucified for me, not only in audible words and preaching or in the words of the liturgy but in these visible signs. I'm being encouraged to *look* as well as to *listen*, to see how much He has loved me and loves me still. And now I have the privilege of feeding on Him as I eat the bread and drink the wine. And then I have the privilege of offering the bread and wine to my neighbor beside me, and perhaps even saying to him or her, "Do this, remembering that Christ died for you, and feed on Him in your heart with thanksgiving."

That is amazing. It's as though each of us can apply Paul's words about the supper to what we are doing at the table: "I received from the Lord what I also delivered to you" (1 Cor. 11:23). What a wonderful privilege we have.

But the word *proclamation* represents only one privilege, and we'll think about another one tomorrow.

2

The Cup of Blessing

YESTERDAY, WE WERE THINKING ABOUT this question: "What do you think about when the Lord's Supper is being celebrated in your church?" Our minds can easily drift toward a kind of hazy dreaminess, can't they? Therefore, it helps us to have a particular truth on which to focus, like nails we can hang our thoughts on that will help us to fix our eyes on the Lord Jesus. After all, we need to receive more than just a small piece of bread and a tiny drink of wine. We need the blessing of meeting with the Lord Jesus Himself.

The word we are going to reflect on today is *blessing*. Paul specifically uses this word in connection with the supper when, in 1 Corinthians 10:16, he speaks of the cup in the supper as "the cup of blessing that we bless."

Paul uses a word that comes from the Greek verb *eulogeō*, "to bless." It's a verb that today has lost the full weight of its biblical meaning, but we need to recover its significance if we want to understand what the Lord's Supper means.

One of the most helpful ways to do that is by thinking about what may still be the most common use of the verb *to bless*: It's when someone sneezes, and we say, "Bless you."

Why do we do that? It may well go back to the Middle Ages, when the bubonic plague swept away large proportions of the population of Europe. It was regarded as an indication of the curse and judgment of God, and sneezing was one of its common symptoms. Therefore, saying "Bless you" was actually a kind of prayer, meaning in effect: "May you not be under the curse. May you be blessed. May the curse be turned away from you."

That, of course, is what God has done for us in Jesus Christ. That is what happened at the cross. Christ took the curse in order to give us the blessing. That is how Paul put it in Galatians 3:13. Christ became a curse for us that the blessing promised to Abraham might come, not only to the Jews, but also to the gentiles.

At the Last Supper, Jesus took the final cup of the Passover meal, which was called the "cup of blessing." He gave it to His disciples and said that He would not drink of the fruit of the vine until He drank it anew in His Father's kingdom.

So did our Lord not drink the cup of blessing, but instead give it to His disciples? Why would that be? If we read on in the Gospels, we find the answer: Jesus was about to go to the garden of Gethsemane. He had said to His disciples, "Take and drink," and His Father now pressed into His hands another cup and said, "My Son, take and drink." That cup was filled with the judgment curse of God against our sins, and Jesus drank it to the last bitter dregs. He said, "The cup that My Father gives Me to drink, the cup of the divine cursing, shall I not drink it so that my disciples may drink of the cup of blessing?"

What a wonderful picture of the gospel. Jesus drinks my cup, the cup of cursing. He gives me His cup, the cup of blessing.

This helps us understand the Lord's Supper better. It fills us with awe that Christ Jesus drank the bitter cup for our sake and out of deep love for us. And now He gives us the cup of blessing, which we want to bless. And as we receive it, we have fellowship with Him, and we are able to praise Him for the wonder of His love.

3

Participation in Christ's Body and Blood

WE HAVE BEEN REFLECTING ON SOME of the New Testament words that help us to understand and enjoy the Lord's Supper. Thus far, we've thought about *proclamation* and *blessing*. Today's word is *participation*, or if you prefer, *communion*.

Paul asks the Corinthian Christians: "The cup of blessing that we bless, is it not a participation in the blood of Christ? The bread that we break, is it not a participation in the body of Christ? Because there is one bread, we who are many are one body, for we all partake of the one bread" (1 Cor. 10:16–17). The Greek word that lies behind the word *participation*, or *communion*, is *koinōnia*. It's the word for fellowship, communion, sharing in something. So Paul is saying that when we receive the supper, we are sharing in—we're having communion in— the Lord's body and blood. But what does that mean?

Paul is echoing here what Jesus said when He instituted the Lord's Supper. He gave the disciples the bread and the wine and said: "This is my body. . . . This is my blood of the covenant, which is poured out for many for the forgiveness of sins" (Matt. 26:26–28). What did He mean by that? The best way to think about this is not to leap to conclusions— something we're tempted to do because this question has proved to be controversial—but to build up our answer step by step.

First, it should be clear at the outset that Jesus wasn't identifying the bread and wine as His body and blood. His body and blood were present at the table. The bread and the wine were in His hands. It must have been obvious to the disciples that they weren't one and the same. What He was really saying was something like this: "Here at this table, what I give you expresses My love for you. This bread and wine represent Me. They express Me as incarnate in flesh and blood. And so when I offer you this bread and wine, I'm offering you nothing less than Myself. Correspondingly, when you eat and drink, you are accepting Me, receiving Me, taking Me, and trusting in Me, the incarnate Son of God, and doing that because you know I'm the One who sheds this precious blood for you to bring you forgiveness of sins."

Jesus was also saying this: "Listen, loved ones. In this ritual, in this little drama, just as by eating the Passover lamb you expressed your share in the exodus, so now by taking the bread and the wine you're expressing your share in the new exodus I'm going to accomplish. You're expressing your share in Me. In the old Passover, you took the exodus as your own. But now in the supper, you're taking Me as your own."

Jesus said that unless we eat His flesh and drink His blood, we have no life in us (John 6:53). He had earlier explained what He meant by eating and drinking as coming to Him, believing in Him, having communion with Him. And it's exactly the same here.

How does that help us understand what we're doing at the Lord's Table? The New Testament wants us to understand that we're not just eating bread and drinking wine, nor are we just trying to remember what Jesus did for us. The bread and the wine are not merely an aide-mémoire for us, helping us think about how Jesus died for us. If that were the case, then the supper should really have been described as a time of reflection. But it's more than that: it's a time of communion. It's Jesus offering Himself to us by means of these love-gifts of bread and wine, saying: "Come to Me, and you'll find rest. Receive Me. Trust Me. Love Me. Enjoy being with Me. Have communion with Me."

In a marriage proposal, a man takes a ring out of a box and offers it to a woman as a way of saying: "I love you, body and soul. I love you, and I offer myself to you to be your husband. Will you receive me and welcome me?" In the same way, Jesus Christ meets us at the table.

When we take the bread and the wine as His engagement ring of love, then we're receiving Him and having communion with Him. But there is even more, and we'll come to that tomorrow.

4

A Meal of Anticipation

WE HAVE BEEN THINKING ABOUT the meaning of the Lord's Supper in terms of the New Testament words that describe it. The next word we'll look at is *anticipation*. The Apostle Paul says, "As often as you eat this bread and drink the cup, you proclaim the Lord's death until he comes" (1 Cor. 11:26).

When Paul says "as often," he is not saying, "You should do this often," although that may be true. What he means is, *"Every time you do it,* you're proclaiming the Lord's death until He comes again." That means that the church is to celebrate both baptism and the Lord's Supper all the way to the end of the age, and to do it everywhere.

Sometimes you may meet professing Christians who suggest that they are "fine" without baptism or the Lord's Supper. But clearly Paul didn't think that way. One of the reasons is this: each time we celebrate the Lord's Supper, it reminds us that there is still more to come. Perhaps, just as many Christians today say "amen" out loud at the end of a prayer in church, the early Christians would say out loud together at the end of the Lord's Supper: "Maranatha! Our Lord, come!"

We noted last week that one of the most basic structures of the New Testament is that it stresses there is an *already* and a *not yet* about the gospel. We've already been raised into new life with Christ, but we've not yet been finally resurrected with Him. The *not yet* is still to come when He returns. So in a way, it's not surprising that this basic element of the gospel is also expressed at the Lord's Supper. In fact, this element of *not yet* has almost a physical expression at the Lord's Supper.

The word that is translated "supper" actually means a meal. But is the little piece of bread and sip of wine that we consume really a meal? It's almost as if the drama of the supper is designed in part to make us say, "Surely there must be more than this." And the answer is "yes," there is more. For now we meet Jesus at the table. We see Jesus by faith, by means of His Word, with the help of the Spirit, through the bread and the wine, and we love Him. In the full physical sense, we don't yet see Him face-to-face. But as Horatius Bonar expressed it in his beautiful communion hymn:

Here, O my Lord, I see thee face to face;
Here would I touch and handle things unseen,
Here grasp with firmer hand th'eternal grace,
And all my weariness upon thee lean.

And that is right—the believer can experience the presence of the Lord Jesus wonderfully at the supper. But in a way, it's only in a secondary sense that we see Him face-to-face. We certainly may feel that we see Him more clearly and love Him more dearly and want to follow Him more nearly because we've been to the Lord's Supper. But it's not face-to-face yet. Nevertheless, the supper teaches us that one day it will be.

So even as the Lord's Supper can bring us into the presence of Christ and give us a wonderful taste of His love, and a time to express our love for Him, it's also a reminder to us that we're not yet home. That is meant not to discourage us but to reassure us there is still more to come. It's saying: "This is food for the pilgrimage. He has prepared this table for you in the presence of your enemies. His cup already runs over with blessing. So keep on going and know that what awaits you is not this simple supper, but the glorious marriage banquet of the Lamb."

Perhaps the Apostle Peter put it best: "Though you have not seen him, you love him. Though you do not now see him, you believe in him and rejoice with joy that is inexpressible and filled with glory, obtaining the outcome of your faith, the salvation of your souls" (1 Peter 1:8–9). Then you'll see Him face-to-face and be made like Him. And then you'll have a seat at the marriage banquet of the Lamb.

That is why Bonar's wonderful hymn ends like this:

Feast after feast here comes and passes by,
Yet passing, points to that glad feast above,
Giving sweet foretaste of that festal joy,
The Lamb's great bridal-feast of bliss and love.

5

A Consecrated Feast

PROCLAMATION, BLESSING, PARTICIPATION, AND ANTICIPATION—we've been looking at these big words this week because the New Testament uses them all in connection with the Lord's Supper. They help us both to understand it better and to enjoy it more. I suspect we might be shocked if someone handed us the bread and the wine at the Lord's Supper and then said what the waiter might say in a restaurant: "Enjoy."

At a church where I once served, the tradition for communion was that the elders would sit around the Lord's Table and serve the congregation from it. On my left hand sat one of the senior elders who had served the longest in the congregation. I remember coming home one day and my wife saying to me, "It is wonderful to see a man sitting beside you at the Lord's Table who looks so happy to be there." She didn't mean that he was flippant and superficial, just that there was a sense that he belonged there with Jesus.

John Knox's successor, Robert Bruce, used to say that we don't get a better Christ at the Lord's Supper than the Christ we get in the preaching of the Word, but we do sometimes get the same Christ "better." But we can do that only when we remember another word that helps us to understand the supper. It's not used by Paul, but it's obviously implied when he tells the Corinthians that they can't go to feasts where the food has been consecrated to idols and then come to the Lord's Supper, in which they are consecrating themselves to Him anew. Therefore, today's word is *consecration*.

The Lord's Supper, like baptism, has often been described since at least the time of Augustine as a *visible* word, a sermon in dramatic form. We might even think of it as a kind of mime in which we've been given program notes that help us understand every movement. What Paul means is that when you reach out to take the bread and wine into your hands, you can't also be holding other food in them that doesn't belong to the Lord Jesus. He says: "You cannot drink the cup of the Lord and the cup of demons. You cannot partake of the table of the Lord and the table of demons" (1 Cor. 10:21).

You can't take hold of Jesus and cling tightly to something else that He doesn't favor. In Corinth, that meant that the Christians couldn't share in pagan celebrations, because those banquets served food offered to an idol. They couldn't do that and then come to worship with Christians who were sharing in the Lord Jesus Christ. It's the *Lord's* Supper, after all. And when we receive it, we're joining ourselves to the community that says, "Jesus Christ is Lord" and shouts out: "Maranatha! Our Lord, come!"

But Paul says something else that is intriguing. He says: "Shall we provoke the Lord to jealousy? Are we stronger than he?" (1 Cor. 10:22). What does this mean? I think one thing it means is this: If you're really a Christian, you need to know that Jesus Christ loves you with a very deep passion, and you mustn't get entangled with other lovers. He is determined that He will have all of you and that He'll never let you go. He is jealous with a holy jealousy, a proper jealousy, and He knows that you're doing yourself harm. And in that holy jealousy, He will have to break that relationship that you've established. And in the process, things will happen that will inevitably cause pain and grief.

Paul is saying: "Don't let yourself get caught up in a foolish compromise situation. Instead, when you take the bread and wine and in faith come to the Lord Jesus at the table, receive His love. Tell Him you trust Him. Take Him with both hands. Let everything that He does not favor drop out of your hands and give yourself without reserve to Him."

The supper is meant to help us do that because as often as we eat this bread and drink this cup, we're saying to the Lord Jesus: "You gave everything for me, body and blood. You are giving Yourself entirely to me now. Lord Jesus, I receive You, and I give myself to You in return."

And so we're able to sing with Isaac Watts:

But drops of grief can ne'er repay
The debt of love I owe;
Here, Lord, I give myself away,
'Tis all that I can do.

Here's the message of the Lord's Supper. Jesus says: "Behold, I stand at the door and knock. If anyone hears my voice and opens the door, I will come in to him and eat with him, and he with me" (Rev. 3:20).

So if you're having the Lord's Supper in church this coming Lord's Day, or the next time you do, remember these words: *proclamation*, *benediction*, *communion*, *anticipation*, and *consecration*.

WEEK 42

Christian Family Life

1

The Christian Family and the Church

THIS WEEK, WE'LL REFLECT ON FAMILY LIFE. We would surely all agree that this topic is important, although we certainly don't all have the same experience of family. Some have had good experiences, while others have had bad experiences. Many of us have had a mixed experience. And some may have little or no real experience of family life at all. Therefore, it's important to begin in the same place, with the family to which every believer belongs. One of my former colleagues used to call it "the worldwide, eternity-long family of God." That is the family that every believer has been brought into, and that is the family that lasts.

We sometimes say about family relationships that blood is thicker than water. That is also true theologically. We've been brought into the family that Christ has created by the shedding of His blood, and that blood is thicker than water. That is why sometimes Christians feel closer to members of the family of God than to some members of their natural family.

But there is another wonderful thing to remember here. In the family of God, none of us is a natural member. We've all been adopted. None can demean a brother or sister by saying, "I *really* belong to this family, but you're just an adopted member." I remember hearing once about an adopted boy who was mistreated by his friends at school. The other children would say to him, "You are only adopted." The boy developed a great reply. He responded: "My parents chose me. Your parents just had to get whatever came!"

So the first thing to say about families and family life is that we need to get our priorities right. There is a lifelong family, and there is an eternity-long family. Most of us belong to a lifelong family with its privileges and obligations, and that family life is a sphere all its own. It has its own structure, and it differs from society in general or the state. It also differs from the church.

All these various structures have their place in our Christian lives. The state has a responsibility to serve its families, but it doesn't have the right to usurp the role of the family or to interfere with it in a way that is contrary to Scripture. Unfortunately, many states today do just that and overreach their authority. By the same token, the church family doesn't have the right to usurp the structure of our family life or to lay down laws for us that are additional to or contrary to Scripture's teaching on family life. That said, we do want our family to take part in the life of the world around us as salt and light, and we also need to fold our family life into the family of the church.

Folding our nuclear family into the church family is a fundamental principle for growing as a Christian family. I've sometimes seen families whose attitude is something like this: "We are sovereign in our family, and we will allow the church only the space that suits us." But that tends to put our family *over* the church, not really *in* the church. And actually, the more biblical picture is of families being folded *into* the family of the church.

Those of us who are parents need to realize that God never intended two parents to have all the gifts and graces necessary to raise one child for Jesus Christ. It takes a church to do that. Our children get a very limited view of the gifts and graces of the Lord Jesus just from us. Surely we don't think we have all the gifts, graces, or wisdom that our children need. It's a long haul to grow a family, adapt to each new stage, and take account of each family member. It happens over many days, weeks, months, and years, and we need all the help we can get. And the best help comes when our family is folded into the larger church family, our local congregation. Then all the gifts and graces the Lord has given to the church will be used for the blessing and strengthening not only of ourselves, but of our children, too—just as we also want our gifts and graces to serve the larger family of the church.

It's surely one of the greatest privileges we have as Christians—not only that we have our nuclear family, but that we can fold that nuclear family into a family that loves us, cares for us, encourages us, strengthens us, and protects us.

More about that tomorrow!

2

Raising Children in the Church

I'VE OFTEN NOTICED THAT WHEN YOUNG COUPLES are beginning to establish their family and raise their children for the Lord Jesus, they are very likely to get some Christian books on the subject. Yet we must be discerning about books that teach us how we should raise our family. The very best books will do us good. But the best help we'll find is not from books, but from other parents whom we respect in our own church family, especially the older parents who have seen the fruit of how they've raised their children for Christ.

I suspect that the best of these parents will not provide you with a formula, although that is what we sometimes want. We want people to just tell us what we have to do to have a good family. But older, wiser parents will share with us what they've found helpful, where they made mistakes, and what they've seen and learned about applying biblical principles to their unique family life and to each of their unique children. Most of all, they will focus on what we can never get from a book—the importance of the atmosphere of love.

It used to be said that young people didn't fully become themselves until they were well into their twenties. This means that parents often don't see the long-term effects of their family life or the way they've raised their children until the children have actually grown up. That is one reason why we should be cautious about listening to a child-rearing guru whose children are still young.

I remember asking once about a woman who was speaking at a Christian conference on children. Even though I hadn't heard her speak, I had the impression that she wasn't all that old. I asked if she had children. It turned out that she did. My next question was to ask someone if they knew how old the speaker's children were. They responded that her children were young. I can't remember if they were even beyond the early teens. I'm a little embarrassed to say that I blurted out (although quietly), "Then she doesn't really know anything about the effects of her own child-rearing." It's not really right for a young man or woman to be known as a child-rearing family-life teacher or counselor or guru. While a young minister may still be responsible for expounding biblical passages that deal with family life, he does this not as a guru, but as a member of a church family, where there are living illustrations of how these principles are applied in different families.

So here's a biblical principle that we need to take to heart: God has given us our church to help us raise our children for Christ. That is why a lot of the instruction in the New Testament about family life is found in letters that were to be read out loud in the presence of the whole church. In the church family, the Lord has given us older men to help us when we're young fathers. He has given us older women to teach younger women how to be wives and mothers by befriending them, encouraging them, and sharing their experience and their hard-won wisdom. Maybe one of the best things that could happen to our youngsters is that they get to know old Mr. or Mrs. Smith who sit at the side of the church, and they become an additional grandfather or grandmother who cares for them and takes a lively interest in them and prays them into Christian adulthood.

Incidentally, that is why one of the great tragedies of the contemporary church is that many churches have lost a second service on the Lord's Day. It was often in the lingering behind at the end of that service that youngsters naturally mingled with and got to know and love the older members of the church. If someone asked me what I thought helped my wife and me raise our children, I would be bound to say, "Sunday night church." It's not rocket science; it's just one of the sweet and natural ways that God works to bless us.

So let's take this to heart and fold our family into the church family. Because not to do that would be cutting off a supply of life for both of these families.

3

Honoring Our Parents for Life

IT'S A TREMENDOUS AMOUNT OF WORK to be a parent, isn't it? But God willing, we also have these moments when it seems the sun breaks through and we realize what an amazing thing it is to have a family. What a blessing that God has set the solitary in a home. It wasn't good for Adam to be alone, and it's not usually very good for us either. One of the things that strikes me as a wonderful expression of God's love for our families is that He devoted one of the Ten Commandments to family life.

The fifth commandment is a unique commandment in the sense that it's addressed to a particular human relationship, a family relationship: "Honor your father and your mother" (Ex. 20:12). That is a great key to happiness in the home, and it's a beautiful thing to see when children honor their parents. But there are several intriguing things about this commandment.

The first is that it's the only commandment that doesn't have a negative element in it somewhere. The second is that although it's the fifth commandment, it's the first commandment about our relationships with others. Commandments one through four have to do with our honoring of the Lord. But the third thing to notice is that it's a lifelong commandment. Notice that it doesn't say, "*Children,* honor your father and your mother." Rather, it says in effect, "Everyone, honor your father and your mother." It doesn't just apply to years one through eighteen.

At the same time, it is important to note that the way that we honor our parents changes over the years.

When we're children in our parents' home, honoring them takes the form of learning to be obedient to them in the Lord. Luke tells us that Jesus did just that. Even after His parents had misunderstood Him, He was submissive to them because, apart from anything else, He knew that was His heavenly Father's commandment.

But then when we grow up—and especially when we've established our own home and family—the nature of honoring our parents changes. This is why the commandment doesn't say, "Obey your father and your mother" but "*Honor* your father and your mother." We're no longer under their authority in later life, and they should no longer issue commands for us to obey. But we still need to find ways of honoring them.

Sometimes that subtle difference can be challenging to negotiate. Alas, some Christian parents have never noticed that the commandment calls us to *honor,* not to *obey.* Some of us may have to find ways of honoring our parents when they wrongly overstep the mark or tell us that we are to obey them. That is going beyond Scripture and can produce difficult situations. But if we understand this difference between childhood obedience and lifelong honoring, then we will find ways to express appreciation and love and to bring blessing and care to our parents. And it will help us through all the challenges. At the end of the day, we will never, ever regret keeping this commandment.

But there is a fourth thing that we can draw from this commandment, and it's as wonderful as it is helpful. When Christian parents teach this commandment to their children when they are still very young, then by keeping this one commandment, the children will, in a sense, naturally keep all the others. They'll honor and imitate their parents and their parents' love for the Lord in their worship of His name and in living lives that please Him. They will breathe in the atmosphere of love for Christ that their parents breathe out.

Yes, we want to help our children memorize the Ten Commandments. The amazing thing is that there are only ten, so it's not beyond their powers to do that. But right from the very beginning, if they honor their parents, the other commandments will fall into place.

It is a wonderful blessing for our family life that embedded in the Ten Commandments is this one simple command that helps our children focus on loving their parents—and in so doing, learning to love the One whom their parents love.

And that, after all, is just Family Life 101.

4

A Husband's Integrity and a Wife's Respect

YESTERDAY, WE LOOKED AT THE FAMILY-LIFE commandment that focuses on honoring our father and our mother. Today, we'll look at another commandment. Though it is directed to wives, its fulfillment is related to both husband and wife. In the Apostle Paul's teaching on marriage, he says, "Let the wife see that she respects her husband" (Eph. 5:33). The verb that Paul uses here is often translated as "fear," but Bible translators are right to translate this occurrence as "respect." Here's a major key to married life: a wife should respect her husband.

When couples have come to talk to me about marriage, I've always looked for this basic grace: Does the woman respect this man? I'm not asking if she is head over heels in love with him. On its own, that could easily blind her to his faults. It's *respect* that matters. And respect means trust. Respect means that his character leads her to believe that his love is true, that he will keep his word, that he is faithful, and that there are qualities in him that she can appreciate and admire.

It's the sense that Ruth had about Boaz. She thought he was the kind of man with whom she would be at home, safe, and secure. It means that a woman feels that this man will be her very best friend in all the world. And if she doesn't respect him before she marries him, it's very unlikely that she'll respect him after she marries him.

When I was a seminary professor, I often found myself at church conferences where I was hosted over a few days by a husband and wife. One of the things that I secretly rather enjoyed was trying to work out why they had gotten married in the first place. For example, what could I see in the husband that had caused his wife to respect him?

If you think about it, superficial things don't produce that respect. They might produce physical attraction, but they don't produce respect. You don't respect someone because of their good looks or their bank balance, but because of their character. And it goes without saying that this presents a challenge to young men—and later to husbands—to be worthy of respect because of who we are as Christians.

Sometimes couples want to write their own marriage vows. Personally, I don't see how they think that they can write better vows than people who were great masters of theology, had tremendous experience of marriage, and were skilled in the use of the English language. Some of these self-written marriage vows make sense to nobody but the couple, and they'll sound trite in a year's time. But having said that, I confess that I wouldn't mind adding this simple question to the groom in the wedding vows: "As you take this woman to be your lawfully wedded wife, do you promise to live worthy of her respect?" It's not rocket science to see that when children live in a home where that is true, they'll feel safe and loved, and they'll also get a glimpse of the Lord Jesus.

It could be that some of us need to go back to the ABCs of married life and ask the Lord to help us to begin again. Thank God that He is able to do that.

5

When Two Become One

EARLIER THIS WEEK, I MENTIONED THAT many look for help from Christian books when it comes to raising children. Specifically, I had in mind books written by supposed gurus who have a very definite formula for how to do that. I suggested that we need to be discerning and, in some cases, very cautious about them because there is no one-size-fits-all when it comes to marriage or family life. Scripture is full of great principles, but sometimes the gurus turn their own applications of those principles into the principles themselves, and that is a very bad way to handle Scripture. It can also lead to off-center guidelines for marriage and family life.

I'm inclined to say the same thing about books on courtship and marriage—there is no one-size-fits-all. Certainly, in more recent decades, the gurus' ideas about courtship and married life often seem to have more to do with Hollywood than with Scripture. For example, it has often struck me that the courtship in the Song of Solomon wasn't exactly plain sailing, and sometimes that is the case with us, too. We need to be cautious about prejudging the ways of God with individual Christians and instead learn to be confident in God's faithfulness and His sovereign providences in our lives.

But what is marriage, after all?

Recall how Genesis 2 describes the first courtship and marriage. Adam was on his own. He saw in Eve someone he recognized as belonging to him in a special way—someone who was like him, someone who would complete him, someone with whom he felt he could be fully himself. Although I know it doesn't sound complimentary, Genesis says that God "built" Eve for Adam. But if you think about it, it's actually a beautiful way of thinking about God's ways. Eve suited Adam; Adam suited Eve. We sometimes talk about the way people "clicked" with each other. That happened to our first parents. They locked together. I remember a friend who was struggling with the commitment involved in asking the woman he loved to marry him. He said he eventually came to the realization that they could be more together than the sum total of what each of them would be without the other.

So in a word, marriage is a friendship of a very special kind. So special that, as Scripture says, the two become one. There is the unity of the duality, a harmony of the differences, and it's an amazing reality. And what makes it even more amazing is that it's a gift that God has so freely given to us.

I sometimes laugh to myself when I think about unpleasant people who are married to each other. It's a gift of God's general grace to them. It can be sarcastic to say that they deserve each other, but isn't it remarkable to think of the generosity of God in that? On the big screen, it's always the beautiful people who marry each other. But in God's generosity, marriage is not just for the beautiful people but for the plain people as well. How is that possible? Because for all our fallen condition, God in His providence allows something to click. People find a friend with whom they want to live permanently to be their very best friend in all the world.

I'm always interested in people's "atmospheres," in the kind of life aroma that a person gives off. I suspect that is what influences and shapes our children more than anything else, even more than the words we speak. They breathe in the atmosphere that Mom and Dad breathe out—in their relationship with God, in their relationship with one another, in their mutual respect, and in their friendship with each other. And where that is present, where a couple really belong to each other in that way, there is the making of a stable home and family life in which the children can flourish.

Hopefully, you have tasted this to one degree or another. But even if that has not been the case in your own family, remember what we were thinking about at the beginning of this week: the real family, the big family, the lasting family, is the family of God to which we all belong if we're Christ's. Because in Him, we've been adopted into the family of God.

Let's pray that in God's grace and goodness, we'll grow our families for the Lord Jesus Christ.

WEEK 43

Covenant

1

The Promised Covenant of Grace

EARLIER IN THE YEAR, WE SPENT A WEEK discussing how Genesis 3:15 is like a spine that holds the whole Bible together. To use a different word picture, we could say that this verse is like a seed from which a massive tree eventually grows. This week, we will develop that idea in a slightly different way.

In Genesis 3:15, God says that ongoing hostility between the seed of Eve and the seed of the serpent will continue until the ultimate seed of Eve, Jesus Christ, crushes the head of the serpent, having His own heel crushed in the process. Theologians call that the first announcement of the gospel, the *protoeuangelion*. But theologians and Bible students through the ages have also looked back to Genesis 3:15 as expressing a new covenant that God was making.

Although it isn't explicitly stated (except perhaps in Hosea 6:7), it seems clear that God's original relationship with Adam and Eve was covenantal. It involved a bond that God made with them in which He promised the rich blessings of life and fellowship as they lived in harmony with Him, but also the curse of profound loss, alienation, and death if they turned against His purposes. What Hosea 6:7 says about God's people is that like Adam, they transgressed the covenant.

In His wonderful love, God made a first covenant in which He promised life. But that covenant was broken. And as Paul says in Romans 5, sin and death have come into the world—and come to each of us. But rather than leave the world in that condition, God gave another promise. He made a new covenant that would later be sealed in the blood of the seed of the woman, our Lord Jesus.

When we think of Genesis 3:15, we can echo the words of the mathematician-philosopher Alfred North Whitehead, who said that the history of Western philosophy can be summarized as a series of footnotes to Plato. Similarly, we can say that the story of the Bible can be summarized as a series of footnotes to Genesis 3:15. That becomes clearer when we see that embedded in the curse on the serpent is a promise of our deliverance and salvation.

Genesis 3:15 embodies what we sometimes call the *covenant of grace*.

Some Christians argue that there is a whole series of different covenants, not just the one covenant of grace. But this isn't really an either-or situation. It's both-and. Because in one way or another, every covenant God makes that is related to His purposes of salvation is simply a further outworking of Genesis 3:15. There is progressive revelation, and there is also cumulative revelation, so that by the end of the Bible, the serpent has grown into a great dragon, and the seed of the woman is the incarnate Son of God.

What can we learn from this covenant of grace in Eden? Surely the first thing is that God is taking matters into His own hands. The plan is His, and the promise is His. The content of the promise is about Him, and its outworking is His. That is, it's a covenant *entirely* of sovereign grace.

Second, the salvation in view is described first of all in terms of the defeat of our enemy. We mustn't lose sight of this. The conflict of Genesis 3:15 is between the serpent and his seed, and the seed of the woman, who is ultimately our Lord Jesus Christ. That conflict is one of the major themes of the Gospels. If we read them remembering that Jesus has come to defeat God's enemy and ours, we'll notice in a new way just how much of our Lord's ministry involves conflict with opposition. The Apostle John sums it up this way: "The reason the Son of God appeared was to destroy the works of the devil" (1 John 3:8).

There is something more. In Genesis 3:15, we see a hint not only that there will be conflict, but also that sacrifice will be necessary. The bruising of the heel of the seed of the woman will be the means of His victory over the serpent. Reading the Bible and seeing how it points to the Lord Jesus is, in some ways, simply a matter of keeping our eye on how this first promise of the covenant of grace unfolds.

There is something here that is really worth thinking about. This is God's longest-standing promise, but more than that, it's also the promise that required the greatest sacrifice ever made. And the marvel is that He has kept this promise.

We will think more about that tomorrow.

2

Safeguarding the Promise of Grace

YESTERDAY, WE LOOKED AT THE ORIGINAL promise of what is often called the covenant of grace. It's a promise that holds the whole Bible together from Genesis 3:15 right through the end, and it is sustained, clarified, and developed as it unfolds in a series of further covenants. This is the case with the covenant that God made with Noah, saying, "I will establish my covenant with you" (Gen. 6:18).

The word "establish" in this verse might carry the sense of "confirm"—as though God is saying, "I will make sure that My covenant remains standing." In other words, the function of the covenant that God makes with Noah is to ensure that the covenant of grace He had already announced would not collapse, even though the world was almost going to collapse in the flood. It's striking that when Noah emerges from the ark, the words that God speaks to him echo what God had said in the garden of Eden. The promise that God gives to Noah that He will never repeat the flood safeguards the promise He had earlier given to Adam and Eve that the serpent would be defeated.

But it doesn't take many more chapters before we discover that the seed of the serpent kept fighting. In Genesis 11, we read the story of the Tower of Babel, which was a concerted effort to achieve a type of world unity that would establish its own authority over against the authority of God—the seed of the serpent against the seed of the woman. God dealt with that opposition by confusing the languages of the people and dispersing them over the face of the earth. The flood would not be repeated, but once again, it looks as though the seed of the serpent has almost annihilated any faithful seed of the woman.

But then the second half of Genesis 11 traces the seed of Shem through many years until we come to a man named Terah. The genealogy in Genesis 11:10–26 makes us feel as though God was watching a moving dot on the screen of history, going along from one generation to the next, all the while knowing where He was heading: to Ur of the Chaldeans and to Terah's son, whose name was Abram. Abram was a seed of the woman to whom God would give another covenant promise.

In this way, God kept developing the original covenant of grace through a series of subsequent covenants, first with Noah, and now with Abram. Terah had two other sons, but it was on Abram that God had set His eye. He was the son who would carry forward the promise, and part of God's covenant purpose was that in Abram—that is, in his seed—"all the families of the earth shall be blessed" (Gen. 12:3).

We mustn't ever minimize the significance of that word "bless." It's a covenant word. When God's covenant is made, it leads to either blessing or cursing, salvation or condemnation. The presence of these words in various parts of Scripture is an indication that God's covenant is in action and that He is being faithful to His commitment.

There were also new elements in the nature of God's covenant relationship with Abraham, of course. He promised that his descendants would inherit a land and He gave the sign of circumcision. These are important, but they are not the essence of the covenant. They are more like appendices to and confirmations of it. The Apostle Paul saw that clearly. He says in Romans 4 that Abraham's circumcision, the sign of the covenant, wasn't a sign of a piece of land, but of the righteousness of faith: "He received the sign of circumcision as a seal of the righteousness that he had by faith while he was still uncircumcised" (v. 11). And as we have noticed before, these words also make clear that his circumcision wasn't so much a sign of his faith, but of the righteousness that God provides—the new relationship with God into which Abraham had been brought through faith.

The story of God's faithfulness to His covenant promise is thrilling. Sometimes it must have looked as though He had completely lost sight of it or totally forgotten it. But God knew exactly what He was doing. He is a covenant-keeping God as well as a covenant-making God.

Let that encourage us today as we remember this: God will never forget His covenant promise to us.

3

The Covenant Made at Sinai

THE SCRIPTURES CONTAIN THE OLD TESTAMENT (or Covenant) and the New Testament (or Covenant) of our Lord Jesus Christ. Despite that reality, the fact that the Bible is a covenant book about a covenant God who makes and keeps His covenant of grace is often a new concept to many Christians. That is why we are reflecting on how important God's covenant is.

Thus far, we've seen that the covenant of grace was inaugurated in Genesis 3:15. It was further developed in the covenant with Noah, and again later on in the covenant with Abraham. But the next big covenant is one that people sometimes struggle to understand: the covenant that God made with Moses at Sinai.

Why would there be misunderstanding? It may be because this is the covenant that has the Ten Commandments and all the laws that governed the life of Israel, containing so many detailed regulations. The biggest misunderstanding with the Mosaic covenant is probably in thinking that the Old Testament (or Covenant), and especially the covenant that we find with Moses, teaches that we are saved by what we do, by obeying the law. Whereas by contrast, the New Testament (or Covenant) teaches that we are saved by grace—not by what we do, but by what God has done for us in Christ.

This is a disastrous misunderstanding of the covenant with Moses, and it turns the teaching of the Bible upside down. It couldn't really be further from the truth. How can we be sure of that? If we read the book of Exodus from the beginning rather than starting right at chapter 20, we see that the giving of the law was set within the context of the covenant of grace that God had made. Then the covenant was more fully expressed in the covenant that God made with Moses.

When God commissions Moses at the burning bush, He declares Himself to be the God of Abraham, Isaac, and Jacob. He says that He will remember His covenant and bring the Israelites out of Egypt, taking them as His people. It's the covenant-making and covenant-keeping God of grace who inaugurates the exodus. It is a work entirely of His sovereign grace, and it's in that context that He gives the law.

Therefore, the covenant with Moses hardly teaches salvation by works! Rather, it's all about God's promise—about covenant grace and mercy, and our response to it.

This point is made crystal clear when God gives Moses the Ten Commandments. The very first words He says amount to this: "Moses, I've been keeping My covenant, haven't I? I've done what I promised. I've remembered My promises. I've brought you out. I'm taking you as My people." Notice how Exodus 20 begins: "God spoke all these words [to Moses], saying, 'I am the LORD your God, who brought you out of the land of Egypt, out of the house of slavery'" (vv. 1–2). Only *after* those first words does God give the Ten Commandments.

The pattern is unvarying: God saves His people, and then He calls them to live in a way that pleases Him. He makes His covenant with us and binds Himself to us, and then He summons us to live in a way that conforms to His wonderful grace. And as we do so, we enter into His promised blessings.

The covenants with Noah, Abraham, and Moses, each with its own distinctive elements, belong together as the unfolding elements in the covenant of grace that are ultimately embedded in Genesis 3:15.

Perhaps the big lesson to learn about the Mosaic covenant is that the law of God is set within the context of the saving grace of God. Therefore, it provides us with the map that leads to blessing and to life.

We need to taste more of the grace of God's law, don't you think?

4

God's Law and Grace

YESTERDAY, WE REFLECTED ON THE COVENANT that God made with Moses. We stressed how important it is to see the Mosaic covenant as an expression of God's covenant of grace, and that we must avoid the drastic mistake of thinking that the covenant with Moses—and the rest of the Old Testament along with it—teaches that we're saved by works. As Paul points out, the law of God was given centuries after God's covenant with Abraham. It didn't annul that covenant of grace, but rather was given within the context of it.

But when we read the small print of the Mosaic law, it does seem to focus on what we do. There are so many details and so many restrictions. It can all sound so legal—laws, commandments, instructions about sacrifices and offerings—that sometimes people get the impression that pleasing God must have been very hard work. And so the idea that the Mosaic covenant seems mainly to be about good works can perhaps too easily persist in people's minds.

This can be problematic, not only in how we understand the Old Testament, but in how we think about God Himself. Is that what He is really like? Constantly scrutinizing us with a multitude of dos and don'ts—and mainly don'ts?

This is by no means the case. Everything becomes clearer if we remember a couple of things. First, have you ever noticed that the only part of the law that was placed in the ark of the covenant, in the holiest place, was the tablets with the Ten Commandments on them? It's interesting that inside that sacred box were written the words about God's delivering His people from slavery. And on top of that box was a covering of solid gold called the mercy seat. It was there that once a year the high priest sprinkled the blood of the sacrifice on the Day of

Atonement. What does that picture say to you? To borrow the words of a hymn, it surely says this:

Grace, grace, God's grace,
Grace that is greater than all our sin.

The second thing to notice is that while the Ten Commandments were placed in the ark, the rest of the law was outside it. The simple reason for that difference is that the rest of the law was the *application* of the commandments to the people of Israel—a distinct people at a certain time in their history—until Christ, the seed of the woman, came. In other words, these particular laws were meant for them while they lived in the promised land. They were meant to keep them together and distinct as a people until the fundamental promise to Abraham was fulfilled in our Lord Jesus Christ.

The psalmist understood this when he wrote that he loved God's law. He understood that these applications had a special purpose for a special time. And according to Scripture, that special time would be fulfilled when Jesus came.

The Mosaic covenant looked back to the covenant of grace, and it also looked forward to the coming of Christ. In this in-between time, the Ten Commandments were applied in a variety of ways to preserve Israel as a very special people and to preserve the promise among them until Christ came. Then in a sense, we can say that the Lord Jesus picked up these applications and carried them away. Of course, we can still learn from them, but as the New Testament tells us, we're no longer under them.

When we begin to see these hints that the Scriptures give us, we learn that it's a great thing to see that there is grace in God's law.

5

What's New in the New Covenant?

ALL THIS WEEK, WE'VE BEEN REFLECTING ON the topic of God's covenant of grace. It goes back to Genesis 3:15, and then all the way forward until it is fulfilled in the Lord Jesus Christ, who is Himself God's covenant.

Entire books have been written on the covenant, but we've simply been looking at a few ways that God's one covenant of grace unfolds in a series of other covenants. They each have a distinct shape and style, but all of them are the unfolding of one single promise. What becomes clear to us is that in all these different covenants, grace is the foundation for our response of unreserved, total, joyful obedience to the Lord.

Sometimes God gives us detailed instruction about what we are to do, such as in the Mosaic administration. Sometimes He gives us principles, such as in the Ten Commandments, that are carried over into the new covenant. He binds us to Himself so that we'll become like Him and reflect His character in our lives—in other words, so that we'll become more and more like the Lord Jesus. The Apostle Paul says that God has predestined us to be conformed to the image of His Son (Rom. 8:29), and that is what He has in view in making His covenants with us.

What makes the new covenant so new? It's not that it presents a different way of salvation from the old covenant. Rather, it's new in the sense that it fulfills everything that was promised in the earlier covenants that God made. It's new in the sense that when it comes, it makes all previous covenants seem old.

The great promise about the new covenant is found in Jeremiah 31:31–34, a passage referred to on several occasions in the New Testament, not least by Jesus Himself when He inaugurated the Lord's Supper and said, "This . . . is the new covenant in my blood" (Luke 22:20).

Consider two features of this promise given through the prophet Jeremiah.

First, God promises a special *location* for His law. In the old covenant, it was placed inside the ark of the covenant. In the new covenant, God says, "I will put my law within them, and I will write it on their hearts" (Jer. 31:33). What God is saying is that through the Spirit's ministry, what was written originally into Adam's heart—the instinct, desire, and power to live in fellowship with God—will be rewritten into the hearts of believers.

The Decalogue itself, which was hidden in the ark of the covenant, couldn't do that. Paul makes that point in Romans 8:3–4 when he says that the Spirit, working within us, accomplished what the written law couldn't do because of our sinfulness. The result is that the righteous requirements of the law begin to be fulfilled in us as we walk according to the Spirit.

Second, in the new covenant, God says, "And no longer shall each one teach his neighbor and each his brother, saying, 'Know the LORD,' for they shall all know me, from the least of them to the greatest" (Jer. 31:34).

This does not mean that the Lord wasn't known in the old covenant. After all, Jeremiah speaks about people's knowing God in the Old Testament days. What is meant here is that in the old covenant, there was a sense in which the knowledge of God came secondhand to ordinary believers. It was mediated to them through their contact with the prophets, priests, or kings, who were all living pictures of the Lord Jesus Christ. It was necessary under the old covenant for someone to say to you, "Know the Lord; let me share His revelation with you." But now that Jesus Christ has come as the King, when we come to know Him, we've come to know the Lord.

The Apostle John puts it this way: "The anointing that you received from him abides in you, and you have no need that anyone should teach you" (1 John 2:27). This doesn't mean that we don't need pastors to teach us God's Word. After all, John was teaching the people who read his letter! The Scriptures are full of teaching, and there are teachers in the church. What John means here is that we no longer need the prophet, the priest, and the king. Now we all know the Lord Jesus, and we know Him directly by the Spirit and through the Word. We no longer need mediators because we have one Mediator between God and man, the man Christ Jesus.

In the book of Isaiah we read that the Lord Jesus Himself *is* the covenant: "I will give you as a covenant for the people" (Isa. 42:6; see also 49:8). That is probably why the word *covenant* doesn't appear very often in the New Testament.

The revelation of the covenant of grace in the Old Testament was *wonderful*. But in Jesus Christ, it's *surpassingly wonderful*. It brings us eternal life, which Jesus said involves knowing the Father through the Son by the ministry of the Spirit.

Let's rejoice and revel in that today. And let's thank God together for the covenant of grace.

WEEK 44

Big Moments in Jesus' Life

1

Living under the Shadow of the Cross

WHAT HAVE BEEN THE BIGGEST MOMENTS in your life? Most of us have them, and the Lord Jesus was no exception. This week, we'll think about a few of those moments in Jesus' life.

The older we get, the more it strikes us that some events in our lives loom especially large. There are crisis points, turning points, moments of special accomplishment, and moments of loss and pain. We remember the details of those moments even years later. Some events become major chapter headings in the story of our lives.

All this is simply part of what it means to be human, and our Lord Jesus must have had similar memories, too. Certainly, He had big moments in His life—moments that the preacher G. Campbell Morgan described in a book titled *The Crises of the Christ*. For all of us, such moments underline that God has a unique plan and purpose for us. The same was true of our Lord Jesus. He experienced these things as well by taking on a human nature.

In the introduction to his gospel, the Apostle John says that the Logos, the Word of God, became flesh and dwelt among us. That is magnificent theology. The divine person of the Logos was with God and was God, but He also became flesh and dwelt among us (John 1:1, 14). And not all moments in His life were the same, any more than they are in our own lives.

The fifth-century theologians who wrote the Chalcedonian Definition of AD 451 said that the Son of God is "acknowledged in two natures unconfusedly, unchangeably, indivisibly, inseparably; the difference of the natures being in no way removed because of the union, but rather the properties of each nature being preserved." This means that Jesus had a human mind, a human will, a human memory, and human sensations. He felt as we do. He remembered in ways that are similar to the way we remember. But He did all of this sinlessly, of course. And it's clear that He saw some events in His life as big moments.

One of them was very literally crucial—the cross. It loomed so large in Jesus' thinking that He spoke about it regularly before He experienced it fully. Indeed, He said that He felt His whole life was hemmed in until His crucifixion took place (see Luke 12:50).

Holman Hunt, an English pre-Raphaelite painter, created a piece titled *Jesus, the Light of the World*. It portrays Christ as holding a lantern and standing at the door of a house. When I was a teenager, a number of my friends kept a postcard-sized version of it in their Bibles. Hunt did another painting of Jesus titled *The Shadow of Death*. Here, he represents Jesus as a young man stretching at the end of the day in the family carpenter shop. The light falling on Him casts on the wall the silhouette of a man stretched out as though hanging on a cross. The message of this painting is certainly suggestive. While there were big moments in our Lord's life, His entire life was lived in the shadow of the cross. It wasn't only at the end of His life, but throughout it, that He was taking up the cross for us. Yes, there were moments of crisis. But there was never a moment when He was relieved of being our Burden-Bearer and Savior.

We cannot begin to fathom what it must have been like for Jesus as a young man on the hills of Galilee to meditate on Psalm 22 or on the Servant Songs of Isaiah, thinking to Himself: "These passages are speaking about Me. The crisis moments are coming."

For all eternity, we'll admire Him for enduring those moments. And for all eternity, we'll praise Him for what John Calvin described as "the whole course of His obedience."

In one sense, Jesus' entire life was a big moment. But in another, it was made up of a series of individual big moments throughout His life. And we'll look more at some of those this week.

2

Baptized into the Sins of His People

THROUGHOUT THE YEAR, WE HAVE OCCASIONALLY reflected on some of the big moments in the life of our Lord Jesus. When we were thinking about baptism, we explored the importance of Jesus' own baptism. Today, we'll think a bit more about His experience on that day.

It was a very big moment. In fact, it was so important to Him that when He looked forward to His passion, He described it as a baptism: "I have a baptism to be baptized with, and how great is my distress until it is accomplished!" (Luke 12:50).

John the Baptist said something intriguing, even enigmatic, about his own ministry of baptizing. He commented that its purpose was that the Messiah would be revealed—as indeed He was when the Spirit came upon Jesus in the form of a dove and He was identified as the Servant King by the voice of God. When Jesus appeared in the crowds to be baptized, there was something about Him that gripped John. We know that John didn't want to baptize Jesus. He said it should be the other way around because he wasn't worthy to untie Jesus' sandal.

But after Jesus' baptism, John the Baptist began to see what had happened. The dove and the voice had identified Jesus as the Lamb of God. Yes, He was spotless; He didn't need to be baptized. But He was the spotless Lamb of God who had come to take away the sin of the world. And so it was, as Jesus had said to John, "fitting" that they should "fulfill all righteousness" (Matt. 3:15). It was fitting with respect to God's purpose that the sinless One become the Sin-Bearer, and that He should be baptized as though He were a sinner Himself—indeed, as though He were *the* sinner.

Two things made this a big moment in Jesus' life. One was the event itself. To this point, Jesus had lived a relatively private life. We know almost nothing about Him between the ages of twelve and thirty, except what we can derive from things He later said and the character He displayed. After all, His holy character didn't drop from heaven the moment He was baptized. But at His baptism, Jesus sensed that He was being set apart, newly equipped, and reassured by His Father for the next stage.

In the book of Genesis, Joseph began his work as mediator and physical savior of the ancient Near East at the age of thirty. In the Mosaic administration, priests entered fully into their ministry when they were thirty years old (see Num. 4). In a similar way, the baptism of Jesus at around the same age (Luke 3:23) was His moment of ordination for His public ministry as Savior. The words spoken by God at His baptism made that clear. And after reading Isaiah 61 in the synagogue at Nazareth, Jesus made it clear that He understood His mission. The Spirit of the Lord had come upon Him to anoint and equip Him for this new public stage of ministry.

For that very reason, this event also marked a new stage of commitment on the part of the Lord Jesus. He was stepping into a new phase of His messianic task. The One who did not need to be baptized was voluntarily submitting to John's baptism. The One who had no sins to repent of, no sins to ask God to forgive, came to be symbolically drenched in the sins of others that He might carry them from the river Jordan to the cross of Calvary.

From one point of view, John was right to sense the incongruity of the situation. He was doing to Jesus what Jesus didn't need for Himself. But then it began to dawn on John what Jesus already understood. He had come to do what we sinners need done for us. And so in baptizing our Lord, John used the very water of the Jordan into which he had symbolically washed the sins of the people. The water that was symbolically polluted, full of sin, now drenched the head of the only One who didn't need the baptism. Jesus could easily have used words familiar to us from 2 Corinthians 5:21 to describe His experience: "I am being symbolically made sin, so that in Me, sinners might be made the righteousness of God."

No wonder, then, that our Lord's water baptism was a big moment in His life. He was coming as the spotless Lamb of God who would take away the sin of the world. He was being baptized into the sins of the people so that they could be baptized into His righteousness. Here, the gospel was being set forward in the form of a drama. No wonder Jesus later said, "I have a baptism to be baptized with, and how great is my distress until it is accomplished!" (Luke 12:50).

His baptism was a big moment for Him. It expressed His absolute commitment to love us to death literally—to His death.

That is why that big moment in Jesus' life is a big moment in our lives, too.

3

The Turning Point in Jesus' Ministry

YESTERDAY, WE LOOKED AT ONE BIG MOMENT in Jesus' life: His baptism in the river Jordan. Today, we'll reflect on another big moment that took place at Caesarea Philippi.

We get so used to seeing this word in the Gospels that sometimes we forget that it's *Caesar*-ea. It's somewhat like Washington, D.C., to Americans. We say the names of these cities and sometimes forget that there is a reason for them. If we're Americans, then perhaps *Washington* reminds us of the privileges of independence. But *Caesarea* reminded God's people of the opposite. They weren't the land of the free; they were under the yoke of Caesar of Rome, and most of them certainly didn't feel that they lived in the home of the brave.

There were two Caesareas in Israel. One was the port of Caesarea, located on the Mediterranean coast about sixty-five miles from Jerusalem. But this other Caesarea was in the north, in the territory of Herod's son Philip. It had earlier been called *Paneon* because the Greeks had built a shrine there to the god Pan. Herod had also built a temple there, not dedicated to Yahweh, but to Rome and to Caesar Augustus.

It was in this region that another turning point took place in our Lord's ministry. It had three main elements.

The first was Simon Peter's confession that Jesus is the Christ, the Son of the living God. Jesus made a point of telling Simon that he hadn't come to that conclusion on his own—although knowing Peter, he probably thought that he had. Rather, the heavenly Father had opened Peter's spiritual eyes, along with those of the rest of the disciples. They now knew who He was, even if it soon became clear that they didn't understand what that fully meant.

The second element was Jesus' declaration, "I tell you, you are Peter, and on this rock I will build my church, and the gates of hell shall not prevail against it" (Matt. 16:18). What Jesus is saying is this: "Here, where Satan has ruled at Caesarea Philippi, I am announcing My manifesto: Nothing on earth or in Hades will be able to prevent Me from building My church."

The third element is that it marked a significant turning point for Jesus. We're told that He then began to show the disciples that they were beginning a journey to Jerusalem. This journey would end in His suffering, His judicial execution, and His resurrection.

In one sense, it's clear that Jesus' true identity was beginning to be recognized by the disciples. Therefore, Jesus knew it was time to explain His purpose. They needed to know that His ministry would not be fulfilled in the way that they wanted, but rather in the only way possible if He was to be their Savior. Simon Peter vigorously resisted this whole idea. He seems to have physically manhandled Jesus in expressing his opposition. Jesus was building His church on enemy-occupied territory, and no sooner were His plans known than Satan opposed Him through His own chief disciple.

It's clear from the Gospels that the disciples looked back on those days as a big moment in Jesus' life. In fact, Luke, who wrote the third gospel, must have interviewed one or more of the disciples who remembered that, shortly after this, they began to notice that something had changed in Jesus' whole demeanor. From this point, Jesus set His face like flint to go to Jerusalem.

Our Lord didn't go straight from His incarnation to heaven, or even straight from His baptism to His crucifixion. It was a progression, and part of that progression was the hard work of helping His disciples understand and yield to the way of the cross. Part of this was His being willing to patiently go through with the Father's plan—a plan that involved the buildup of opposition to Him and the perfect timing of His crucifixion and resurrection.

I don't know how our Lord bore both of these tremendous strains with such grace and dignity. But I know He did it day by day for you and me. The big moments were for us.

So let's be thankful today for the obedience of our Lord Jesus all through His life, and not least in these big moments.

4

A Foretaste of Christ's Glory

THIS WEEK, WE HAVE BEEN CONSIDERING some big moments in the life of Jesus. We have looked at His baptism in the Jordan and His time with the disciples in the region of Caesarea Philippi. Today, we'll consider Jesus' time in the highlands, traditionally on Mount Hermon—often called the Mount of the Transfiguration.

Just before the transfiguration, Jesus said that some of the disciples would not see death before they saw "the kingdom of God" (Luke 9:27), "the Son of Man coming in his kingdom" (Matt. 16:28), and "the kingdom of God after it [had] come with power" (Mark 9:1). These words are linked by the Gospel writers to the transfiguration by a rare time marker—the transfiguration took place just a week later. Perhaps His words include something greater than the transfiguration, but they certainly include the experience Peter, James, and John (the inner circle of disciples) had on the mountain when they saw a foretaste of what was still to come.

Perhaps you have experienced that odd feeling that "something is going to happen"—and then it does. I remember watching a Philadelphia Flyers ice hockey game years ago. One of their star players got the puck in his own half and began to make his way toward the opponent's goal. From where I was seated up above, I could almost trace in the ice where he would need to weave his way through the defenders to get there. I'm certainly not an ice hockey expert, but amazingly, he did exactly what I had envisaged and scored a brilliant goal. I felt a bit like a chess grandmaster seeing ten moves ahead!

In a way, the transfiguration was like that. It was a moment that prophesied the future. It was a real, unique, historical event. But it was also a glimpse of what was to come, a kind of preview of the final glory of the Lord Jesus.

In John 17:24, Jesus prays that believers would be with Him to see His glory—the glory He had with His Father before the world began. Peter and his two friends were getting a glimpse of that. He says later: "For we did not follow cleverly devised myths when we made known to you the power and coming of our Lord Jesus Christ, but we were eyewitnesses of his majesty. For when he received honor and glory from God the Father, and the voice was borne to him by the Majestic Glory, . . . we ourselves heard this very voice borne from heaven, for we were with him on the holy mountain" (2 Peter 1:16–18).

It was such an overwhelming experience that it seems to have emotionally drained the three disciples who were with Jesus. They could hardly stay awake. But nevertheless, they recognized that Moses and Elijah had appeared and that they were talking with Jesus about the new "exodus" He was going to effect in Jerusalem—the redemption and salvation He would accomplish by His death and resurrection. The glory cloud of the presence of God came down and enveloped them, and God spoke very directly, "This is my beloved Son, with whom I am well pleased; listen to him" (Matt. 17:5). Then Moses and Elijah disappeared from view, and Jesus was there in solitary glory.

We don't know if this kind of experience was common for Jesus when He was praying privately. But even if it was, this was a big moment because He wanted Peter, James, and John to be with Him to see it. When John wrote the words found in John 17:24, he must surely have remembered that day years before when he saw Jesus, His whole being full of glory.

But why did Jesus want these three men in particular to witness this? No doubt it was to reassure them that He truly was the Son of God incarnate. But perhaps it was also because He knew that these same three disciples would later be stationed near Him in the garden of Gethsemane on the evening of His crucifixion. There, they would see Him in the depths of agony as He faced the shame and humiliation of the cross and asked that, if possible, the cup might be removed from Him. He surely wanted them to see that these two times of prayer were connected. The sight of His glory must have made the sight of His shame almost unbearable, but He wanted them to see where that shame would eventually lead. The glory required the shame. The shame led to the glory.

So the transfiguration was a big moment for Jesus and a big moment for these three disciples. And it's a big moment for us, too. It reminds us that the One who is Himself glorious, the Son of God, came:

Bearing shame and scoffing rude,
In my place condemned he stood,
Sealed my pardon with his blood.

Yes, indeed: "Hallelujah! what a Savior!"

5

The Cup That Could Not Pass

WE HAVE BEEN REFLECTING THIS WEEK on some of the big moments in the life of our Lord Jesus. The Apostle John says at the end of his Gospel that if everything Jesus did were written down, then "the world itself could not contain the books that would be written" (John 21:25). He must have had a smile on his face when he wrote that. It's a nice way of saying just how great and glorious the Lord Jesus really is.

John himself doesn't record all the big moments in Jesus' life that the other Gospel writers do, probably because he knew they had already recorded them. But as John Calvin says so well, the other Gospels show us Christ's body (that is, they tell the story), while John shows us His soul. That is one reason that we love John's gospel so much. But that said, there are one or two moments in our Lord's life not recorded by John that really show us Christ's soul.

One of them is surely in Matthew 11:28–30, where Jesus invites His hearers to come to Him and shows them His soul. "I am gentle and lowly in heart," He says. Additionally, while John tells us in John 12:27 and 13:21 that Jesus was deeply troubled in His spirit as the dark shadow of His passion loomed ever nearer, he doesn't mention our Lord's experience in the garden of Gethsemane.

But the garden of Gethsemane was certainly a very big moment for Jesus. He had just celebrated the Passover meal with the disciples and instituted the Lord's Supper. He had passed around that final cup of the Passover meal, "the cup of blessing," but doesn't seem to have drunk it Himself. For Him, the last cup to drink was the one that His Father was pressing into His hands in Gethsemane, "the cup of cursing," filled with the wine of the divine judgment curse.

Jesus said in Gethsemane, "My Father, if it be possible, let this cup pass from me" (Matt. 26:39). Perhaps we tend to rush too quickly to the words that follow—"Nevertheless, not as I will, but as you will"—and we don't linger long enough on the words "not as I will." When Jesus said, "Let this cup pass from me," that was an expression of His human will. In other words, He didn't want to drink the contents of the cup. Our holy Jesus, in His humanity, *couldn't* want to drink the contents of that cup, for this was the cup that the prophets had spoken about—the cup that when drunk led to alienation and a sense of God-forsakenness because of sin.

The cup that was in the Lord's hand was the cup of divine judgment. It was a cup of desolation that contained such judgment that it would undo those who drank it, utterly desolating them, making them stagger like drunk men who have been overwhelmed by what they have been drinking (see Isa. 51:17, 22; Jer. 25:15, 27; Ezek. 23:32–34; Hab. 2:16). Our holy Savior Jesus did not actively desire to experience the outer darkness of a sense of God-forsakenness—the experience He had on the cross. He had lived forever in the presence of God, so He *couldn't* desire to drink that cup. That is what makes the last part of our Lord's prayer so overwhelming: "Nevertheless, not as I will, but as you will."

The words of the Gospel writers confirm the agony of Jesus' experience. On the same night when Simon Peter was cold enough to come out of the shadows to warm his hands at a fire in the courtyard, great bloody globules pressed their way out of Jesus' body. In fact, Mark employs language that one of the greatest of the nineteenth-century New Testament scholars described in this way: "It describes the confused, restless, half-distracted state caused by physical confusion or mental derangement."

Perhaps like me you are reminded of the words of the hymn "There Were Ninety and Nine That Safely Lay," which describe Jesus the Good Shepherd seeking and finding His lost sheep:

> But none of the ransomed ever knew
> How deep were the waters crossed;
> Nor how dark was the night that the Lord passed thro'
> Ere he found his sheep that was lost.

We don't know fully, do we? We'll never plumb the depths of what that meant for our Savior. We will surely be in awe of it and in awe of Him and His love for us throughout all eternity.

How could He love us so much? And yet He did, and He still does.

WEEK 45

Romans

1

The Letter That Changed the World

DO YOU HAVE A FAVORITE BOOK OF THE BIBLE? I would guess that there are several competitors for our affections. Of course, we might wonder if this is a proper question to ask, since all Scripture is breathed out by God. But clearly there were some parts of Scripture that were more significant for Jesus than other parts, and the same is true for the Apostle Paul. So while all Scripture is God-breathed, it has particular mountain peaks. That brings us to this week's theme: Paul's letter to the Romans.

This letter is one of the soaring peaks in the Himalayas of Scripture. Some would say that it's the Mount Everest of the Bible. In the interest of full disclosure, I should probably admit that Romans is not my own favorite book in the Bible, so I'm not trying to persuade you to make it yours. But it's surely the most important book or letter that the Apostle Paul ever wrote, and it's arguably the book that has had more influence on the history of the church than any other.

Think back to the way in which Augustine describes his conversion in his *Confessions*. He was sitting in a garden and overheard a child's voice saying, "*Tolle lege*—take up and read." He picked up the New Testament and read Romans 13:14: "Put on the Lord Jesus Christ, and make no provision for the flesh, to gratify its desires." That was just a single moment in God's saving work in his life, but Augustine's influence in the Western world has been incalculable. We might even say that the whole course of Western history has been influenced by the impact of that one verse in Paul's letter to the Romans.

You're probably also familiar with the story of Martin Luther, the sixteenth-century Augustinian monk who was struggling with a burden of guilt despite the enormous efforts he made to please God. He was terrified of the righteousness of God because he was so conscious of his sin and his inability to make any compensation that would relieve his conscience.

Luther wrote that he hated Paul's words about the righteousness of God's being revealed in the gospel. But then he had his breakthrough, and light dawned. Paul was speaking about the righteousness of God in Christ, in which God counted sinners righteous because Christ had died and risen for them. Jesus Christ—not Martin Luther—had borne God's judgment. Luther said that when he discovered this he felt as though the gates of paradise had been flung open and that he'd been born again. And the rest, as they say, is history.

Perhaps like the experience of Augustine or Luther, a section or verse in Romans has changed your life—either you were converted through it, or it stimulated your progress in the Christian life, or it comforted you in a difficult period. But for this week, I want to ask you a question: "If someone were to ask you what is in the book of Romans and what it's about, how would you answer?"

I wonder what percentage of Christians could give a half-decent answer, or if, instead, most would be able to recollect only a few verses or passages here and there. In one sense, that would suggest that what Paul wanted to communicate in writing to the Romans isn't so important to us as the scattered gems that we'd found valuable in our own lives. Of course, God wants to bless us through individual verses. But don't you think He wants us to be blessed by the whole book of Romans and by its basic message?

Romans divides fairly neatly into four main sections, so looking at them one by one is going to be our task this week as we take a fairly quick helicopter ride through what is undoubtedly the greatest letter ever written.

2

None Is Righteous

TODAY, I'D LIKE TO PROPOSE A simple division to the book of Romans that may be helpful to us.

The first section of the letter runs from Romans 1:1 to 3:20.

Romans 1:1–15 is an introduction. Paul had never been to Rome, but he had long desired to go. At the end of the letter, he indicates that he hopes to visit the Romans soon. He felt that his ministry, which had stretched from Jerusalem all the way around to Illyricum, was now drawing to a close and that God was calling him to go west to Spain. He hoped to visit Rome en route. It appears that Paul was also hoping that the churches in Rome might help support him in his new mission in the same way that the church in Antioch and some of the other churches had helped him.

One of his reasons for writing Romans was to present his credentials, as it were, saying, "This is the gospel I preach." He knew that what he taught was sometimes twisted by people, and he wanted to set the record straight. In addition, as is clear from chapter 16, he seems to have known a remarkable number of church members in Rome. He had probably heard from them about some of the issues facing the church, and he wanted to help them. There is a lot going on in Romans!

In Romans 1:16–17, Paul begins his exposition of what he calls "my gospel" (Rom. 2:16). He is not ashamed of the gospel because it's the good news of God's saving righteousness. Sinners can be justified by faith in Christ, and by faith *alone*. In other words, the gospel answers the question, "How can a sinful man be righteous before a holy God?"

Then from Romans 1:18 to 3:20, Paul presents a massive argument to demonstrate the sinful and lost condition of everyone in the human race. Romans 1:18–32 is a devastating analysis of the human condition. We've been made as the image of God for the glory of God, but we've exchanged His glory for idols. We've exchanged the truth about Him for the lie. And as a result, we find ourselves under His wrath and judgment.

In Romans 2:1–16, Paul exposes the self-righteous people who agree with that judgment. He seems to talk first about gentiles (perhaps with one eye on his own people, the Jews) and then more specifically about Jews. God will judge us all according to the truth. Jesus Christ will be both the Judge and the standard of judgment, not our good opinion of ourselves. People sometimes say, "God will judge us according to the light we have had." And Paul says: "Yes, indeed, that is true. But you need to understand that means that we all stand condemned."

All who have sinned without the law (that is, the law given to Moses and the Israelites at Sinai) will perish without the law. But it isn't *not having the law* that makes us sinners. Rather, it's the way we've rebelled against the God who has revealed Himself in creation and providence and shown His eternal power, divine nature, and amazing kindness. We should have sought Him out and worshiped Him unreservedly, but we've swapped His glory for our own idols and His truth for our own lie.

Then this argument develops into a more detailed exposure of the sin of those who have had the special revelation of God recorded in the Bible and who have had the signs of God's covenant of grace, such as circumcision. Paul exposes the mistake of thinking that these privileges themselves provide us with security and make us immune from God's judgment and condemnation. "No," he says, "those who have the law and still sin will be judged and condemned by the law for that sin."

He brings all this to a crescendo in chapter 3 with a series of quotations, mainly from the Psalms, that strike like hammer blows on the casket of our dead self-righteousness: "None is righteous, no, not one" (Rom. 3:10).

The section concludes by telling us that every human being in the world is accountable and guilty before God and condemned by Him.

Paul says, "Every mouth will be shut" (see Rom. 3:19). That is actually the first step toward discovering our need of God's grace—when our mouths are shut and we realize that we have nothing to plead. We are guilty. We can't say, "We've done enough." We know we can't compensate. Our problem is guilt, and there is nothing to say in our defense. That is the message. Righteousness is lacking in us—we have none.

Thank God that this is not Paul's last word. There is good news to come. And we'll discuss that more tomorrow.

3

The Wonders of the Gospel

YESTERDAY, WE TRACED PAUL'S ARGUMENT FROM Romans 1:1 to 3:20. The conclusion is this: we're all guilty before a holy God. We stand condemned, and there is nothing we can say in our defense. Our mouths are shut. We are hopeless and helpless. Our mouths are shut and we want to look down in shame, but then we see these glorious words of Romans 3:21: "But now the righteousness of God has been manifested apart from the law."

You'll never feel the wonder of these words just by memorizing this one verse. But if you meditate on Romans 1:18–3:20, you will begin to see what overwhelmingly wonderful good news these words really are. The righteousness that is lacking in us has been provided by God. It's absolutely staggering. The holy God we have offended to the point of our condemnation is the very God who delivers us from it. In Jesus Christ, He counts us righteous through faith. And He does this without compromising His own righteousness. This is what makes grace amazing to us.

But that leaves us with a big question, of course. How can God be just and at the same time justify ungodly sinners? Paul's answer is found in Romans 3:21–24, which is often called the gospel in a nutshell. In Christ's death for our sins, God's wrath is propitiated. We are justified. The price of our redemption—our liberation from bondage to sin and Satan—has been paid.

Paul then works out in detail what this means for us in Romans 3:22–8:39.

First, he says that it means there is no boasting. Second, he says that it's consistent with the teaching of the Old Testament and the experience of Abraham and David. He does this through chapter 4. Then in Romans 5, he goes on to explain that the blessings that flow from justification and a new relationship with God mean that we now rejoice in the hope of glory, and that we can rejoice even in our sufferings. Best of all, we learn to rejoice in God Himself, though we once hated Him. And this, he says in Romans 5:12–21, is because we're no longer united to Adam but to the Lord Jesus Christ.

This leads Paul to the wonderful teaching in Romans 6–8. In simple terms, what he is saying here is that our union with Jesus Christ has staggering implications for our lives.

In chapter 6, he tells us that we have died to sin in our union with Christ, although sin has not yet died in us. But because we have died to its dominion, we're now in a position to resist it and, by God's grace, seek to overcome it.

In chapter 7, he says that we've also died to the law in Christ, and that we're set free from guilt and from the condemnation of sin, even though we are not yet made perfect according to the law's standards. As long as that is true, we will still be conscious of sinfulness within and long for the final deliverance, which only Jesus Christ can bring.

Then in chapter 8, he reassures us that we're no longer living in a state of condemnation as the result of sin. That is to say, the Christian life isn't a prison sentence. Instead, in Christ we live in the power of the Spirit and in the joy of knowing Him as the Spirit of adoption.

But the Spirit has not yet completed His work. Until He does, we will experience a kind of ache, a groaning within, as we await the day when our salvation will be consummated. But in the meantime, we know that nothing can overcome our faith, for we are more than conquerors through Him who has loved us with a love from which we can never be separated.

Trying to summarize five and a half chapters of Romans in a few minutes may leave us all feeling a bit breathless. But Paul's explanation of the gospel, the sheer wonder of God's way of salvation in Christ, *should* leave us breathless, shouldn't it? If Romans 1:18–3:20 shuts our mouths permanently, Romans 3:21–8:39 leaves us thinking: "What can I say? The glory of the gospel leaves me almost speechless." But then we remember that Paul says we do have something to say, and here it is: "What then shall we say to these things? If God is for us, who can be against us? He who did not spare his own Son but gave him up for us all, how will he not also with him graciously give us all things?" (Rom. 8:31–32).

Here's the message: righteousness is lacking in us, but righteousness has been provided for us in Jesus Christ. That is Paul's gospel. That is the gospel. That is our gospel.

Praise God for His glorious gospel.

4

The Unfailing Promises of God

WE'RE HALFWAY THROUGH OUR HELICOPTER TOUR of Paul's great letter to the Romans. Today, we've reached Romans 9–11. What are these chapters all about?

When we read Paul's letters, it's always important to ask, "Why did he move from saying *that* to now saying *this*?" How is the glory of Romans 8:31–39 related to the apparent gloom of the opening verses of Romans 9, where Paul seems to be in some distress?

Chapter 9 begins with Paul's being heartbroken because his kinsmen according to the flesh, the Jewish people who have had so many spiritual privileges, by and large have not come to faith in the Lord Jesus Christ. He even echoes Moses' words and says that he'd be willing to be accursed himself, if that were possible, if it would lead to their salvation. I suspect that being in the spiritual heights in Romans 8:31–39 may have triggered in Paul's emotions the realization that he, a Jew, had tasted the grace of Christ, but that his own people, the people he loved, for the most part wanted nothing to do with the Savior.

In addition, Paul seems to have been aware of the tensions—or at least the potential tensions—in the Roman churches between Jews and gentiles. That wasn't altogether surprising because sometime before, Claudius Caesar had expelled Jews from Rome (partly because of some conflict with the Christians). It seems that Jewish Christians had been sent away, too. They'd been allowed to return, but in the meantime, the churches in Rome must have become very gentile churches. As a result, we can imagine that perhaps the Jewish Christians who returned may have felt that they no longer really mattered. Therefore, Paul's concern for the Jews, and then his extended exposition of God's purposes for Jews and gentiles in Romans 9–11, is not only biblically and theologically significant, but also pastorally important.

What is Paul's argument in these chapters? It's this: God's Word hasn't failed. His promises have not been broken. His purposes for His ancient people need to be understood biblically. For the truth has always been that belonging to God's people has never been merely a matter of physical descent. God's grace has always worked in fallen humanity in a distinguishing election through the response of faith, as in Isaac and Ishmael or Jacob and Esau.

Paul says that what is happening in his own day is actually the fulfillment of Hosea's prophecy: God is making those who are not genetically His people become His people, and vice versa. In doing this, God acts both sovereignly and righteously. But alas, Paul's kinsmen, who had the promise of justification by grace through faith, had mistakenly tried to establish their own righteousness instead of receiving God's righteousness. Not only that, but the Old Testament had indicated that God's purposes all along had been to call gentiles to faith and salvation.

The Jews' own Bible had said that *everyone* who believes would be saved, *not just every Jew* who believes (although that was certainly true). This believing comes through hearing, and hearing comes through preaching, and preaching comes through God's sending preachers—exactly what was happening in Paul's mission to the gentiles. How sad, then, that God says of Israel, "All day long I have held out my hands to a disobedient and contrary people" (Rom. 10:21).

These words bring us to Romans 11. Gentiles have received the gospel; Jews by and large have rejected it. Has God, then, simply rejected His ancient people? No, Paul says. He himself was a Jew, and there were other Jews, a remnant, who believed in the Lord Jesus. But Paul says that a hardening had come upon others. The prophet Isaiah had already spoken of this in his day, as had King David in his.

Is this, then, the end for the Jewish people? No, Paul says, and woe be to any gentile who thinks that it is the gentiles who are now the special people. In fact, the Jews' rejection of Christ led to the gentiles hearing the gospel. Now it's Jews who see gentiles experiencing the promises of salvation that the Jews had first received. And if that makes them jealous and they turn to Christ, then, says Paul, the conversion of Jews will be like "life from the dead" (Rom. 11:15). That was his great hope and comfort.

Bible students and scholars discuss and debate exactly how Paul believed this would happen. But the great thing is that it will happen. Jewish and gentile believers will be united in Jesus Christ in the church. So it's no wonder that Paul ends up marveling at the depth of the riches and wisdom and knowledge of God.

If your head is spinning as we land the helicopter today, don't forget these last words. And join us for a slightly less intense ride tomorrow, when we'll think about the fourth—and the last—section of this great letter.

5

How Does the Gospel Work in Our Lives?

TODAY, WE COME TO THE FINAL SECTION in Paul's letter to the Romans: chapters 12–16. So far, we've seen Paul expound that righteousness is lacking in gentile and Jew, that righteousness is provided for us in Jesus Christ, and that God's righteousness has been established in both Jew and gentile in His providential ways in history. Now in these closing chapters, he wants to teach us how righteousness is realized and applied in the lives of Christian believers. In other words, he is now answering the question, "How does this gospel work out in our lives, not least in the capital city of the Roman Empire?"

Many of us understand the significance of Romans 12:1–2: the gospel transforms us as we yield ourselves to the Lord without reservation, because our minds are renewed through it by its truth. It is in this way that we learn to understand and discern the will of the Lord. Then our lives begin to manifest the righteousness to which we are called. We can summarize Romans 12–16 by saying that it teaches us about the application of righteousness in a series of concentric circles.

First, in our different spheres of life, we learn personally and individually to have a sober estimate of our gifts, and we use them for the blessing of others (12:1–8).

The way that we engage in personal relationships with others then begins to change (12:9–21). We're called to a sincere love—love that isn't hypocritical and doesn't pretend. Yet it's not a weak kind of love, because this love doesn't tolerate evil. It has a gritty stickability, as well as a wonderful freedom from self-interest. This kind of love, Paul says, is manifested in our reactions as well as in our actions.

In Romans 12:14–21, Paul probes how the believer is to react to a series of situations: to persecution with blessing (v. 14); to others' success with joy (v. 15); to others' grief with tears (v. 15); to those who are difficult by seeking harmony (v. 16); to those who are lowly, without conceit and with pleasure (v. 16); and to those who do us evil by behaving with honor (v. 17). But how is this possible in a hostile world? Paul answers that it is possible because we know that we ourselves have been under God's judgment and the Lord showed us mercy. And so we're able to leave things to the Lord and love our enemies as the Lord Jesus Christ did.

Then in Romans 13, Paul speaks about the way that this new righteousness is expressed in our attitudes to authority. The basic principle is this: the lordship of Christ liberates us to serve. We know that God has appointed a twofold ministry for us: one in the state, the other in the church. The spheres differ, but He is the Lord of both.

On the one hand, the calling of magistrates is to recognize and yield to His lordship. And on the other, our calling is to be faithful and respectful citizens. This is why Christians should make the best citizens, even in a state that is hostile toward them. The Christian remembers that the law of God is always fulfilled by a life of love. Like Augustine, we put on the Lord Jesus Christ, and we live according to the Spirit, not according to the instincts of our native flesh.

This in turn leads to another circle of teaching in Romans 14:1–15:13. This section deals with how the consecration of Romans 12:1–2 affects our life together as believers, not least when our practices differ from each other because of our personal, and sometimes strong, convictions. Here, Paul is especially thinking of Jews and gentiles who had become Christians but who had different convictions about kosher food and the observance of the Jewish calendar with its many holy days. But the principles he enunciates apply more broadly.

Paul says that freedom is for service and calls us to remember that Christ is the Lord of other believers. We are not. We all stand or fall before Jesus. He is Lord. Therefore, Paul calls us to be loving, patient, self-controlled, and self-denying, and never to flaunt our liberty. That is an important principle. You are truly free only if you don't *need to* express your freedoms. But if you *need to* flaunt those freedoms before others, you're actually still in bondage.

This finally leads Paul to share his hopes for his own ministry—a ministry that he hopes will be in partnership with the Romans.

He closes his letter by sending loving greetings to a surprising number of Christians in Rome whom he already seems to know.

We've described this week as a helicopter ride through Romans. But now let me change the imagery. I hope it's also been like one of those tour buses you find in most cities. We've just driven around to all the main sites and are at least a little familiar with them. And now it's time to go back to them one by one and spend more time at each of them.

I hope you'll do that with Paul's great letter to the Romans.

WEEK 46

Romans 8:30

1

A Golden Chain—Or Is It?

LAST WEEK, WE TOOK A QUICK TOUR of Paul's letter to the Romans. I suggested at the end that it had been like a whole-city tour-bus ride. I suggested that we could all go back and look at the wonderful sites we'd seen and spend more time on each one of them. This week, we'll do just that by spending more time in Romans 8:30: "And those whom he predestined he also called, and those whom he called he also justified, and those whom he justified he also glorified."

This verse has often been referred to as the "golden chain" or the "chain of salvation." The expression goes back at least four hundred years, and it is easy to see why it's been so popular. In this verse, it's as though Paul is describing four links in a chain that has been forged.

Notice the sense of completion. When we read the words out loud, they exude certainty. They sound like the thump, thump, thump of a well-disciplined troop of soldiers marching across the parade grounds, reliable, certain, and unconquerable: "Those He *predestined* He *called*, those He *called* He *justified*, those He *justified* he *glorified*."

That is exactly what this verse is meant to sound like. Paul has been speaking about the trials of life. A few verses later, he'll talk about situations that might threaten our sense of security in the love of Christ: tribulation, distress, persecution, nakedness, danger, or sword. That last threat was, in fact, the final threat Paul himself faced—execution by beheading, under the emperor Nero.

But Paul's confidence in the face of these facts lies not in himself and in his own plans. Rather, his security and confidence rest in God, in the reliability of His purposes, and in His ability to accomplish them. For God's purposes cannot be broken. They will not fail.

That said, it's helpful to note that Paul doesn't actually mention a chain here. Many of us are used to looking at Romans 8:30 in that way, so this observation may sound a little odd, perhaps even almost heretical. After all, this is the golden chain! I don't want to spoil that idea, because it has helped many Christians. But Paul doesn't really mention any chain here.

It's worth noting this point because seeing these words as four links in a chain can actually distort Paul's own perspective. For example, I've heard people say something like this: "Romans 8:30 is the golden chain. Predestination causes calling, calling then causes justification, and justification then causes glorification."

My question is this: "Where is the Lord Jesus in this chain?" I hope you understand my point. When we see these words as a chain, we relate predestination, calling, justification, and glorification to *each other*, one link closing around the next link, and that link closing around the next, and so on. The problem, maybe even the danger, is that by linking them to each other in this way, we haven't left any room for the Lord Jesus. We focus on predestination, calling, justification, or glorification as though somehow they existed on their own apart from Christ.

But there is something in Romans 8:30 that really helps us here. It's the very first word: "and." This indicates that God's actions—predestination, calling, justification, and glorification—don't exist in splendid isolation. Rather, they belong to something else. They are aspects of something even bigger. But what could be bigger than these things? It's this: "Those whom [God] foreknew he also predestined to be conformed to the image of his Son" (v. 29).

In other words, these wonderful privileges in Romans 8:30 are actually four aspects of our union with Christ and lead to our becoming like Him.

So if you want to think about Romans 8:30 as a golden chain, remember that it's the Lord Jesus Christ Himself who is the gold.

2

Predestination: He Loved Us First

ROMANS 8:30 SPEAKS OF FOUR GLORIOUS CONCEPTS: predestination, calling, justification, and glorification. Today, we'll look at predestination. It means deciding the destination of the journey before it actually begins. My church history professor in university didn't publish much, but he did write a book on the Scottish Reformer John Knox. One of the chapters is on Knox's teaching on predestination. As I recall, my professor noted something like this: "The Bible is a book about predestination."

That simple sentence arrested my attention. Of course, God didn't just let creation happen. Such an idea is nonsensical. Rather, God planned it—that is to say, He predestined it. He had a plan even before He created anything. The cosmos didn't one day think to itself, "It would be a good idea if I existed." That is a laughably incoherent idea.

But God's purposes, plans, and predestination involve more than the original creation. They also include our existence. That wasn't *our* decision, was it? Nor do we believe that our existence was just our parents' decision. Their actions were sovereignly superintended by the planning of God.

Occasionally, an evangelical Christian has said to me, "I don't believe in predestination." I suppose the right reply to that is: "So you don't really believe the Bible? You don't believe the Apostles? You don't believe the Lord Jesus?" Usually, they'll sputter. But hopefully, they'll also go away and think about it. Why would a Christian not believe in predestination?

It may be because, on one hand, they are prejudiced against predestination by preachers and teachers they've heard or books that they've read.

But along with that, predestination can be an unsettling teaching. How so? Because it is what we might call a bottom-line doctrine. If it's true, it means that I'm not the one who is in charge. If it's true, it means that I depend entirely on God for my salvation. If it's true, it means that God is Lord and I'm not. And so in all these different ways, it humbles us. And none of us really likes being humbled. But of course, that is exactly what we need as sinners. And so predestination is a spiritually helpful doctrine to us. And once we accept that it's the Bible's teaching, predestination becomes a wonderfully comforting and encouraging teaching.

It's always seemed a bit odd to me that the Arminian Methodist Charles Wesley could write in a hymn that he was

> Fast bound in sin and nature's night;

but that

> Thine eye diffused a quick'ning ray;
> I woke, the dungeon flamed with light;
> My chains fell off . . .

This is actually a confession that we're not able to save ourselves. Indeed, as Jesus says, we're not even able to see and enter the kingdom of God ourselves (John 3:3, 5). God needs to bring us to new birth. And all that means that we need God to be acting first. And if He is the first actor, then He surely planned to act beforehand—and that is predestination.

We should think of this often as Christians: Even before we were born, God had set His heart on us (incidentally, that is what "foreknew" means in Romans 8:29). Even before I was born, He had planned my salvation. He planned that He would take my broken and marred life and transform it by His grace so that the Lord Jesus would be reflected in me.

Isn't that amazing? What love, what grace, what security—and yes, what planning. And this reassures me that even though I am weak, His purposes stand forever.

Martin Luther's superior in his monastery was a man by the name of Johann von Staupitz. Staupitz once said to Brother Martin when he was troubled by this doctrine of predestination, "Martin, seek predestination in the wounds of Christ."

There is something wise about that, I think. I can't climb to heaven and pry into the mind of God and His plans. I won't find any answers to my questions about predestination in myself either, except why I so badly need it. But when I take hold of Jesus Christ in faith and come to love Him, He surely responds to me, "Yes, My child, but I loved you first." We love Him because He first loved us. That is the heart of predestination.

So thanks be to God that those whom He predestined, He also called, justified, and glorified.

3

Calling: Awake, O Sleeper

AS WE CONTINUE OUR STUDY OF Romans 8:30, today we'll focus on *calling*.

Calling is a word that right from the beginning indicates God's sovereign grace. Earlier in Romans 4:17, Paul described God as the One who "calls into existence the things that do not exist."

Theologians have sometimes distinguished between what they call the *general call*, the *gospel call*, and the *effectual call* of God.

Psalm 19, for example, describes this *general call*:

The heavens declare the glory of God,
     and the sky above proclaims his handiwork.
Day to day pours out speech,
     and night to night reveals knowledge. (Ps. 19:1–2)

This is the teaching that we find in Romans 1:18 and following: God has so sufficiently revealed Himself in the created order that, through it, we are summoned to know Him, to trust Him, to love Him, and to worship Him.

By *gospel call* we mean the proclamation of the good news about Jesus as Savior and Lord. Just as Jesus Himself said, "Come to Me," we continue to issue His call, His summons, His invitation to come in faith to Him, to trust Him as Savior, and to live for Him as Lord.

Sometimes the much-loved words of Revelation 3:20 have been used to express this. In the gospel call, Christ stands at the door and knocks, seeking our response of faith and repentance. If anyone opens the door, Christ will come in and eat with him, and he with Christ.

Of course, these words were first addressed to professing Christians. But it's still legitimate for us to use them as a presentation of the gospel to those who are not yet Christians. Yet we always need to remember that according to Ephesians 2:1–2, all those to whom that call is addressed are dead in trespasses and sins. To put it bluntly, Christ calls us, but we are unable to hear, get up, or open the door.

Therefore, this gospel call on its own doesn't necessarily prove effective. It needs to be accompanied by the work of the Holy Spirit, who enables us to respond, to open the door, and to welcome the Lord Jesus.

That is what theologians mean when they speak about the *effectual call*, and this is what Paul is talking about in Romans 8:30: those whom God predestined, He also effectually called to Himself. It's not that there are two different messages—a gospel call, and also an effectual call that is very different from the gospel call. Rather, it's one message. But what theologians have distinguished is that apart from the work of the Spirit, the message of the gospel call falls on deaf ears and blind eyes, and it will therefore be ineffectual in terms of bringing us to salvation.

How, then, do we experience the effectual call?

Our spiritual forefathers liked to use a biblical picture here. They spoke of being *awakened*. It's a picture that Paul uses in Ephesians 5:14, perhaps quoting the verse of an early hymn:

Awake, O sleeper,
and arise from the dead,
and Christ will shine on you.

It's a great picture, isn't it? We're spiritually sleeping the sleep of death. But there's a voice calling us in the proclamation of the gospel, a voice like the one that called to Lazarus when he slept in death. This voice is so powerful that the dead begin to hear it.

Perhaps this picture brings back memories of your mom or dad's waking you up in the morning by calling your name. Sometimes they'd been calling your name for some time before it penetrated your ears and you began to hear it. The voice then woke you up. You recognized your name, opened your eyes, and saw your mom's face looking at you. A new day had begun.

It's like that when we are effectually called. There is a call—perhaps it's been repeated in our hearing again and again—and then, wonderfully, we are awakened. We realize that it's Christ who's calling us by name to come to Him. Then we can sing, with my favorite Scottish hymn writer, Horatius Bonar:

> I heard the voice of Jesus say,
> "Come unto me and rest;
> Lay down, O weary one, lay down
> Your head upon my breast."
> I came to Jesus as I was,
> Weary and worn and sad;
> I found in him a resting place,
> And he has made me glad.

I hope that you're among the awakened, that you've heard that voice, and that its call has been effectual in your life, too.

4

Justification: Final and Irreversible

SOMETHING VERY FUNNY HAPPENED YEARS AGO when several of the Ligonier teaching fellows were sitting around a table recording a program.

Right at the end of the recording, we were talking about how to read the Bible. I used an illustration of how when I was young, peppermints were the standard candy. When I was given one, I tended to crunch it so that it was gone in a couple of minutes, whereas older people sucked them and could make them last for half an hour. I wanted to make the point that we should meditate and suck slowly on verses of Scripture. Right at the end, I made this confident pronouncement: "So when it comes to reading the Bible, we shouldn't be *crushers*; we should be *suckers*." There was a kind of stunned silence. Nobody spoke. For a moment, I thought they were amazed at my insight and brilliant illustration. Then I realized what I'd said!

I'm not sure if the outburst of laughter was at the look of horrified realization on my face or at the fact I'd mistakenly thought I'd used a tremendous illustration. I hope my insight was edited out. And since the teaching fellows are my friends, they don't constantly remind me of the occasion, and I think they've forgiven me.

I'm not going to use that terrible illustration ever again, but I mention it today because it is so terrible that it might actually remind you of the point I was so badly illustrating: that we need to linger on the teaching of Scripture. That is what we're doing this week. We're sucking its theology from Romans 8:30, like bees gathering nectar.

Paul is teaching us that we're united to Christ in order to be transformed into His likeness. For this to happen, it must begin in the Lord's own plans and purposes in His predestination. Then we must be drawn into that plan by His effectual calling. By His Word and Spirit, we are awakened to faith in the Lord Jesus, so that now in Christ every spiritual blessing becomes ours.

At the heart of these blessings is the one that Paul now mentions: "Those whom he predestined he also called, and those whom he called he also *justified*" (emphasis added).

This means a great deal. So much so that Paul has spent several chapters in Romans explaining why we need justification, and then he goes on to explain the amazing privileges it brings, saying, "Therefore, since we have been justified by faith, we have peace with God through our Lord Jesus Christ" (5:1). He speaks about our rejoicing in the hope of glory, rejoicing in our sufferings, and rejoicing in God Himself.

I sometimes think that this section of Romans is like a suitcase that a wife has packed for her husband before he goes on a journey. When he is preparing to come home, he tries to get everything back into the suitcase and realizes that there seems to be more in it now than there was when he left home. Romans 5:1–11 is like that—blessing upon blessing tumbles out of the suitcase of our justification.

But today, I want to emphasize this point: Paul uses a completed tense: *justified*. He could have said *justifies*: "Those He calls He justifies." But by speaking of a completed action, he gives a wonderful sense of finality. It's done. It's complete. It's irreversible.

We need to linger on this because it's an element in the gospel that feeds our assurance. The criminal trial, the court of law—it's all past. The verdict has been pronounced. There is no double jeopardy. In Christ, the penalty for my sin has been paid. He took my guilt so that I might be counted righteous, justified in His righteousness.

Paul had said earlier that Jesus "was delivered up for our trespasses and raised for our justification" (Rom. 4:25). His resurrection was the equivalent of God saying to Him: "You have paid the penalty for the sins that were not Yours, but theirs. The debt is cleared." And now the prison doors are flung open for Christ, and He emerges from the tomb, never to die again, and never *needing* to die again. He was once condemned. Now He is forever, eternally, fully justified.

Here's the truly wonderful thing about the gospel: when we believe into Jesus Christ, we, too, are fully and finally justified. From the moment you trusted in Christ, you were as justified as He now is—as completely, permanently, irreversibly, eternally justified as the Savior because you're justified with His righteousness and His justification.

Even if you are a new Christian, you are as justified as the holiest saint in Christian history. The person who became a Christian yesterday is as justified as the person who became a Christian fifty years ago. That is the sheer wonder and glory of being justified by faith. It's yours now. It's perfect and complete because Jesus Christ has given you His righteousness.

Isn't the gospel absolutely amazing?

5

Glorification: Perfected in Christ

THIS WEEK, WE'VE BEEN REFLECTING ON the words of Paul in Romans 8:30. Their sheer power is amazing. I heard it said once that Charles Spurgeon read them on one occasion when he was preaching and commented, "Brethren, there is no stopping this God." It's absolutely wonderful. And Paul has kept the best for last: *glorification*.

There is kind of a Russian-doll effect in this verse. Open up predestination in Christ, and you find calling by Christ inside. Open up calling, and you find justification in Christ inside. Open up justification, and you find glorification and likeness to the Lord Jesus inside. It also reminds me of the famous long-running BBC TV series *Doctor Who*. The gospel is like Doctor Who's time machine. On the outside, it's an old, battered London police phone box. But it's larger on the inside than it is on the outside. And it's full of marvels.

Isn't that true when we think about the gospel and its effect on us? On the outside, we are basically nobodies—specks of dust in a vast cosmos. But God has set His heart on glorifying us. Our lives are as big as that. He is putting glory into us, making our humanity eventually glorious—and all because He loves us. What could be more amazing, moving, thrilling, wonderful, and comforting to us than that?

There is a whole new world in this one word "glorified," and today we will reflect on only a couple of details.

The first is this: What is glorification? There is a big answer to that question, but there is also a wonderfully simple answer that we've already seen. On Monday, I pointed out that Romans 8:30 begins with an "and." It's connected to verse 29, and it spells out how verse 29 comes to pass. Verse 29 says that God "predestined us to be conformed to the image of his Son." Verse 30 says that this happens when God, who predestines us, also glorifies us.

Do you see the parallels? The parallelism is between the statements "God conforms us to the image of His Son" and "God glorifies us." Glorification is simply the final reality of our conformity to the likeness of Jesus. God is creating a new family, and all its members will need predestining, calling, and justifying. But all those actions are preliminary to our bearing the family likeness.

Of course, each of us will retain our individuality. The disciples on the Mount of Transfiguration could recognize Moses and Elijah. I think that suggests to us that although we're all members of the same family, and all will be made like our Elder Brother, Jesus Christ, it will still be our unique selves as individuals who will have become like Him. In that new world, we'll be able to recognize one another. But maybe when we see one another for the first time, we'll say, "Wow, you really are like Jesus now."

There is something else here that you're bound to have noticed and perhaps even been a little puzzled by. Paul doesn't say, "And those whom He called He also justified, and those whom He justified He will one day in the future glorify." Rather, he says, "Those whom he *justified* he also *glorified.*" All these verbs are verbs of completion.

Paul speaks in 2 Corinthians 3:18 about our being transformed into Christ's likeness "from one degree of glory to another." That means that there is already a degree of glory in our lives. So it is possible that in Romans 8, Paul means that the glory we look forward to has already begun. It's not just a thing of the future; it already has a here-and-now dimension. That is part of our experience of living in the already accomplished work of God and looking forward to its finalization.

That may well be the right interpretation, and it may be that putting the whole sentence in the past helped Paul communicate the way that all these blessings we receive in Jesus Christ belong together. You don't receive one of them without receiving all of them. Maybe that is why he didn't put it in the present tense and say, "Those He justified, He is also now beginning to glorify," in case anyone made the mistake of thinking that it had started but might not actually be completed.

Most commentators on Romans tend to believe that Paul says "glorified" in the completed tense because he wants to underline that the work of God that has started is absolutely secure and so certain to be brought to completion that it's as good as finished. It's guaranteed for everyone who is in Christ.

If you've been justified, then you *will* be glorified. Your justification can't be repealed. It can't be reversed. It can't be added to. But one day it's going to be crowned, and that is glorification. And that glorification is as certain as though you already had it now.

What amazing privileges are ours in Christ. So let's enjoy them. And I hope if you've never memorized Romans 8:30, you now know it by heart.

WEEK 47

The Four Last Things

1

Identifying the Four

WHEN WE'RE CHILDREN, THE END OF THE YEAR and the Christmas holidays seem to come so slowly. But the older we get, the more likely we are to say, "Where did the year go, and what have I accomplished?"

Long before Einstein's theory of special relativity, people used to say, "Time is relative." And the fact is, the more time there is in your past, the faster you seem to hurtle into the future. This week, we're going to think about that future, but not in the sense of making plans for the holiday season. Rather, we'll talk about the future that we sometimes, perhaps even often, don't like to think about: our own individual, ultimate future.

The big theological word that describes these final realities is *eschatology*—thinking or talking about the last things. Theologians sometimes subdivide that topic into *corporate* and *personal* eschatology. *Corporate eschatology* refers to what will happen to the whole cosmos at the end of history, while *personal eschatology* refers to what happens to us as individuals at the end of our lives. It's the latter that we will reflect on this week.

Christians have often spoken about personal eschatology in a fourfold way. In some church traditions, ministers were expected to preach about these topics on the four Sundays before Christmas as a way of preparing people for the celebration of Jesus' birth. I suspect that if our ministers were to do that this year, some people in our churches might be a bit upset. These pastors might be seen as the Rev. Mr. Grinch stealing Christmas. But perhaps that says more about us than about our forefathers. Maybe we don't want to be that serious at Christmastime. Yet such a series might have a very beneficial effect on our Christian lives and help us to live more clearly to the glory of God.

The "four last things" are *death, judgment, heaven,* and *hell*. These are words that can send a little shiver down our spines. We can be quite resistant to them. Certainly, three out of four of them are not pleasant thoughts for sinful men and women. We might say, "Well, the people who thought about these things in the past lived much nearer to these things than we do." Of course, in one sense that is true of death. In those days, people almost always died at home without the pain relief that is available today, surrounded by their family members and usually conscious. But the death rate wasn't any higher in the seventeenth century than it is in the twenty-first century. It's still 100 percent.

But that alone wasn't the reason that Christians were encouraged to think about these things. Rather, it was the sheer frequency with which the Bible itself refers to them.

There was another deeply biblical reason that meditating on these things was encouraged. It's because our Christian lives are shaped by the way that we think about the future. It's not possible to think about these themes without becoming a more serious Christian. And since life is short and eternity is long, meditation on the four last things weans us off our addiction to the things that are seen and temporary and helps us focus our gaze and reorient our lives to the things that are unseen and eternal. Our modern times constantly encourage us to look through a microscope at the things of this world, when what we truly need is to be looking through a telescope at the world to come.

So meditation on the four last things helps to transform us from being this-world-oriented and microscopic in our Christian vision, and it turns us into Christians who are oriented to the world to come. As C.S. Lewis once famously commented that the Christians who make most impact on this world are usually the ones who think most of the world to come.

That is what we will try to do this week.

2

Death

AS WE LOOK THIS WEEK AT THE SUBJECT OF the "four last things," today we will try to think about the first of them: death.

Death is not a subject on which most of us want to linger. There are good reasons for not wanting to think about it: one is that we don't want it to happen. We love life, and we love the people in our lives. Life is such an amazing gift from God. We didn't choose to have life, and we didn't contribute to its beginning. Even our parents didn't know who they were going to get. But we love being alive, and if we're Christians, we love the world in which we live because it's God's creation. We see people who go through enormous trials, privation, and suffering, yet they still love life because they love the Lord, and they love being in the world He made.

One of the most fascinating things about God's common grace is that people who seem to be quite unpleasant individuals are still given the gift of loving life. We have an inborn love for and concern about our world, and family and friends mean so very much to us that we don't want to lose them. We are made to love life, not to hate it.

When we no longer love life, something has become disordered either in our bodies or in our minds. And death itself, from a biblical point of view, is a disorder. Sometimes we read of someone famous who "died of natural causes." But nobody truly dies of natural causes. Death is not natural, according to Scripture; it's unnatural. It's disruptive of the created order. It's an enemy of the life that God created human beings to enjoy.

Because of that, it's quite natural for us to hate death because it leads to disintegration. That is why Paul says in a magisterial statement in Romans 5:12 that sin came into the world through one man, and death through sin. Sin is the reason why we all die—Adam's sin, others' sin, and our own sin.

Sin is the sting of death, and it injects corruption into our mortal bodies. We were wonderfully created out of the dust, given the breath of life, and created as the image of God (Gen 2:7; 1:26–28). But now it is as though we had received a lethal injection. The result is that death will work its way into every particle of our physical being, and we will disintegrate into the dust from which we came.

So when we love life as Christians and learn to think properly about death, then we hate it for what it is in itself and for what it does. We're going to die. Our bodies are going to disintegrate. The future for our bodies is bleak, and it's worse than bleak for someone who isn't a believer.

People who say that they love life but view death with equanimity must therefore be self-deceived. A more realistic depiction of a proper response to death is seen in the famous poem by the Welsh poet Dylan Thomas, where he speaks of his agony about the way his father died:

Do not go gentle into that good night,
Old age should burn and rave at close of day;
Rage, rage against the dying of the light.

How wonderful it is when the gospel of Jesus Christ bursts onto the stage as a message of hope, faith, and love. How blessed the day when Jesus' death removed the sting of death! How blessed the day when, in His resurrection, death was defeated. And how blessed will be the day of His return, when He will finally destroy death. Death and Hades will be thrown into the lake of fire, never to appear again (Rev. 20:14).

That is why, for believers, the same death that is our enemy also becomes an entrance into life eternal with Jesus Christ, who has conquered death.

When we breathe our last, we will be able to say to those whom we love in Christ: "I go gently into this good night to be with Christ. I love you, and I will see you in the morning."

3

The Coming Judgment

THE "FOUR LAST THINGS" THAT WE are discussing this week help us to see how much we need the Lord Jesus.

Yesterday, we looked at death, and today, we will think about judgment. Hebrews 9:27 says, "It is appointed for man to die once, and after that comes judgment."

Have you ever heard someone say, "I don't believe in judgment"? People can certainly try to convince themselves to believe something that they know isn't true. But Paul says in Romans 1:18–32 that we all know that God exists. We know there is a judgment, but sinners suppress and eventually deny that truth. Paul goes on to say that however hard we try to suppress the knowledge that our lives will be judged, we can never finally do it.

But what is that judgment of God? Since God is the Judge of all the earth and does what is right, it ought to be important to us to know something about His judgment. And He doesn't leave us in the dark. He tells us about this judgment in His Word. One of the fullest passages is Romans 2:1–16, where the Apostle Paul makes a series of powerful points.

The first is that God's judgment is always righteous. When He judges, He judges rightly (v. 2). On the last day, "God's righteous judgment will be revealed" (v. 5).

Second, God's judgment will assess what we have done. "He will render to each one according to his works" (v. 6). That really does mean each and every one of us. As Paul says in 2 Corinthians 5:10, we will all appear before the judgment seat to receive what we have done in the body. The great Scottish church leader Thomas Chalmers was right to say that there is a present justification for Christians according to grace and a future judgment or assessment according to works.

Third, God's judgment will be impartial: "God shows no partiality" (Rom. 2:11). On that day before God's judgment seat, no one will be able to say, "But don't You know who I am?"

Fourth, God's judgment is discriminating in the sense that it is discerning and judicious. His judgment sees through our professions to our practices. It detects the difference between seeking His glory and honor and seeking our own.

Fifth, God's judgment will be fitted to the revelation we have received. Sometimes it's said that we'll be judged according to the light that we had. In one sense, that is true. But it's vital to notice Paul's bottom line here. He says that even people who have not had the special revelation that God gave to Israel in the law are still made in the image of God, and they still have the remnants of the law written on their hearts. They will be judged according to the light that they've had, and there will be only one possible verdict: guilty as charged, and condemned.

Sixth, Paul says that God's judgment has a norm, and that norm is the Lord Jesus Christ: "God judges the secrets of men by Christ Jesus" (v. 16). Jesus' life is the standard. We need to understand what that means. It won't be possible to say to God, "You didn't understand," or "Your standards were inhuman," or "We had to face all kinds of difficulties that You don't know anything about." We won't be able to say any of those things standing before the Lord Jesus.

Seventh, God's judgment will result in glory and honor for those who are His but wrath and fury for those who have rejected Him.

That is sobering, isn't it? It underlines how foolish it would be to think that we could say to God, "I know You sent Your Son to die to save us from condemnation, but I found my own way to be counted righteous before You." "There is no other name under heaven given among men by which we must be saved" (Acts 4:12). If it was necessary for the Son of God to die to bring us into the presence of God with joy, who on earth do we think we are that we can find our own way?

Judgment is an enormously serious subject. Let us thank God that He has found a way to bring the forgiveness of sins to us.

4

What Will Heaven Be Like?

TODAY, WE COME TO THE THIRD OF THESE "four last things"—death, judgment, and now heaven.

It's been a week of heavy reflections, and there is still one more to come. But today, the clouds part, the sun shines, and glory appears—heaven is our theme. And who doesn't want to go to heaven?

That is a more searching question than we might at first think. Years ago, I was driving some distance in Scotland to speak at a weekend conference. As I was listening to BBC radio in the car, I was surprised to discover a program about heaven. Of course, it attracted my interest immediately. For the next thirty minutes, I listened to a series of interviews with very well-known personalities who were all asked the same question: "What do you think heaven will be like?"

I began to notice a consistent pattern in their replies. It was the same in every single interview. It wasn't what was said. Rather, it was what *wasn't* said, not even once. Not once in all the descriptions of heaven did anybody mention the presence of God. I was reminded of the words of the psalmist: "God is in none of his thoughts" (Ps. 10:4, NKJV).

What a staggering illustration. If you don't want God at the center of your life now, then you won't want Him at the center of the world to come. The person who lives without God naturally imagines a heaven without God. But as we'll see tomorrow, a future world without God can't possibly be heaven.

That series of interviews serves as an illustration of a puzzle we often encounter: Why do people who haven't wanted God during their earthly lives think that dying will change all that? Why do they think that they'll suddenly start to trust, love, and adore Him? And the answer to those questions, affirmed by the content of the interviews, is this: They won't. They don't want life with God; therefore, they don't really hope for heaven. The tragic mistake is to live without God and then die without God.

But what does heaven mean for those who do walk with God in this life? It means being in the presence of God in a way that we can only barely glimpse here on earth. It means experiencing the reality that is so beautifully pictured for us in John's vision in Revelation 4–5. That is why the central message of the book of Revelation is actually easy to grasp, even if some of the details seem mysterious. Heaven is where God is enthroned in glory, where the Lord Jesus is seen as the Lion-King who became the slain Lamb, where the presence of the Spirit feels like rivers of fresh water, and where amazing supernatural creatures are soloists in leading the heavenly anthems. It's a place where elders and martyrs lead a choir of innumerable size, where angels and men agree and sing from the same hymnbook.

Of course, all this is symbolic language. But the important thing to grasp is that the reality is greater than the symbol. And when we experience the reality, we will see that it's totally consistent with the pictures that we've been given—only greater, more real, more wonderful, and more beautiful.

I remember as a teenager dreaming that I'd died and gone to heaven and was being greeted by Christian friends who were already there.

I saw myself pushing them aside (I'm not sure if pushing is actually allowed in heaven, but this was a dream, after all). And I still remember saying to them: "Let me get to Jesus. I want to see Jesus." That will be heaven. He is at its center. And we need to understand that there is no other heaven than the one in which our Lord Jesus is present and reigns.

We have many questions about heaven. Here there is space to answer only two of them.

The first is, "When do Christians go to heaven?" The answer is, "The moment we die" (Luke 23:43; Phil. 1:23).

A second question often asked is, "Will we recognize each other in heaven?" The answer to that question is "Yes." After all, we'll recognize Jesus. But it may just take a few minutes before we recognize our dearest friends who have been transformed into His likeness. Then we'll say: "*That is* who you are. That is absolutely glorious."

And all this awaits those who trust in Jesus Christ.

5

The Reality of Hell

TODAY, WE'LL WRAP UP OUR WEEK OF CONSIDERING "the four last things." We've already looked at death, judgment, and heaven, and today our subject is hell. We've kept to the traditional order in which these four things have been covered historically during Advent, but I suppose many of us would rather have reversed the last two.

People sometimes say that we don't know much about heaven, but that is not strictly true. We haven't experienced much of it, but the Bible has a lot to say about it. We could say that we know even less about hell, which is true. Nevertheless, the Bible does have quite a lot to say about it. It's often said with some degree of truth that Jesus spoke more often about hell than anyone else in the Bible. The fact that our loving Lord Jesus did so is a sobering fact about a sobering truth. But He spoke about it because He loves us.

I once heard a story that a member of the British royal family asked a clergyman in the Church of England if there is a hell. The clergyman apparently replied, "Your Highness, the Bible says so, Jesus taught so, and the articles of the Church of England affirm so," to which the member of the royal family reportedly responded, "Then why in God's name do you not tell us about it?"

What is hell? The Bible doesn't try to answer that question in subtle philosophical terms. Rather, it paints pictures because its basic concern is to tell us how to avoid it. It also tells us *why* we need to avoid it. To be in hell means to be separated from all the privileges and blessings not only of God's saving grace, but of God's common grace. What that means can't fully be described in terms we can grasp. It's too awful to understand. All we know is a world in which God is present and kind in His common grace, even to those who are rebels against Him. That is why our Lord paints these pictures for us—pictures we can understand, feel, and sometimes almost smell.

Today, we'll focus on just one statement that gets us to the heart of the Bible's teaching. In 2 Thessalonians 1:9, Paul speaks about God's final judgment on those who reject Him. He says, "They will suffer the punishment of eternal destruction, away from the presence of the Lord and from the glory of his might."

That is a very densely packed statement. Notice some of its features. Hell is being "away from the presence of the Lord." That is simply a way of saying that hell is ongoing life in death. It is life separated from the blessings that flow from the One who is the source of all blessing. It is existence that has nothing positive about it—only everlasting negativity.

Hell is also an existence of punishment. That suggests that people in hell know why they are there: their own rebellion against the loving

God who offered life, which they rejected and despised. In the words of C.S. Lewis: "There are only two kinds of people in the end: those who say to God, 'Thy will be done,' and those to whom God says, in the end, 'Thy will be done.' All that are in Hell, choose it."

Perhaps that is why Jesus refers to the "weeping and gnashing of teeth" (Matt. 8:12), the sobering thought of the permanent regret, the anger against God that has grown to its fulfillment. That is why we understand from Scripture that God takes our response to Him with utter and eternal seriousness.

Paul says that hell is "eternal" or "everlasting destruction." By this, he doesn't mean annihilation, but rather the deconstruction and demolition of life as it was intended to be. It reminds me of the words of the Puritan writer Thomas Brooks:

> Oh—but this word Eternity! Eternity! Eternity! this word Everlasting! Everlasting! Everlasting! this word Forever! Forever! Forever! will even break the hearts of the damned in ten thousand pieces. . . . Impenitent sinners in hell shall have end without end, death without death, night without day, mourning without mirth, sorrow without solace, and bondage without liberty. The damned shall live as long in hell as God himself shall live in heaven.

What a sobering word that is in the Advent season as we approach Christmas. Yet it does have this effect of showing us why the coming of our Lord Jesus was so absolutely necessary and why it is the most glorious news in the world. He is called *Jesus* because He will save His people from their sins.

I hope that you are trusting Him as your Savior and following Him as your Lord.

WEEK 48

Titles of Jesus

1

Knowing Jesus

THERE IS MORE THAN ONE WAY to answer the question, "Who are you?" For example, in the United Kingdom, plumbers seem to be very difficult to find. So if someone appeared at the door of my house and replied to my question by saying, "I'm the plumber," I might be ecstatic. But in a different situation, I might not be satisfied with that reply. I might say: "No, I mean, *who* are you? What's your name?" Even then, I may not be satisfied just with a name.

When we ask this question, what we really want to know is the person himself or herself. We're seeking information on questions like these: "What's your character? What are you like? If I get to know you, what am I going to discover? Should I trust you? Will I like you? Will I want you as my friend?" Of course, a person's name, occupation, and character are all involved in answering the question, "Who are you?" The answer to this question also tends to determine the kind of relationship we will have with a person and, in turn, how we answer someone else's question when they ask, "Do you know so-and-so?"

People often ask me that question, "Do you know so-and-so?" I don't mean to be awkward and irritating when I sometimes reply, "Well, it depends on what you mean by *know*." And even when the answer is, "Yes, I know them," I don't know someone as well as his closest friends do or his wife does. And we recognize that even in the case of the person we know best, we still don't fully understand who and what they are. That is true even of those who are our dearest friends. Even in the case of the person we know best, there is still so much more to know about them. Therefore, our knowledge can keep growing.

If that is true in the case of our day-to-day relationships, it's also true of knowing the Lord Jesus Christ. What do you say when someone asks, "Do you know Jesus Christ?" Of course, knowing Christ is not the whole of the gospel because the gospel is "the gospel of God" (Rom. 1:1). It's not only Christological (about Christ); it's theological (about God the Trinity). There is ultimately no gospel without the Father and the Spirit. But knowing Jesus Christ is certainly at the heart of the gospel, because it's in and through Jesus Christ that we have access to God and come to know Him.

As Paul puts it in Ephesians 2:18, it's through Christ and by the Spirit that we have access to the Father. This echoes the teaching of Jesus: "No one knows the Father except the Son and anyone to whom the Son chooses to reveal him" (Matt. 11:27). These words immediately precede His great invitation to all who labor and are heavy laden to come to Him and to find rest (v. 28). Therefore, knowing Jesus Christ means resting in Jesus Christ.

At the beginning of His High Priestly Prayer in John 17, Jesus says that eternal life is to "know you, the only true God, and Jesus Christ whom you have sent" (John 17:3). Therefore, knowing Jesus Christ is Christianity 101.

Today, we'll consider just one point on this topic, but it's a big one: the New Testament was given to us ultimately by the Lord Jesus Himself, through His Apostles, so that we can get to know Him. That is what our Lord told the Apostles in the upper room just before His crucifixion, although they didn't understand this truth until later. He said that He was going to send the Spirit to them, and when the Spirit came, He would glorify Jesus by showing Him to them.

Jesus said that this would happen in three ways. First, the Spirit would remind the Apostles of everything Jesus had taught them. Second, He would lead them into all the truth about Himself. And third,

He would show them the things that were still to come (John 14:26; 16:13–14).

If you think about it, that is an amazing summary of the whole New Testament. The Gospels tell us what Jesus taught by word and deed. Acts records how the Spirit led the Apostles into the truth, while the letters expound that truth. And Revelation (along with some other parts of the New Testament) tells us the things that are still to come.

This helps us understand the basic answer to the question, "How do I get to know Jesus?" The answer is this: Read and reread your New Testament. Of course, knowing the New Testament isn't the same thing as knowing Jesus, but you can't get to know the Author without reading His Book. That is something we will need to think more about tomorrow.

2

Who Do You Say That I Am?

YESTERDAY, WE STARTED TALKING ABOUT KNOWING CHRIST. We noted briefly that our access to that knowledge comes through the pages of the New Testament. Since we can't cover the whole New Testament in one week, we'll focus our gaze the next few days on something that our Lord Himself said to help His disciples. He asked them at Caesarea Philippi, "Who do the crowds say that I am?" The disciples answered, "John . . . , or Elijah, [or] one of the prophets." Then Jesus asked them a more direct question: "But who do *you* say that I am?" (Luke 9:18–20, emphasis added).

It's interesting that the crowds didn't simply say, "Well, He is Jesus of Nazareth." That would have been true. But there was something about Jesus that made people look for a different category of answer. It seems that everyone Jesus encountered during His public ministry realized His uniqueness. His name was *Jesus*, but there was something bigger about His identity.

His opponents certainly wished that He could have just been described as "Jesus." Pontius Pilate probably thought that. But Pilate also felt compelled to ask, "Tell me who You really are." Everyone who met Him sensed that they needed to reach beyond their ordinary ways of describing someone if they were to discover who Jesus really was. They were intrigued by Him. He was like one of His own parables. There was a mystery, a puzzle, about Him that many were trying to solve.

When Jesus asked the disciples about His identity, Peter blurted out the right answer: "You are the Christ, the Son of the living God" (Matt. 16:16). It almost immediately became clear that Peter himself didn't understand his answer very well. But we know he gave the right answer because Jesus said to him, "Flesh and blood has not revealed this to you, [Peter,] but my Father who is in heaven" (v. 17).

What's interesting is that the crowds were struggling to identify Jesus by thinking in terms of specific individuals from the Old Testament. Was He perhaps one of the prophets of the old covenant? King Herod wondered if Jesus was John the Baptist, whom he had executed. But Simon Peter identifies Jesus by using not personal names but titles. And these were not titles he had made up himself. We don't know whether these ideas about Jesus had been slowly germinating in his mind or if they came to him like a light bulb being turned on in an "*aha* moment."

What Peter had come to realize was that Jesus was someone about whom the Old Testament had already spoken. He did not need to make up new categories that would help him understand Jesus. Those categories had already been given to him in the Hebrew Scriptures. We could even say that when Peter blurted out his answer, he was at last discovering the meaning of some very important passages in his Hebrew Bible. It was as though now that he was face-to-face with Jesus, he could at last say: "Oh, that is what these passages really mean. That is who they were talking about. That is who Jesus is."

What are these titles? "You are the Christ, the Son of the living God." We'll explore these titles over the next few days. But today, let's close by reflecting on how wonderful it is when people's eyes have been opened to discover who Jesus really is. Perhaps they've known about Jesus, but then the heavenly Father, through the Holy Spirit, works in their hearts, and they recognize at last the truth about Him.

I wonder if you're one of those people who have known about Jesus all their lives, but it's only recently that the Father has revealed His Son to you.

If that hasn't already been your experience, then please begin to ask God to do it for you just as He did it for Peter.

3

Christ, the Anointed One

YESTERDAY, WE LOOKED AT SIMON PETER'S answer to Jesus' question, "Who do you say that I am?" He replied, "You are the Christ, the Son of the living God" (Matt. 16:15–16).

Near the beginning of his gospel, John tells us that when Peter's brother, Andrew, first brought him to meet Jesus, he said to him, "We have found the Messiah" (John 1:41). So although we often think of Peter's confession as a kind of sudden moment of revelation, it looks much more likely that it was the flowering of a seed that had been planted in his mind by his brother. But now for the very first time, Peter was saying it out loud, and he was saying it to Jesus. That was a big moment.

But what did Peter mean?

Christ, or its Hebrew equivalent, *Messiah*, means "anointed one." We know that certain individuals and objects in the Old Testament were anointed with oil to set them apart for God's use. For example, Exodus 29 tells us how Aaron and his sons were anointed with oil. The ritual was so sacred that a unique recipe was used to make the oil. That particular oil was never used for any other person or for any other purpose, under penalty of excommunication.

All those who were anointed were intended to point beyond themselves to the One who was still to come. He was the Promised One who would accomplish what they could do in only a symbolic way. He was the One whose heel would shed blood as He crushed the head of the serpent. This One would be the final Prophet like Moses, but far greater. He would be the Priest after the order of Melchizedek rather than after the order of Aaron. He would be the King greater than David whose reign would extend from east to west and north to south.

And so in the Old Testament, a whole series of anointed ones appeared like dots to be connected in a child's puzzle book. When all the dots were joined together, it would become clear whose picture they were displaying: Jesus Himself.

It was the prophet Isaiah who had the immense privilege of learning that the One who was to come would be anointed not with oil, but with what that oil symbolized—the Holy Spirit. Isaiah prophesies this:

> There shall come forth a shoot from the stump of Jesse,
> > and a branch from his roots shall bear fruit.
> And the Spirit of the LORD shall rest [or stay, or remain] upon
> > him. (Isa. 11:1–2)

That was how John the Baptist was told he would recognize the Messiah: the Spirit would descend on Him and remain on Him (see John 1:32). Almost at the end of his prophecy, Isaiah hears an echo that seems to bounce back from the future. He hears this Anointed One saying:

> The Spirit of the Lord GOD is upon me,
> > because the LORD has anointed me

to bring good news to the poor;

he has sent me to bind up the brokenhearted. (Isa. 61:1)

These were the words that Jesus read in the Nazareth synagogue. Luke tells us that after He had finished reading, Jesus closed the scroll, handed it back, sat down, and said, "Today this Scripture has been fulfilled in your hearing" (Luke 4:21). Jesus is the Messiah, the Christ, the Anointed One.

What Peter was beginning to see but didn't fully understand is that when we come to know Jesus, we discover that He is the Messiah. He is anointed to fulfill the three great offices of God's grace. He is God's Prophet, who communicates the Word of God to us and is Himself the Word of God. He is the true High Priest, whose sacrifice for our sins will be nothing less than Himself offered in our place. And He is the anointed King, who has come to restore the dominion that Adam lost and to reign over all His and our enemies.

So when Simon Peter said, "You are the Christ," he was only at the beginning of understanding these things. He stumbled more than once, but at last he had the key, and the door was swinging open into an ever-deepening knowledge of, and love for, the Lord Jesus.

I hope you know these things, too, and that the same will be true of you. I hope that you're able to say, "You are the Christ, the Son of the living God."

4

Son of the Living God

WHO IS JESUS? THAT IS THE question we've been thinking about this week. To find an answer, we've been reflecting on Simon Peter's response to Jesus' question, "Who do you say that I am?" The first part of Simon's answer, which we looked at yesterday, was, "You are the Christ." The second part of his answer was, "You are . . . the Son of the living God" (Matt. 16:15–16).

That is a striking description of God, isn't it? *The living God.* It's reminiscent of the divine name revealed to Moses, "I AM WHO I AM"—the One who is all life in Himself and of Himself (Ex. 3:14). And so Peter makes this monumental confession, "You are . . . the Son of the living God."

As we noted yesterday, when Peter declared that Jesus is the Christ, it may not have been a sudden thought that came to him, even if it was the first time he actually said it out loud. The same may also be true of "You are . . . the Son of the living God." Peter's brother, Andrew, may well have been at Jesus' baptism and may have told him of the voice that spoke from heaven, "You are my beloved Son" (Mark 1:11). Maybe Peter had been thinking about that for months. But even if he had, he needed to think more deeply about it, because soon, on the Mount of Transfiguration, he would hear for himself the very same voice saying, "This is my beloved Son, with whom I am well pleased; listen to him" (Matt. 17:5).

This reminds us that it takes time for who our Lord Jesus Christ really is to sink in: He is the Son of God. That is the testimony of the voice from heaven. It's the testimony of Simon Peter. It's the testimony of the Apostle Paul, who once denied and rejected it. It's the testimony of the Gospels. It's the testimony of the letter to the Hebrews. It's the testimony of James and Jude, probably our Lord's half-brothers. Although they don't use that title, James calls Him the "Lord of glory" (James 2:1), and Jude refers to Him three times as "our Lord," *kyrios*, the word that the Greek version of the Old Testament always used to translate the great divine name, *Yahweh*.

Jesus is Lord because He is the Son of God. Did Peter fully understand what that meant? Well, the truth is that only our Lord Himself understands all that it means. But Peter must have understood this: the Old Testament taught that there is only one personal living God. But it also gives us various indications that there was something wonderfully mysterious about the Lord. He was one Lord who led His people through the wilderness. And yet Peter's Old Testament also told them that it was the messenger of God, the *malakh Yahweh,* who did that. The prophet Isaiah also explains that it was the Holy Spirit who did this. The exodus was the work of the three who are one and the one who is three.

Peter must also have known that Psalm 2 promised that when the Messiah came, He would be the Son whom God would set on His throne. Isaiah had spoken of Him as the Wonderful Counselor, the Mighty God, the Everlasting Father, the Prince of Peace (Isa. 9:6). Peter didn't yet fully understand, but these kaleidoscopic pieces of the Old Testament revelation were all coming together in a single pattern that was becoming clear. That pattern told him that the Jesus he knew was God's own Son.

It was God's own Son who had come to be the promised Prophet, and Priest, and King. And beginning to see that clearly doesn't happen naturally—not to Simon Peter, not to me, and not to you. It happens only when the Father opens our eyes through the ministry of the Spirit. When we say to Jesus, "You're the Christ, the Son of the living God," we're not simply saying words. Rather, we're embracing Him. We're trusting Him as our God and as our Savior. I hope you are.

But before we leave Peter's confession, there is another title for Jesus mentioned in this story. And we'll look at that tomorrow.

5

The Triumphant Son of Man

ALL THIS WEEK, WE'VE BEEN REFLECTING ON the question that Jesus asked the disciples at Caesarea Philippi: "Who do you say that I am?" We've thought about the two great titles that Simon Peter used in his answer: "You are the Christ, the Son of the living God" (Matt. 16:15–16). But yesterday, I mentioned a third title of Jesus used in this passage.

But it wasn't used by Peter. In fact—and this is significant—it's not a title that is ever found on the lips of any of the Apostles, although it appears frequently in their writings.

Apart from what amounts to a quotation in John 12:34, only two people have ever used it. One is the martyr Stephen, who used it in the moments just before he died. He said, "I see the heavens opened, and the Son of Man standing at the right hand of God" (Acts 7:56). The other person who used it was the Lord Jesus Himself. He used it at Caesarea Philippi when He asked the disciples, "Who do people say that the Son of Man is?" (Matt. 16:13).

Son of Man is an expression that occurs around eighty times in the Gospels. We could say not only that it's *uniquely* Jesus' way of describing Himself—because almost no one else uses the title—but that it's also Jesus' *favorite* way of talking about Himself and His own ministry.

Many Christians have been taught to think that the title *Son of God* refers to Jesus' deity, while the title *Son of Man* refers to His humanity. But that is not the whole story. Certainly, *Son of Man* can simply mean "man." But Jesus doesn't talk about Himself as simply *a* son of man, but as *the* Son of Man, the *well-known* Son of Man. And what He means by that is the Son of Man spoken of in the Hebrew Scriptures.

I have no doubt that Daniel 7 was in Jesus' mind when He referred to Himself in this way. Daniel had a vision of God in His majesty, seated on a throne of fire, with thousands of thousands serving Him and ten thousand times ten thousand standing before Him. It was a throne-room scene, and it was also a courtroom scene. Daniel saw God's enemies being subdued, although opposition to Him was not yet finally destroyed.

Then in the night, he saw something amazing: on the clouds of heaven, a symbol of the presence of the Spirit of God. He saw "one like a son of man" coming to the throne and being presented to God, the Ancient of Days. And this "son of man" was given dominion. All peoples, nations, and languages would serve Him. His dominion would be secure and everlasting, His kingdom indestructible (Dan. 7:13–14).

Later on, as the vision was explained, Daniel learned that the Son of Man shares His riches with His people, who are described as "saints of the Most High" (vv. 18, 22).

That is who Jesus is talking about. The Son of Man is Himself. That is who He really is. In His incarnation, life, death, resurrection, and ascension, this vision has become a reality. Jesus is the One who's going to the throne of God in triumph. He is the Son of Man.

But where does the Son of Man go first before going to the throne? Of course, that is what Jesus then makes clear to Simon Peter and the other Apostles: He is going to the throne of the Most High through His suffering and death. For through His death and resurrection He will regain the kingdom that Adam was called to rule over (but lost).

This isn't primarily a picture of Jesus' second coming, although it's often understood that way. He is not coming *from* heaven; He is going *to* heaven. It's a picture of His ascension. It's a vision of His going to His coronation. It's the picture of Psalm 68:18: "You ascended on high, leading a host of captives in your train and receiving gifts among men." Paul tells us in Ephesians 4:8 that at that point, the Lord Jesus, through the Spirit, would then distribute those gifts to men. He'd share His victory and His kingdom with the saints of the Most High.

What a glorious picture of Jesus Daniel is seeing, a vision of the Savior who would take our humanity as the Son of Man to undo what Adam did and to do what Adam failed to do—to regain dominion over all things and to bring to completion the purposes of the Most High. And when He had done that, He would ascend on the clouds of heaven to be crowned as Lord at the Father's right hand. Then when all authority in heaven and on earth was given to Him, He would spread His dominion by reigning in our lives.

And so Jesus is the Christ, the Son of the living God, the Son of Man, who for our sakes became incarnate, was crucified, dead, and buried, and was raised, and is now ascended and reigning at the right hand of the Majesty on high.

As the hymn "All Hail the Power of Jesus' Name" says, "Let angels prostrate fall . . . and crown Him Lord of all." I hope you want to sing that, too.

WEEK 49

The Return of Jesus

1

Looking to Christ's Return

THOUGH IT HAS DIED OUT IN MANY PLACES, there is a tradition in the Christian church that on the first Sunday of Advent—which celebrates Jesus' first coming—Christians have also paused to reflect on His second coming.

Why did this tradition became such a fixture in the old Christian calendar? Our spiritual forefathers knew that the incarnation of Christ intersects history, but that it also looks beyond the moment of the incarnation toward the end of history. The birth of Jesus was the beginning of something new. The humbling of the Son of God led to His humiliation on the cross. But that was the prelude to His exaltation and glorification, and ultimately to His return.

Think of it this way: at Christmastime, we're reminded of a very small number of Jewish people who came to worship Jesus—the aged Simeon and the shepherds—and a handful of gentile scholars from the East. But the Scriptures teach us that these people were merely the firstfruits. They were tiny shoots pressing through the soil of history, indicating what will one day take place in the final harvest. Then all the nations will see the glory of the Lord Jesus when He comes again and ushers in the final stage of His kingdom.

That is the united testimony of the New Testament authors. They don't all mention the details of Jesus' birth, but they all write in light of the fact that Jesus is going to return. They tell us that when He does, it will be in majesty and glory.

But it wasn't just the New Testament authors that looked forward to this. Every New Testament Christian was expected to eagerly look forward to Christ's coming. Indeed, they were so eager for it to take place that some of them mistakenly gave up their day jobs, wrongly imagining that He was going to come immediately.

When I was a young student, an older friend told me about something he had learned as a student of early church history. He said, "In the early church, it was almost regarded as a sign of apostasy not to long daily for the return of the Lord Jesus." I'd like to say that I've never forgotten that challenge, but I have to confess, there are days in my Christian life when I probably don't give much thought to the fact that my Lord Jesus Christ is going to return.

Therefore, at the beginning of Advent season, it's spiritually healthy for us to remember that the Jesus who came at Bethlehem is going to return again in majesty and glory.

So let's pray that we'll learn to say with the early church: "Maranatha! Our Lord, come!"

2

Proclaiming His Death until He Comes

AT THE FIRST ADVENT OF OUR LORD, Jesus inaugurated His kingdom. But it is only at His second advent, or coming, that He will consummate it. That is why we pray each day:

Your kingdom come,

your will be done,

    on earth as it is in heaven. (Matt. 6:10)

One day, God's will is going to be done on earth perfectly, as it is already in heaven, when Jesus comes again to reign. But some of us may get a little nervous when we hear people talking about the second coming.

There are several reasons for that. One is that some Christians become so fixated on the details of the second coming that its details almost become a test of orthodoxy as far as they are concerned. They become obsessed with whether Jesus will come before the tribulation or after the tribulation, or whether the rapture will be secret or public. Therefore, it's important for us to see that there is a big difference between convictions about the teaching of the whole of Scripture and a fixation on one particular element in it.

One way that we could try to describe this fixation is to say that there is no theology without psychology. For example, there is a problem when someone has an almost neurotic interest in one facet of truth but doesn't commit the same emotional weight or energy to topics such as the biblical teaching on the humanity of the Lord Jesus or the holiness of God. Such people have an emotional commitment that is out of proportion and disjointed. And for some reason, that often happens in connection with the Lord's second coming.

As we look this week at the second coming of Christ, we will not stray beyond what the New Testament teaches as the fundamental elements of this doctrine.

That is probably a good litmus test of whether we really are balanced Christians. For example, does it overly disappoint you that I'm not going to talk about the rapture? You might think that is a cop-out or even a compromise. But let me ask you this: Are you equally enthusiastic about the doctrine of the Lord's Supper? Or the nature of sanctification? Or the knowledge of the holiness and grace of God? Or the daily significance of your baptism? It's a good checklist for us to ask if we are really committed to everything that is central in Scripture.

One sign of such imbalance can be seen in a person who loves to talk about the details, chronology, or geography of the second coming more than he or she loves to talk about the Lord Jesus Himself as the One who is coming. It's always possible to be taken up with the *doctrines* of grace more so than we are with the *Christ* who is the grace of those doctrines.

So where's a good place to begin? The answer might surprise you, but I think that the place to begin is the Lord's Supper—yes, the Lord's Supper. It was celebrated frequently in the early churches, and it reminded believers of the heart of the gospel. Every time it was celebrated, the believers remembered Jesus' death "until he comes" (1 Cor. 11:26). Their invitation to enjoy communion with the Lord Jesus at the table always looked forward to the communion they would enjoy with Him at the final marriage supper of the Lamb, when He returns in glory and majesty.

I suspect that is an element in the celebration of the Lord's Supper that is often forgotten. However, the supper is meant to be a repeated reminder to us that while we live looking *back* to the incarnation and *up* to the presence of Christ, we also look *forward* to His return. Ask yourself these questions: Do I fix my mind on and fill my heart with the Lord Jesus, who is going to return? Do I focus on the fact that it's the Lord Jesus Himself who is coming? Do I remember Paul's statement that the crown of righteousness is laid up for all those who love His appearing (2 Tim. 4:8)? The emphasis here is on Jesus Himself.

So when we think of the second coming, let's never let ourselves be diverted from the Lord Jesus Himself.

3

Delivering the Kingdom to the Father

TWO WEEKS AGO, WE REFLECTED ON what is sometimes called *personal* eschatology: death, judgment, heaven, and hell. But this week, we're thinking about *corporate* eschatology—that is, what's going to happen at the end of history when Christ returns.

The angels told the Apostles after Jesus' ascension, "This Jesus, who was taken up from you into heaven, will come in the same way as you saw him go into heaven" (Acts 1:11). This is the most important thing to know about the future: this *same* Jesus is going to return, the Jesus who is the same yesterday, today, and forever (Heb. 13:8).

But that is not all we know about the future. The Apostle Paul gives us a basic theological map of the future in 1 Corinthians 15:20–28, the great chapter on the resurrection. He provides a taxonomy of Christ's future triumph and tells us that there is an order to what's going to happen.

First, the bodily resurrection of our Lord Jesus has already taken place as the firstfruits of our resurrection.

Second, when the Lord Jesus returns in majesty and glory, our bodily resurrection will take place.

Third, Jesus will destroy all opposition to Him and His kingdom, and He will put all His enemies under His feet—and in particular, the last enemy, death. Then the "end" will come.

End is an interesting word, in that it can have multiple meanings. On one hand, it can mean: "That is the end. There is no more. It's finished and done." But there is another meaning to the word *end*. The first question of the Westminster Shorter Catechism asks, "What is the chief end of man?" Here, *end* means "purpose" or "goal."

In this passage in 1 Corinthians, perhaps Paul means both. Christ's return will be the end of the present story, the close of history. There will be no more opportunities to hear the gospel or to respond in faith and repentance.

But the end will also come in the sense that the goal will have been reached. The destiny for which God created the world in the first place will have been accomplished. Everything will be under the dominion of the Lord Jesus. And at that point, Paul says, "Then comes the end, when [Jesus] delivers the kingdom to God the Father after destroying every rule and every authority and power" (1 Cor. 15:24).

The Apostle goes on to say, "When all things are subjected to him, then the Son himself will also be subjected to him who put all things in subjection under him, that God may be all in all" (v. 28). What a vision that is! But what does Paul mean by saying that "the Son himself will also be subjected" to the Father? Does he mean that Jesus is a second-rank deity, eternally subordinated to the Father?

That is not what Paul is saying here. Rather, he is talking about the way that we all die in the first man, Adam, but we'll all be raised through Jesus Christ, whom he describes as the second man and the last Adam. Do you see the idea here? It is that Adam was made in God's image to exercise dominion over the earth and to expand the garden of Eden into the whole earth. But Adam failed, sinned, and fell, so he was never able to bring the completed work back to the heavenly Father and say, "It is finished, Father, and we offer it to You as our gift."

But now the Son of God has taken on our human nature. He has become the second man and the last Adam, and He has undone what Adam did and done what Adam failed to do. And at the end, as the second man and the last Adam, He will take it all back to His heavenly Father, fulfilling what He first said on the cross of Calvary: "It is finished, Father, and we bring it to You as our love gift." And then leading the whole creation, He will bow in our humanity before the Father and crown Him Lord of all.

That is why Jesus has regained all authority in heaven and on earth and brought everything under His dominion. He has done it for our sake so that, at the last, we might give everything back to the Lord. And then as the second man and the last Adam, along with all those whom He has saved, He'll lead us in worship of His Father and ours. What a day that will be.

No wonder Paul speaks about loving the appearing of the Lord Jesus Christ.

4

We Shall Be Changed

WHEN ADAM SINNED, HIS LIFE WAS THRUST FROM forward gear (obedience to God) into reverse gear (disobedience and rebellion). Have you ever tried to drive in reverse gear? It's not easy. It's a lot harder to go straight, and it's not a very fast or smooth way to go. Perhaps we can think of what will happen at the return of Christ in the same way: He will thrust everything from reverse gear into forward gear. Everything will be transformed. It will run more smoothly, efficiently, comfortably, and easily. It will be as it ought to have been. That is what the resurrection will be like.

Years ago, I used to keep an old golf club (a "driver") in the trunk of my car. If I had a spare thirty minutes, I might go find a driving range. One day, I was happily hitting golf balls at a driving range in Philadelphia close to where I worked. There was an older man in the next bay, and he was using a top-of-the-line, latest-technology driver. He leaned over and said to me, "Have a try with this one, son." Somewhat reluctantly, I took up his offer. I immediately felt the difference between my driver and his. This one felt and looked fabulous, and it was easy to swing. The ball flew off the club face, sailing past the balls I'd hit with my own driver. It seemed effortless, easy by comparison. I handed it back to him a little reluctantly, knowing it was a far more expensive club than I was ever likely to buy.

But then I had a heart-lifting thought that made up for having to hand back that driver to its owner. I thought: "Wow, I think I've just experienced the nearest thing to the resurrection of the body that a golfer can experience! One day, it will seem the most natural, the most wonderful, and the easiest thing in the world to live every moment to please God. My body will feel different. My mind won't be distracted from Jesus. Obedience will be completely natural." Or to put it in the words of the hymn, "all the ransomed church of God" will be "saved to sin no more."

It's almost unimaginable. We will one day live in the presence of the Father completely happy, under the direction of the Holy Spirit, free from sin, and finding it easy and joyful to serve Him without reservation. Doesn't that grip your mind and flood your heart with anticipation of the return of the Lord Jesus?

Some time ago, I met someone I hadn't seen for ages, and he introduced himself to me. It turned out that he had asked a mutual friend if he would still recognize me if he saw me. My friend said, "You will, but he wears eyeglasses now." But I had to look twice to recognize him. I would never have imagined that the person he turned out to be would be so self-assured, so composed, so well-spoken, so urbane. But I could still see he was the same person I'd known half a century ago—but now wonderfully changed and quite improved.

The resurrection will surely be something like that. Yes, we'll maybe have to look twice at our resurrected fellow believers to recognize that what we are seeing is the inside ministry of the Holy Spirit in their lives turned outside as they are made more and more like Christ. Then we'll see who they really were and who they really now are. That is something to look forward to, isn't it? The Apostle John tells us that "what we will be has not yet appeared; but we know that when he appears we shall be like him, because we shall see him as he is" (1 John 3:2).

What a day to look forward to!

5

Our Lord, Come

AS WE'VE REFLECTED TOGETHER THIS WEEK on the return of the Lord Jesus, we have deliberately focused our attention not on obscure or controversial details but on the Lord Jesus Himself. The great biblical scholar Geerhardus Vos was surely right when he wrote that there are prophecies in Scripture about Christ's return whose best and clearest exegesis will be discovered only at their fulfillment. Only then will everything be clear to us. Therefore, it's wise to be modest in our statements and to focus on the most important things. As the Westminster Confession reminds us, the main things about our salvation are usually clearly stated in Scripture, and often in several places.

Before His crucifixion, Jesus prayed that all His people would one day be with Him to see His glory. I think you can understand why He wanted that, even from a human point of view. After all, His closest friends, the Apostles, had been and would be with Him through the days of His suffering and see Him in the depth of His humiliation. They would also come to taste suffering for Jesus themselves. So of course, He wanted them to see Him in His glory and triumph.

Jesus wants the same for us, too, because there is a sense in which almost all of us have seen and experienced Jesus being humiliated by others, and we've also been humiliated with Him. That is one of the things that make us long to see Him as He really is on that day.

We know that Jesus will come, but *how* will He come? The central answer is this: He'll come gloriously.

There are three New Testament words that express this.

First, His coming will be an *apocalypse*—literally, an *unveiling*. Jesus is now glorified at the right hand of His Father, but we don't see that yet. But on that day, the thin veil between earth and heaven, between time and eternity, will be drawn back, and we will see Him as He is. And surely we will gasp with awe at the glory of His person.

Second, the New Testament says that Jesus' coming will be an *epiphany*, an actual appearance. Every eye will be able to see Him. How that will be, we simply do not know. But that it *will* be, we are promised in Scripture. Think of it: every eye will see Him.

Third, the New Testament speaks about Jesus' coming as a *parousia*. This word was used for the arrival of a king coming into his kingdom or a general returning in triumph.

Jesus' second coming will be all three of these words rolled into one: *apocalypse*, *epiphany*, and *parousia*. And because of the way it will come to pass, it will be the single most glorious moment in the history of the whole cosmos.

In addition, there are three things to look forward to, according to the Scriptures. First, Jesus will return *visibly* and every eye will see Him. And He will not come alone. He will be accompanied by His holy angels.

It's wonderful to think that this world is already populated by angels who are God's ministering spirits. We do believe in extraterrestrial life after all. But their ministry is largely invisible to us. But on that day, that other world, that heavenly branch of God's family that is invisible to our naked eyes, will become visible. And it may seem to us as though there is no space left in the heavens, as the army of the Lord of Hosts accompanies Him at His return.

Second, Jesus will return *audibly*. In the Old Testament in the Year of Jubilee, the Sabbath year of Sabbath years, everything was symbolically restored to its proper condition. That was announced by the blowing of a trumpet—and that is what the New Testament says will happen when Christ returns. The trumpet will sound, Christ will come with a cry of command, and the dead will rise (1 Thess. 4:16). The early church fathers used to say that if Jesus had not cried out specifically, "*Lazarus*, come forth" (see John 11:43), everyone in the graves would've come forth. But on that day that is still to come, there will not be that limitation. For at the cry of command, all the dead in Christ will rise.

Third, Jesus will return *triumphantly*—so triumphantly that He will destroy the man of sin by the breath of His mouth (2 Thess. 2:8). He'll simply blow him away. Then every knee will bow and every tongue confess that Jesus is Lord. At that point, Jesus' prayer in John 17:24 will be finally and fully answered. We will see Him in the glory that His Father gave to Him before the foundation of the world. Surely that makes us say with the New Testament church: "Maranatha! Our Lord, come!"

And one day, indeed He will.

WEEK 50

Angels

1

What Is an Angel?

AS WE APPROACH CHRISTMAS, it's a fitting time to reflect on the subject of angels.

We'll begin with a few facts. The first is that the word *angel* appears in the Bible three times as often as the word *Apostle*. Additionally, by my reckoning, at least two-thirds of the traditional Christmas carols refer to angels. Despite these facts, we tend to give angels very little consideration (although some people give them too much), but they punctuate the story of our Lord's life and His ministry.

Angels appear at the beginning of the Gospels in connection with

Jesus' birth. They appear again at the end of them in connection with His passion and His resurrection. And of course, they'll appear again when they accompany Him in His glorious return. Their presence underlines His glory, but it also underlines the fact that He is their King as well as our King. It's a bit like England and Scotland: two peoples with one and the same king.

But what are angels? What do they do? And what is their significance for us? These are some of the questions we will explore this week.

First, let's consider the basic question, "What is an angel?" The words used in the Bible to designate angels—in the Old Testament, *malak*, and in the New Testament, *angelos*—both mean "messenger." In the Old Testament, the word usually refers to human messengers. When it refers to a heavenly messenger, it's usually to the Angel of the Lord. The Angel of the Lord is a *theophany*, a physical manifestation of the presence of the Lord Himself. Many Christians have believed that the Angel of the Lord is specifically a *Christophany*—that is, a preincarnate manifestation of the Son of God—although this identification is not specifically made in the New Testament.

In the New Testament, however, the word *angelos* usually refers to heavenly beings. Angels are created beings, and according to Colossians 1:16, they were created by Christ. They are heavenly beings. They are spirits, yet they are capable of appearing in physical form. We even know the names of two of them: Gabriel and Michael.

This raises an interesting question: "Are angels *persons*?" My view is that if we can use that term of both God and man, then we can probably also use it of angels. They certainly seem to have the characteristics of persons. They are rational and volitional beings, and there are hints that they experience affections such as joy (Luke 15:7, 10). In addition, they speak, direct, obey, serve, show interest in earthly activities, and worship.

It's more accurate to say that many but not all angels worship, because there are two categories of angels now. There are the faithful and the fallen. There are elect angels associated with God and His heavenly assembly (1 Tim. 5:21). In the book of Job, they are described as "sons of God" (Job 1:6). They are members of His heavenly family. But there are also fallen angels. Matthew 25:41 speaks of the devil and his angels. He was a liar and murderer who fell from his original status and brought with him other angels. We read of them in 2 Peter 2:4 and in Jude 6.

Scripture also teaches that there are huge numbers of angels. Jesus spoke once about twelve legions of angels waiting to minister to Him. There were between three thousand and six thousand in a single Roman legion, so clearly there are many angels. There is also a vivid picture in Revelation 5 of myriads of angels, thousands and thousands of them. That is a huge population of extraterrestrial life, isn't it?

The Bible wants us to see that we are not alone in the universe. There is an entire world of extraterrestrial beings. And the wonderful thing is that so many of them want to serve our Lord Jesus Christ. They do that by serving His people in ways that are beyond our understanding because so often they minister in ways that are invisible to us. Perhaps one day we'll discover how marvelous their ministry has been.

Can you imagine what pleasure and joy we will have in heaven meeting some of these angels who have invisibly served us?

That is something to look forward to.

2

Different Kinds of Angels

THERE IS MUCH WE DON'T KNOW about angels, but that shouldn't prevent us from reflecting on what we do know. And one thing we do know is that it seems there are different orders of angels, and perhaps even different kinds of angels.

We know that there is at least one archangel, because he is referred to in that way in connection with the Lord's return—when the Lord Jesus will overwhelm His enemies and destroy death itself (1 Thess. 4:16). We also know that his name is Michael, and he is said to have contended with Satan over the body of Moses (Jude 9). He appears again in Revelation 12:7 as the one who fought against the dragon, and in Daniel 10, he is described as the "prince." He always seems to appear in a military context, serving on behalf of God's kingdom as the guardian and protector of God's people, like a general among the hosts of heaven.

We also know the name of another angel, Gabriel, from Daniel 8–9. Since Michael is referred to as *one* of the chief princes in Daniel 10, perhaps Gabriel is another. Gabriel's honored position is underlined by the fact that he is the angel who appeared to Zechariah to announce John's birth and to Mary to announce Jesus' birth. He seems to be less of a military leader and more of a royal herald, a communicator and interpreter of the divine will.

Therefore, these two chief princes, or archangels, express God's purposes in deeds and in words. One guards the people of God, and the other communicates God's will to the people of God at crucial moments.

In addition to these ranks and roles, there seem to be different kinds of angelic beings. There are cherubim, who appear first in Genesis 3:24, guarding the way to the garden of Eden. They were later symbolized in the two cherubim who overshadowed the mercy seat on the ark of the covenant. They are guardians of the glory of God. On a number of occasions, the Lord is described as dwelling "between the cherubim." The book of Ezekiel describes them as having four faces. In chapter 1, the faces are like an ox, an eagle, a lion, and a man. But in chapter 10, they are described as having the faces of an eagle, a lion, a cherub, and a man. They bear away the glory of God from the temple when man has defiled it. It makes one wonder who first thought of the idea of calling children's church or children's choirs "Little Cherubs," since according to Scripture, cherubs seem to be extraordinarily powerful creatures!

Then there are the seraphim, who appear in Isaiah 6. They are described differently from the cherubim. They are servants of the holiness of God, as well as ministers of His goodness and grace.

These heavenly creatures appear in visions in Isaiah and in Ezekiel. Neither prophet claims to have actually met a seraph or a cherub. But the cherubs in Genesis 3 are not represented as a vision. They are actual beings, and we should assume the same of the seraphim. They are real and majestic beings. Ezekiel describes the cherubim by using analogies to put into words what he saw in his visions. He says: "Their appearance was *like* burning coals of fire, *like* the appearance of torches moving to and fro among the living creatures. . . . The living creatures darted to and fro, *like* the appearance of a flash of lightning" (Ezek. 1:13–14, emphasis added). They transcend simple description. We might even wonder if these creatures are angels at all or if, instead, there are other kinds of creatures in this extraterrestrial world in addition to angels and archangels.

There are many mysteries to God's heavenly creatures, but here are two things that we can reflect on.

First, think for a moment about how rich and full the heavenly world of God really is.

Second, ask yourself this question: "Have I assumed too easily that the present world I live in is the real and substantial world, the one that really matters, whereas the heavenly world is kind of empty, ephemeral, and insubstantial?" The truth is, *that* world is very substantial, very real, and full of glorious life.

We are only one branch of the amazing family that God has created through His Son, Jesus Christ. There is another heavenly branch to the family, and one day, those two families will meet together in the new heavens and new earth. No wonder those who are already in heaven must have discovered that it's full of amazing and wonderful surprises.

That is something to look forward to.

3

Angelic Appearances

WHEN WE THINK OF THE AMAZING CREATURES that angels are, we realize how ludicrous it is that they've been portrayed as though they were children's toys. It makes one wonder if that is a tactic of Satan—to ridicule the angels and thus ridicule God. To combat this inaccurate view of angels, we're reflecting this week on who these heavenly creatures are and what they do.

In general terms, we know that they are servants of God who establish His purposes. Psalm 103:20 says that they are "mighty ones who do his word, obeying the voice of his word!" Think of how powerful these angels are. They destroyed the wicked city of Sodom (Gen. 19:13). Think of the angel of death's visitation in the last plague and first Passover before the exodus (Ex. 12:23). Think of the angel who opened prison doors to rescue Peter from prison (Acts 12:7–10), or the angel who rolled away the stone before the tomb of Jesus (Matt. 28:2–4).

It's especially interesting how angels seem to appear at strategic points in biblical history. They appear at creation (Job 38), at the time of the fall (Gen. 3), and at the establishment of the covenant line and family of Abraham (Gen. 19). They also appear in the exodus from Egypt, in the angel of the Lord's appearing to Moses, and in leading the Israelites in the pillar of cloud and fire. Angels appear in connection with the giving of the law (Gal. 3:19). They are there when the Israelites enter the promised land (Ex. 23). They appear in the days of the judges with Gideon and Samson. Later, we meet with angels in the establishing of the prophetic ministry and Elijah and Elisha, in the visions of Isaiah and Ezekiel, and in the experience of Daniel at the time of the exile.

As we turn to the New Testament, we meet angels at the promise of Jesus' coming and in His birth, ministry, death, and resurrection. Angels appear to the Apostles. We also read of them in the book of Revelation, which describes the conflict between the powers of darkness and the power of God. And finally, we read about them in connection with the return of our Lord Jesus.

When we trace the presence of angels through the narrative of Scripture, something becomes clear. No doubt the angels are constantly at work serving the Lord in many different ways, but these specific angelic appearances are far from haphazard. What they have in common is similar to what unites the apparently spasmodic outbreak of the supernatural that takes place in miracles. The appearance of angels is not a constant, everyday occurrence, any more than the occurrence of miracles is. They seem to be limited to specific periods in the story of the kingdom of God—we have listed some of them. The common factor is that these were all periods of strategic defense or advance of the kingdom of God.

It's interesting that in the book of Daniel, angels are described as the "watchers" (see Dan. 4:13). They are watching out for God's kingdom and for God's people in times of crisis or in moments of great advance. That is a great way to think about the angels and their ministry. They are observing what's happening in the world. Their eyes are fixed on the situation in the kingdom of God. In fact, Peter says that they are watching us being saved and wondering, "What must it be like to be a sinner for whom the King, the Lord Jesus, was willing to die?" (see 1 Peter 1:12). They are ready at a moment's notice to go in the service of their King, to protect His people in days of danger and in days of advance.

I'd love to have been a fly on the wall of heaven to sense the atmosphere among the angels when they heard the voice from the throne say: "Gabriel, it's time. Go now." The watchers saw Gabriel go to Zechariah to tell him that his wife, Elizabeth, would have a son. They must have held their breath in awe, and perhaps fallen totally silent, when a few months later the voice spoke again and said: "Gabriel, *the* time has come. Go now to Nazareth. There you will find a teenage girl called Mary. Tell her: 'Do not be afraid, Mary, for you have found favor with God. And behold, you will conceive in your womb and bear a son, and you shall call his name Jesus. He will be great and will be called the Son of the Most High.' " Stunning, isn't it?

No wonder the hymn "Praise, My Soul, the King of Heaven" says, "Angels, help us to adore him."

4

The Angels That Ministered to Jesus

THE GOSPELS RECORD THE WONDERFUL ministry of angels in Jesus' life. That may not be surprising, since He is their Creator and King. We have already discussed how angelic appearances in Scripture come in clusters, especially when the kingdom of God has reached a crucial point of either advance or severe conflict.

We find both in the life of Jesus.

We noted yesterday that angels are called "watchers" in Daniel 4. They were certainly watching over Jesus during His earthly ministry. Recall that Jesus said He could call down twelve legions of angels and they would come at a moment's notice (Matt. 26:53). He didn't actually call for their help at that time, but there are a couple of occasions mentioned in the Gospels when the angels did come, and they came specifically to minister to our Savior. These are moving incidents, and today we'll reflect on them.

The first occasion took place early in His ministry. Jesus was baptized and then led by the Spirit into the wilderness to face the devil. In a sense, it was a rerun of the garden of Eden, but our Lord was in the wilderness, not in a garden. He was surrounded by wild beasts, not by tame animals. His situation was the very antithesis of Adam's. Matthew tells us that when the devil left Jesus, "Behold, angels came and were ministering to him" (Matt. 4:11). He must have been absolutely exhausted. We don't know how many came, but we can imagine how privileged they must have felt to attend to Him.

I once worked with a wonderful associate minister who preached a children's sermon on Jesus as the Light of the World—the Light that couldn't be extinguished. He brought along a very realistic everlasting candle and invited the children to blow it out. The first tried and failed, then the second, and then the third. There was such eagerness among the children to be the next to try. Each child was confident that he or she could do it, and I thought for a moment that there would be a riot in the church. It was fantastic.

When I think of the enthusiasm of those children, unable to contain their cries of "Let me try," I can imagine the eagerness that the angels must have felt: "Let me go to minister to my King!" He was hungry and weak, tempted, and surely physically exhausted as the temptations climaxed; the angels could see Him in His fragility. So it's a good thing that there was no jealousy among these angels in heaven when the Father said to only some of them, "Go to My Son and minister to Him."

It's both interesting and important to notice that it wasn't the angels who overcame the devil or resisted the temptations. They didn't act for Jesus or instead of Jesus. He won the victory, and they ministered to Him.

I wonder how they did that. Was it perhaps just by being there because they loved Him? Perhaps one of them knew what to do because he'd been in charge of the ravens who had looked after Elijah. And maybe one day, we'll know, too. For the only person who could let others know about the visit of those angels is the Lord Jesus Himself.

When we turn to the end of Jesus' ministry, we find another angelic visitation. This time, only one angel was sent.

In the garden of Gethsemane, Jesus was praying that if possible, the cup of judgment and dereliction might be removed from Him. But it wasn't possible for Him to be saved from death if we were to be saved from condemnation. Luke tells us, "There appeared to him an angel from heaven, strengthening him" (Luke 22:43).

Again, we don't know exactly how the angel did that, but I wonder if you've ever noticed the rather surprising words that follow. We might expect to read that, thus strengthened, Jesus resolutely committed Himself to drinking the cup. But instead, this is what is recorded in Luke's account: "There appeared to him an angel from heaven, strengthening him. And being in agony he prayed more earnestly; and his sweat became like great drops of blood falling down to the ground" (vv. 43–44).

Far from easing the strain, far from diluting the challenge, far from somehow making it easier for Jesus, the angel's presence only strengthened Him to face the depth of the challenge that awaited Him as He now experienced it in an even more overwhelming way. Who knows if the angel said anything; all we know is that he came to strengthen Jesus. And surely all the angels watching must have been holding their breath at the suffering of their King and wondering how He was willing to undergo that for us.

The famous Scottish minister Alexander Whyte used to say that after he had seen the Lord Jesus in glory, he would most of all want to meet the angel who strengthened Him in Gethsemane.

I think you can understand why he said that, because this is the angel who was so close to Jesus as He made His way to the cross of Calvary.

What a great Savior our Lord Jesus really is.

5

Worship with the Angels

WE ARE CONCLUDING OUR WEEK OF reflections on angels with a feature of their ministry we rarely think about: angels serve as ministers of praise in the worship of the heavenly sanctuary.

It's clear in Scripture that angels are *not* to be worshiped. In fact, the worship of angels was an element in what's sometimes called the "Colossian heresy" that Paul warns about in Colossians 2. In the last chapter of Revelation, John was so overawed by the presence of an angel that he fell down to worship at his feet. The angel said to him: "You must not do that! I am a fellow servant with you" (Rev. 22:9).

Angels are not to be worshiped, but they are worshipers. They worshiped at creation. God tells Job that the angels, the heavenly sons of God, shouted for joy when He laid the foundation of the earth (Job 38:4–7). They certainly worshiped at the incarnation of Jesus (Luke 2:13–14). The psalmist looks up through the heavens to address the angels and says, "Praise him, all his angels; praise him, all his hosts!" (Ps. 148:2).

In the early years of my Christian life, I used to read through Revelation 4–5 every Sunday morning to prepare for the worship services that day. I don't suppose I fully understood what the passage was saying, but I had a sense that this was true worship and I longed for it—the throne of God surrounded by the four living creatures, reminiscent of the cherubim, and surrounded by the twenty-four elders. All were giving thanks and worshiping Him who lives forever and ever, casting their crowns down before Him.

In Revelation 5, when the Lamb takes the sealed scroll and is worshiped, a new song of praise breaks out. The entire congregation of cherubim, elders, angels, and eventually every living creature praises God. What a help to us to join in that heavenly worship with the angels of God.

There is another passage in the New Testament that we ought to place alongside Revelation 4–5. We might say that Revelation gives us a picture, but Hebrews 12:22–24 gives us its theology: "You have come to Mount Zion and to the city of the living God, the heavenly Jerusalem, and to innumerable angels in festal gathering, and to the assembly of the firstborn who are enrolled in heaven, and to God, the judge of all, and to the spirits of the righteous made perfect, and to Jesus, the mediator of a new covenant."

That is what we're doing when we attend worship together. This is the church we're really going to. We are joining with the angels as they conduct the worship of the Lord Jesus Christ. Interestingly, earlier in Hebrews, Jesus is called the *leitourgos*, the priest who leads the liturgy (Heb. 8:1–2). And so these angels form a kind of heavenly choir, now singing in harmony with the redeemed saints who have joined them. As John Owen once wrote, all true worship takes place in heaven. In our worship, we join our hearts and voices—"lifting up our hearts," as some of the liturgies say—and we join in the magnificent worship of holy angels, cherubim, and perfected saints.

In 1 Corinthians 11:10, the Apostle Paul makes an enigmatic statement on our behavior in worship. He comments on what the angels will think. Perhaps He is referring to a general principle—namely, that we need to remember where we are. We're in church, and the church that we're ultimately in is the church in which the angels worship. We're worshiping their King as well as our own King. We're worshiping along with these amazing creatures, and with the company of those who have now been "saved to sin no more." So we must remember where we are, remember the angels, and worship with them.

Thinking about angels should lead us to greater awe of and deeper devotion to our Lord Jesus in our worship services—not because we worship angels, but because we have the privilege of worshiping together with them the One who is both their King and our King, the One who humbled Himself in the incarnation and is now crowned Lord of all.

So let's look forward to enjoying this coming Lord's Day as we are led in worship on Sunday—not only to sing here on earth, but to sing with the angels in heaven.

WEEK 51

Christmas

1

Recovering Christ at Christmastime

IT WILL SOON BE CHRISTMAS DAY. For many people, especially those who are mothers, this is one of the busiest weeks of the year. Some of us revel in the holiday season and all the events; we love planning, and we enjoy doing. But others dread it, feeling pressure and exhaustion rather than anticipation and joy. No matter what people try to say to us about keeping things simple, we still hear an accusing voice telling us that we haven't done enough, that we need to do more, and that we need to do it better.

When it comes to Christmas, there are also two kinds of preachers: those who love it and those who dread it. After all, the more familiar the story, the greater the pressure most ministers feel preaching about it. The weight of the occasion can crush them rather than carry them. But underneath these different feelings we can have about Christmas, we all need one and the same thing. We all need the real message of Christmas.

Ministers may often tell their congregations that Christmas is the most secularized time of the year and warn them not to fall into that trap. But I suspect that is really a counsel of despair, because law never works grace. What we need is more than a warning. We need what Thomas Chalmers called "the expulsive power of a new affection."

It's impossible to overemphasize how important this principle is, not just at this frenetic time of the year or in connection with Christmas. It's true of the entire Christian life. And although Chalmers' sermon called "The Expulsive Power of a New Affection" was on John's words in 1 John 2:15—"Do not love the world or the things in the world"—it's perhaps especially the Apostle Paul who emphasizes how important this principle is in helping us to not love the world.

How can we do this? That is the million-dollar question, not least because it's surprisingly easy for us to turn this principle into another rod to beat our backs. We can be tempted to say to ourselves: "I need to get a new affection. I need to try harder to get it. Thomas Chalmers tells me I need it."

Years ago, when I was a minister in Scotland, I developed a personal tradition on Christmas Eve. I'd park a little distance from the church and walk across the brightly lit and decorated city square as I headed to the late-night Christmas Eve service. It was a way of preparing my spirit for what I would preach—preaching to people who scarcely ever, perhaps, went to church.

One year, I noticed two police officers standing beside the life-sized nativity scene in the square.

"Guarding the manger?" I said to them, thinking that a friendly conversation might begin.

To my surprise, one of them said: "Yes. Last year, someone stole Jesus."

Those were prophetic words, for that police officer was saying more than he likely realized. He had put his finger on the heart of the problem: we've allowed Jesus to be stolen at Christmastime (and often during the rest of the year). But it is Jesus alone who is the power of a new affection.

But before we think about how to recover Him at Christmastime and experience the power of a new affection for Him, there is something else important to note.

Perhaps the reason that He is not central to us at Christmastime is that He has been stolen from our lives long before Christmas. So the first issue to settle is really this: Is Jesus central in my life day by day during the rest of the year? If not, why would I imagine that He will suddenly become central to me on Christmas Day?

Perhaps today we need to pray Richard of Chichester's famous prayer: "Lord, for these three things I pray; to see Thee more clearly, to love Thee more dearly, and to follow Thee more nearly, day by day."

2

Renewed Affection for Christ

THOMAS CHALMERS' SERMON "THE EXPULSIVE POWER of a New Affection" cut to the heart of how our lives can't be transformed by all the efforts we make to produce the strength or courage to stop doing something or to overcome a sin and start doing something else. Yes, sin needs to be expelled. But the gospel doesn't transform us by creating a vacuum in which we simply get rid of things in our lives. If we try to do that, we'll be like the man in Jesus' parable who swept the house clean of an evil spirit. When the spirit discovered that the house had been swept clean, it fetched another seven spirits more evil than itself and occupied the house. The result, Jesus said, is that "the last state of that person is worse than the first" (Matt. 12:45).

So how do we get out of this vicious cycle?

To put it another way, perhaps (like me) you've often sat on a large airplane and thought, "How on earth is this thing going to fly with all these people on board, with their luggage, and with the weight of the plane itself?" Apparently, a fully fueled, ready-to-go Boeing 737-800 weighs about 130,000 pounds—and that is before you stepped onto it! Can air-traffic control suspend the law of gravity and enable that plane to fly? Of course not. The plane flies because it's designed to employ the laws of aerodynamics. When these principles are thrown into operation, the power of gravity (in a sense) is nullified. And spiritually speaking, what we need is something just like that.

Our tendency toward sin doesn't totally disappear when we're regenerated. What we need is for Christ's indwelling us—His presence in our hearts and lives, and our love for Him—to affect this new powerful affection that will overcome the down-drag of sin and the gravity of our disordered affections.

But how does all this apply at Christmas? If we're going to enjoy Christmas in the midst of all the busyness, it's only the expulsive power of a new affection for Christ that is going to help us. Then we'll see other things in their proper place.

What I've found in my personal experience of being a minister is this: in all the pressures of Christmastime and the many services and responsibilities of a pastor, the more I had to *preach* the Christmas message, the more I actually *enjoyed* Christmas. If you'd been a sympathetic member of the same church family as me, you might occasionally have had this thought: "I should think about my minister. He is preaching four or five Sundays on the Christmas message. He is preaching in the middle of the week on the Christmas message. He has Christmas Eve sermons to prepare on the Christmas message. The poor man must be exhausted."

But no, even if he is a bit exhausted, he feels that he is the richest man in the church family because he has very little time to think about anything else except Jesus! His calling has given him the blessing of the expulsive power of a new affection: love for the Savior who came at Christmastime. With so little time to think about anything else, everything else gets put into its place.

I'm not suggesting that we all become preachers, but the same principle applies. When our hearts and minds are fixed on the Lord Jesus Christ and we have the expulsive power of a new affection for Him, then things begin to fit into place. When the center holds, everything else will find its proper place in our lives.

So let's pray for God's grace to have our hearts and minds fixed on the Lord Jesus Christ this Christmas week, and then we'll be able to enjoy it in a fresh way.

3

A Friend Who Sticks Closer

AS CHRISTMAS APPROACHES, WE'VE BEEN REFLECTING ON a simple biblical principle that is applicable year-round, but it's especially relevant to this frenetic season of the year. Specifically, it's the principle that what we need in Jesus Christ is the expulsive power of a new affection for Him.

This is also true if Christmas is a lonely time for us—and it sometimes is that, even when we're surrounded by other people. Perhaps some of us feel that the words of Lamentations 1:12 are our words, too: "Is it nothing to you, all you who pass by? Look and see if there is any sorrow like my sorrow." Maybe we feel that because this Christmas we have a personal burden that nobody around us really shares. If we've had some special loss this year, we may well feel that while the rest of the world seems to have moved on, we are left on our own.

But whatever our situation—anxious and burdened, sad, or excited and full of eager anticipation—what we all need is a new affection for the Lord Jesus. But that is not something we can work up. Only the Lord Jesus Himself can give us that new affection through His Holy Spirit. It needs to come from the outside to the inside and not the other way around.

I very rarely mention my family when I preach. If I did, they would give me a very hard time! I learned this lesson on one occasion when I told our congregation that one of our children had done something, and then I added, "I won't tell you which one she is." Since I have three sons and only one daughter, I never made the same mistake again! But I think I'm safe in telling you this story from our family history.

It was Christmas season, and in the Sunday school classes in church, the children were making Christmas cards for their moms and dads. One of our young sons came home and cheerfully handed his creation to us. It was the statutory stable scene, and inside, a carefully chosen Bible verse. Our son had come up with a text that was just a little different for Christmas. We opened the card to find stretched across the inside the words from Proverbs 18:24 in bold letters: "There are friends who pretend to be friends . . ." (RSV).

When we saw only those words on the card, it almost felt as though he was exposing us as pretend friends. But then he added in smaller letters the words "But there is a friend," followed by a series of dots that ran to the edge of the card and left us anticipating what might be on the back. After a moment of puzzlement, we turned over the page to find the conclusion of the matter: "There are friends who pretend to be friends, but there is a friend . . ." and on the back, the single word, "Jesus!"

We smiled with a twofold joy, partly at the sheer imagination of our little boy in making use of a relatively obscure text in Scripture at Christmastime, but largely because of the message itself. I don't know how much he knew as a little boy about seeing how the Old Testament points to Christ, but he'd certainly nailed it there, hadn't he? Yes, there is a friend who sticks closer than a brother. And yes, His name is the name that He was given from His birth, Jesus, because He came to save His people from their sins.

I still think about that Christmas card and the emotions that were encapsulated for me in just a few seconds. There is a friend who sticks closer than a brother, Jesus, and it's knowing this that leads to the expulsive power of a new affection.

I know that is a trivial story. Family stories can mean a lot to us when they mean almost nothing to anybody else. But I think this story might help some of us this year. It might contribute to dispelling the gloom or the sense of loneliness that we feel at Christmastime for whatever reason. So here is a Christmas card. It has a stable scene on the front. It has unusual wording inside, and you read, "There are friends who pretend to be friends." Perhaps you feel that keenly. But read on: "There is a friend who sticks closer than a brother."

Is that it? Well, not quite. You need to turn the page, because on the back page of my card, you will find this one word, this one name: *Jesus.* He is the expulsive power in your life of a new affection that will dispel loneliness, even if you're on your own.

Let us pray that that will be true for all of us today.

4

The Savior's Lowly Birth

THIS WEEK, WE'RE THINKING ABOUT THE CHALLENGE at Christmastime to keep Jesus Himself at the heart of things. That kind of talk can sometimes devolve into a sense of duty or responsibility, or perhaps even a burden. It's always struck me as a paradox that is difficult to wrap our heads around. The very season when the church celebrates the One whose yoke is easy and whose burden is light is a season when many Christians feel an excessive sense of burden. No doubt, one of the reasons for that is the false expectations we are encouraged to have.

Here's one example. Christmas Eve services often begin with the words of Luke 2:15, usually in the King James Version: "Let us now go even unto Bethlehem, and see this thing which is come to pass, which the Lord hath made known unto us."

I have to confess, I've given up trying to get to Bethlehem on Christmas Eve because we can't get there. I think I know what people are trying to say when they use this verse. But I wonder if the great hymn writer Horatius Bonar had the same experience. He wrote a little hymn about looking for Christ in which he says, "We went to Bethlehem," but Christ wasn't there. That is to say, we can't generate this new affection we need by making an imaginary geographical journey to where Jesus was born. He isn't there any longer.

So maybe we need to think in a different way about our struggles to feel like Christmas. After all, there were certain elements in the first Christmas that didn't feel very Christmassy: a long journey away from home for a young woman, almost certainly still in her teens. expecting a child, no Holiday Inn, no Hampton Inn, and certainly not the Ritz for Joseph and Mary. Instead, they went around Bethlehem looking for somewhere to rest, trying to find a place for Mary to wait for the imminent birth of her son.

It makes me wonder, "Was Jesus' birth possibly (humanly speaking) premature because of their journey and their struggles to find a place?" Not premature from God's point of view, of course. How difficult it must have been for Mary. In addition, her mother almost certainly wasn't there to help. And then I don't know how many times we need to sing, "The cattle are lowing, the baby awakes, but little Lord Jesus, no crying he makes," to realize that that couldn't possibly be wholly true. Later on, there were the warnings about Herod and the exodus in reverse that Mary and Joseph experienced as they hastily bundled up their little son one night and made their way down to Egypt. There is not much that feels Christmassy about that, is there?

And yet understanding their hardship creates the expulsive power of a new affection, because the gospel tells us that this was all for us. And this is what the best Christmas hymns are all about: how Christ's suffering and impoverishment were all for us.

Thou who wast rich beyond all splendor,
All for love's sake becamest poor.

Or perhaps you know the hymn by the seventeenth-century metaphysical poet Richard Crashaw:

Gloomy night embraced the place
Wherein the noble Infant lay:
The Babe looked up and showed His face;

In spite of darkness, it was day!

. . . .

Great little One! Whose lowly birth
Lifts earth to Heav'n, stoops Heav'n to earth.

Or perhaps you know the lovely Gaelic carol:

Child in the manger,
Infant of Mary;
Outcast and stranger,
Lord of all;
Child who inherits
All our transgressions,
All our demerits
On Him fall.

Or:

He came down to earth from heaven
Who is God and Lord of all,
And his shelter was a stable,
And his cradle was a stall:
With the poor, and mean, and lowly,
Lived on earth our Savior holy.

Or perhaps you know another seventeenth-century carol by Thomas
Pestel:

Behold, the great Creator makes
Himself a house of clay,
A robe of human flesh He takes
Which He will wear for aye.

I wonder if these words about the amazing humiliation and suffering of the Son of God, our Lord Jesus, create a new affection in your heart for Him.

I hope so. May it be so.

5

Should We Celebrate Christmas?

IT'S IMPORTANT FOR US TO UNDERSTAND that there are no special holy days now for believers. In the Old Testament, the life of an old covenant believer was punctuated by holy days because God's people had national holidays. They had many such days, but they were religious *holy days*. That is where the word *holiday* comes from.

Before the Protestant Reformation, the church had created a whole calendar of holy days, Christmas being one of them. The Reformers, especially in my own country of Scotland, reacted against that because it appeared that the church had been insisting on observations that went beyond Scripture—and sometimes against Scripture. And so all these special days came to an end, including Christmas. When the Scottish commissioners went to the Westminster Assembly in the mid-seventeenth century—the assembly where the famous confession and catechisms were written—they were appalled to discover that people were not working on Christmas Day. Even when I was growing up in Scotland, Christmas Day was only a half-day holiday.

I have Christian friends who maintain that old tradition because Scripture doesn't command us to celebrate Christmas, and therefore, they think that the church shouldn't. Sometimes rather sadly, that can be expressed in a rather mean-spirited and even spiritually superior way, suggesting that those who do celebrate the incarnation at this time should feel guilty about doing so.

But there are several considerations that have led me to believe that it's legitimate, appropriate, and helpful for us to celebrate Christmas.

One is this: Scripture doesn't tell us that our pastors, our elders, or the congregation as a whole, for example, should decide that we will have sermons in September on sanctification, or that the last Sunday in some month in the year will be "Missions Sunday," or that another weekend will be the church anniversary weekend. Our pastors and elders make those decisions for the spiritual well-being of the congregation. And if we have *that* liberty, then surely we have the liberty to have a time in the year when we concentrate on the incarnation of our Lord Jesus Christ—thinking about, celebrating, and applying the momentous event of the birth of the Savior of the world.

We're not saying that these are special *holy* days. We're not binding anyone's conscience any more than when we have a month of sermons on sanctification. In fact, my general observation is that Christians and congregations that *don't* mark the incarnation in this way are actually likely to hear fewer sermons and have less concentration on the conception, birth, and early days of our blessed Lord than those who do. But surely these topics are really important.

There's something else. It's often said that Christmas is actually a pagan holiday based on the Roman holiday of Saturnalia. But that is a bit like saying that Reformation Sunday is a pagan celebration because it coincides with Halloween. Some churches started holding a Reformation Day service as a direct contrast with the events associated with Halloween.

Historically, there were similar reasons that Christmas came to be celebrated around the time of the Roman festival of Saturnalia. It was a way of pointing the pagan world to a better story, to an infinitely greater God than the Roman god Saturn. It was saying, "You are worshiping the creature, and we want to encourage you to worship the Creator." It was meant to be a powerful witness to the incarnate Son of

God, our Lord Jesus Christ. And in fact, so powerful was that witness that at least on one occasion a church gathering on Christmas Day was deliberately and maliciously firebombed by Christ's enemies. Therefore, it's both muddleheaded and ungracious to say that Christmas is a pagan celebration.

So yes, Christmas Day isn't any more holy than any other day of the year. Christmas dinner isn't more sacred than yesterday's dinner. But like that food, it can be sanctified in special ways by the Word of God and prayer and praise, because the Lord Jesus came into the world to be our Savior.

It's knowing this that helps us to enjoy Christmas to the full.

WEEK 52

Looking Back on the Year

1

Coming Face-to-Face with Christ

FOR SOME OF US, THIS TIME of year may be proving to be very difficult. Perhaps we're experiencing special struggles or feeling the loss of someone who was very dear to us. But the message of the coming of the Lord Jesus is that He is able to be with us, to help us, and to save us no matter who we are, where we are, or how we feel. He does this precisely because He became one with us. Right from the beginning of His human life, He came face-to-face with everything that we have to face. So today, let's take a moment to think about Him and to listen once again to His story.

Years after the gospels of Matthew and Luke had been written, the aged Apostle John sat down to write his gospel. No doubt he'd read the other Gospels and could still remember being an eyewitness of the events they described. He'd long pondered the meaning of the incarnation of the Lord Jesus.

But I think John also remembered the promise that Jesus had given the disciples in the upper room the evening before the crucifixion.

Jesus told the Apostles that the Spirit would come to them and remind them of everything Jesus had said. The Spirit would also show them the things that were still to come and lead them into the truth about Jesus. And so John wrote his gospel so that we might understand the truth about Jesus that the Spirit of God revealed to His much-loved disciple—the truth about the coming of Jesus into the world.

John Calvin insightfully wrote that the other Gospels show us Christ's body, but John shows us His soul. That is, John gives us the inner story of the incarnation. The other writers describe the outside—the events in which Joseph and Mary, the shepherds, the magi, and Simeon and Anna were involved. But John tells the story from the inside—in a sense, from Jesus' own point of view and from John's observations.

Listen to John's wonderful words:

In the beginning was the Word, and the Word was with God, and the Word was God. He was in the beginning with God. All things were made through him, and without him was not any thing made that was made. In him was life, and the life was the light of men. The light shines in the darkness, and the darkness has not overcome it.

There was a man sent from God, whose name was John. He came as a witness, to bear witness about the light, that all might believe through him. He was not the light, but came to bear witness about the light.

The true light, which gives light to everyone, was coming into the world. He was in the world, and the world was made through him, yet the world did not know him. He came to his own, and his own people did not receive him. But to all who did receive him, who believed in his name, he gave the right to become children of God, who were born, not of blood nor of the will of the flesh nor of the will of man, but of God.

And the Word became flesh and dwelt among us, and we have seen his glory, glory as of the only Son from the Father, full of grace and truth. (John bore witness about him, and cried out, "This was he of whom I said, 'He who comes after me ranks before me, because he was before me.'") For from his fullness we have all received, grace upon grace. For the law was given through Moses; grace and truth came through Jesus Christ. No one has ever seen God; the only God, who is at the Father's side, he has made him known. (John 1:1–18)

The Son of God was always face-to-face with God His Father. That is what John means by saying, "The Word was *with* God." The preposition he uses means *toward* God. But the Son who was face-to-face with God came to be face-to-face with us. Therefore, all that is left for us to do is to look face-to-face with Jesus, who is face-to-face with God.

Turn your eyes upon Jesus,
Look full in his wonderful face;
And the things of earth will grow strangely dim
In the light of his glory and grace.

May we know His presence and peace.

2

Making Christmas Last

WHEN I WAS A CHILD, *BOXING DAY* STRUCK ME as a very curious description for the day after Christmas. But despite how the name sounds, it was not the one day in the year when you were allowed to fight with your big brother. Instead, people seemed to consider it as a kind of "tidy up the mess" day after Christmas.

I had my own version of celebrating Boxing Day because, apart from small gifts on my birthday, Christmas was the one time in the year when I would get a special present. We looked forward to it, anticipating it for weeks in advance. It was a magical day.

And so on Boxing Day I would try to recapture the feelings of the day before by putting my presents back into their boxes and then opening them up again. But of course, it was never the same. It could never be the same. Christmas Day was Christmas Day. Twenty-four hours only once a year, unrepeated until near the end of the next long year. Another twelve months to wait for the excitement, the joy, and the presents. As a child, I hated this letdown and the demands it made on my patience. And try as I might, I could not make Christmas last.

When I later became a Christian, I couldn't help asking myself this question: "Is it possible to make Christmas last?" That is where the words of Hebrews 13:8 have come to mean so much to me: "Jesus Christ is the same yesterday and today and forever."

We've noted before that the author of Hebrews thinks of "yesterday" not as the day before today but as what he elsewhere calls "the days of [Jesus'] flesh" (Heb. 5:7). And "today" is not just this period of twenty-four hours. Rather, it is the "today" he refers to in Hebrews 3:13—where he quotes Psalm 95 and says, "Today, if you hear his voice, do not harden your hearts as in the rebellion" (Heb. 3:15). That "today" is still true in all our todays. It refers to all the days between the ascension of Jesus and His future return in glory. He is the same today and tomorrow and the next day.

And He will be the same "forever." He will forever be the person He was when He came and lived among us in the days of His flesh. He'll be the same Jesus who was born in Bethlehem, who walked the dusty roads of Galilee, who was crucified outside Jerusalem, who rose again and ascended and is seated at the right hand of God, who makes intercession for us, and who one day will come again in glory. That is the Jesus whose coming we celebrate at Christmastime. And He has not changed.

As a child, I thought Boxing Day had to do with the boxes in which my presents had come. But it's called Boxing Day for another reason entirely. It's because the day after Christmas Day was traditionally when Christians would put food and other items in boxes and distribute them to the needy. In a way, it was saying (at least symbolically): "In His birth, the Lord Jesus gave Himself to us. And in His death, He gave Himself for us. And now He lives to take care of us in our need. And so in response, in Jesus' name, we want to take care of you in your need." That is surely one way that we can make Christmas last. That is how we can extend what it means to us beyond ourselves and beyond the one day we celebrate it.

Did you get enough at Christmas this year? More than enough? Then remember that inasmuch as you do something for one of the least of Jesus' brothers, you do it for Him who has done so much for you.

And regardless of whether Boxing Day is celebrated where you live, perhaps you should take just a moment to think of one simple way that you can make Christmas last, not just for yourself but also for others who so deeply need to know our Lord Jesus Christ, God's inexpressible gift.

3

Living between the Times

THE TIME BETWEEN CHRISTMAS DAY and the beginning of a new year is a kind of no-man's-land. We're still feeling the events (and the effects) of Christmas, but we are not yet at the fullness of the end of the year and the beginning of a new one.

You probably know that the month of January is named after the Roman god Janus. It's odd that despite the impact of the Christian faith, we still use pagan names both for the days of the week and for the months of the year. Perhaps in God's providence, it's a reminder to us that we live between the times—like the time between Christmas and New Year's Day—between the first coming of Christ and the return of Christ. We're part of God's new creation. We're new men and women in Christ. But we are still living in a world that is alienated from Him. Even the names of the days of the week and the months of the year are a constant reminder of that fact.

Janus is the god who faces both ways. He looks backward to the past, and he looks forward to the future. Even if we don't especially like the fact that the coming month is named after a Roman deity, I think we can understand that experience of looking both ways. As Christians, we, too, live facing both ways as we look back to what the Lord Jesus did in His first coming and look forward to what He will do at His second coming. That is why we have sometimes said that we live between the times. We live the Christian life between the *already* of what Christ has done and the *not yet* of the completion of His work. We're reminded of that every time we take the Lord's Supper: we proclaim His death until He comes again.

So for a moment today, let's look back. That is one of the practices that our spiritual forefathers encouraged. If you've ever read John Flavel's wonderful book *The Mystery of Providence* or a similar Christian book from the past, you'll know that these wise old pastors often encouraged their people not only to *observe* God's providences in their lives but then also to *record* them. They knew how forgetful we are.

Perhaps like me, you've sometimes experienced something and thought at the time, "I'll *never* be the same again after that." And yet before too long, it's as though the event never happened.

The other day, I was reading about ministers in the seventeenth century who kept journals of God's dealings with them. One of them recorded some selections of God's providences in his life in another book so that he could reflect on them in his declining years. He wrote that they were "things that might be of use to me from what I have found of God's love in the days of old, and He is the same, and His compassions fail not." This man was like a squirrel storing up nuts for the winter of old age.

That would be a good spiritual exercise for all of us in these in-between days from Christmas Day to New Year's Day. It may even be something that you were taught to do as a youngster if you were brought up in church or Sunday school and learned to sing "Count Your Blessings":

When upon life's billows you are tempest tossed,
When you are discouraged, thinking all is lost,
Count your many blessings, name them one by one,
And it will surprise you what the Lord has done.

It may not be the greatest poetry in the world, but it's terrific counsel. So I suspect it would be very helpful for us to find time later today or in this time between Christmas and the beginning of the new year to do a bit of spiritual counting of the blessings of the past.

If you do, perhaps it will surprise you what the Lord has done, and then you'll be able to say with the psalmist, "The LORD has done great things for us; we are glad" (Ps. 126:3).

4

Remember Jesus Christ

YESTERDAY, WE REFLECTED ON THE PRACTICE of noting the providences of God in our lives. The old spiritual masters meant this quite literally. They encouraged writing them all down in a notebook so that we can remember them. But this practice wasn't just good advice geared toward Christians who lived a few hundred years ago. It's actually a biblical directive that we find in Scripture. God's people were told many times to "remember" or "do not forget."

We are all prone to forget, and that is why it is so important to actively remember.

Two passages come to mind. The first of them is Deuteronomy 8. In the first seven chapters of Deuteronomy, Moses gives an account of God's redeeming grace to His people in the exodus and the way of life that God called them to through His commandments. He drives this home by saying, "Remember" (Deut. 8:2), "Take care, lest you forget" (v. 11), "You shall remember" (v. 18), and "If you forget" (v. 19). There is a kind of melody here, isn't there? The life of faith has this underlying rhythm. It's the drumbeat to which the Christian marches: remember, don't forget; remember, don't forget.

The same principle holds true not only in life in general, but in our worship in particular. Psalm 103 underlines this:

Bless the LORD, O my soul,
and forget not all his benefits. (Ps. 103:2)

Observing, understanding, appreciating, noting, remembering, and fixing in our minds and hearts the providences of God in our lives—all of these are part and parcel of living well as a Christian believer.

Remembering is our privilege, and it's also our responsibility.

But how are we to do this? This is where we see the realism of the Scriptures. We are God's children, and sometimes we think that we are older and more spiritually mature than we actually are. But the Scriptures teach us that God remembers our frame because we are dust (v. 14). To put it pointedly, He knows that we can be careless, forgetful, and even cool-hearted children. Our minds easily wander to other things, and we forget what God has done for us.

The result is that when we should have greater confidence in the Lord—both because of His promises and because of the way He has providentially kept them to us—we end up forgetting. We become like people who lose their appetite, not realizing that they are unwell, and then wonder why they feel so weak and lacking in energy. It can be quite a challenge to take in just how forgetful we can really be.

Imagine someone's saying to you, "Remember Jesus Christ, risen from the dead." You might be inclined to say: "You don't need to remind me of that. How could I possibly forget that?" But these are among the last words the Apostle Paul wrote to his son in the faith Timothy (2 Tim. 2:8). He wasn't imagining that Timothy didn't know about the risen Christ, but he was hinting that it's very easy to be diverted.

It's surprisingly easy to live without the gospel's making a profound and constant impact on our mind, will, emotions, and entire life. That is true because this kind of remembering isn't just a matter of how good our memory is. It's a matter of making the Lord Jesus Himself central in our thinking, feeling, willing, and living.

So here's a good watchword for us, not only for the days between Christmas and the new year, but for every day of our lives. We're living between the past of Christ's first coming and the future of His second coming, so don't forget Him.

Remember, remember, remember: Jesus Christ is risen from the dead.

5

Renewed Day by Day

OVER THE PAST YEAR, WE'VE THOUGHT ABOUT biblical and doctrinal themes, pastoral themes, and personal themes. And because we're all wired differently and are in different stages in our spiritual experience, some of these daily reflections will have been more helpful to us than they were to others (and vice versa!). But what we share in common is this: when the clock strikes twelve on New Year's Eve, we will be in a new year—and at least from our human point of view, at another new beginning. The old year will have gone forever.

That is quite a thought, isn't it? *Gone forever*. It underlines the importance of putting into practice Paul's encouragement in Ephesians 5:16 about "redeeming the time" (KJV) or, as the English Standard Version translates it, "making the best use of the time."

One of my earliest memories of New Year's Eve is my parents telling me to go into the bedroom and decide on ten New Year's resolutions—yes, ten. I think the number probably had something to do with the Ten Commandments. Or perhaps I was so difficult a child that they assumed that there would be at least ten ways I could easily come out of the room slightly improved. But to be honest, after I got the first few obvious ones written down, I struggled to get to ten. I suppose I just didn't know myself very well. It wouldn't be so difficult today for me to find ten points needing improvement.

But when I looked back in later life, what struck me was that while my parents loved and cared for me very deeply, they didn't yet understand that my life would be transformed not first by laws that told me where I needed to change, but by the grace of the Lord Jesus Christ transforming me. We were a moral family, certainly, but not yet a churchgoing, gospel-hearing-and-understanding family. And this might be a good place to bring our year to a conclusion, because it brings us back to a theme that, in a variety of ways, has been part of the background music to this daily devotional.

The theme is this: We don't get God's grace by what we try to do. It's God's grace that *transforms* all we do. We don't become acceptable to Jesus by our efforts to follow His example or to live according to the Sermon on the Mount. It's really the other way around. It's only when we come to recognize our own spiritual bankruptcy and entrust ourselves to Him as our Savior and embrace Him in all His saving sufficiency that our life begins to change.

That is exactly what Paul is saying in Romans 8:3–4. What the law with its commands couldn't do because of our sinfulness, God Himself did for us by sending His Son to take on our flesh, so that He might take our place and bear our sins. And then when we come to Him in faith and are united to Him, the very things we couldn't do—the righteous requirements of the law—begin to be fulfilled in us through the ministry of the Holy Spirit.

Then, instead of crushing us, we find that God's law becomes light on our path. It becomes like the tracks on which a train runs. It's the path along which the Spirit of Christ directs us and empowers us to live for the glory of the Savior. And that is how we begin to glorify God and to enjoy Him forever.

Perhaps those famous words of the Shorter Catechism are a good way to end our year together, praying that the Lord Jesus will come to mean more and more to us as we go on in the Christian life glorifying God.

But maybe we should leave the last words to the Apostle Paul:

So we do not lose heart. Though our outer self is wasting away, our inner self is being renewed day by day. For this light momentary affliction is preparing for us an eternal weight of glory beyond all comparison, as we look not to the things that are seen but to the things that are unseen. For the things that are seen are transient, but the things that are unseen are eternal. (2 Cor. 4:16–18)

ABOUT THE AUTHOR

Dr. Sinclair B. Ferguson is a Ligonier Ministries teaching fellow, vice-chairman of Ligonier Ministries, and Chancellor's Professor of Systematic Theology at Reformed Theological Seminary. He previously served as senior minister of the historic First Presbyterian Church in Columbia, S.C.

Dr. Ferguson is a native of Scotland and earned his Ph.D. at the University of Aberdeen. He is author of numerous books, including *Devoted to God*, *The Whole Christ*, *The Holy Spirit*, *In Christ Alone*, *The Sermon on the Mount*, and *Devoted to God's Church*.